TALES AND LEGENDS

TALES AND LEGENDS

OF NATIONAL ORIGIN
OR WIDELY CURRENT IN ENGLAND
FROM EARLY TIMES

WITH CRITICAL INTRODUCTIONS BY

W CAREW HAZLITT

BENJAMIN BLOM, INC.
Publishers New York 1972

First published London, 1891
Reissued 1972 by
Benjamin Blom, Inc.
New York, N. Y. 10025

Library of Congress
Catalog Card Number 72-80500

Printed in the
United States of America

1748422

CONTENTS.

---◆---

SUPERNATURAL LEGENDS.

FEUDAL AND FOREST LEGENDS.

ROMANTIC LEGENDS.

DESCRIPTIVE AND HUMOROUS LEGENDS.

INTRODUCTION.

An assemblage of fictitious narratives, presenting romantic adventures, supernatural episodes, and dark, if not even immoral, scenes, might seem to recommend itself only to an illiterate age or to a time of life when the opportunity for study and investigation has not yet been given. But nothing can well be more certain than the fact that tales of a fabulous cast have at all periods possessed an irresistible fascination alike for old and young, and that the knowledge of their unreality does not sensibly or generally impair our affection for these compositions. All the wondrous myths which have come to us from the East, and all the creations of Western fancy and belief, constitute for ourselves the same inexhaustible treasury of reading and meditation which they have been to our foregoers in this land from a period almost immemorial; and as society grows more and more artificial and prosaic in its day by day routine, with a more powerful admixture of archæological feeling, we may perhaps expect to see a more widely diffused sympathy with stories and traditions which owe much of their charm to their strong contrast with existing conditions and possibilities.

The new interest and rank lent to the Legend in ballad or other shape by its recognition as an agent in elucidating or confirming many obscure features in the national life of the past in no wise displace it from its ancient home in all our hearts as a picture and reflex of bygone ages and people. It may for a season discharge a twofold function ; but probably the day will arrive when the vast majority of readers will prefer to view this species of production from the philosophical side. The study of such romantic epics as *Robin Hood, Doctor Faustus, Friar Bacon, Friar Rush*, and *Virgilius* should not prove less attractive to an educated intelligence because evidence of a trustworthy character is adduced that there is in these and in other analogous stories something beyond the superficial meaning conveyed by the text. The exploits and sentiments handed down to us in these fictions ought, on the contrary, to acquire in our eyes an augmented charm and worth, when we discover so much mineral riches beneath the surface, and are enabled to add them to the material for tracing the development of our country and our race.

The compositions which form the volume before us were the product of times and conditions so immeasurably different from those with which we have grown up, that it demands a very considerable effort to realize the circumstances contributory to their existence and popularity, and it is necessary to follow the clew backward till we do our best to succeed in making ourselves part of the age which favoured and witnessed the rise of narratives partaking of the common nature of all folk-lore in their unequal admixture of fable and fact and in their servility to local or contemporary costume.

The bulk of our popular literature owes its derivation to four leading sources : the political vicissitudes formerly so frequent, the Forest Laws, maritime and commercial adventure, and superstition. The interesting epic of *Robin Hood* may be considered as falling under the first and second of these categories or divisions, since at the period of life which the outlaw and his friends had apparently attained when they embraced a career fraught with so much hardship and peril nothing less than necessity could have induced them to forsake their homes and renounce the protection of the laws. To the same group belong the *King and the Hermit*, the *King and the Tanner*, the *Pinner of Wakefield*, and *Adam Bel*, of all of which the scene is laid amid the dense woodlands and in the townships bordering on them. *Chevy Chace*, the *Battle of Otterburn*, and perchance the *Nut-brown Maid*, may be almost classed with this highly interesting family of legends.

The stories of *Whittington*, the *Blind Beggar of Bethnal Green*, *Tom à Lincoln*, and *Thomas of Reading* offer examples of romantic inventions originating in the early mercantile enterprise of our country and its relations with others ; and into this section we should probably not err in admitting the *Squire of Low Degree*.

A very conspicuous feature in the present volume is the remarkable series of Tales of Magic and Enchantment, which, like the others, we have for readier study and comparison arranged in consecutive order. No one who possesses a fair amount either of sensibility or cultivated taste can peruse without being strongly impressed with the contents such relics as *Virgilius*, *Robert the Devil*, *Friar Bacon*, *Friar Rush*, *Doctor Faustus*, the *Friar and the Boy*, and the *Child of Bristol*, of which nearly all are obviously products of a foreign soil, but which have grown by length of use as familiar to us as our own indigenous creations.

The endeavour to render these pages a representative selection necessitated the choice of a few of those traditions of a domestic tenor which are plentiful enough in our ballad lore, but are generally too brief or fragmentary to yield material for a narrative even of the most sketchy character. We hope that we have been successful in gathering a few satisfactory illustrations however of this attractive kind of fiction, and need do little more than refer to the portion of the book in which they are all brought together. There is in some, beyond the mere humour or fun, considerable power of structure and cleverness of plot ; and the *Monk of Leicester*—of which Marlowe borrowed one of the incidents in his *Jew of Malta*,—the *Miller and the Tailor*, and the *Maltman of Colebrook* may be recommended as masterpieces in their way.

Our inborn proneness to a love of the marvellous and unarguable, which has originated in our imperfect acquaintance with the laws of nature and our own being, does not appear to suffer diminution as education and culture advance ; for it is found to co-exist with the highest intellectual development and the most refined critical temper. To the generality of readers and thinkers our romantic and legendary lore is, and will probably long remain, a mere repertory of names and abstractions ; and we have not to go back many years to meet with an epoch when our most learned countrymen discerned in the popular literature of England little beyond a source of entertainment, with the slenderest basis or nucleus of history and truth. The tales of silvan or domestic life, of stirring adventure, and of mystical enchantment, of which there are such abundant printed and manuscript remains, were regarded by Bishop Percy and his immediate contemporaries and followers as poetical amplifications of the chronicles, and even as collateral vouchers for the statements found in their pages. But it is not too much to assert that, to the world at large, a ballad or other like relic was what a primrose was to Wordsworth's *Peter Bell* :

> " A primrose on a river's brim
> A yellow primrose was to him,
> And it was nothing more."

There was no suspicion of an inner sense or an occult moral. There was no surmise that beneath the rugged surface of a few homely stanzas lay (hitherto ungotten) some precious hint or germ, illustrating the thought of the primitive era with which they had kindred and touch.

The average Englishman or Englishwoman who takes up a volume of popular tales, whether in prose or verse, is still apt to lay it down again with an ingenuous homage to the quaintness of the contents and a stricture on the morality or the spelling. The presence of a hidden meaning and value does not occur to them. If they have arrived at the point of having heard of such things, it is to be entered to their credit. The circulating libraries are not often asked for books of this class, and of our private homes how few possess them !

A century since, the ballad and the nursery-rhyme enjoyed a wider vogue and a more loyal allegiance ; but except in the most sequestered districts the minstrel and old-wife have become matter of the past. On the other hand, a strong and wholesome feeling has arisen for trying to build up out of existing material something better than the old-fashioned library of garlands and broad-sheets, with their bountiful admixture of corrupt and even spurious ingredients, and to question these records in a different spirit and from a higher standpoint.

The admittance of Folk-lore to a place among the sciences, and the espousal of that important movement by students in various parts of the world, have gradually led to a very fruitful inquiry into the genesis of all these stories and their international correlation. The result which has been thus far attained, although it is unexpectedly great, is yet very incomplete ; but more than sufficient is ascertained to convince reasonable persons that our ideas and conclusions on these subjects will have to be considerably modified. We hardly required to be told that *Reynard the Fox* was an apologue, and that *Whittington and his Cat* should not be quite literally interpreted, But every one was not prepared to learn that *Doctor Faustus, Robin Hood,*

Jack the Giant-killer, and many more, stood in a similar predicament, and that much which we took to be true was otherwise, while a good deal which we passed unobserved was pregnant with religious, social, and political significance. Here, as almost everywhere else, it now appears that we are inside the threshold of a revolution in thought, which may prove fatal, if it has not already done so, to a host of traditional beliefs and associations.

In works of a supernatural complexion, the whole region outside fact and science is at the command of the inventor or romancist, whose resources are barely capable of exhaustion ; but from the paucity of fictions of a high order of excellence in this department we easily judge that its wealth of material forms a condition of difficulty, if not of failure, although dramatic fitness and concord are not incompatible with the wildest extravagance. It is in so few cases that the unity of the story or conception is sustained throughout ; and in *Virgilius, Faustus*, and other celebrated legends, there is a disappointing leaven of puerile contradiction. A background or thread of serious incident is an indispensable foil to the miraculous, and at the same time is bound to be unceasingly in conflict with it.

In the narratives which we have selected and printed below, we have purposely refrained from introducing criticism and argument, and have contented ourselves with presenting a series of readable and genuine texts. To the ordinary reader archæological learning and detail constitute a deterrent feature in a book. But at the same time it seemed desirable not to let the opportunity pass of offering some preamble explanatory of the principal stories, especially where it happened that there was a hidden moral or a philosophical aspect material to a complete appreciation of the subject. For advanced scholars there may be nothing fresh in all that is put forward ; but to many it will be serviceable to find in our introductions certain suggestions and statements explanatory of some of the fictions which the volume includes.

The series has been arranged in four classified divisions : Supernatural Relations ; Feudal and Forest Tales ; Romantic Stories ; Descriptive and Humorous Stories.

We regret our inability to include in the present collection an authentic text of the famous story of *Herne the Hunter*—made so familiar to English-folk by its occurrence in the *Merry Wives of Windsor*—not so much on account of its originality or novelty, as on that of its importance as the English type of a world-wide legend and idea. The Wild Hunter myth is spread over the whole of Europe, especially in those countries which continued down to the historical era, as they do indeed still, to be covered by immense tracts of forest-land.

The origin and texture of the Herne story may be surmised, however, from those of the kindred German traditions ; and we perceive in the case, for example, of the *Hunter of Hackelnberg*, in Roscoe and Grimm, that the belief, if it did not originate in persons of narrow culture and children, was at least chiefly entertained by such, and consequently amounted to folk-lore in its normal acceptation.

In the *History of Fulke Fitzwarin*, an epic of
the Plantagenet times, one of the incidents is laid
in Windsor Forest, where the outlaw and his
followers are said to have been on familiar ground.
But there seems to be no further clew to any link
between the Fitzwarren cycle and Herne ; although
we may remember that the forest was at that time
of vast dimensions, and lent itself more readily than
now to weird or romantic reports of former fre-
quenters of the scene.

So far as the general reader is concerned, and
indeed such as feel an interest in Percy's *Reliques*
and other collections of the same character, the
probability is that many of the ancient tales here
found present themselves for the first time in an
intelligible form. For in their metrical dress the
uncouth orthography and the redundant doggerel
are apt at once to mystify and repel ; and stories,
which might as well have been allowed to remain
in MS. or in black letter, when the spelling and
style are equally archaic, are susceptible by faithful
and judicious handling of yielding to the lovers of
the ballad and the folk-tale a store at once of
entertainment and instruction.

As regards the tone and style which have been
adopted, a considerable amount of care has been
taken to strike a middle course between modern
diction and phraseology and a vocabulary too archaic
and obscure. To observe a certain genuine quaintness of language and expression, and at the same
time to avoid antiquarianism, proved a task of
some difficulty, as the process necessarily narrowed
the choice of terms and figures of speech.

It is to be regretted indeed that for so many of our early fictions we have to resort to poetical texts, which are at once more diffuse and less exact than those in prose, the requirements of rhyme or even metre necessitating the modification of the sense, on the one hand, and the employment of redundant pleonasms on the other. But the reduction of stories to this form was dictated by the feeling that it rendered them more attractive to popular readers and audiences.

Correctness and grace of versification are rarely found in these metrical productions, even where the writer was capable of developing and sustaining a plot, and possessed a tolerable power of description. The ruggedness of the lines, the infelicity of the phrases, and the superfluous expletives contribute to render our early poetical romances very tedious and disagreeable to modern taste and to an ear which has been educated and refined by a succession of masters of style and melody from Waller to the present day.

The practice of altering the original forms of compositions to suit a variety or change of fashion is very ancient. The *Roman de la Rose* was digested into prose. Some of the stories of the *Decameron* were versified. Plays were turned into novels, and novels into plays ; and the ballad was amplified into a prose chapbook.

In estimating the descriptions of persons, circumstances, and accessories in the following series, the reader will do well to bear generally in mind the discrepancy between the costume of the period concerned and our own, no less than the vein

of hyperbole which usually pervades romantic narratives, and the tendency to exaggerate in dealing
with heroic topics.   This warning is all the more
requisite, inasmuch as even the *Little Gest* represents in language and feeling a fifteenth-century
modernization and conception of a fourteenth-
century epos.   The distance between passed ages
and our own, and the development of science and
art in the interval, have contributed to qualify the
accounts which we get, not only in these fictions,
but in the ancient chronicles, of architecture, furniture, dress, ceremonial, pomp, martial or knightly
prowess, and the poetry of the early English life.
It is as with the relative valuation of the currency
—we have to allow for the difference of standard.

Again, in such stories as have been taken from
ballads, we ought to see that we invariably get in
this form of composition selected scenes only, as in
an ordinary play.   A ballad or a romance is not an
exhaustive biography, or even a biographical outline ;
it merely seizes salient points and characteristics,
and presents them in a more or less consecutive
order, and with more or less fidelity to life.

The treatment to which we have had recourse
is recommendable by its preservation of the temper
and mind of the old texts ; but it is feasible only
where, as, it is to be hoped, in the specimens selected,
there is a fairly pronounced vein of intrinsic interest
and permanent worth.   The divestment of inferior
compositions of their antique cerements in spelling
and type is a descent to sheer nakedness.

SUPERNATURAL LEGENDS.

THE KNIGHT AND HIS WIFE.

(*Fifteenth Century.*)

[*This is a short fable of engaging beauty and interest, and illustrates the old and steadfast belief in the ascendency of Christianity over the principle of evil by virtue of faith and prayer; but, although the feeling and spirit are congenial, here we have a special example of mariolatry, with the miraculous transfiguration of Our Lady for a beneficent purpose.*]

THERE was in a certain country a knight, who was at one time very rich, and every year he held a great feast in honour of Our Blessed Lady. But he spent so largely, that he by degrees became poor. A good woman he had to his wife, who held the Virgin as dear as he did ; and sorely the fiend grudged therefore.

The season came round for the yearly jubilee to Our Lady, and the poor knight had not wherewithal to discharge the cost of the same ; and he was abashed, that he betook himself to the forest, to dwell there in solitude till the feast-day was passed and gone.

The Devil saw the poor knight's case, and of his wife was he secretly enamoured ; but nought might his unholy passion prevail through that lady's virtuous living and the love which Our Lady bare unto her.

3

One day, while the knight her lord was still in the green forest, came the fiend to his side in human guise, and asked him why he walked there, and why he wore so dejected a mien.

Then the poor knight related to the stranger his story. "I was once," quoth he, "a rich man; but now all is lost. I was wont to celebrate every year the feast of Our Blessed Lady, and at present I lack money—yea, for my very livelihood."

The stranger answering him said: "If thou wilt grant me my will, I will give thee greater riches than ever thou haddest before. Go to the place that I shall bid thee, and thou wilt find gold in store. Then come back hither, and speak with me again, and bring thy wife with thee along."

The poor knight wist not that he was a fiend that spake thus unto him, and he promised to do as he bad him. So home he went, and found there forthwith money enough, as the stranger had foretold. Right fain was he hereof, and Our Lady's feast was held with greater spending of gold and silver than had ever been remembered.

The time passed away, and the day arrived when he was to meet the stranger once more, and to bring his wife with him. That gentle lady durst not do other than his bidding, and she made herself ready accordingly, and they mounted their palfreys and rode forth toward the forest. On the way, by the roadside, stood a chapel of Our Blessed Lady, and the knight's wife said unto her lord, "Let us enter this chapel, and pray to God to keep us in His fear." But the knight was full of glee and jollity, and recked nought of prayer, and to his lady quoth he: "Thou mayest get down, if thou listest, and pray; but for me I will proceed on my journey. Do not tarry long, however, or I shall wax wrath."

The lady promised not to overstay, and into the chapel she hied, and placed herself nigh an image of Our Blessed Lady, where she reclined, and a drowsiness overtook her, so that she fell asleep.

Now Our Blessed Lady, to requite that good wife of the poor knight for all her love to her, transformed herself into her likeness, and riding on the palfrey rejoined the knight, who wist not that it was Our Lady that rode beside him. But when they came where it had been appointed that they should meet the stranger, he stood there; but because he was in truth a fiend, he knew her to be, not the knight's wife, but the Holy Virgin; and he cried to the knight: "Traitor, I bad thee bring thy wife with thee, and in her room thou hast brought Christ's Mother! Hanged shouldest thou be by the neck for thy falsehood!"

These words made the knight wax fearful; and he descended from his horse, and sank on his knees before Our Lady, shedding tears and imploring forgiveness.

Our Lady said unto him: "Knight, thou hast erred. Thou hast delivered thyself to the fiend. Return him his gift. Bestir thyself henceforth in the service of God, and He will reinstate thee in thy goods." She uttered these words and vanished.

The knight leapt on his palfrey, and rode to the chapel, where his wife yet slept by the altar.

THE CHILD OF BRISTOL.

(*Fourteenth Century.*)

[*There are perhaps few more favourable and
more striking specimens of early popular mythology
than the little production which we now introduce.
It is the story of a rich and covetous father who is
redeemed from eternal punishment by the practical
piety and charity, as distinguished from the mere
adjuration or prayers, of an affectionate son; and
the writer of the narrative has brought to his task
no mean literary skill and no ordinary insight into
human nature.   The father who is thus emanci-
pated from hell by his offspring was a rich franklin
or yeoman, who by his avarice had unconsciously
brought about a catastrophe which put to the test the
loyalty and love of his young heir.   The good deeds
of the Child gradually release his parent from
bondage and pain, and he reduces himself to poverty
in order to restore to its owners property which the
dead man had misappropriated.   The father ultimately presents himself in the likeness of a naked
child; or, in other words, is brought back by prayer
and almsdeeds to his original beauty and innocence.*

*The term attorney, which more than once occurs
here, must be understood in the sense of an attorney
"in fact," or agent, exercising what is commonly
known as a power of attorney; and the employment
of the word is probably a very early one.*

The tale breathes an air of unquestioning and unshaken faith germane to the priest-ridden and benighted century which produced it. In the introduction to the two existing versions of it in Hazlitt's "Popular Poetry," 1864–66, the editor has adduced the principal analogues and imitations of it in various collections and poems.]

HE who made both heaven and hell in seven days bless us all that are here assembled together, old and young, great and small, if so they lend good ear to my tale! The best tale that ever was told is worth little enough, unless some listen thereto. So, I pray you, as many as are now present, to desist from your talking, and to hear what I am about to say.

There dwelled in England in old days, in the fair city of Bristol, a very rich lawyer, who had gotten into his hands great possessions, and was a lord of many townships, castles, and forests, and of much cattle ; and he used his craft in law to beguile the poor man, for he had not the fear of God before his eyes.

This rich man, who was both a merchant and an usurer, had one only son, a comely child, of rare promise, and by him he set all his store. For his sake he heaped up riches, and oppressed his neighbours far and wide ; for he looked to make him, whenso he himself should die, even richer than he was, and more powerful and great than any in all that country.

It happened, when this youth was twelve years old, that his father sent him to school to learn clergy; and the Child grew wise and witty and in mislike of all ungodliness. Then his father devised in his thought how it would bestead his heir, so that he might not be deceived by men when he came to full estate, and stood in his father's place, to have some learning in law; and accordingly he called the child to him, and said to him thus: "Son, I have it in my mind to cause thee for a twelvemonth's space to learn so much of the law of this land as will hinder thy neighbours and all others, when thou comest to manhood, from doing thee wrong."

But the Child answered softly: "Father, many prosper well in this world that are no lawyers, and so I trust that I may do. That craft will I never study which may put my soul in jeopardy, and be to God's displeasure. I am loth to follow any calling which is contrary to my spiritual well-being. Ever hath it been my wish to live by merchandise, in which a man may advance himself by honest means in the sight of heaven. Here at Bristol liveth one who is a good and true man, as I hear tell: let me be his bound prentice seven year, and learn his business, and dwell under his roof."

So his father, seeing his bent, rode to Bristol, and made covenant with the said merchant to take his son for seven years; and the boy went unto that merchant, and by his courtesy and honesty won his love, and the love of all those that came into those parts to buy and to sell their goods.

Now, meanwhile, the Child's father pursued his godless ways, lending out moneys to use, robbing the parson and the vicar of their tenths, and wringing from the poor man all he might, with intent to

leave his estate so that his heir would be lifted by
his riches above all others without a peer.

But, as all things will have an end, this usurer,
who was waxing in years, fell sick and lay on his
bed, and doubting that his life might draw to a close
suddenly, he summoned to his side some of the
chief men of the country, that were his neighbours
and acquaintance, and besought them out of charity
to be his executors.   Then, because his goods had
been so, ill-gotten, and the fear of the Lord was not
in him, no one among them all assented to be made
his executor, saying that they would not have to
do with his affairs from dread of the wrath of God
upon them.

This sick usurer lamented sorely his case, that
none would for conscience' sake be executor to him ;
and seeing that he drew nigher and nigher to his
end, he sent for his son, where he lay at the good
merchant's house, seven mile thence, and when he
had come to him, he shewed him how it was, and
begged him, as he was heir to all his fair lands and
goods whatsoever, to take that office upon him.

Quoth he : " Son, I have gathered all this together for thee, than whom I have no other heir,
and I see well that in friendship there is no trust.
Do thou therefore this thing for me."

His son turned away from him, uttering not a
word ; and then the dying man, when he perceived
his unwillingness, further said : " I charge thee, as
thou wilt have my blessing ere I go, obey my
behest."

" Ah ! father," cried the boy, " thou layest on me
a heavy charge, and thy command I cannot gainsay.

But on my part, lo! I enjoin thee, on the fourteenth day after thy passage, to appear before me, and let me behold thy spirit, and see whether it be saved or damned; and further I pray and require thee, both thou and any that shall bear thee company at that time, to do me no trespass."

"Son," answered the father, " I agree."

"Alas," thought the boy, "that for any gold or land of mine a man's soul should stand in peril to be lost!"

The priest came, and gave that rich usurer, as he lay on his death-bed, the glorious sacrament, and shrove him, and prayed to God to be merciful unto him; and when God was so pleased, the sick man passed away.

Then his good son brought his father to burial, and spread largesse among young and old, and gave much store of gold to holy priests, so that there was great mourning and many a dirge for the rich usurer; and the boy, who began to draw toward man's estate, sold his father's cattle and houses and lands, and with the money he kept in his service a hundred priests, causing them to say for his father's soul thirty trentals of masses. So this pious youth dispossessed himself of almost all that rich usurer's goods, till gold he had none, and where he was heir to so much riches there was, as the fortnight drew near to completion, no poorer man than him in the whole land.

Now, when the day arrived wherein he had appointed to meet his father, he repaired to the chamber in which his father had died, and remained there in prayer nearly to noon; and toward midday, as he knelt praying, there came a flash of lightning and a peal of thunder, and he muttered *Benedicite!* and called upon God for succour.

And as he thus knelt and prayed, his father's spirit appeared to him, as he had enjoined, flaming like a glowing coal, and the devil led it by the neck in a gleaming chain.

The boy said : " I conjure thee, whatever thou art, speak to me."

The spirit answered : " I am thy father that begat thee.   Now thou mayest perceive my sad estate."

" It pierceth my heart, father," answered the boy again, " to behold thee in such sorrowful plight."

The spirit replied : " Son, I fare thus, as thou seest me to-day, because I got my estate by deceit and extortion ; unless it be restored, I shall go in this guise a hundred year henceforward.   Ease me therefore of my bond, for till then my soul is in durance."

" Nay, father, not so, if God will give me grace. Pledge me that this same day fortnight ye will return to me in this place, and I shall labour all I can meanwhile to bring thy soul into a better state."

The spirit gave its assent, and in a clap of thunder vanished ; and on the next day following the boy went to Bristol to seek his former master, the good merchant.   To whom : " I have served you, sir," quoth he, " many a day ; for the love of God, be my friend.   My father has passed ; and I need a little sum of gold, until I have found a chapman for the residue of my heritage."

But the good merchant blamed him for parting with his patrimony, and said to him thus : " If so it is that need presseth, I will lend thee a hundred marks, and I will not ask for the same again this seven year."

The youth avowed that he must find some one to buy his lands that still remained to him ; and when he told the good merchant that his steward held them to be worth a hundred pounds, the other said unto him, "I will give thee three hundred all truly told"; and when the youth consented, he fetched the gold, and counted it out to him, and the son of the rich usurer was right glad in his heart, and thanked his master, and went his way.

So now he caused it to be proclaimed and pub- blished in all churches and all markets, that whoso, man or woman, had suffered loss by his father, should come to him, and he would satisfy them to the full. And he did as he made promise till the money was all spent, and the second fortnight passed away.

Then he prepared to meet the spirit, as he had done before, and knelt down and prayed against the hour when it behoved it to appear ; and when the youth beheld him, the burning chain was no longer on his neck, and the red flame in which he had been wrapped was turned to blackness.

"Now, father," said the youth, "tell me how it goeth with thee."

"All the better for thee, son," quoth the spirit ; "blessed be the day that I begat thee! Yet I live still in much pain and woe, and so must continue till my term is fulfilled."

"Father," answered the youth then, "say to me now what goeth most grievously against thee?"

"Tenths and offerings, that I refused, son, and never would pay," returned the spirit, "are the cause why I remain, all thy good almsdeeds notwithstanding, thus wretched and forlorn. Give me back my pledge, for there is no remedy, and I must be gone."

The youth replied thus : "I shall still once more essay what I may do, father. Promise me again that thou wilt be visible to me a fortnight from this day in the same place, and I will against then try what to amend thy cheer I can do."

To his old master, the kind merchant at Bristol, he betook himself, and said to him : "Sir, it is so, that I lack yet a little sum of money, to make another bargain." And as he spake he wept.

The merchant replied : "Thou art a fool ; thou hast been among bad company, and hast lost money at cards or dice. Thou hast nought left that thou canst sell. Thou art, I doubt, an unthrift."

But the youth offered to become a bondservant to the merchant, himself and all his heirs for ever, if he might have for which he prayed ; and the good merchant softened toward him once more, saying, "How much wouldest thou ?"

He said : "Forty marks will supply me."

That burgher loved the youth so well in his heart, that into his inner chamber he went and fetched the money, and he gave it to him, saying : "Thou didst ask me for forty marks, and, lo ! forty pounds herewith I give thee ; and God bless thee to boot ! "

The youth departed, light of heart, and to all the churches far and near where his father owed tenths and offerings he went on pilgrimage, and paid them one and all whatso they demanded, till his money was utterly spent; and as he returned home hungry and penniless, he met an old man by the way, who said to him: " Sir, it is so that your father owed me for a measure of corn. I beg thee pay me therefore."

The youth humbled himself before the man, and said to him, kneeling on one knee, that gold he had none; but he stripped off his own doublet, and laid it on the shoulders of the other, saying, " It is all, father, that I have"; and he went on his journey in his shirt and breeches, till he came to his own house, where his father's spirit was to visit him.

He knelt and prayed long, and presently he became aware of the gladdest song that ever was heard, and when it was ended, by a light which burned more brightly than a thousand torches, a naked child, led by an angel of God, stood before him.

" Son," said the vision, "blessed be thou, and all that shall be born of thee!"

" Father," he answered, " I rejoice to behold thee in that state in which thou now art, and I trust that thou art saved."

" Son," the vision answered, " I go to heaven. God Almighty reward thee, and make thee prosper! Now yield me up my pledge that I gave to thee, and I go."

And the youth discharged his father from that hour, and to heaven he went.

Then the Child, thanking God and Our Blessed Lady, went anon to Bristol; and he was in his

poor array, for his gay clothes had he given for the
measure of corn.   And when the burgher, his old
master, espied him, he asked him what he had done
to bring himself to such a pass.

He said : " I have come to yield myself to thy
service to my life's end."

But the merchant would not take that answer,
and said to him : " Now, tell me, son, by the love
which is between us, why thou goest thus, and how
thou makest thy thrift so thin."

" Sir," answered the young man, then, " all my
goods have I sold to get my father into heaven ;
for through his covetous and unholy life so many
had he set against him that no man would be
his executor or attorney."   And he set before
him the whole story of his father's appearances,
and how at length he was admitted to bliss.   " And
so," he said, " now all my sorrow, sir, is healed and
assuaged."

" Son," quoth the kind merchant, " blessings on
thy name, that thou couldest so impoverish thyself
to save thy own father's soul !   All the world shall
do thee honour.   Thou art a steadfast and true
friend, the like whereof I have seldom seen.   Few
sons would thus save their fathers after they were
gone.   Executors know I many an one, but none
such as thou art.   Now I say unto thee, I make
thee partner with me in Bristol to buy and to sell
for me as I should myself do ; and seeing that I
have no child to come after me, thou shalt be to
me a son, and shalt inherit all my goods when I
am dead."

And the merchant wedded him to a rich man's

daughter of that country, and in the process of time dying left to him, as he had said, all his lands, cattle, and goods; so that he became greater in wealth than before, and through the blessing of God the treasure which he had restored to holy Church and the poor was given back to him twofold.

THE FRIAR AND THE BOY.

(15*th*–16*th* *Century.*)

[*This story is probably of German origin, and in its present shape belongs to the first quarter of the sixteenth century. Subsequently the references to the idea in our literature are almost innumerable, and the narrative in a curtailed form, under the title of Tom Piper, gained a permanent place in the nursery library. Although, no doubt, the legend is derived from a Teutonic source, there is an indication that the English writer in this case was immediately indebted to a French text which lays the scene in Orleans. In Hazlitt's "Popular Poetry," iii. 54–59, (1849) will be found a detailed account of the various phases through which the belief in the enchanted properties of a horn, tabor, or other object passed in the course of time in different countries ; and perhaps the myth of the " Rat-catcher of Hamelen" comes nearest to the present composition, which is one of the large series reflecting on the lax morality of the Popish clergy just prior to the Reformation. The friar, it may be noted, is not clothed with any power of invocation or exorcism to extricate himself from the dilemma in which he is placed by the boy.*]

GOD that died for all give them a good life and long that listen to my tale !

A. L. ¹⁷ C

There was a man in a certain country who in process of time had three wives. By the first he had a son, who was a light-hearted lad ; but by the other twain issue had he none.

His father loved this boy well ; but his stepdame looked upon him with an evil eye, and stinted him in his victual, and did him many a shrewd turn.

At length she said unto the goodman : "I heartily pray you, sir, that you would put away this boy, who is a cursed plague to me, and let him serve some one else who will give him his desert."

Her husband answered her, saying : "Woman, he is but a child. Let him abide with us another year, till he is better able to shift. We have a man, a stout carl, who keeps our beasts afield ; look, the boy shall take his place, and we will have the fellow in the stead of him at home."

To which the goodwife agreed.

So on the morrow the little lad was sent to tend the sheep, and all the way he sang out of the gaiety of his heart ; and his dinner he carried with him in a clout. But when he came to see what his stepdame had given him to eat, he had small lust thereto, and he took but little, thinking that he would get more when he returned homeward at sundown.

The boy sat on a hill-side, watching his sheep and singing, when there came along an aged man, and stood still, when he espied the child, saying unto him, "Son, God bless thee !"

"Welcome, father," the boy replied.

The old man said : "I hunger sore ; hast thou any food of which thou mightest give me even some ?"

The child returned: "To such victual as I have thou art welcome, father."

So he gave the old man the rest of his dinner, and thereof he was full fain. He ate, and grudged not. To please him was not hard.

Then, when he had finished, he said: "Gramercy, child; and for the meat which thou hast spared me I will give thee three things. Tell me now what they shall be."

The boy thought in his mind, and anon: "I would," quoth he, "have a bow, wherewith I could shoot birds."

"I will find thee incontinently," said the stranger, "one that shall last thee through thy whole life, and shall never need renewing. Thou hast but to draw it, and it will hit the mark."

Then he handed him the bow and the arrows; and when the child saw them, aloud he laughed, and was mightily content.

"Now," said he, "if I had a pipe, if it were ever so small, then I should be glad."

"A pipe I here give thee," the old man said, "which hath in it strange properties; for all whosoever, save thyself, shall hear it, when thou playest, must dance to the music perforce. I promised thee three things. Say, what is to be the last?"

"I seek nothing more," replied the boy.

"Nothing?" quoth the stranger. "Speak, and thou hast thy will."

"Well," said he, musing, "I have at home a stepdame—a shrewd wife she—and she oftentimes looks ill-favouredly at me, as though she meant me no love. Now, prythee, when so she looketh in that wise, let her laugh till she fall to the earth, and laugh still, unless I bid her to desist."

"It is granted," said the stranger. "Farewell!"

"God keep thee, sir," said the boy.

The evening drew on, and Jack wended homeward in great glee. He took his pipe and played it, and all his beasts and his dog danced to it in a row. He played as he went along, and the sheep and kine followed at his heels and the dog, dancing all the way, till they came to his father's abode; and he put by the pipe, and saw that all was fast, and then walked he into the house.

His father sat at his supper, and Jack said unto him, "I am a-hungered, sir; my dinner I might not eat, and I have had charge of the beasts the whole day."

The husbandman threw a capon's wing toward him and told him to eat it. The goodwife sorely grudged that he should have so fair a morsel, and eyed him sourly. But she straightway fell to laughing, and she laughed, and she laughed, till she could no longer stand or sit, and fell on the floor, laughing still, and she ceased not till she was half-dead; and then the boy said, "Dame, enough!" and she laughed not a whit more, which made them both amazed.

Now this goodwife loved a friar, who oftentimes came to the house; and when he next shewed himself she made complaint to him of the boy, and told him how Jack had caused her to laugh, and had mocked her, and she prayed this friar to meet him on the morrow and beat him for his pains.

" I will do thy pleasure as thou desirest," quoth
the friar.

" Do not forget," quoth the goodwife. " I trow
he is some witch."

So the morning following the boy went forth
to drive his father's beasts to the field, and he took
with him his bow and his pipe. And the friar rose
betimes likewise, lest he might be too late, and he
approached the boy, and thus he accosted him :

" What, forsooth, hast thou done by thy step-
mother, Jack, that she is angered at thee ? Tell me
what it is ; and if thou canst not satisfy me, surely I
will beat thee."

" What aileth thee ?" asked Jack. " My dame
fares as well as thou. Have done with thy chiding.
Come, wilt thou see how I can bring down a bird
with my bow, and what other things I can do ?
Though I be a little fellow, I will shoot yonder bird,
and yours it shall be."

" Shoot on," said the friar.

The bird was hit surely enough, and dropped into
a thorn-bush.

" Go and fetch it," said Jack.

The friar stepped into the middle of the brambles
and picked up the bird. Jack put the pipe to his lips
and began to play. The friar let the bird fall and
set to dancing, and the louder the pipe sounded the
higher he leapt, and the more the briars tore his
clothes and pierced his flesh. His dress was now
in shreds, and the blood streamed from his legs
and arms. Jack played all the faster, and laughed
withal.

" Gentle Jack," gasped out the friar, " hold thy

hand. I have danced so long that I am like to die. Let me go, and I promise thee I will never again offer thee harm."

"Jump out on the other side," quoth the boy, pausing, "and get thee gone."

And the holy man made all the haste he could for shame's sake ; for the thorns had almost stripped him to the skin, and covered him with blood.

When he reached the house they wondered where he had been, and how he had fallen into such a sorry plight. The goodwife said : "I see well, father, by thine array that thou hast come to some mischief. What has befallen thee ?"

"I have been with thy son," he replied. "The devil overcome him, for no one else may !"

Then entered the goodman, and his wife said unto him : "Here is a pretty matter! Thy dear son hath well-nigh slain this holy friar. Alack! alack!"

The goodman said : "*Benedicite !* what hath the boy been doing to thee, friar ?"

"He made me dance willy-willy among the briars, and, by Our Lady, the pipe went so merrily that I might have danced till I burst myself."

"Hadst thou met with thy death so, father," said the goodman, "it had been a great sin."

At night, at the usual hour, the boy came back, and his father called him unto him, and questioned him about the friar.

"Father," said Jack, "I did nought, I tell thee, but play him a tune."

"Well," answered the goodman, "let me hear this pipe myself."

" Heaven forbid ! " cried the friar, wringing his hands.

" Yea," quoth the goodman, "give us some music, Jack."

" If," entreated the friar piteously, " thou wilt indeed have him play, first bind me to some post. If I hear that pipe I must fain dance, and then my life is nought worth. I am a dead man."

They fastened him to a post in the centre of the hall, and they all laughed at his distress, and one said, " The friar is out of danger of falling now."

" Now, boy," said the goodman, " play on."

" That will I do, father," he replied, " till you bid me hold, and I warrant ye shall have music enough."

As soon as the boy took up the pipe and laid his mouth to it, all began to dance and jump, faster and faster, and higher and higher, as though they were out of their wits. Even the friar struck his head against the post and screamed with pain. Some leapt over the table ; some tumbled against the chairs ; some fell in the fire. Jack passed out into the street, and they all followed him, capering wildly as they went. The neighbours started at the sound, and came out of their houses, springing over the fences ; and many that had gone to rest jumped out of bed and hurried into the village, naked as they were, and joined the throng at Jack's heels. A phrenzy was upon them all, and they bounded into the air, and looked not whither they plunged ; and some that could no longer keep their feet for lameness danced on all fours.

The goodman said to his son, " Jack, I trow it is best to give over."

" Let it be so," said the boy, and he desisted from his playing accordingly.

" This is the merriest sport," said the goodman, " that I have known this seven year."

" Thou cursed boy!" exclaimed the friar, when they returned to the house, " I summon thee before the judge.   Look thou be there on Friday."

" Good," answered the boy; " I will.   I would with all my heart it were already come."

Friday arrived, and friar Topas and the step-dame, and the whole party, appeared, and the judge was in his place, and there was a goodly gathering of people, for there were many other cases to be heard.   The friar was fain to wait till his turn came, and then he addressed the judge, saying to him :

" See, my lord, I have brought a boy to thee who hath wrought me and others many grievous trouble and sorrow.   He is a necromancer such as in all this country hath not his like."

" I hold him for a witch," put in the goodwife, and scowled at Jack ; and forthwith she set to laughing till she fell down, and none could tell what she ailed, or whence her great mirth arose.

" Woman," said the judge, " tell thy tale."   But she could not utter another word, though Jack stayed her laughter as he had power given to him to do so by the stranger on the hillside.

Then spake Friar Topas, and said: " My lord, this boy will worst us all unless you soundly chastise him.   He hath, sir, a pipe that will make you dance and hop till you are well-nigh spent."

The judge said, "This pipe I fain would see, and know what sort of mirth it maketh."

"Marry! God forbid!" quoth the friar, "till I am out of the hearing of it."

"Play on, Jack," said the judge, "and let me see what thou canst do."

Jack set the pipe to his lips and blew, and the whole room was quickly in motion. The judge sprang over the desk and bruised both his shins; and he shouted out to the boy to cease for God's sake and the love of the Virgin.

"Well," said Jack, "I will if they will promise me that they will never again do me trespass so long as I live."

Then as many as were there, the friar, the step-dame, and the rest, sware before the judge that they would keep the peace toward the boy, and help him to their power at all seasons against his enemies; and when they had done so Jack bad the judge farewell, and all proceeded merrily home.

And thus it may be seen how the boy, because he was courteous and kind to the old man whom he met on the hillside while he tended his father's beasts, prospered, and kept every one in his country in his fear for evermore. For the old man was in truth a magician.

THE SMITH AND HIS DAME.

(*Sixteenth Century.*)

[*This is one of those strange inventions which belong to the period of transition from Eastern fable and mediæval demonology to a revival of the miraculous intervention of Christ in response to prayer.*

The prevalent superstition was and is, that invocations to the Deity are efficacious in producing desired results both internally and externally ; and this belief is an exact inversion of the real nature aud value of prayer, the operation and virtue of which are limited to its influence on our feelings and conduct.

A blacksmith, who is filled with impious pride on account of his masterful knowledge of his craft, incurs the displeasure of Our Lord, who visits him for the purpose of humiliating his presumption. It eventuates in Christ undertaking to do what the man with all his experience considers to be impossible. The smith has a\ mother-in-law, who has been bed-ridden upward of forty years, and Christ engages to bring her back to youth by laying her on the forge, and hammering her out. The miracle is performed, and the old woman is restored to vigour and beauty.

But the smith unluckily essays without Divine

intervention to achieve a similar triumph in the case of his wife, and burns her to death. But prayers are addressed to Jesus; and He reappears, resuscitates the woman, and from the flames is seen to emerge the subject of the second experiment, " bright as a blossom," and a thousand-fold younger than she was before. Of course, one can only look on such a narrative as a piece of whimsicality, since the central incident at once removes it out of the category of prodigies accomplished by leechdom or legerdemain. To the Elizabethan reader, for whom the little tale was written, the particulars may have presented nothing beyond a humorous exercise of fancy. The serious side was not considered.

The proposal made by Jesus to the smith to enable a blind man to guide himself by means of a rod of steel has probably some reference to the ancient theory of magnetism.

The description of the blacksmith himself imports a person of much higher social and financial consideration than an operative of that class at the present day; and the hero of the story, in fact, belonged to a period when the calling was far more lucrative and prominent, owing to more primitive travelling conditions and the universal use of horses for nearly all purposes. In England it was the same as elsewhere: the forge and the smithy were an essential feature in every locality, great and small; and the leading members of the trade formed from the seventeenth century a Guild, which still exists, though shorn of its original significance and practical value.]

GOD that died on a tree yield His grace unto them that will hearken unto me, and I shall tell of a marvel.

In Egypt there dwelt a smith, who prospered long and well, and had land and fee, and husbandmen at his bidding. This smith was a cunning artificer, and could, by my troth, work in any metal ; and he was wont to boast that, save himself, there was none that followed that same craft worth a straw.

Now Our Blessed Lord was wrath with this smith by reason of his pride and vain-glory, and thought how He might compass his chastisement. And so it happened on a day, that, as he stood at his forge working, Our Lord came unto him secretly, and said unto him : " Lo, I have a thing for thee to do ; and if thou canst do it, thou shalt be well paid, i' faith."

" Say on," replied the smith, as one that wist not who spake thus unto him, " for I am a master of all this cunning ; and whatever thou shalt be pleased to command, it shall be done to point."

Then said Our Blessed Lord unto him : " Canst thou make a yard of steel to lead a blind man, so that he may never fall ? If so thou canst this accomplish, then I will salute thee a master of thy calling."

Then the smith fell into a study, and presently answered the stranger thus : " Sir, I trow thou art mad or something worse to talk of such things. If a man be blind, he must have a fellow who can see to lead him in the way. For if two blind men walk together, they commonly both fall into the ditch ; and how should a blind man with a blind rod, be the steel never so hard, find his way ?   Nay ; it is false."

"Well," said Our Blessed Lord unto the smith, 'I can make such a rod, or I can restore an old man to his youth, as he was before."

"I have an old quean here with me," the smith said ; "she is my wife's mother, and it is forty years or more since she set foot to ground.   By my faith, if thou couldst make her young again, then right glad were I."

Our Lord said : "Where is she ?   Let me see her, and I shall shew thee a feat beyond thy reach."

The smith hastened to fetch his dame, where she lay a-bed.

"Mother," quoth he, "art thou asleep ?   I have come for thee, that thou mayest be made young again."   And he pulled her out of the place where she lay, and carried her on his shoulders back to the stranger, and her cries and struggles heeded not.

Our Lord said unto him : "Verily, smith, it shall be done unto her as I say.   Take her now, and put her on thy forge, and make her fast, that she fall not therefrom, and with thy bellows blow thy best."

He blew as he was commanded by the stranger, till the fire roared, and the old wife was as red as a hot coal ; yet pain suffered she none.

The smith said : "Now is it all over.   She will never eat meat more.   I have blown till I sweat."

"Let me alone," quoth the stranger.   "Thou shalt behold anon a full fair woman in place of thy old beldame."

He blessed her, and said unto her, "Dame, awake."   And he bad the smith to strike her with his hammer, and straightway she arose, and was comely and young to the sight.

Our Lord said to the smith : " She is whole once more.   We have made her young again with hammer and bellows.   There is none in Egypt that may surpass her.   Behold, one that was an old crone is now as though she were but thirty years of her age. Now acknowledge me for thy master."

" Sir," then quoth the smith, " I dare well say that, an' a man were dead, thou mightest make him live again by thy excellent craft and mastership. Now what shall I pay thee, ere thou goest, to teach me this art ? "

Our Lord rejoined : " What thou seekest is in vain ; thou canst never compass these things.   And I prythee do not essay them, lest thou shouldest be deceived.   But leave thy boasting ; for whatsoever thou knowest, there is ever much to learn.   My name is Jesus, and I now depart from thee to go into another country."

And Our Lord was lost to view.

When Our Lord was no longer manifest to the smith, the smith went and called his wife Joan, de-siring her to come to him ; who cried out, and asked him if he wist not well that she was in no case to come, as he bad her, for she was lame and might not walk, and she was waxing in years, so that her sight failed her and her bones ached.   She feared to fall at every step she took.

The smith was forgetful of the admonition which Our Lord had given to him, and thought that he might do with her even as Christ Jesus had done with the old wife his mother ; and so he sent unto her : " Come forth, and at a stroke I will make thee young as thou wast before. Look ! thy own mother, that could neither walk nor see, is as merry as a bird, and her complexion is like a rose."

Then when the woman came, and saw her mother, how she was young and lusty, she said unto her, " Art thou my mother indeed ? "

" Yea," quoth she, " *benedicite !* "

" Who made thee whole, then, mother?" she asked.

" Even one," she answered, " that came this way. Men call his name Jesus."

" Verily he has worked a wonder by thee ; for even yesterday thou wast but a feeble trot."

" Wife," said the smith, " had I a right hot fire, I could make thee as thy mother is." And he fetched a quarter of coals, and took his bellows, and blew till there was a white heat.

" Lo," cried the smith, " there is none in all this country can do this save I." And he laid hold of his wife to place her on the forge.

" What art thou doing, thief, with me ? " she cried. " Knowest thou not that I am thy own wife ? "

" I go to burn thee, as I did thy sweet mother," quoth the smith.

" Traitor, if thou burnest me, thou shalt hang on a tree," she shouted. " Curses upon thee ! Did we not keep thee, when thou hadst nought ? and goest thou about to burn me ? "

" Fear not," said the smith ; " thou shalt with the fire and the hammer be made as when I saw thee first. Come." And he took her by the middle, to fasten her on the forge. But she struggled and kicked and sware, and when he had her at last well on the furnace, she caught him by the hair, and smote him in the eye, and called loudly for help.

He waxed wrath hereat, and cast her clean into the flames, and once she rose, and twice, essaying to rend him with her nails. But he heaped on the coals, and then the water, and set to work with his bellows, and blew as hard as he could. " Ha! ha ! " he cried ; " I shall make thee young again yet, I see well."

Then, when she lay still, he raised her up, and hammered at her with all his might, till both her legs dropped from her.

" What is this ? " he said, aghast ; " wilt thou not be young, wife ? What ! thou art not dead ? Come, speak a word. Say *Bo*."

But she uttered no word, and anon an arm fell into the flame ; and the smith threw down his hammer, and ran into the street like one distracted, shouting for Jesus to come to him.

Then incontinently Our Lord appeared unto the smith, and said unto him, " Man, what hast thou done ? "

" I sought to do as thou hadst done by my dame before, and make my wife young by burning her in the furnace, and beating her with the hammer."

" Did I not shrewdly avise thee, man," quoth Jesus, " not to venture herein ? Thou hast burned thy wife, and slain her."

" Ah ! good Lord," answered him the smith, " I cry for mercy. I disobeyed you, Lord."

" Thou repentest thy sin," said Jesus ; " and as thou prayest, so it shall be done."

And He blessed her, and bad her arise ; and she

arose straightway, and seemed as bright as a blossom, and a thousand-fold fairer than she was before.

She sank on her knees, and prayed to God on high, and the smith fetched his mother ; and all those three knelt together, and held up their joined hands, to give praise and glory to Heaven.

Our Lord then said to the smith : " See that thou never do this thing more, for it is a craft which thou canst not learn. But I grant unto thee this boon, that over all thy fellows in the mystery which thou professest thou shalt have lordship, and that none, save he seek thy counsel and aid, may prosper."

These words He delivered to the smith, and again He enjoined him in no wise, to his life's end, to intermeddle with such things as belonged not to man ; and so He departed into other lands, to do like acts of grace and mercy.

Let us all give thanks that there is such a Lord, and pray that He may bring us to His bliss!

So endeth the tale of the smith, which that burned his dame, and made her whole again by the help of Christ Jesus.

VIRGILIUS.

[*It is well known that the poet Virgil, who in his
works has included descriptions of the infernal regions,
and who was supposed to have been the grandson of a
magician, from an ignorant misreading of* Maius *for*
Magus, *shared the fate of many scholars, both during
the Middle Ages and at a later period, in being
invested with the character and power of a wizard.
The most singular fables were current in southern
Italy about his miraculous exploits at Naples and
elsewhere in the same vicinity, when, on the revival
of literature under monastic auspices in the thirteenth
century, the compilers of books began to collect
material for their purposes, and eagerly availed themselves of stories relative to such a famous personage,
handed down from age to age, and gradually magni-
fied and distorted by a variety of agencies.*

*"Virgilius" may be considered as belonging to the
same family of tradition as Bacon and Faustus,
and presents to our view a remarkable illustration of
the slow tangle of Roman or Italian folk-lore with
heterogeneous Middle-Age empirical beliefs and ideas.*

*When a nucleus was obtained, as in this case and
in those of Bacon and Faustus, and many others,
there was no limit to the accumulation round it of
fabulous growths, and the question of historical or
literary propriety did not enter into the thoughts of*

34

those who identified exploits or opinions with cele-brated names. 1748422

It may be surmised that the prophetic and mys-tical cast of the fourth "Eclogue" of Virgil and the account in the "Æneid" of the hero's descent into hell were primarily instrumental in surrounding the Roman bard with an atmosphere of romance; and if the same fortune befell Horace in his own home, the phenomenon becomes less surprising and less abnormal. In the present instance, we have to bear in mind the dense ignorance and the puerile credulity prevalent in Italy generally, and especially in the south, at this moment, when we weigh the facilities which existed in what are called the Dark Ages for the propagation of the most childish and most incon-gruous theories.

The short preamble, in which the origin and sur-roundings of the Gothic Virgilius are gravely and circumstantially set forth, is worthy of the remainder of the production, and is as distant from the first draft of an authentic view of Roman history as the latter is from that at present accepted. It seems almost incredible that the true facts, so far as they are, or can ever be, known at all, should have been overlaid by such a stratum of illiterate fable; but the same fate befell every branch of learning and archæology during the transitional period when western civilization was effaced by the decline and fall of Roman ascendency.

One striking peculiarity in "Virgilius" is the resort of that reputed magician, for the accomplishment of some of his designs, to the agency of water and air under what appear to be impossible conditions. But *the storyteller has at no time been hampered by the laws of nature or limits of science.*

One explanation may be offered of the presence of these notions; and it is that the description was borrowed from the observed localization of mist or vapour in a compact form by the action of the wind, and from the atmospheric phenomenon known as a mirage.

A second special feature is the association of the mystery of working in metals and the production of automata *with occult philosophy—an Homeric idea, which continued to flourish through the Middle Ages, as we see partly exemplified in the legend of Wayland Smith, down to the more recent period with which the singular story of the " Smith and his Dame" connects itself. The pieces of mechanism ascribed to Virgilius were probably some species of clockwork, and would at the present day be considered rudimentary devices.*

The description which we find here of the walls of Rome is so far curious, that it was probably derived from the personal observation of the romancist, and points to the practice, where towns were not walled or fortified, of surrounding them with palisades.

In the adventure with the Soldan's daughter "the side of France" is quoted as the country where Virgilius had his orchards; but by such a phrase we are merely to understand a locality in that direction.

The version of the origin of Naples, and its foundation on eggs, is apparently connected with an attempt to explain the volcanic nature of the soil underlying and surrounding that city.

The extraordinary account which we get of the death of the enchanter reads like a jumble of the ancient belief in rejuvenescence, which was usually by fire, with some legend of the murder of a rich man by his servant for purposes of plunder. Even the emperor in the story does not credit the defence set up by the man, and executes him as an assassin.

The costume of the narrative, in short, is that of the period to which it belongs ; and by studying particulars which are not perhaps otherwise of great interest or importance we may gain many serviceable glimpses of the social and political life of former ages, even where it is no weightier matter than the custom of schoolboys being sent between their lessons to play in the fields.

Many of the incidents have their analogues in the fabliaux *and in Eastern traditional folk-lore, which were only available in a manuscript or oral shape when " Virgilius " was written and published in the early years of the sixteenth century.*

Certain of the scenes or adventures recall the coarser passages in Owlglass and Scogin.

The English text which we have employed was in all probability indeed derived from a Dutch original, of which a copy is before us, with a series of woodcut embellishments of a commonplace character, except indeed that one of them depicts the ordeal imposed by Virgilius on the gentlewoman in the market-place. There is also a French version.

In one passage we note the reference to a July fruit and corn harvest. It is always difficult and hazardous to rely on these clews in popular tales ; but we seem to discern here an indication that the

writer observed the unities rather unusually, or that
the work before us had an Italian original, with
which we have not so far met, although such a phrase
as "town-house" applied to the Capitol at Rome
bespeaks rather a Flemish or Dutch source and a
literal translation of Stadt-huis.]

I.

In the city of Rome, in old days, there dwelled
two brothers, named Romulus and Remus ; and
because that city was too strait and small for two
kings, as these twins were, Remus departed, yielding up to Romulus his heritage, and went and
founded in Champagne the fair city of Rheims,
which he embattled with fair and high walls.

Now it happened that Remus came on a time
to Rome to see his brother, and because the walls
of Rome were so low that a man might leap over
them, Remus made sport thereof, and at a run leapt
over them in a certain place, which so angered his
brother that he slew him, and, leading his army
into Champagne, destroyed the said fair city of
Rheims. But the wife of Remus and her son, that
bare his father's name, escaped.

Then the wife of Remus, that was a lady of high
lineage and richly allied, rebuilt the city, when
Romulus his brother had departed ; and anon her
son, that was named Remus, repaired to Rome, and
slew his uncle Romulus, and reigned in his place,
and was called emperor.

In his court this emperor had many knights ; but
there was one that had espoused the daughter of a
very rich senator, and was a man of great power and

renown ; and by this lady had he one son, who was called Virgilius.

Whenas that child was born, the city of Rome shook, and he shewed himself of much promise and of a rare wit, and he was put to school at Tolentum, where he studied diligently ; and soon after his father died, whom his mother the senator's daughter loved so well, that she would not consent to wed again.

One day Virgilius and his fellows had leave, according to the usage of those times, to go into the fields for to play ; and it fortuned to Virgilius that, as he strayed among the hills, he espied a great hole, into which he crept, and all was in darkness ; and he went a little farther, and it wox lighter again ; and so he advanced inward till he heard a voice saying, "Virgilius! Virgilius!" But he looked about, and could see nobody.

He cried, "Who calleth me?"

The voice answered and said, "Virgilius, seest thou not that board beside thee with the word marked thereon?"

"Yea," he replied.

"Remove it then," said the voice, "and let me out."

"Who art thou," then asked Virgilius, "that liest there-beneath?"

"I am a devil," quoth the voice, "that was conjured out of the body of a certain one, and am banished and imprisoned hereunder till the day of doom, unless I be delivered by the hand of man. So I pray thee, Virgilius, enlarge me from this bondage, and I shall shew unto thee many books

of magic, that thou shalt grow to be the greatest
necromancer of all men, and shalt be able to help
thyself and thy poor kinsfolk which were deprived
of their heritage.   Surely it is a small boon that I
ask for so great a reward."

Virgilius, who knew that his mother had been
wronged by her kindred, and of the emperor could
in no wise gain redress, was tempted to do as the
devil would have him ; and when the devil had
upon his asking shown him the books that he
purposed to bestow upon him, he slid away the
board, whence-beneath that devil glid like an eel,
and came and stood straightway before Virgilius
in the semblance of a big man, that Virgilius was
astonished, seeing so great a man issue forth from
so small a hole.

Then, when the devil had delivered the books to
Virgilius, Virgilius said unto him : "Might ye fall
back into that hole once more ?   I warrant not."
The devil said he could, and when he had shown
Virgilius how it was possible, Virgilius shut down
the hole suddenly, and cried, "Now thou shalt
abide where thou art till the hour appointed"; and
although the devil besought him, he left him there
lamenting and chiding.   And thus it was that
Virgilius became a famous sorcerer and expert in
the black art.

II.

The mother of Virgilius, as she wox old and deaf,
began to long for the sight of her son, whom she
wished to incite to the recovery of his heritage,
which certain withheld from him, and which having
he might be the greatest in all Rome.   Wherefore

she sent one of her servants to the school where he yet was ; and the man found him teaching scholars from all countries, among them many great lords' sons ; for I assure ye he had grown a fair and wise youth, and was proficient in all arts.

The messenger shewed unto Virgilius the case, and took his answer that he could not come at that time, but sent his mother four sumpters laden with money and other choice gifts ; and soon after, when he had arranged his affairs, he set out to Rome, where he saluted his mother, who had not beheld him these twelve years, and she was glad enough to see him again.

But the enemies of Virgilius misliked his coming, and would not eat nor drink with him ; and Virgilius was wrath, and gave money and lands to all his poor kindred, and yielded hearty thanks to all those who had shown his mother kindness in his absence, and of such as denied him entrance on his heritage he made complaint to the emperor.

The emperor took counsel with such as held Virgilius in despite, and they advised him to pay no heed to one who was but a schoolmaster, and to leave the land with those who might aid him in his needs ; and the emperor said therefore to Virgilius that he would take four or five years to consider well whether he were the true heir or no.

Thereat Virgilius fretted sorely, and he assembled together all his poor kinsfolk, and gave them meat and drink, and wherewith to make merry till the harvest, when the corn and fruit should be ripe. And when it was so that the corn and fruit were ripe, Virgilius by his art did enchant the air over

the lands that were held by his enemies, so that all
their corn and fruit were gathered into his garners,
and they had not a whit. Whereupon his enemies
mustered together in such a throng that the emperor
for fear fled out of Rome. But Virgilius encompassed his lands with a wall of air, that none might
enter thereinat without his leave gotten ; and when
his enemies approached to take him and smite off
his head, the air so enveloped and bound them
that they could neither stir backward nor forward.
At which when they chafed and marvelled, Virgilius
came to them, and said : " Lo! so long as I live, ye
shall have no profit from the lands whereof ye have
disinherited me ; and ye may tell the emperor that
I am tarrying his pleasure against such time as he
shall determine if I am true heir or no, and that
meanwhile I shall take my belonging as I may, nor
care for what he may do."

When the emperor learned the words of Virgilius,
he gathered together his army, with the intent to
beleaguer his castle and burn all his places, and do
him to death for his treason ; for he was sorely
enraged that he should have thus defiantly spoken.
But as soon as all the host was before the castle,
Virgilius laid a spell upon it that it stood motionless,
and presently the emperor imagined that he and all
his soldiers that were with him were surrounded on
each side by water.

Then Virgilius appeared in the sight of the
emperor, and spake unto him these words : " Lord
emperor, you have no power to do me harm nor to
profit by my lands whereof you have disinherited
me, whereas I should be one of your greatest lords

and nearest of your kinsmen, and in the day of need might help you more than all other." The emperor threatened him, but he feared him not; and Virgilius and his folk dressed victual and ate it, so that the host outside could see them so do, but the emperor and his folk had nought whereof to eat.

Now while they were in these straits, one that also professed necromancy came before the emperor, and made offer to cause all the folk that were with Virgilius, and Virgilius himself, to fall into a sleep, so that this spell might be relaxed. And so it was; and Virgilius had much ado to keep himself from sleeping; and he saw how the emperor and his soldiers moved once more, and approached the walls, raising ladders against them. Then Virgilius looked into his books, and found how this might be averted, and made the enemy stand still again, some that were on the ladders or the walls, or one foot on either, remaining void of faculty to go upward or downward.

The emperor asked his conjuror if he might not deliver them from their distress, but he answered him Nay; and Virgilius defied the emperor, and imprisoned him and his army in a circuit of air a whole day. When the night drew on, Virgilius came secretly to him, and shewed him what dishonour it was to so mighty a prince to fall into so low a state, for that he had undertaken what he could not fulfil.

The emperor answered and said that if Virgilius should free him out of this danger wherein he was, he would restore him all his lands, and acknowledge him for his kinsman; and he sware by his crown

to be true to his pledge. Virgilius then brake the
spell, and the emperor and his folk entered into the
castle, and were right nobly entertained and feasted ;
and Virgilius was reinstated in his lands, and became
the greatest lord in Rome after the emperor.

III.

Now Virgilius, when he had so gotten again his
goods, fell enamoured of a fair lady, and by his art
made her understand his mind ; whereupon she,
meaning to beguile him, appointed a time when he
should come to her house that stood in the market-
place, and she would let down a basket from the
tower, wherein he might come to her chamber. But
when Virgilius had entered into the basket, and
had been drawn up half-way to the gentlewoman's
window, she left him to hang there, making fast
the cord.

"Lo! to-morrow, sir," quoth she, "it is market
day, and ye will be seen and mocked of all."
And so it happened. But the emperor, when he
understood how it was, commanded the lady to
release Virgilius ; and he departed his way, saying
that he would be avenged on her for her false
dealing.

He incontinently used his art, and extinguished
all the fire in Rome, that none but he had fire ; and
when the emperor sent to him to ask how they
might have fire again, he answered so : "Ye must
have a scaffold set up in the middle of the market-
place, and place the gentlewoman that hung me in
the basket thereon in her smock only ; and then
make cry throughout Rome that whoever needeth

fire may come and fetch it from between the gentle-woman's legs ; nor other fire shall ye have any."

So all the multitude went, as Virgilius bad them, and got their fire and lit their candles there, both rich and poor. And soon after this Virgilius married another lady, and built for himself a marvellous palace with four angles ; and he took the emperor into each angle by turn, and he heard all that the people said in that quarter, albeit they but whispered.

The emperor, thus perceiving the might of Virgilius and his great subtlety, demanded of him on a day howso he might cause Rome to prosper, and to have many lands subject to the same ; and likewise to know when it was within the purpose of any land to rise up against it. Virgilius answered at that time, " Lord emperor, that shall I do " ; and forthwith he set him to place in the Capitol divers carved images in stone, that we name idols, of all the gods appertaining to such lands as were to Rome obeissant ; and in the midst he put one god of Rome, and to every god his bell, to the intent that when any other land should make war upon Rome, all the gods might turn their backs on the god of the Romans, and the god of that land which willed war might clink his bell. Then, ere the people of the land could muster in array and come to Rome, the emperor, thus avised, might go into that land and subdue it.

Now the folk of Carthage, that were very cunning and expert, had secret knowledge of this device, and were sore at heart by reason of the great hurt that Rome had wrought them ; and so they sent forth three trusty messengers, provided with much abundance of gold and silver, to essay to destroy the work of Virgilius.

These three men repaired to Rome, and first of all they buried, deep in the earth, a great pot full of money, and sank in the Tiber, by the bridge, a barrel of golden pence. Then they proclaimed themselves soothsayers and dream-expounders, and reported unto the Senate of Rome that if they might have leave to dig in a certain hill, and to cast nets in the river, they would come upon a marvellous treasure, whereof they had dreamed ; and the Senate gave them leave, and they found the pot of money and the golden pence, and made to the senators costly gifts in recompense.

Anon they came again to the Senate, and prayed it, whereas they had discovered that beneath the Capitol there was buried a treasure far greater than the other two, to grant liberty to them to dig in quest thereof. And the Senate granted them liberty, who assembled labourers, and took away as much ground as underlay the Capitol, which was called *Salvatio Romæ*, or, the *Salvation of Rome*, and privily departed ; and the next day after the Capitol fell down, and all the great labour of Virgilius was lost, to the amazement and dismay of those lords of Rome, who thus saw how they had been deceived by the men of Carthage.

Yet once more the emperor prayed Virgilius of his good counsel, that the thieves and night-walkers in Rome, which did great mischief and committed many murders, might be stayed and abolished ; and Virgilius wrought hereupon a horse of copper, with a man of copper on his back, and bad the emperor

cause proclamation to be made that whoso, after ten
of the clock at night, should range the streets, and
should be slain, there should be no inquisition thereinto. But the thieves and other evil-doers lent no
ear to that proclamation, and did as before; and
when at ten of the clock the bell rang, and none
marked it, the man of copper on his copper horse
galloped through the streets, leaving none overlooked, and slew every man and woman whom he
met withal, slaying in one night two hundred or
more.

The thieves and night-walkers misliking this
gin, they devised how they might escape from
the copper man upon his copper horse; and they
contrived ladders with hooks, which, whenso they
should hear the copper man drawing nigh, they
could fix to the houses, and climb beyond the
danger thereof; which they did, and the streets
returned to their former perilous estate. And the
emperor sought out Virgilius, that he might aid him
to find a remedy, who made two copper hounds,
which should run beside the copper horse; and when
the thieves and night-walkers thought to climb their
ladders, these copper hounds sprang thereto, and
tare them in pieces. After which none durst go in
the streets of Rome by night, and the evil-doers
were clean destroyed.

A while after, in order to discover the more
effectually false swearers, Virgilius devised a metal
serpent : and whoso into the mouth of that serpent
should put his head, and had falsely sworn, might
not withdraw it again ; but if it was so that the oath
was true, then he might pluck it back without harm

done. And many tried that ordeal till a certain lady, that was a knight's wife in Lombardy, beguiled Virgilius by means of her lover, whom she caused to disguise himself in a fools'-coat. And Virgilius in despite brake the serpent to pieces; for with all his cunning and necromancy women still had the better of him by their mother-wit.

Then, by cause that the city was plunged in darkness, when the day waned, Virgilius studied how he might make a light to burn for ever in the very middle of Rome for the special good of the common sort that had no lamps nor candles; and he set up a mighty pillar of marble, and between the pillar and his palace he built a bridge, over which Virgilius passed from his palace to the top of the pillar; and thereon he placed a lamp of glass that would burn to the world's end, and no man could put it out: which lamp lighted all the streets of Rome, so that all might see, even in the smallest, by night as well as by day. And on the walls of the palace Virgilius placed a metal man that held in his hand a metal bow, wherewith he ever aimed at the lamp as though he would put it out. Yet he did not; and the lamp gave light to all Rome during the life of Virgilius and three hundred years after; and to this day would so have done if one of the burgesses' daughters had not, as she sported with her fellows on the roof of the palace, touched the metal bow, which made the bolt shoot out and break the wonderful lamp that Virgilius had fashioned.

But Virgilius in his time did many other strange and marvellous things. Whereof one that we shall rehearse was an orchard, wherein he planted all

manner of trees that bare fruit and blossom, and set
every sort of bird and tame beast, with a fountain
in the midst and great plenty of fish ; and the birds,
which came within this garden, might well enter,
yet could in no wise fly out, for it was encompassed
about with a wall of air.

But, above all, beneath the orchard he made a
secret chamber, where he placed all his money and
goods that he had, for he was so exceeding rich,
that he scarce wist how much good he possessed ;
and two metal men, that perpetually smote on two
anvils with great hammers, kept this chamber, that
none could come near it, or Virgilius had quickly
lost the whole of his treasure.

IV.

So great power had Virgilius over the air, that he
made an image, and suspended it therein, that none
in Rome might open door or window, and not see
that image ; and it had this property, that no woman,
after she had looked upon it, had any bodily lust
thenceforward. Which when the women of Rome
understood, they prayed the wife of Virgilius to use
sleight, that the image might fall. Who thereupon,
to do them pleasure, passed over the bridge of air,
and cast down the image, so that all the women
were as before.

But when Virgilius perceived that it was so, he
was wrath, and knew who had done this deed, for
none might compass such a thing save his wife
alone ; and he demanded of her if she had cast it
down. Who answered, "Nay"; and Virgilius set
it up once more. Then the women complained

again to his wife, that it was even worse than heretofore with them, and begged her to throw it down
a second time. But Virgilius lay in wait, where he
might see her ; and when it was accomplished, he
cried in anger that he would throw her down after
it. But he did not. Yet he said that he would
not meddle with women hereafter, and from that
time he misliked his wife.

Oftentimes it had been reported to him how fair
was the Soldan's daughter ; but he had never seen
her ; and now he crossed over to her on a bridge
through the air, and spake with her, and so ordered
her mind that she consented to his love. And this
lady said unto Virgilius one night, that she would
fain return with him into his own country, and see
what manner of man he was, and where he dwelled.

Virgilius answered and said, " Thou shalt cross
over many lands, and shalt not touch the ground ";
and he bare her through the air by means of the
bridge which he made, and brought her to Rome.
He demanded of her how many she saw, and she
said, only him alone. Then he shewed her his
palace and orchard, and the metal men that guarded
his riches, and for ever smote with their mighty
hammers on their anvils ; and he let her see his
treasure ; and after, when she had tarried with him
a certain space, he carried her back through the air
to her father's country ; and the Soldan was a glad
man, for he wist not whither his daughter had gone.

Virgilius gave her of the fruit of his orchard
to bear with her along, and the Soldan knew,
because they were walnuts and such like fruit, that
the strange man who had taken her away was a

Frank from beyond the sea.   So he commanded his
daughter, if so he came again to her, to give him to
drink of a certain sleeping potion, but in no wise to
partake of the same ; and when Virgilius repaired
to her again, she gave him thereof that he slept, and
was taken, and adjudged by the Soldan to die.

But Virgilius defied the Soldan, and caused him
and all his lords suddenly to find themselves in a
great river that ran thereby, where they swam and
plunged like ducks ; and they thus remained under
his spell, until such time as he had risen into the
air with the Soldan's daughter, when he made the
river abate, and so set them free again, to their great
marvelling.   And he, with that lady whom he loved
so well, came safely to Rome over the bridge of air.

Now he was of this lady, the Soldan's daughter,
mightily enamoured, while his own wife for certain
sufficient reasons he had disdained and eschewed.
Yet he thought not to marry her, but to raise her to
a high estate, and to find for her a husband of like
degree ; and first of all he imagined how he might
found in the midst of the sea, in her honour, a fair
town with large possessions thereto pertaining.

The foundation of it was eggs ; and in it he built
a four-cornered tower, on the top whereof he set an
apple, which hung by its stalk from a chain, nor no
man could remove the apple unless he brake it ;
then above the apple he placed a bottle, and on
the bottle, again, an egg, where they yet continue.
And so the town was finished by his cunning in
short space, and he called it Naples.   And when
the egg stirreth, the tower quakes ; and if the egg
should break, the town shall sink into the sea.

Here he brought a part of his treasure, and placed his mistress, the Soldan's daughter ; and he gave her the town, and all belonging to it, and married her to a Spanish lord.

The emperor, when he heard what a noble town it was, sorely coveted it, and within a brief time lay siege to it. But the Spanish lord that had married the Soldan's daughter defended the place with great valour, and Virgilius so ordered that all the water in the rivers outside the town was turned to rain, and the emperor and his host were discomfited, for that they had no water ; and so they returned again to Rome.

Then Virgilius removed all his goods to Naples, save his treasure which he left in care of the two metal men, who smote on the anvils with their mighty hammers day and night ; and he made the town the abode of scholars and merchants, with harbours, and schools, and baths, to which all might alike resort ; and the schools he endowed with much land, to the intent that the scholars should have and enjoy it, each his share, so long as he continued in that place, and no longer ; and Virgilius himself taught necromancy therein, for he was the most learned and apt man in that science that ever was born ; and in his days Naples was the fairest city in the whole world.

V.

Yet the emperor was so loth to part with Virgilius, that he was fain to dwell at Rome, all this notwithstanding ; and being there he promised the emperor that in good time he would perform in his behalf

many other marvels : as, namely, to make the trees
bear thrice a year, and ripe fruit and blossom at
once ; to cause ships to sail against the stream ; to
enable men to earn money as quickly as spent ; and
to let women bring forth children without travail ;
and many another wonderful matter, put-case in the
meanwhile Virgilius should not happen to die.

And Virgilius about this time built another castle,
whereinto was one entrance, and no more, and round
about flowed water on every side. It stood without
the city of Rome, and the gate was kept by four
and twenty metal men, that held four and twenty
flails, which were made to work day and night, so
that no one could enter, till Virgilius commanded
the flails to cease, or he was slain.

Then when Virgilius looked upon this castle,
and upon the treasure that he had privily removed
thither, and considered that he was waxing old, it
came into his thought how he might so contrive by
his mastery to renew himself, and be young again.

Virgilius had among his servants a fellow that
above all the rest he in especial trusted ; and while
his mind was occupied with this thing, he called him
one day, and took him with him along to his castle
without the city. And when they were come to the
gate, Virgilius said unto him, " Get you first into
the castle." The man answered and said, " Sir,
an' I should enter, the flails would slay me to a
surety."

His master thereupon shewed to him the manner
in which the flails worked, and how they might be
made to cease ; and he made them to cease, and
they both passed into the castle. Then Virgilius

turned the vices, and the flails once more stirred and quickened as they were wont.

As soon as they were within, Virgilius led his servant into the cellar, where he kept a fair lamp ever burning, and spake to him thus : " Dearly beloved friend, whom I above all others trust, see you that barrel that standeth below the lamp ? Ye must therein put me ; but ye must first slay me, and hew me small, and cut my head into four pieces, and lay it at the bottom of the cask, and my heart in the centre ; and ye must salt them all, and for nine days together see that the lamp is filled, and that the leakage therefrom fall into the cask upon me. And when nine days are come and gone, and ye have done all this as I bid, I shall be renewed, and be young again, and live many winters more, unless it be that I be taken above."

But when the servant heard this speech, he was exceeding sorrowful, and would not by any means be consenting to the death of Virgilius, nor would not slay him. Nevertheless his master urged him, saying that it must be done, and there was none else that might do the same ; and so the man did as he was charged, and went each day in and out of the castle, and made the flails cease and fed the lamp.

The emperor missing Virgilius for the space of seven days, he marvelled what had become of him, and he sent to his servant and questioned him, who said that Virgilius had gone away this sevennight, he wist not whither, and would not let him bear him company. The emperor deemed that the fellow lied, and threatened him with death if he did not tell him shortly where he was. The man said that his master and he went together to the castle, and when they came thither Virgilius entered, but would in no wise suffer him so to do. The emperor commanded him to go with him to the castle, and when they were before the gate, they might not enter for the flails; and the emperor enjoined him to stay them, and if he did not so do, he should die; and the servant through the fear of death stayed them, and they entered in.

The emperor made search everywhere about the castle, and at length descended to the cellar, where the lamp burned above the barrel, and in the barrel lay the body of Virgilius hewn small; and the emperor enraged cried, "What made thee so hardy as to kill thy master?" and drawing his sword he smote off the head of the servant. Then, after this had come to pass, the emperor and the folk that were with him beheld a naked child, that ran thrice round the barrel, saying these words, "Cursed be the time that ye came ever here!" and so vanished, and was no more seen.

So ended the life of Virgilius, for which the emperor, and the town of Naples that he had founded, and all the scholars of the same, and all his kindred, long and sorely grieved.

ROBERT THE DEVIL.

[*This singular fabulous compilation was originally written in French, in the fifteenth century; and relates to the birth, alleged misdeeds, repentance, and holy end of one of the early dukes of Normandy, whom the romancist arbitrarily, and indeed erroneously, makes in order of time anterior to Charlemagne. The hero of the legend before us was really the younger son of Richard the Good, Duke of Normandy* (996–1027) *and the father of William I. of England; he succeeded his brother, Richard III., in* 1028, *and reigned till* 1035. *His wife is said to have been the daughter of a skinner or currier at Falaise.*

From the account it is easy to perceive that the direction which the excesses of the duke took in early life, during his father's and brother's reigns (996–1027), *in the spoliation of the Church, was naturally apt to awaken resentment in the mind of the class then most influential in shaping the public estimate of persons and events, and to blacken the fame of the duke. But as he subsequently relented and made his peace with God, we are to understand that, after a suitable process of humiliation, he was readmitted within the sacred pale and his offences condoned. The Church, it is to be observed, makes its own classification of monarchs into good and bad, as they have sacrificed the interests of their subjects to clerical rapacity, or the contrary. This is only just beginning to be appreciated, and will involve much rewriting of history.*

The legend has assumed a variety of forms, and the same string of inventions has served to illustrate incidents in the lives of several real or fictitious personages, who were supposed to have transgressed in a similar manner against God and the Church.

At present, the particulars given of the life and fortunes of Robert the Devil are chiefly valuable as proofs of the strange credulity of former ages, and at the same time as a serviceable and interesting picture of manners and thought. But a certain interest attaches itself to his name, by reason of his nearness to the founder of our Norman line of kings.

The romance is divisible into three portions : Robert's birth and period of sin; his term of penance; and his restoration to spiritual health and accession to the ducal throne in 1028.

The clerical spirit is strongly manifest throughout, in the subordination of political to spiritual circumstances, while the distortion of historical facts very signally demonstrates the writer's want of knowledge, or his disrespect for that of others.]

I.

IT befell, in time passed, that there was a duke in Normandy that was called Hubert, which duke was passing rich in goods, and of virtuous life, and loved and feared God above all things, and did great alms-deeds, and exceeded all other in righteousness and justice and in deeds of chivalry, and in notable exploits.

Duke Hubert held his court at Naverne on the Seine upon a Christmas Day, and thereto all the nobles of Normandy resorted ; and because the duke was unmarried,. his lords besought him to take unto him a wife, to the intent that his race might be continued, and he might have an heir to enjoy his estate and place after his decease. To whom the duke graciously signified his readiness to do their pleasure, if so that he might find a consort fitting his condition ; and they commended unto him the daughter of the Duke of Burgundy, which that Duke Hubert sought and obtained in marriage accordingly, and he brought her to Rouen in Normandy, where he dwelled.

But it came to pass that the duke and duchess lived together for the space of eighteen years child-less, albeit this duke prayed to God, so often as he intermeddled with his lady, that they might be blessed with a son, who should honour and serve God, and fortify their lineage. But in no wise could they compass their desire.

The duchess exhorted her husband to be patient, and to submit himself to God's decrees ; but he sorely chafed at the lack of issue, and it happened that, when he returned on a day from hunting, moody and discontented, as though the devil had possessed him, he came to the duchess, who was in like manner vexed and moved, and embraced her, saying his orisons in this wise following, " O Lord Jesu, I beseech Thee that I may get a child at this hour, by the which Thou mayest be honoured and served." But the lady, being angry, spake thus foolishly : " In the devil's name be it, since God hath not the power ! and if I conceive at this very moment, I give the child to the devil, body and soul."

The duchess suffered great travail, and had not alms-deeds, good works, and penance been done for her, she had surely died ; and when the child, that was a man child, was at length born into the light, the sky wox so dark, and it thundered and lightened, that men feared lest the heavens should open, and the world should perish. For the winds blew from all the four quarters, and the palace was shaken, and a piece of it fell to the earth ; and there were sundry other fearful signs and tokens.

But, as it pleased God, after a while the weather was composed, and the child proceeded to his christening, whom they christened by the name of Robert ; and he wox so shrewd, that he bit off the paps of the nurses that gave him suck, so that they were fain to feed him through a horn, and by such time as he was twelve months old he could speak and walk better than other children of three years ; and he was shortly dreaded by all that sought to play with him, for he brake their legs and arms, and scratched their eyes out, wherein only he found pleasure and delight ; and the common people gave him the name of Robert the Devil, which he kept during his life, and will so long as the world lasteth.

II.

Anon Robert had by his father and mother assigned unto him a schoolmaster to teach him good learning ; but because this schoolmaster would have chastised him for his cursed conditions, the boy gat a bodkin, and thrust it into the man's belly, that he died ; and cast his book against the wall, saying, "Now have I taught thee that never priest nor clerk shall correct me, nor be my master." And from that time forward no man durst gainsay this Robert, whatsoever he did ; and he followed no manner of virtue nor grace, but mocked both God and the holy Church.

For when he came to the church, and found the priests and clerks singing God's service, he came privily behind them, and threw ashes or dust in their mouths in despite of God ; and if he saw any one in the church kneeling in prayer, he would steal to them and give them a jerk, that they fell on their faces. Nor did he eschew any sort of vice and mischief.

The duke and duchess were marvellously aggrieved that their son was of such a disposition, and the duchess counselled her lord that, since he was now of an age to bear arms, he should be made a knight, to the end that he might be moved thereby to forsake his evil life; and at a high feast of Whitsuntide his father accordingly made him a knight, and prayed him to demean himself fitly in that estate and leave his dishonest courses. And a tournament was proclaimed in honour of this Robert being so made, whereat he by his strength and prowess overthrew all that were opposed to him, and had no peer.

But, all this notwithstanding, Robert continued steadfast in his former mischievous practices, and went about his father's dominions slaying men, ravishing women, and pillaging churches ; and when his father sent out soldiers to take him, and made proclamation of outlawry against him, he defied him and slew all that sought to arrest his body ; nay, he killed seven holy hermits that were virtuous and of good living, and martyrs in the service of God, in a great wood, crying : " I have found a nest of popish rascals, and have shorn their crowns. They were wont to kneel on their knees, and now they lie on their backs ! " A truly cursed deed and bloodshed in scorn of God and holy Church.

III.

Now when Robert the Devil had thus murthered the virtuous hermits, he rode till he came to the Château d'Arques, and all that saw him fled at his approach. Some ran and shut themselves up in their houses ; others took shelter in churches. This Robert, when he perceived how the people dreaded him, was touched with remorse and sighed. " O mighty God ! " he cried, " how is it that every man flieth me-from ? Now I see truly that I am the most mischievousest and the most cursedest wretch in the world, and seem rather to be a Jew or a Saracen than a Christian man. Alas ! I begin to loathe my ungracious life." And while he thus meditated and spake to himself, he came to the castle and lighted down from his horse.

But there was none there that would stay to hold his horse for him, and he left it standing at the gate and entered the castle, where, when his mother the duchess espied him coming, she would have likewise fled. Yet when he cried out to her piteously, say-ing, " Sweet lady mother, stay till I can speak with you," the duchess awaited him ; and when he came to her he prayed her to let him know what it was which made him so vicious and cursed, for that he had such conditions either of her or of his father, and besought her to acquaint him with the truth thereof.

Then when the duchess signified to Robert how she had given him to the devil, body and soul, at his birth, he fell down to the ground in a swoon ; and when he had somewhat recovered himself, he spake in manner as follows : "The fiends of hell use great diligence to have me to their own ; but from this time forth I forsake and eschew them and all their works, and will amend my life, quitting my sins, and doing therefore holy penance. So, O most reverent, holy mother mine, have me heartily recommended to my father ; for I will shortly take the way to Rome, to be assoiled of my sins."

Robert therefore straightway went to his companions and reproved them for their misdeeds, and shewed them how he and all of them had offended in the sight of God by robbing churches and priests, and by murthering great numbers of virtuous people ; and for that his followers would not consent to leave their wickedness, and that one of them mocked him, saying, "Lo, the fox would turn monk!" he wox wroth, and therewith slew them all.

As he rode along on his way to Rome, and was not yet far from his father's castle, he came to an abbey that he had (among many others) formerly robbed, and when the abbot and the rest saw him they fled. But when he shewed them by signs that he would speak with them, they paused, and he addressed them so piteously and graciously that they were no more afeard. Then he spake to the lord abbot, shewing his lordship how he had repented him of his acts, and praying him to have him recommended to his father, the Duke of Normandy, who would restore all that he had taken, which was stored in a certain house, whereof his father had the key; and he besought them to deliver back to every one that which of right was his; and he was about to visit our holy father the pope, to plead to him for remission of his trespass against God and holy Church.

IV.

This Robert, which some called the Devil, arrived in Rome on Shere Thursday at night; and the next day, as the custom was, the pope himself celebrated the Divine service in St. Peter's church. Robert pressed through the throng to reach the pope, and the more they pushed him back and smote him, the more he was importunate; and when he at length got nigh the pope and fell down on his knees, crying, "Holy father, have mercy on me!" the people would have still driven him away, but the pope, seeing his great earnestness, took pity on him, and suffered him to abide, to whom he said, "Good friend, what is your desire? and what aileth you that you make this stir?"

Then quoth Robert: "O holy father, I am the greatest sinner that this world knoweth, and am bound and laden with my offences against God, that, as ye are he that giveth aid and comfort to such as have need, I beseech you, for the passion of Our

Lord Jesus Christ, to purge me of all my abominable misdeeds, whereby I am deceived and defeated of all the joys of heaven."

The pope, hearing these words, mused within himself whether this were that Robert the Devil of whom he had heard such strange and heavy reports, and axed him if he was that Robert that he had heard so much speaking of, the which is of all men the worst.

Robert answered, " Yea."

The pope said : " I will assoil you ; but I conjure you to do no man hurt."

Robert gave him hearty thanks, and the pope afterward took him apart, and shrove him, learning how his mother at his conception had given him to the devil, which caused the pope to be sore afeard. Nevertheless he enjoined Robert to go three miles away out of the city to a hermit, which was his ghostly father, and to say to him that the pope sent him, and the same would assoil him.

When he came to the place where the holy hermit dwelled, he let him know that our holy father the pope had desired him to repair thither ; and as soon as the hermit had welcomed him, Robert confessed all his sins to him, setting forth at large every each thing that had happened to him since his birth, and the evil conditions that he followed, till he repented him ; and the hermit prayed him to rest there for that night in a little chapel hard by, and on the morrow he would speak with him again.

All that night the hermit prayed for Robert that God might pardon his great sins against Him, and as he slept the Lord sent an angel unto him, who said unto him thus : " Holy father, take heed to the commandment of God. If that Robert be willing to be purged of all his trespasses, he must counterfeit the ways of a fool, and feign dumbness, nor eat no manner of meat, but he take it of the dogs ; and so he must continue till it please God to declare that he hath forgiveness." And whenso the hermit awoke, he made Robert understand the matter ; and Robert was merry and glad at the thought of being assoiled by God, and without more ado returned to Rome to fulfil the ordinance of the angel, holding it a light penance enough, when he viewed all the abominable deeds of his whole life forepassed.

V.

Robert tarried in Rome a certain time, and dissembled according to the command which he had received from the angel of God, and ran about the streets like a fool, at whom the children threw dirt and stones, and the burghers of the city from their windows laughed at him and mocked him.

Whence, after a while, he departed to the emperor's court, and since the gate lay open, he entered into the hall, and he hopped and jetted up and down, never staying long in one place, till the emperor, marking him as he thus played the fool, and seeing he was a well-favoured young man, commanded one of his servants to give him to eat. But Robert spake not a word, nor would eat, neither would he drink; yet presently, whenas the emperor cast one of his hounds a bone, Robert rose and sought to take it from him, and when he could not, he gnew one end and the hound the other. At last he got the bone all alone,

and gnew it right hard, for he was sore a-hungered. And the emperor cast a whole loaf at another
of the hounds, which Robert seized incontinently
and brake in twain, giving the hound half, and keeping half, which made the emperor deem that he was
a natural fool and a very noddy; and all present
laughed at him for being such an innocent. And
when he had eaten fully, he went to a fountain in
the garden and drank therein, and afterward smote
with his staff, as he wandered about, on stools and
benches, as he had been mad; and at last, when it
was night, he lay down under a stair with the dogs,
and slept.

Now a strange accident befell when Robert was
thus doing his penance in Rome; for the emperor
had a daughter which was born dumb, and had never
spoken since her birth; and nevertheless, because
she was heir to her father after his death, the great
seneschal sought her in marriage, and when the
emperor denied him, he led a great host of Saracens
against Rome.

The emperor, assembling his lords, prayed them
of their counsel how he might withstand these
heathen dogs, and they advised him to muster all
his power and might and drive them away; and
when the emperor had made proclamation through
all his lands, and had assembled a great army, he
marched against those heathen caitiffs.

Robert remained at home, and was drinking at
the fountain in the garden on the same day on which
the emperor should give battle to the Saracens,
when a voice came down to him from heaven, saying: "Robert, God commandeth you by me that

you put on this armour incontinently, and mount upon this white horse that He hath sent you likewise, and ride as swiftly as you may to rescue the emperor and his people."

Robert, hearing the commandment of God, which he might not disobey, aroused himself, and leaping into the saddle, took his way toward the emperor ; and as he departed, the emperor's daughter beheld him from a window, and would have spoken, but might not, for that she was dumb. Robert spurred his horse forward with all speed to the field, and saw how the Christian host was being pressed on each side by those cursed hounds the Saracens ; and suddenly throwing himself into their midst, he made such havoc among them that it was a world to see the ground strown with the limbs of the dead. Those damned dogs were constrained to yield, and the emperor returned joyously to Rome. But Robert was there before him, and he had a scar in his face, yet was otherwise whole.

The emperor was glad to see Robert again, for, albeit he was a fool, he loved him well enough ; and marking the wound on his face, he thought that some had done him hurt through envy while he was at the battle, and he straightway notified to all that none should harm Robert, or he should rue it, as he would make him an example to the rest.

Then the emperor began to axe among his knights if it were so that any of them wist who the knight upon the white horse was, that came privily on the field. But they could not tell him ; and thereupon the emperor's daughter pointed to Robert, yet spake not. Her father sent for her governess,

and axed her what his daughter meant by her pointing. The governess answered and said : " Your
daughter means that ye have gotten the battle this
day through the help of your fool Robert, and the
scar that he hath on his face he hath gained it
on the field." But the emperor rebuked her, and
advised that she should teach his daughter more
wisdom than to think so foolishly ; yet was it in truth
as the emperor's daughter signified. And a second
and a third time came the Saracens in greater
numbers than before to besiege and take the city,
and were discomfited only by the marvellous valour
of the knight on the white horse : nor none could
tell the emperor whence he came or whither he
went ; albeit, after the third battle, a certain knight,
that had lain in wait for Robert in a wood, wounded
him in the thigh with a spear, and left the spear
head there, yet nevertheless could not overtake him,
nor discover who he was.

VI.

But when Robert came again to the fountain, he
drew the spear-head out of his thigh, and hid the
same between two great stones there-by ; and he
dressed his wound with grease and moss, deeming
that none marked him. But the emperor's daughter
saw him do these things, as she stood at her
window ; and for that he seemed a fair and well-
favoured young knight, she began to nourish an
affection for him.

The knight who had wounded Robert, as is
aforesaid, counselled the emperor that he might
discover who the knight upon the white horse was,

if he published his proclamation that whoever had been hurt in those battles against the heathens, riding on a white horse, and should bring with him the spear-head wherewith he was wounded in the thigh, would receive in marriage the emperor's daughter, and half the empire with her.

Whereupon the seneschal, weening that he might by stratagem gain his desire, which was to espouse the emperor's daughter, caused to be procured a white horse and white armour, and wounded himself in the thigh with a spear-head. The emperor, to whom he presented himself, was at the first loth to give ear to his tale; but he persuaded him, until he thought that, whereas he had judged him to be a false and forsworn knight, he was a wise and true one; and consented to the marriage of his daughter him-with.

After a while the seneschal set out to go to Rome to espouse the emperor's daughter, of which thing there had been proclamation and cry made, and he took with him a goodly company; and at the same time God sent an angel to command the hermit thitherward to wend, in order to see Robert, and make known unto him that his term of penance was concluded. Whereat the hermit was exceeding joyful, and accordingly went.

But when the emperor's daughter well understood that she was appointed to wed the seneschal, she was as she had been distracted and forlorn, and tore her hair and rent her garments. But nought hereof availed her; and the day was named, and everything held in readiness.

VII.

The emperor and his daughter that was born dumb, as ye have afore heard, and the pope of Rome his holiness, and their retinue, and the seneschal and his company, assembled in the church, and the bride and bridegroom stood by the altar, and the ministering priest would have begun the service, when our Lord did a fair miracle ; for by the grace of God, the young maid, that had never spoken since her birth, opened her mouth, and said as follows : " Father, I hold you not wise, in that you believe what this proud traitor telleth you, whereas all that he saith is false ; but here in this city is a holy and steadfast one, for whose sake God hath bestowed on me this day my speech ; and him I do love in my heart, and have ever noted his valiance and devotion, yet when I pointed only with my finger, no man would believe me."

The emperor was in an ecstasy, when he heard the voice of his daughter for the first time, and he knew by the words which she delivered that the seneschal had deceived him ; and the seneschal, dreading his wrath, suddenly made out of the church, and mounted his horse, and departed his way with all his folk.

Then the pope his holiness axed the maiden who the man might be whereof she spake ; and she rose up, and led the pope his holiness and the emperor her father to the fountain, where Robert had been wont to arm and unarm him ; and there she drew out from betwixt the two stones the spear-head that Robert had hidden there, which, when the spear was brought, the two joined together point-device, and quoth the emperor's daughter: "Thrice we have had the victory against the Saracens by him, and thrice I have seen him arm and unarm at this fountain, and when he had so done, lie down again among the dogs. Yet who brought him the white horse and the white armour, that know I not. This is he, notwithstanding, that hath given you, sir, the victory against the heathen; therefore, if ye will, we will even go together, and have speech of him."

So they went, and found Robert among the dogs, and did him reverence, commanding him to speak; but he answered no word, as he understood them not, and played many strange pranks to make them sport. Then the pope his holiness conjured him, in the name of God who died on the cross for our redemption, that he would lift up his voice; but Robert only rose like a fool, and gave the pope his blessing.

But anon he espied behind him the hermit, that at the bidding of God had set him his penance; and when the hermit drew near to him, he cried unto him: "My friend, hearken unto me. I know full well that ye be Robert that men call the Devil; but, lo! now ye be once again in grace with Almighty God, and in place of that foul name ye shall be termed the Servant of God. It is ye that have delivered this land from the Saracens, and I bid ye henceforward serve and worship God; for Our Lord sendeth me to you, commanding you to speak, and no more to counterfeit a fool, since it is His will and pleasure that all your trespasses shall be forgiven, and your penance determined."

When Robert heard these words of the holy hermit, he fell on his knees, and lifted up his hands toward heaven, giving praise unto God for His infinite mercy. Yet albeit the emperor saw his noble valiance and courtesy, and the emperor's daughter loved him exceeding well, the hermit would not at that time that Robert should marry that lady, saying that if it was the will of God, it would come to pass in due season ; and so each departed to his own country.

In very sooth, ere Robert, that was no longer a fool, but the high and puissant Duke of Normandy, which kept his state at Rouen in France the Fair, had long time returned home among his lieges, who loved him well enough for the gentleness and benignity of his rule through the grace of God, Our Lord charged him to repair again to Rome, to the intent that he should wed the emperor's daughter, his dearly beloved mistress ; which marriage was royally kept, and the Romans, that were so beholding to the White Knight on the White Horse, were glad that it had so in the end fallen out. And when Duke Robert brought his noble spouse, the emperor's daughter, home to Rouen in Normandy, all the people did her honour and reverence, and made her many rich gifts.

The remainder of his life Duke Robert, that was now named the Servant of Our Lord, spent in well-governing his realm, and maintaining the same in peace, so that he was beloved of every degree ; and he had born unto him of that great lady, the emperor's daughter, a son, who was called Richard, and who did many and divers deeds of arms in the wars of Charlemagne, king of France, and afterward reigned in Normandy, and was beloved of all, as his father Robert before him.

FRIAR BACON.

[*The investiture of a scholar, whose works have
been collected, and of whose true character and attain-
ments we are at present able to take more correct
measurement, with supernatural attributes and associations is the customary incidence and lot of every
career cast in an illiterate and priest-ridden epoch,
when an overwhelming majority of people could not
comprehend faculties and opinions transcending their
own, and the Church discouraged and suppressed by
every means at its command a tendency to free inquiry and independent thought. The circumstances
attendant on the mythical biography of Roger Bacon
have a good deal of affinity with those which sur-
round and disguise the actual Faustus of history.
It was readily taken for granted that studies and
disclosures so far removed beyond the general reach
must be under the auspices of some spiritual or
demoniacal agency, and the clergy spared no pains to
throw discredit on a movement which they felt to be
antagonistic to their own welfare and prestige.*

*At the same time, Bacon was, no doubt, fundamen-
tally a good Catholic, and credited many points of
belief which such a man would now-a-days view with
different eyes; and very possibly the notions which*

were affiliated on him respecting Julian the Apostate were such as he might have entertained, just as it would jump with his academical training to put faith in the submarine tour of Alexander the Great under the auspices of Aristotle, the last a proceeding which is readily traceable to the knowledge by the ancients of the science of diving.

In the case immediately before us, we hear how the priest who taught him discerned betimes the receptive tone of Bacon's intellect, how his father desired to keep him to the plough, and how the boy escaped from home to become a prominent figure in the literary annals of his native land. The growth of information has long enabled us to read such a story as that below between the lines, and to arbitrate between Bacon and the period which produced him. It was no consolation to such men, that we, coming so long after, gladly and proudly accord to them their real place in the domain of intellect, and in the ranks of those who led the way in promoting secular education ; yet it was something if they escaped the halter or the fagot. Bacon flourished at a transitional period, and was fortunate enough to inspire wonder, without incurring super-stitious dread and hatred.

Portions of this narrative are obviously borrowed from earlier sources, such as the supernatural power conferred on Miles's tabor, which is a loan from the " Friar and the Boy" : and the scene where rare fruits are exhibited before the court out of season, which is in Boccaccio and in Painter's " Palace of Pleasure," and which recurs in the " History of Faustus"; and again the friar is invested, when *occasion serves, with the mischievous or tricksome attributes of Robin Goodfellow.*

It may be observed that the idea of presenting the dancers before the king was probably suggested to the compiler by the antic-masques at court and elsewhere which became so frequent and fashionable during the reign of James I. In fact, Bacon exhibited a masque of the Five Senses; and a second occurs as a sequel to the marriage of Millisant to her truelove by the agency of Bacon. This was just such another performance—an antic masque of Apes. One or two of the adventures narrated are from the jest-books; and the story of " How Friar Bacon did Help a Young Man to his Sweetheart" reads like an analogue of Robin Hood and Allen à Dale.

The illogical incongruity of the supernatural features in this romance is common to nearly all narratives of the class. We have noticed it in " Virgilius," and it is discernible in " Friar Rush" and " Faustus."

Miraculous circumstances and adventures constituted, of course, an attractive feature among readers of our popular literature; and the confused notions of sorcery and magic in the minds of the latter were not unfrequently shared by the authors of the fictions, who, besides, might be desirous of reconciling the objections of the most squeamish by making the devil and his friends come off second-best at the last.

The confines of the normal and supernatural are necessarily unadjusted by any fixed or recognised law, and are at the mercy of any particular writer's fancy or convenience; and the harmonious and effective fusion of two distinct elements has always proved

beyond the reach of average literary workers. Hence
arises the whimsical and vexatious jumble which
these stories of enchantment display.]

I.

THERE once lived in the west country a rich farmer,
who had an only son. The farmer's name was
Bacon, and his son was called Roger ; and, not
because his father looked to make him a holy clerk,
but for that he should get learning enough to enable
him to use his wealth wisely, this Roger was put with
the parson of the town where he was born, to learn
his letters and to become a scholar.

But the boy discovered so rare an aptitude and so
quick a wit, that his master could, after a short time,
teach him no more ; and as he judged it to be pity
that young Bacon should lose what he had gained,
he went to the farmer, and exhorted him to suffer
Roger to go to Oxford, that he might shew, by
taking upon him that charge, his thankfulness to
God in having sent him such a son.

The father said little ; but as soon as Roger came
home, he asked for his books, and taking them and
locking them up, gave him a cart-whip in place
thereof, saying to him so :

" Boy, I will have you no priest ; you shall be no
better learned than I ; you can tell, as it is, by the
almanac when it is best to sow wheat, when barley,
peas, and beans, and when the gelding season comes ;
and how to buy and sell I shall instruct thee anon,
for fairs and markets are to me what his mass and
Ave, Maria, are to Sir John. Take this whip ; it

will prove more useful to you than crabbed Latin. Now do as I bid, or, by the mass, you will rue it."

The young fellow thought this hard measure ; but he made no reply, and within a short space he gave his father the slip, and entered himself in a cloister some twenty miles off, where he was heartily entertained, and continued his studies.

And ere many years had passed he made such progress in all kinds of learning that he grew famous, and was invited to go to the University of Oxford, where he perfected himself in all the sciences, and was known for a master of the secrets of art and nature throughout Christendom.

Now the king of England, hearing of this learned friar, and of the wonderful things which he was able to perform and to answer, sent for him at such time as he and the queen were sojourning in Oxfordshire ; and he said to the king's messenger :

"I pray you thank his grace from me, and say that I am at his grace's service ; but take heed lest I be at the court two hours before thee."

"Scholars, old men, and travellers," answered the messenger, "may lie with authority. Scarce can I credit such a thing."

"To convince you, I could tell you the name of the wench you last lay with ; but I will do both within four hours."

The gentleman departed in haste ; but, whether he took the wrong road or not, the friar was there before him.

The king warmly welcomed him, and told him, from what great marvels he had heard of him, that he had long desired to see him. The friar declared that report had been too flattering, and that among the sons of learning there were many worthier than himself. The king prayed him not to be too modest, and to afford him some taste of his skill ; and he said that he should be unworthy of possessing either art or knowledge, did he grudge to make his grace and the queen witnesses of his ability. So he begged them to seat themselves.

Friar Bacon then waved his wand, and forthwith there arose such ravishing music that all were amazed.

" This is to please," quoth he, " the Sense of Hearing. All the other senses shall be gratified, ere I have done."

He waved his wand again, and the music waxed louder ; and, lo ! five dancers entered, the first like a court-laudress, the second like a footman, the third like an usurer, the fourth like a prodigal, the fifth like a fool. And when they had given great content by their antics and positions, they vanished in the order in which they came. This was the indulgence of the second Sense, or the Sense of Sight.

He waved his wand the third time, and the music was changed, and before them appeared a table covered with all manner of delicious fruits, many not to that season belonging ; and when they had partaken fully thereof, they were suddenly removed from view. And this was the Sense of Taste.

Then the wand once more moved, and the most fragrant perfumes filled the air. And this was the Sense of Smell. And presently for the fifth and last time Friar Bacon exercised his mastery, and men of divers nations, as Russians, Polanders, Indians,

Armenians, were seen bearing the richest furs, which they offered to the king and the queen to handle, and for softness they surpassed all that had ever been seen of that nature. And this was the Sense of Touch.

When it happened that these wonders were at an end, Friar Bacon demanded of his majesty if there was any other thing in which he might do him service ; and the king thanked him, and said no, not for that time, and he took a costly jewel from his neck, and gave it to the friar of his royal bounty. And when the friar was about to take his leave of the court, he cast his eyes round, and espied the messenger hurrying in with all speed, covered with mud, for he had ridden through quagmires and ditches, through mistaking his way.

" Be not wrath," said the friar to him ; " I shall now fulfil my word, that I pledged to thee." And he lifted the hangings, and there stood a kitchen-maid, with her basting-ladle in her hand.

" I trow," quoth the friar, " you have no great store of money in your purse, and I will bear the charges of your wench's journey home." And at his bidding she disappeared, and all laughed at the gentleman's greasy sweetheart.

Now Friar Bacon had one servant to wait upon him, and his name was Miles ; and he was none of the wisest. So the friar being yet at Oxford in residence with other scholars, all were wont to fast on the Friday ; and none so devout as Miles, for when his master offered him bread to eat, he would refuse it, saying that it was holier and meeter not to eat ought. But the friar, knowing his craft, and that he secretly ate meat, served him well for his deceit, and it was in this manner following.

On a certain Good Friday, when the friar was accustomed to partake of bread only, he tendered some to Miles; but Miles with a grave aspect turned away from it, and desired leave to fast altogether. Then he left his master, and went where he had a delicate black-pudding, that he had made the day before, and began to eat the same. But the friar his master so contrived by his art, that when his man had set the end of the pudding in his mouth, he might in no wise remove it again; and when he pulled and pulled, and it stirred not, he cried out for help. The friar ran to him, and taking the other end of the pudding, drew him to the hall, where all the other scholars were, and shewed them how Miles would not eat meat on Fridays for conscience' sake; and he tied him by the pudding for a while to one of the window-bars, where he looked like a bear fastened by his nose to a stake.

II.

Friar Bacon now began to accomplish many other strange and marvellous works. Whereof one was the deliverance of a gentleman in Oxfordshire, that had been a prodigal, and had brought his estate to ruin. This gentleman scarce knew at the last how to earn bread enough to keep him during the rest of his miserable existence, and so he wandered about here and there. Then came to him one day an old penny-father, and besought him that he would say why he was in this piteous case.

A. L.   G

The Oxfordshire gentleman told the stranger everything, and the other said that, if he would fulfil certain conditions, he would furnish him with money enough for all his creditors; and when he said that he would swear to return the money, the old man rejoined that it was not oaths he would have, but bonds.

So the gentleman met him the next morning in a wood, as they had appointed, and he was attended by two serving-men carrying money-bags. Then he dictated to him the conditions on which he would lend him what he needed; and they were, that he should discharge all his debts, and when he was no longer indebted to any man, he should become at a word the slave of the lender.

That gentleman, in the plight in which he found himself at that time, yielded to this treaty, and paid all his mortgages and chief creditors, and became richer than he had ever been before. But he was secretly troubled in his mind when he remembered how he had bound himself to the stranger, and had consented to submit to his will; and after a time the old penny-father appeared, and claimed his bond, saying, "Thou hast paid thy debts, now thou art mine." But he replied, "Nay, sir; I have not yet discharged them all." And the usurer therefore waxed wrath, and transformed himself into a horrible shape, and cried, "Thou shalt not so deceive me; I will come to-morrow morning and prove to thee thy falsehood, till when I leave thee to despair." And he vanished, and the gentleman now knew that it was the devil with whom he had made that compact.

This caused him to be so sorrowful and downcast, that he would have thrown himself on his sword, and so ended his life, had not Friar Bacon happily interposed, and comforted him ; and when he unfolded to the friar what had passed between the devil and himself, the friar said unto him so : " Sir, appoint to meet the devil to-morrow in the wood, and for the rest be content."

So the Oxfordshire gentleman met the devil in the wood, and the devil in sore anger upbraided him with his falsity, and commanded him to tarry no more, but to follow him. Then the gentleman asked him whether he would suffer some one to be judge in the case, and to deliver an award ; and the devil agreed thereto. Whereupon suddenly Friar Bacon was seen by the gentleman walking near at hand, and he called him, and set out how the matter was. Friar Bacon considered, and asked the gentleman whether he had ever paid anything to the devil for all his great goodness to him, and he answered that he had not. Then he told him, as he valued his life, never so to do, for he was his chief creditor ; and thereupon the devil vanished with a loud cry, and the Oxfordshire gentleman thanked Friar Bacon for the great boon which he had conferred upon him in so wisely judging between them.

III.

The next exploit which Friar Bacon sought to achieve proved him a loyal subject to his prince and a dear friend to England. For reflecting how often England had been invaded by Saxon and Dane and

Norwegian, he laboured with a project for surrounding the whole island with a wall of brass, and to the intent that he might compass this, he first devised a head of brass which should speak. And when he could not for all his art arrive at this, he invited another great scholar, Friar Bungay by name, to aid him therein; and they both together by great study made a head of brass, yet wist not how to give it motion and speech; and at last they called to their succour a Spirit, who directed them, but gave them warning that, when the head began to speak, if they heard it not ere it had finished, all their labour would be lost.

So they did as the Spirit had enjoined them, and were right weary; and bidding Miles to wake them when the Head spake, they fell asleep.

Now Miles, because his master threatened him if he should not make them aware when the head spake, took his tabor and pipe, and sang ballads to keep him from nodding, as, *Cam'st thou not from Newcastle? Dainty, come thou to me*, and *It was a rich merchant-man.*

Presently the Head spake, saying, TIME IS! but Miles went on playing and singing, for the words seemed to him to import nought. Twice and thrice the head said TIME IS! but Miles was loth to wake his master and Friar Bungay for such a trifle; and there, surely enough, came in one of his ditties, *Dainty, come thou to me*, and he began to sing,—

> " Time is for some to eat;
>   Time is for some to sleep;
>   Time is for some to laugh;
>   And time is for some to weep.

> Time is for some to sing;
>   Time is for some to pray;
> Time is for some to creep
>   That have drunk all the day."

At the end of half an hour the Head spake once more, and delivered these two words, TIME WAS! And Miles made sport of them, as he had done before. Then another half-hour passed, and the head uttered this sentence, TIME IS PAST! and fell down amid flashes of fire and terrible noise; whereat the two friars awoke, and found the room full of smoke.

" Did not the Head speak ?" asked Bacon.

" Yea, sir," replied his man; " but it spake to no purpose. I'd teach a parrot to talk better in half the time."

" Out on thee, villain !" cried his master; " thou hast undone us both. Hadst thou roused us, all England would have been walled about with brass, and we had won everlasting renown. What did it say ?"

" Very few words," answered Miles, " and I have heard wiser. It said, TIME IS !"

" Hadst thou called us then, we had been made for ever."

" Then in half an hour it said, TIME WAS !"

" And thou didst not wake us then !" interposed Bungay.

" Alack, sir," answered Miles, " I was expecting him to begin some long tale, and then I would have awakened you; but anon he cried, TIME IS PAST ! and made such an uproar withal that he woke you himself."

Friar Bacon was greatly incensed at what his servant had done, and would have beaten, and maybe slain him; but Friar Bungay pleaded for the fellow, and his master said, "Well, his punishment shall be, that he shall be struck dumb for a month."

So it was that England was not girded round with a brazen wall, as had nearly come to pass.

IV.

Friar Bacon, this mishap notwithstanding, ever grew more famous as time passed; and it so fortuned that, when the king of England proceeded to his conquests in France, and could by no means take a certain town, but, on the contrary, sustained much loss before it, he wox angry, and offered ten thousand crowns truly counted to any one who should conquer this town and gain it for him.

So when proclamation had been made to such effect, and no one came to essay to do what the king desired, Friar Bacon, leaving his studies, crossed over to France and sought admittance to the king. To whom he recalled how his grace had formerly shown him great courtesy in Oxfordshire, and he was now ready to do his pleasure.

"Bacon," said our lord the king, "alas! it is not art but arms that I now require."

"Your grace saith well," returned the friar; "but be pleased to remember that art doth oftentimes accomplish more than force. And speaking of art and nature, pure and simple, without any magical property, consider how ships are made without oars, and large vessels to cross the wide sea, and only one man to guide them ; how chariots may be built to move with incredible force without human help to stir them ; and how one may fly in the air, and turn an engine ; or walk in the bottom of the sea (as Alexander the Great did) ; and, which is more pertinent at this time, how by means of a mirror you may make one man wear the semblance of a whole army, and what is far off seem near at hand, and what is high, low, or the contrary.   So Socrates did detect the dragon that lurked in the mountains, and destroyed all around.   Then, as Aristotle instructed Alexander, instruments may be contrived by which venomous influences may be brought in contact with a city, and infect its inhabitants every one, even the poison of a basilisk lifted up upon the wall.   These things are worth a kingdom to a wise man."

His grace gave leave to Friar Bacon to do as it liked him, and he should name his reward ; and the friar caused an earthwork to be raised higher than the city wall, and desiring his grace to be in readiness the next morning to attack the town, when he should wave a flag from the earthwork on the morrow, at nine of the clock the friar had, with certain mathematical glasses, set fire to the town hall, and while the people and the soldiers were busy in extinguishing the flames, the flag was waved, and the king took the place with little resistance.

He treated the inhabitants with such clemency, that he won the love of his brother the king of France, who, to divert him, summoned a servant of his, a German named Vandermast, to shew conjuring sleights before both their graces ; and the king of England, understanding what the entertainment was to be, privily sent for Friar Bacon and Friar Bungay to come to him, that they might witness the same. But he bad them keep their counsel.

When the banquet was over, Vandermast asked the king of England if it was so that he would choose to see the spirit of any man that had formerly lived. The king said, "Yea; above all I would see Pompey, who could brook no equal." And Vandermast made him appear as he was attired at the battle of Pharsalia, whereat all were mightily contented.

Then Friar Bacon, all without warning given, raised the ghost of Julius Cæsar, who could brook no superior, and had beaten Pompey at Pharsalia; and Vandermast, not knowing that Friar Bacon was present, said that there was some one in the hall who was skilled in magic. To whom Bacon discovered himself, and declared that he had brought Cæsar to overthrow Pompey, as he did erst; and therefore Cæsar engaged Pompey, and vanquished him. Which pleased all present passing well, and then both disappeared.

The king of England said to the German ambassador, that he thought his man had got the better of Vandermast; but Vandermast said that he would tell a different tale, ere all was done. "Ah!" said Friar Bacon, "my companion, Friar Bungay, shall deal with thee, sirrah; and if thou canst worst him, I will try what I may do, and not till then."

Then Friar Bungay raised the Hesperian tree, laden with golden apples, which were guarded by a fiery dragon stretched beneath its branches. Vandermast conjured up the ghost of Hercules, and said, " This is Hercules, who in his lifetime gathered the fruit of the tree, and made the dragon crouch at his feet ; and so shall he do again."

But when Hercules offered to take the fruit, Friar Bacon raised his wand, and Hercules desisted. Vandermast threatened him, an' he picked it not : but he said, " Vandermast, I cannot ; I am fearful ; for here is great Bacon, that is more powerful than thee." Vandermast cursed Hercules, and again threatened him. But Bacon bad him not fret himself, for since he could not persuade Hercules to do his bidding, he himself would cause him to perform some service ; and he commanded Hercules to take up Vandermast and carry him back straightway into Germany.

" Alas !" cried the ambassador ; " I would not have lost Vandermast at any price."

" Fear not, my lord," answered Bacon ; " he hath but gone home to see his wife, and shall return to you anon."

V.

Shortly after, when Friar Bacon had come again into England, a rich man of that country died, and left his estate to that one among his three sons who loved him best ; and none could say how that was, for each one avowed that it was he, by reason that to him his father was most dear. So Friar Bacon was asked of the king to aid him in this matter ; and that learned and famous man, when the three brethren agreed to abide by his judgment, having caused the body of the father to be taken from the ground, and gotten ready three bows and three

arrows, summoned the sons to attend him, and said
unto them so : " Sirs, there appeared to be no
other method whereby this controversy might be
concluded ; therefore I have brought hither the
dead body of your father, and whoever strikes him
nearest to his heart shall have all his goods and
lands."

The two elder brothers shot one after the other,
and both hit the body, yet did not go near the
heart. But the youngest refused to shoot, saying
that he would liever lose his patrimony ; and Friar
Bacon awarded him the estate, because he shewed
by his loyal act that he loved his father better than
the others : and all men commended the friar's
wisdom therein.

Now, albeit Friar Bacon had seldom indeed taken
any reward for all his great services to our lord the
king and many other, yet the report spread abroad
that in his house he kept a rich treasure ; and certain thieves brake one night thereinat, and demanded
of Miles, who admitted them, and of the friar, what
money they had. The friar answered that he was
but poorly furnished with money ; whereto they
replied, these three thieves, that they must have
whatso there was : and the friar gave them one
hundred pounds each in a bag.

They heartily rejoiced at their good fortune ; and
he said to them that they should have music to
boot, which still further contented them ; and Miles
took his tabor, and began to play thereon. Then
the three thieves rose and set to dancing, and
danced so lustily with their money-bags in their
hands that they grew weary, but could not cease,

for the friar had set a spell on them; and Miles
went out of the door playing the while, and led the
thieves over the fields, and over hedge and ditch,
and through quagmire and pond, till they were wet
to the skin and weary to death. Then Miles
stayed his hand, and they lay down as they were
and slept; and he took the money from them, and
returned home to his master.

Meanwhile Vandermast was plotting how he
could compass the death of Friar Bacon, to revenge
the dishonour which had been cast upon him in
France; and the friar, looking into his books, and
finding that a great danger would befall him in the
second week of the present month, unless he used
some means to prevent it, devised this sleight,
namely, while he read to hold a ball of brass in one
hand, and beneath it was a brass basin, and percase
he should fall asleep, the loosing of the ball from
his hand would wake him.

Now Vandermast had recently hired a Walloon
soldier to come over to England, and to kill Bacon,
and if he did so his reward was to be one hundred
crowns; and when he arrived at Bacon's house, this
Walloon soldier found Bacon dosing, yet the ball
of brass still in his hand; but as he lifted his sword
to slay him, the ball dropped into the basin, and
Bacon woke.

" Who art thou ? " he demanded of the Walloon.

" I am a Walloon, and a soldier, and more than
that, a villain ; and I am come, hired by Vandermast, to kill thee."

" What is thy religion ? "

" To go to an ale-house, to abstain from evil for

want of employment, and to do good against my will."

"A good profession for a devil! Dost thou believe in hell?"

"I believe in no such thing."

Then Friar Bacon raised the spirit of Julian the Apostate, with his body burning and full of wounds, whereat the soldier was almost out of his wits for fear. Friar Bacon asked the spirit wherefore he was thus tormented; and he answered, that he had been happy if he had remained a Christian, but he abjured the true faith, and now endured the doom of all unbelieving wretches.

The Walloon soldier that had come to kill the friar stood trembling all this time, and when the friar dismissed the spirit, he begged him that he would instruct him in a better course of life, which the friar engaged to do; and this Walloon became a true Christian, and died in the Holy War.

VI.

It becomes time to relate how once Friar Bacon had a strange adventure, and helped a young man to his sweetheart that Friar Bungay would have married to another.

An Oxfordshire gentleman had a daughter named Millisant, who was courted by a youth whose love she returned, and whose wife she desired to be; but her father was averse from that match, and would have wedded her to a rich knight.

This knight, when he perceived how loth the maiden was, went to Friar Bungay, and asked him to get her for him, either by his counsel or art;

and Bungay, for that he was something covetous, promised, if he would take the lady for the air in a coach, so to direct the horses that they should bring them to an old chapel in the wood, where they might be secretly married.

But meantime the gentleman had sought Friar Bacon, and implored him to do what he might to further his suit; and Bacon, knowing him to be virtuous and deserving, brought out a beryl, wherein he could see his best-beloved and the knight in the chapel, though it was fifty miles thence, on the eve of being joined together in holy matrimony by Friar Bungay. The gentleman was overwhelmed by grief; but Bacon bad him be of good cheer, and seating him and himself in a chair, they were presently at the chapel door. Friar Bungay was about to join their hands, when Bacon struck him dumb, and raising a mist in the chapel, no one could see his way, but each mistook the other, and amid their bewilderment Bacon led Millisant to the poor gentleman, and they were married by him in the chapel porch, and furnished with good store of money for their journey; and while they went their way joyfully together, the friar by his magic detained the father and the knight in the chapel, until they could not overtake them. And at a certain distance he prepared for them (albeit unseen) a banquet, succeeded by an antic masque of apes with music, wherein first entered three apes, and then three more, dressed in quaint coats, and then six; and all danced in merry and strange wise together, and then, when they had saluted the bridegroom and the bride, vanished.

VII.

News had been brought to Vandermast, where he sojourned in Germany, that at length Friar Bacon was dead ; and accordingly he came over once more into England, and met Friar Bungay in Kent, whom-of he learned that Bacon yet lived.

Now he bare no goodwill to Bungay, for that he was a friend to Bacon ; and when he rose in the morning to leave his inn, he went to the stable where Bungay's horse was, and took it, leaving a spirit in its room. And when Bungay sought his horse to go on his way, he wist not what Vandermast had done, and mounted it, and in the middle of a stream it let him go, so that he perforce returned to his inn, at the door whereof he met the other, who asked him if he had been in a swimming match, and Bungay answered him again, that had he been so well posted as he was when he went to Germany, this would not have so fallen out. Vandermast bit his lip, but said nought. And then Bungay, knowing that this German loved a wench in the house, and spared no pains to get her, shaped a spirit in her likeness, which yielded unto his advances, that he was enraptured ; and when he had gone to bed, the sheet on which they lay was carried into the air, and fell into a deep pond. When Bungay saw him, he asked him how he liked the girl.

" Marry, I wish thee such another," quoth he.

" Nay, the rules of my order forbid it," he replied.

So it came to pass that these two conjurors grew more and more wroth each with other, until at last

the Devil wox impatient of not having received
from them the money for teaching them all their
knowledge, and slew them, so that they were
strangely scorched with fire amid a mighty storm
of wind and rain; and the country people, finding
their bodies, bestowed on them Christian burial,
for that Bungay was a friar and Vandermast a
stranger.

VIII.

You have heard that Friar Bacon, who thus
out-lived both Bungay and Vandermast, possessed
a wonderful glass, in which it was possible to see
what was happening some fifty miles away; and
this glass had been a source of great profit and
pleasure to many, whom Bacon had obliged with
the use thereof; till it happened that two youths,
whose fathers — being neighbours — were absent
from home, wished to know how they did, and
besought Bacon to suffer them to look in his glass.

But those gentlemen, since their departure, had
grown to be foes one to the other, and when their
sons looked, they saw that their fathers were on
the eve of fighting together, and as they fought
one killed the other; and this sight so fired one
of the youths whose father was thus slain, that he
began to quarrel with his friend, and they both
became so furious that they stabbed each other.
Which when Friar Bacon knew, hearing the noise,
he was so grieved, that he broke his mirror, the
like whereof the whole world could not shew; and
then arrived the news of the deaths of Bungay and

Vandermast, which further distressed him, so that he kept his chamber three days.

He now began to repent his wicked and vain life, spent in the service of the devil, and to turn his thoughts to Divine studies : and calling together many of his friends, he addressed them in these words :

" My good friends and fellow-students, it is not unknown to you how by my art I have attained great credit with all, and have done many wonders, as every one knows, both king and commons.   I have unlocked the secrets of nature, and have laid them open to the view of man, whereas they had been buried and lost since the days of Hermes the philosopher.   I have revealed the mysteries of the stars and of every kind of life that is under the sun. Yet all this my knowledge I value so lightly, that I could wish I were ignorant ; for what hath it availed me, save to keep me from the study of God, and the care of my soul, which is the immortal part of man.   But I hasten to remove the cause of all my error, gentlemen."   And, a fire burning in the hearth, before they could prevent him, Friar Bacon threw all his books therein, and consumed them utterly.

Then he gave away all his goods to the poor, and building himself a cell in the church wall, with-drew from the world, and after two years' space died a true, penitent sinner.

FAUST OR FAUSTUS.

[*The material for judging the true character and attributes of the remarkable individual who constitutes the subject-matter of the next item in our collection is chiefly preserved in a German prose book of* 1587, *when about half a century had elapsed since the death of Faustus. Beyond this source of knowledge we have one or two accidental pieces of testimony on the part of persons who either saw our hero or had heard of him in his lifetime; and on this information we have to found our estimate of the alleged magician, for, as we shall explain, the dramatic creations of Marlowe and others, no less than the popular theory, are, one and all, more or less unfaithful to reality. In the introductory remarks, we have ventured to suggest certain notions about the intellectual history of Faustus; and what succeeds is a careful digest of the Elizabethan version of the legend, published only five years later than the German original, compared with a second English text a couple of years later in date.*

The second pseudo-biography, which purports to be the work of an English student at Wittenberg some fifty years after the time, takes serious exception to its predecessor; but it appears to be, on the whole, an inferior production, and to have been very loosely and clumsily compiled. It is neither a supplement to the earlier text nor a revision of it, but a wholly distinct assemblage of stories and adventures, arranged without any ostensible regard to propriety or sequence.

The partiality and veneration for the supernatural and weird which have constantly manifested themselves in the professors of demonology and witchcraft, as well as in those who have gained an indirect knowledge of such studies by hearsay and guesswork, readily explain the estimate which his contemporaries formed of Faust or Faustus, and the discrepancy between our present conclusions as to the nature of his employments, his power, and his fate.

It was not till Faustus had been nearly half a century underground that the idea occurred to a German romancist of utilizing all the current popular myths relating to him, and others of the same stamp, for literary purposes; and there appeared at Berlin in 1587 a volume professing to recount with fidelity the transactions of that rather brief and still more obscure and uneventful career. The book was calculated to tickle the palates of readers to whom the very name of a retired student of a former generation would be in many instances new, and of whose character and achievements the author might confidently propagate the wildest fictions and extravagances with impunity and profit. During the lapse of fifty years all those who were acquainted with the truth had died, and there was no school of analytical criticism to dissect and estimate a plausible tissue of chimerical or mischievous inventions, vamped up jests, and affiliated matter of all kinds.

Under the name of Faustus we find at least four impersonations: (1) the Faustus of real life, so far as we can make him out, the son of poor parents, studying at first for holy orders, then diverting into the occult sciences, and questioning cardinal points of theological doctrine ; a shy, secluded scholar, of whose pursuits and opinions few had any correct knowledge ; living almost in solitude, and dying under conditions which favoured the report that he had been strangled by the devil. (2) The Faustus of German prose fiction, in whom the natural course of things concentrated all the marvels and prodigies current in oral tradition from want of better information, and to lend an air of freshness to a string of fables and jests in circulation about Eustace the Monk and other earlier men of similar tastes and endowments. (3) The Faustus of Marlowe. (4) The Faustus of Goethe.

In order to be in a position to understand the actual facts, which are few enough, we have to try to forget that Faustus ever became a hero and central figure of romance, a puppet, which each succeeding age and school of fiction felt at liberty to turn without scruple to its own account. We are dealing with a biography, which seems to have extended from 1491 to 1538. Faustus died comparatively young ; he is made in the story to lament his premature fate. He was born at Knütlingen in Silesia, and breathed his last at a village near Wittenberg. He could have barely reached his forty-eighth year.

The circumstances attending the birth and education of this distinguished and enlightened man are narrated with tolerable fulness in the history of his career. His relations were evidently anxious that he should go into the Church, and his youthful studies were originally directed to such an object.

But the learning which he acquired in this manner operated in inspiring him at once with a distaste for the calling, and a misgiving as to many points of religious belief. He relinquished the project of joining the clerical body, and proceeded to devote himself to the study of medicine, with which at that period astrology and alchemy were commonly associated.

Of his real progress in his new profession we know next to nothing; but it is said that he, like many other physicians, became at one time a compiler of almanacks and prognostications; and a considerable portion of one epoch of his life was spent in foreign travel. He visited, besides various parts of Germany, France, Italy, and the Levant; but the extent of his observations and experiences are, we suspect, over-stated in books.

He was fond of pleasure; his temperament was voluptuous, and his imagination lively and warm; and he met with many strange adventures, even casting aside the apocryphal incidents which are vulgarly coupled with his name.

We have to exercise a good deal of moral self-restraint, if we desire to realize this man to ourselves as he probably was. The first hint of anything approaching to solid ground occurs in a conversation of Melanchthon respecting him, reported by a third party in a volume printed two years after the reformer's death. Melanchthon was born at a village not far from Knütlingen, and was the junior of Faust or Faustus by several years. He is made to refer to his studies in magic, to which he had been led by attendance at public lectures delivered on that science, and he speaks of his attempt at Venice to fly, and of the devil accompanying him in the likeness of a dog; but he does not even glance at the varied and elaborate exploits which he performed, or at the compact with Mephistopheles.

Melanchthon, as a Churchman, merely cherished, perhaps, a loose persuasion that his contemporary was a freethinker, and so qualified himself for becoming a liegeman of the devil hereafter, and even a correspondent with him during life. Much of this entered then, as now, into common parlance.

The testimony of Melanchthon is valid, at any rate, to the extent of establishing the existence of Faustus and his veritable place of nativity. But he was also personally known to Paracelsus, Cornelius Agrippa, and Conrad Gessner, three men of congenial pursuits, though not sharing his strong passions and manifest proneness to sensual indulgence. The alchemists of Germany, in whom Faustus must have taken a powerful interest, if he did not participate in their researches, were of course men far in advance of their time, and were, in fact, the founders of the modern European school of chemistry.

The ignorance of physical laws, the want of communication and of the means of diffusing accurate intelligence of events, contributed to accredit to the devil any incident which passed the common comprehension. His majesty was heir-general or remainder man to all occurrences for which no key was forthcoming. Our early literature is replete from the first with prodigious accounts of his intercourse with us and his lively interest in our affairs. In 1641, a Coventry musician of parsimonious disposition was said to have made with him such another bargain as Faustus, and to have come to a similar end, " to the terror and amazement of the inhabitants." He made his presence sensible in a diversified form to innumerable persons, chiefly in humble life, whose account of the conference or vision was faithfully reported in type, and you were referred to eye-witnesses of undoubted credibility, if you wished to inquire further.

The singular revelations, which Faustus was invested with the faculty of conjuring up and making subservient to his desires, may have owed their origin to a vivid and unbridled fancy, in the same way as the imaginative vagaries which we see in the pages of Dante, Poliphilo, and our own Blake, all having their prototypes in Virgil and Homer, as these had again in the Hebrew and Chaldæan visionaries. The descriptions of heaven and hell, in the picture before us, are evidently elaborated dreams or reveries.

As far as the notes of foreign travel go, very possibly Faustus may have seen certain portions of the Fatherland at different periods of his life ; but the rest strikes us as purely imaginary, and as the product of hearsay or reading on the part of the compiler of the biography.

A habit of solitude, whether in fact or in sympathy, is apt to throw a man on his own internal resources, and to favour the realization of spectral and other illusions ; the supposititious objects which he embodies by intellectual incubation supply the place of ordinary companionship; and where the mental fabric is not sound, or where the process of solitary contemplation is too continuous, insanity often accrues.

The seers and prophets of antiquity were men of the same cast as Faustus, but with a less keen relish for life and a narrower insight and reach. They were as imperfectly understood by their contemporaries, perhaps, as he was by his.

Looking at the channels through which intelligence of Faustus and his doings might have reached posterity, we naturally turn to his servant Wagner, to whom he left his books, and who must have enjoyed a better opportunity of knowing the extent of his commerce with magic and the black art than any one else. But it is tolerably plain that (with one exception) no use was made of this source and material in framing the account, which was the superficial popular idea of the man, coloured by prejudice and distorted by time; and if we needed a further illustration of the unscrupulous application of folklore to biography and history, we might cite the absurd attempt to palm on the public, about 1712, a German compilation, pretending to describe the life and actions of Wagner, who plays the same part in the Faustus story-book as Miles does in "Friar Bacon."

At the same time, we have always to recollect that the school of biography to which the old account of Faustus appertains considered it a legitimate, or at least a safe and advantageous, feature in their work to heighten the colour or shadow of the portraiture which they presented to view by a free use of borrowed accessories; and some of the achievements of the Knütlingen wizard are mere reproductions of thirteenth and fourteenth century German folk-lore.

The conception of the grandeur of Lucifer and

his original rank in heaven, as second only to God in power and glory, is worth remarking, as one of those hints which may have assisted to form in the mind of Milton an idea of the devil at variance with the popular theory.

When the comic business and horse-tricks were inserted by way of attraction in the earliest surviving record, they had already become matter of tradition; yet, notwithstanding, we are entitled to believe that Faustus permitted occasional trespassers on his privacy and, both at home and in his foreign travels, mixed with all sorts of personages, from crowned heads to good creatures wishful to convert him, and he gratified some of these with an exhibition of his skill in legerdemain, palmistry, and astrology. He was even willing to be interviewed by individuals who sought enlightenment on some point of ordinary science, and he rarely sent them away without a solution. But he did not, it is presumable, admit any participator in his enjoyment of the beauty of Helen of Troy and other famous heroines: these were phantoms of his own seething brain, creatures of his dreams; and it is more than possible that we are indebted for them to wilfully exaggerated entries in manuscript diaries, which may have existed in 1587, *when the first pseudo-biography came from the press at Berlin.*

The accounts of the circumstances attending his death, which are somewhat conflicting, and which bear the strong impress of clerical bias and manipulation, represent him as having been found with his neck twisted, or with his brains dashed out and his body mangled. The probability seems to be that he committed suicide in a fit of despondency, and possibly, as his remains are described in one place as lying in the court-yard, he threw himself out of an upper window. We see that Christian burial is mentioned as a concession. Curiously enough, in 1581, a drama called " The Conflict of Conscience" had been founded on the somewhat analogous case of Francesco Spira, an Italian convert from Protestantism; and in 1587 a ballad was published on the same subject. When the play appeared, Spira had already been dead about three and thirty years, having perished by his own hand, and it is said under the influence of despair.

There is no legitimate room for astonishment that the mysterious labours and tastes of Faustus should have awakened in the minds of his Saxon neighbours and German countrymen generally a sentiment of dread and awe, when we consider how prevalent to this day in most parts of the world superstitious ignorance remains. The demonological portion of the narrative is of course a pure invention, partly based on contemporary gossip, and partly evolved from the fertile brain of the compiler of the German account in 1587. Half a century constituted a sufficient interval for the stealthy growth of myth round his name and his career. The very nature of his researches compelled secrecy and stratagem in such an age; and the inability to comprehend the true character of his occupations and objects tended to encourage fabulous reports.

We have only to remember that four and twenty years taken back from the received date of his decease (1538) brings us to 1514, when he was four and twenty years of age, a wholly improbable period of life for the conception of such a treaty as he is alleged to have contracted with Lucifer; and in our present state of information and opinion, even if we in England are somewhat behind Germany in philosophical analysis, it is almost superfluous to pursue the investigation further, where the corner-stone of the indictment against Faustus is so transparently compounded of idle and foolish fables, concocted by the Church or under clerical auspices to throw discredit on a reader and thinker whose bias was adverse to ecclesiasticism, but who discerned the necessity of extreme caution in ventilating heterodox views, even in the relatively tolerant Fatherland.

This may explain the presence of the jocular episodes in the history, and even the miracle of the grapes. Faustus himself never probably claimed authority over superhuman powers; it was a method adopted by others of accounting for phenomena which they were unable to comprehend; and the attribute of a familiar was nothing more than a loan from the East, when, with an almost equal measure of inconsistency, the attendant genius executes commands involving an universal jurisdiction.

It is not very hard, after all, to divine and understand the relationship between Faustus and his contemporaries. If this celebrated man had had to reckon only with the illiterate majority immediately around him, his taste for inquiry and scientific research would have probably elicited from the neighbourhood a passing expression and sentiment of wonder and curiosity, and he would have been regarded by posterity as little more than Dr. Dee or

Lilly the astrologer. But Faustus entertained and proclaimed heretical theories on religious subjects; he placed himself in antagonism to the clergy. At a period when the Church was beginning to suffer from doctrinal ruptures and a questioning spirit, such a personage was bound to become a marked object of ecclesiastical jealousy and resentment, and in the description which has been delivered to us of the Knütlingen scholar, who feared neither God nor devil, and accomplished a variety of surprising feats by supernatural expedients, we easily recognise the familiar stratagem by which the clerical party has always retaliated on its secular adversaries. At all times, but more particularly in an age of prevailing illiteracy, the Church has been the maker of popular opinion. Faustus, as he is pourtrayed by the novelist and playwright, is not the Faustus of real life, but a masquerading caricature like Guy Fawkes or Marino Faliero; and we are indebted for such a serious distortion of the truth to the reports which were circulated about him by those whose interest lay in discrediting his peculiar opinions.

Faustus, in fact, was a philosopher, whose precise views will probably never be accurately known, as there is a certain amount of contradiction in the account of him, on which we have almost exclusively to rely for our acquaintance with his intellectual training and range. It is tolerably manifest, however, that he was an unusually keen and attentive observer, under grave educational disadvantages, of the laws and processes of nature, and that he deduced therefrom a tissue of theory and speculation alike in conflict with the orthodox sentiment of his day.]

I.

JOHN FAUSTUS was the son of a poor husbandman that dwelled at a little town of Weimar in Germany named Knütlingen; and his father not being able well to bring him up, he went, as soon as he had passed childhood, to an uncle at Wittenberg, that was something richer than his father, and had no issue of his own. This uncle put Faustus to the study of divinity at the University of Wittenberg; and he read the Holy Scriptures, and farthered himself in theological learning, to the intent, as his uncle desired, that he should be a labourer in the ministry.

But Faustus, because he was of a different bent, and in no wise inclined to such a life, engaged by little and little in other exercises, to the great sorrow of his uncle, who reproved him for so neglecting the service of Almighty God, and the fitting himself for a preacher. Yet, while this youth disliked divinity, it was not by reason that he applied himself not thereto; for after he had sojourned at the university a certain space, being straitly examined therein by the masters and rectors, he was found to be deeply versed in all that referred to the Scriptures, and was accordingly admitted to his degree of doctor in that faculty.

At the same time, he commonly passed among his fellow students under the name of the Speculator, because he was ever propounding to them strange opinions, and frequented heretical books in the Chaldæan, Hebrew, Arabian, and Greek tongues, that treated of sundry infernal arts, as soothsaying, witchcraft, necromancy, conjuration, and other. Nor brooked he well the title of doctor of divinity, but chose rather to be called an astrologer, a mathematician, and a physician ; and he began to be known for a worker of notable cures, and for a man learned in the secrets of nature.

Faustus severed himself ere long from his theological studies, and entered on a most unchristian life, fearing neither God nor devil ; and he gave his time to the mastery of the black art, so that he might gain power and sovereignty over the whole world and all things therein.

Now after a while there went a report in Wittenberg that Faustus had seen the devil or his deputy in a wood near at hand, called the Spisser Holt ; and sometimes in his cups he related to his neighbours how he did that the devil might not have the better of him, which were by making a circle in the dust at the crossway, and writing thereon certain characters and signs ; and men surmised that he, Faustus, had entered into articles with the devil through his servant, that was named Mephistopheles, but what the treaty imported none as yet knew.

For Faustus kept his meetings with Mephistopheles secret, and no man wist how he had stood at first in the Spisser Holt, and endured long the fearful tokens and portents, as thunder and lightning, and roaring as of a thousand lions, that went before the appearance of the Spirit to him, who came with a horrible noise, and ran round the circle that he had made like a thousand waggons on a paved way, and a second time in the shape of a mighty dragon, that from his mouth shot a flame as bright and rapid as lightning.

But at length Faustus, through his craft, reduced Mephistopheles, that was the devil's name and a servant to Lucifer, prince of devils, to his will, and made a treaty with him, written with his blood on warm ashes, that he should at all times answer to his summons, and do his pleasure, nor tell him ought that was untrue, from that hour forward to the time of his death, provided that Faustus on his own behalf consented to deliver up his soul at the end of four and twenty years to the aforesaid Mephistopheles, servant to Lucifer, by whom all these articles were confirmed. For in hell, as on earth, all things are ordered in obedience to the command of the prince. And when Faustus had made an end of the writing, he kept one copy for himself, and the other he delivered to Mephistopheles, who thus, with the assent of Lucifer, became the servant of Faustus in all things, at all times, his life during.

II.

Now Faustus had a boy with him in his house at Wittenberg to serve and wait upon him, whose name was Christopher Wagner. This boy Faustus loved well, and taught him his own arts, that he might grow up to be a necromancer such as he was ; and they lived together in the house at Wittenberg which had belonged to the uncle of Faustus, and was now his by inheritance. They both fared exceeding well, and went in sumptuous raiment ; for Mephistopheles brought whatever Faustus commanded him from the cellars of great lords and from merchants dwelling in that country, who lost their wine, and victual, and fine cloth, and all manner of rich goods, and divined not whither they were taken : which were carried by Mephistopheles to Wittenberg to the house of Faustus, his master, secretly ; and Faustus waxed so cunning in his science, that he learned to conjure the birds of the air into his hands, as they flew over his dwelling, and of the dantiest.

But when Faustus desired to enter into wedlock with a fair lady, the Spirit forbad him, saying that he could not serve two masters, for that, whereas he had given his soul to the devil, marriage was a holy institution, ordained of God ; which made Faustus heavy at heart. Then Mephistopheles brought him a book, in which he might look and find the means of doing all things that he lusted, which occasioned Faustus to demand of him how it chanced that Lucifer had so great a fall.

Mephistopheles thereupon answered and said that his prince had been, next to God, the highest and most puissant in heaven, above Michael and Gabriel, that were named Angels of God's Wonders, as they were, again, above the lower degree of angels ; and because he was so high and great, he aspired to put God from His throne, and was cast down, never to return, unless it be so that God summon him ; and Faustus thanked the Spirit, for that he made him aware of these things, and Mephistopheles vanished, as was his wont.

Faustus thereupon came to dream of hell, and he questioned the Spirit further upon the same, as how many kingdoms were therein, and what were the several rulers' names, and especially concerning Lucifer; of whom Mephistopheles satisfied him in all

points, shewing how he once far exceeded all the other
creatures of God for worthiness, pomp, authority,
and shape, and surpassed the very sun in splendour
and brightness, and was for ever before God's
throne, but therefore waxed proud and presump-
tuous, and was banished from the sight of God, and
was thrown down into the fire which no water may
quench. "Alas! alas!" thought Faustus, "and am
I not likewise a creature of God's making? and shall
I suffer a like doom? Ah! woe is me that ever I
was born!" And the wretched Faustus grieved
that he should have forsaken the faith of Christ,
and bound himself to Satan, that he might in no
wise escape from so damnable an end.

Nor he could not now give his thought to anything but hell, of which he thirsted to know more
and more, and could not bear to turn his eyes
upward, for there he beheld the sun and the moon
and the stars, and everything which spake to him
of God; and when Mephistopheles had yet more
fully enlarged upon the nature of hell, and what
was seen there, and how the souls of the damned
lived there in everlasting torment, Faustus asked if
a man that went to hell, and afterward repented,
might be saved. But Mephistopheles shewed him
how this could never be, and that a damned soul
could look for no mercy, no matter if it were soul of
emperor, king, duke, or other whomsoever. Even
Lucifer himself could never be recalled to the
presence of God, albeit he, as they all, had long
cherished a hope of forgiveness and redemption.
And when Faustus heard the Spirit so speak, he
became pensive and sorrowful, and threw himself on

his bed. But he remained not long in this mood, but mixed with his friends, and amidst the pleasures of the world forgot his sad case and fortune.

Yet when he was alone, and began to reflect on his wicked estate, once more he called Mephistopheles before him, and said to him, "Now, if thou wast a man, as I am, what wouldst thou have done to please God?" And the Spirit replied to him, smiling, that if he had been as he once was, endowed by God with all the gifts of nature, he should have humbled himself before His majesty, and taken all pains possible to understand aright His will and pleasure. But in lieu thereof he had denied and defied his Maker, and had sold himself to the devil; and so detestable were his sins in the sight of God, that he could never hope to win back His grace.

III.

Faustus, when he had done with questioning his Spirit on these and like matters pertaining to his future state, fell to the study of astronomy and mathematics, so that among all the men of that age he passed for the most expert in the courses of the sun, moon, and stars, and in the changes of the weather, which he calculated more exactly than had been heretofore practised of any. And he not only fell to be an almanack-maker, but wrote books thereupon, which he dedicated and sent to sundry great lords, who regarded him as a man of excellent learning, seeing that if a plague, famine, mortality, or war were about to happen, he foretold the same, to the astonishment and rare content of all.

These marvels he accomplished with the aid of his Spirit, which taught him all the hidden works of God, save the day of doom, and how God made the world, and why He made man in His own likeness ; and he promised Faustus that ere long he should be able to do all the things which the devils of hell could do, and have all the elements at his bidding. But by reason that it appeared to Lucifer that Faustus demanded of Mephistopheles more than was fit and in his treaty set out, he, with certain other devils, visited him in his chamber, so that Faustus deemed that at length they were come to fetch him away.

They sat by Faustus all on a row.   Lucifer, like a brown hairy man with a tail turned upward in a manner of a squirrel's : Belial like a bear, with curly black hair reaching to the ground, was standing straight up, and all within as red as blood, and flaming, his teeth a foot long and white as snow, and his tail three ells ; and he had wings, one behind each shoulder.   Next to him, Beelzebub, his hair of the colour of horse-flesh, and curled, his head like a bull's, with mighty horns, his ears sweeping down to the ground, his tail like a cow's, and behind his back two wings horned and fiery.

Then there was Astaroth, in form of a worm ; and Cannagosta, with the head of an ass and the tail of a cat, and hoofs like those of an ox, an ell broad ; and Anubis, dog-headed, in shape resembling a hog, but with two feet only, one beneath his throat, the other at his tail ; and he was four ells long, with hanging ears like a bloodhound.   Dithican seemed a huge bird with shining feathers and four feet, and

Brachus was of the shape and colour of a hedgehog,
his back brown, his belly flame-blue, and his tail like
a monkey's. The rest wore the semblance of divers
other beasts; and each, as he came into the hall
of Faustus, made his obeisance to Lucifer, and then
took his place. When anon there came a prodigious thunderclap, which shook the whole house,
and every devil had a muck-fork in his hand, and
pointed it with one accord at Faustus, who recol-
lected the words of Mephistopheles, saying that the
damned souls in hell were cast from devil to devil
with such forks.

Lucifer noted his disquiet, and said to him: "We
cannot change our devilish forms, Faustus mine;
but we can make men believe that we are angels or
men by deceit and enchantment."

Faustus said to him: " I like not so many of you
together."

So Lucifer commanded them to depart, except the
seven principal, which gave Faustus better courage,
and he said: "Where is my servant Mephistopheles? Let me see if he can do the like."

Then presently appeared a fiery dragon flying
round about the house, till he approached Lucifer,
and saluting him changed himself into a friar, who
said, "Faustus, what wilt thou?"

" I will," quoth Faustus, "that thou teach me to
transform myself in such manner as thou and the
rest have done."

Then Lucifer put forth his paw, and gave him
a book, saying, " Hold, do what thou wilt"; and
straightway he was changed into a hog, into a
worm, and into a dragon—which liked him well.

"How is it?" said he to Lucifer, "that so many unclean forms are in the world?"

"They are sent of God to plague men," answered Lucifer, "and so shalt thou be plagued."

The place was then filled with all manner of stinging insects, which stang Faustus, that he cried to Mephistopheles for help. But Mephistopheles came not at his call, and in a moment all had vanished, and he heard the sweetest music that ever fell on mortal ear, which ravished him with delight. Yet it repented him that he had seen no more than he did of that strange company.

IV.

But Faustus did not forbear to ponder in his mind over what had passed before his eyes; and since he had beheld the chief governors of hell, under Lucifer their prince, it entered into his thought that he would procure, if so he might, liberty to view hell itself. Whereunto through his Spirit he was straightway borne on a chair of beaten gold by Beelzebub, in the likeness of a huge, rugged, curly bear; and only this condition was laid upon him, that, whatever he saw, he should keep silence.

And, first of all, Beelzebub carried him into a lake, where Faustus fell asleep, and when he woke again he was in a place full of fire and brimstone, yet he received no more hurt than from the rays of the sun in May; and music was heard in the air, albeit the players were invisible. Other devils presently came to meet Beelzebub, and then ran before him to clear the way, and anon an exceeding great hart, which would have thrust Faustus out of his seat, but was put to the repulse. Next he espied a multitude of snakes, unto which came storks and swallowed them, leaving not one. Whereat Faustus marvelled, but, as he had been straitly charged, said nought.

Next out of an hollow cleft issued a monstrous flying bull, which rushed at Faustus, and overset his chair, that he rolled on the ground, and deeming that his end was at hand, exclaimed, "Woe is me that ever I came here!" But a great ape drew near, and bad him not be afeard; and when the fog that had arisen with the coming of the bull cleared, Faustus saw a waggon drawn by two mighty dragons, and thereinto the ape mounted and lifted Faustus up beside him. The chariot rose into the air, and entered an exceeding dark cloud, where nought could be seen, but the cries of tormented souls were continually heard, with thunder and lightning, till Faustus quaked for dread; and after they came to a stinking lake, into which they plunged, chariot and all, and Faustus lost sight of the ape and the dragons and the chariot, and sank and sank, till he stood on the top of a high rock, where the waters parted, and left him dry; and the rock was as high from the bottom as the heaven is from the earth; and Faustus wist not what he should do, till he espied a small hole in the rock, whence flashed fire; and he thought that he must either sit there in despair, or fall to the bottom, or perish in the flame.

Then suddenly, choosing his course, he leapt into the hole, and albeit he was in the midst of fire, it burned him not; but for the noise that smote his

ear, the like of it he had never heard. And as he
descended lower down into the rock, he came upon
a fire, wherein were many noble personages, as
emperors, kings, and the like, and hard by a clear,
cool water, into which they ran when the heat
wox too great to bear ; but they quickly returned
again, for that the water froze them. And so they
spent their days. And Faustus beheld one that
he thought that he knew, and would have spoken
with him, as he sprang out of the fire, horribly
shrieking ; but he remembered that it was forbidden
unto him.

At length Beelzebub appeared, and said that it
was time to depart, and Faustus seated himself once
more in his golden chair, and was conveyed home
asleep, where his boy Wagner was overjoyed to see
him ; and he felt within himself as though he had
been in a dark dungeon, nor knew certainly if he
had seen hell or no.

V.

It followed nevertheless, that such a man as
Faustus, when he had thus beheld the place where
the devil dwells, and where the souls of the damned
lie in durance for ever, craved to know more of
other things, and moved his Spirit to be gracious
unto him, so that he might view the whole world.
Whereupon he ascended in a waggon drawn by four
dragons straight into the air forty-seven leagues in
height, and looked down on the earth, and all the
kingdoms and countries thereof. And his Spirit
shewed him, when they were above Hungary,
Prussia, Poland, and the rest, and how on their right

hand lay Spain and Portugal, France, England, and Scotland. Soon they flew over Wittenberg, and Vienna in Austria, and Constantinople : Tripoli and Jerusalem, and the frozen zone. And they looked on ships in battle-array, and on some places where it rained and hailed, on other where the sun shone exceeding bright and hot, and on other, once more, where there were mountains clothed with everlasting snow.

But when Faustus gazed upward, and his eyes rested on the heavens, the light was so great that, had not Mephistopheles covered him with a cloud, he had been burnt outright ; and the sun seemed as big as the world by reason of the circumference of its rays, that spread to the uttermost corners of the world. And Faustus felt assured that, whereas men commonly hold that the sun moves round the world, it is indeed contrariwise, and it was the heavens that moved on their axis.

Eight days Faustus spent in his voyage through the air, and was restored to his own home at Wittenberg, as he slept, in like manner as before.

Now, having outrun fifteen years of the four and twenty that were allotted to him by his treaty with Lucifer, he coveted a better acquaintance with the famous cities of the world, and commanded Mephistopheles to carry him, wherever he listed, visible or invisible, as it might please him, till he had seen the most notable places in the whole earth.

So his Spirit, that was bound to obey him, likened himself to a winged horse, whereon Faustus mounted, and visited by turn every state, Scotland and England included, and each town of repute.

At Trent he tarried, having long desired to see that city, but found nought save two fair palaces of the bishop, a mighty large castle, and a church that had sumptuous marble tombs of Simon and the Bishop of Popo. And at Naples he viewed the tomb of Virgil, with the road that he cut through the hill a mile long ; the windmill and castle in the water, and the burning mountain called Vesuvius.

Thence he repaired to Venice, and wondered at many things which he noted there—the water flowing through every street, the beauty of St. Mark's Place, and the good-cheapness of victual, albeit nothing grew near-hand ; and from Venice he proceeded to Padua, for once in four and twenty hours a boat passed from one city to the other ; and from Padua to Rome.

There he had under his eyes much to make him marvel, and not least of all the richness of the pope's court and the luxury of his table ; and when he entered invisible, while they sat at meat, he thought that they seemed such other as himself, proud, wilful, gluttonous, evil-doers in every sort, adulterers, whoremongers, drunkards. "Fie!" he said to himself, "why should not the devil have made me pope?" And he said to Mephistopheles, "I thought I had been alone a hog of the devil's : but he must bear with me a little longer, for these hogs of Rome are ready-fatted ; and he would do right well to spit them all, and summon the nuns to turn the spits, for as none but the friar may confess the nun, so none should turn him save her, while he roasts."

Three days Faustus sojourned in Rome, and

during that space came the Cardinal of Pavia ; and
there was a great feast, whereat the pope kept
blessing and crossing himself, till Faustus could
suffer it no longer, and smote the pope in the
face, yet no man saw who did it, for he was invisible, and the pope gave out that it was some
damned soul, and commanded that mass should
be said to deliver it out of purgatory.

Then when the pope would have tasted of a
dainty dish that was set before him, Faustus cried,
" That is mine ! " and snatched it away, and flew
to the Capitol, where he bad Mephistopheles procure him some wine of the best from the pope's
table, and the very cup whence his holiness drank ;
and he had good cheer.

Leaving Rome, he visited many other places in
Italy, Germany, Switzerland, and the Low Countries,
especially the famous city of Nürnberg, where,
among many other wonders, were relics of Christ
and Charles the Great, and Ravensburgh on the
Danube, where Faustus went into the cellar of an
innholder, and emptied all his beer and wine that
were therein.   But, above all, at Prague he marked
the sepulchre of a renowned conjuror that had lived
there, and that had so bewitched his burial-place,
that no man might set foot in it, and yet die in his
bed ; and he thought of himself, and whether this
wizard were not such another as he was.

Then he ascended into the air, scarce knowing
whither to go ; and below him anon he distinguished
a fair city, which was Breslau in Silesia, and so
clean and comely were the streets that the place
seemed to him a sort of paradise ; and below the

bridge over the river he saw the brazen virgin, which embraced no man to his good.

Now Faustus, having observed all these strange things, betook himself to Constantinople, where he visited the harem of the Great Turk, and compared his service at table with the pope's. He was something discontented that one man should have so many wives; but it angered him more that in his eating and drinking the Turk exceeded so far all those princes whom he had ever known; and while he sat at meat, Faustus hurled flames of fire about the chamber in such sort that all fled save the Grand Signior himself, whom he charmed, and taking the form of the Pope of Rome, he spake to him in manner as follows:

"All hail, emperor! Now art thou honoured, that I appear before thee as thy Mahomet was erstwhile wont to do."

And the chamber was filled with dazzling light, and as Faustus vanished, the thunder shook the palace, and those about the sultan persuaded him that it was Mahomet himself whom they had seen. Whereupon he enjoined them to fall down upon their knees, and give the Prophet thanks for having done them so great an honour.

But Faustus, attended by Mephistopheles, went the next day to the seraglio, where he looked with much pity on those ladies that consume their youth and beauty in giving pleasure to one only man, and were served by such men as were eunuchs. Then his Spirit said to him: "Why, Faustus, shouldst thou not lie with these fair ladies as soon as the Great Turk himself? Do as thy lust prompteth herein, and I will aid thee." And he presented himself among the ladies in the guise of Mahomet, who, when they beheld him, kneeled down and worshipped him ; and he took the fairest by the hand, and led her to a chamber, where he lay with her ; and during six nights he did likewise, and so encompassed that part of the palace where the sultan was with a thick fog, that none could see the way out nor the way in. And it happened on the seventh day, when Faustus had accomplished his ends, that he rose again into the air in the likeness of the pope, and the fog disappeared.

Then the Great Turk went to his seraglio, and questioned those ladies concerning the matter, who said that the Prophet had lain with them ; and he, hearing these glad tidings, fell on his knees, and tendered Mahomet thanks for that he had so honoured him, giving strait charge that those ladies whom he had lain withal might be watched, for he was assured that of the seed of Mahomet should spring a mighty race.

Faustus, when he had thus had good sport among the ladies of the Grand Signior, departed, and by way of Hungary, Lubeck, Magdeburg, Erfurt, and other places, returned home to Wittenberg ; and he had been absent thence a year and a half, and had witnessed by the help of his Spirit stranger and more marvellous sights than ever it fell to him to do before.

Yet it fortuned, as it is commonly wont, when a man has seen certain countries, it moves him to an increased desire of travel ; and Faustus departed from home a second time, and visited most part of

Europe, Africa, and Asia, with the Holy Land and the island of Britain. In the fair waters, warm baths, and metals of the last he took great delight; and when he came to the Orkneys he beheld the tree whose ripe fruit falleth into the water, and there begetteth the barnacle-goose.

Then from the Caucasus he surveyed all the lands and kingdoms round about, and toward the east he became aware of a mighty stream of fire stretching from heaven to earth, even as if it had been one of the beams of the sun. Hard by, four prodigious waters had their springs, one flowing toward India, one toward Egypt, the other two toward Armenia. But he wist not what they were, and he demanded of Mephistopheles, who answered, saying : " It is Paradise that lieth so far in the east, the garden that God Himself planted with all manner of pleasant fruit; and the fiery streams are its wall, and the clear light that thou seest stretch from heaven to earth is the fiery sword of the angel that guardeth it ; and albeit thou conceivest that thou art hard by, thou art indeed farther therefrom than ever thou hast been. The four great waters are called Ganges, Gihon,[1] Tigris, and Euphrates ; and the angel is called Michael, that with his flaming sword keeps the tree of life. But such as I and thou, Faustus, are forbidden to enter therein, or to come nearer than we now be."

[1] The Nile.

VI.

When Faustus had returned from his travels the second and last time, and had gotten a high name among all the folks of that country where he dwelled for a man of great learning and wisdom, many resorted unto him, and put questions on astronomy and like things ; and he quickly resolved them, to their wonder and content.

Among the rest, he was prayed to say how it was that those spirits which vexed men vexed them so greatly more by night than by day. And he replied, that it was because those spirits are of God forbidden the light ; and their dwelling is in darkness, so that the clearer the sun shineth, the farther is their abode from it ; but as the darkness waxeth, they draw nigher and nigher to men, and have their familiarity with them, in like manner as by day we see not the stars, though they be equally there, but by night they are visible to all.

The fame and report of Faustus meanwhile grew in such sort, that many great princes coveted the sight of him, and among others, the emperor Charles[1] prayed him to come to his court, that he might have converse with him.

His imperial majesty greeted Faustus heartily well, and said that he had heard marvellous tales of his skill in necromancy, and that he had a familiar spirit, which did all his bidding. Now this high and mighty prince desired that Faustus should shew him some tokens of his art and experience ; and

[1] Charles V.

when the emperor was asked what above all other
things would do him pleasure, he required Faustus
to make appear straightway before him Alexander
the Great in visage and habit as he lived.

Then Faustus opened the privy-chamber door,
where he had audience, and presently entered a
strong, thick-set man, of middle stature, with black
hair that was thick and curly, both over the head and
beard, red cheeks, a broad face, and eyes like a
basilisk, and he was clad in rich armour. He made
obeisance to Charles, who would have saluted him,
had not Faustus held him back ; and as he left
the room came in Roxana, clothed in blue velvet
embroidered with pearls and gold. She was fair,
tall, and slender, with a face round as an apple, and
the emperor, turning to Faustus, said thus :

" Now have I seen the two persons whom of all
the world I most affected ; yet lest the Spirit should
have deceived me, like the woman who raised the
prophet Samuel, I would satisfy myself that she
hath the great wart behind her neck, which they say
that Alexander's living concubine had."

And taking the hand of Faustus, the emperor
went to her, and when she bowed down her neck,
he espied the wart to his mighty liking ; and then
she and Alexander went out.

Faustus, about this time, exercised himself,
through the help of his Spirit, in many strange and
witty jests, to make sport for noble personages or
other. As, for example, when he saw a knight
leaning out of one of the windows of the palace,
and asleep, he conjured on his head a huge pair of
hart's horns, so that the knight, when he awoke,

might not draw his head in again until Faustus did the horns away ; and when it was so that the same knight would have been revenged on Faustus, and met him in a wood, and charged at him with his horse, Faustus changed the bushes into riders, who surrounded the knight, and for punishment he and his men had to wear for a month each of them a pair of goat's horns, and each of their palfreys a pair of ox's horns.

Another time, he transported three young dukes, that were at the University of Wittenberg, to see the same, to München in Bavaria privily, to be witnesses of the Duke of Bavaria his son's wedding ; and he did it after this manner. He laid his large cloak on the ground, and begged the dukes to sit with him thereon, and they should be in München speedily, and back in Wittenberg the same night. But he enjoined them silence, whatever fortuned. Then a mighty wind rose, and bore the cloak upward into the air ; and all fell out as Faustus had said. But when they would wash, ere they came away, one said to the other, out of courtesy, that he should wash first ; and when they sat on the cloak to return home, he that spake, when the cloak rose into the air, fell off; but the other two, with Faustus, arrived safely at Wittenberg. The young duke that remained behind was cast into prison, for that they knew not who he was, and he would not speak, lest he should his brethren betray, so that the Duke of Bavaria gave order that he should be racked. However, his brethren besought Faustus that he would deliver him, and he repaired thither where he was, and loosed him out of prison, and brought him away, for which he was richly rewarded.

Faustus was making merry with some students at an inn, when there came among others to get entertainment certain Jews, and of one of them he borrowed for sport threescore dollars for a month. But when the time arrived, and the Jew sought him, he had no money, nor meant to have any ; but he said to the Jew that he might have his leg for a pledge on condition that, when he paid the debt, he should have his leg again, and the Jew should set it on as it was before.   The Jew, that was to Christians nothing friendly, consented, and Faustus cut off his leg and delivered to him the same.

But the Jew, doubting that the leg, if he took it home, would grow corrupt and stink, mused with himself what an ass this Faustus was to offer so great a security for so small a matter, and as he went along he cast the leg into a ditch.   Within three days after Faustus sent for him, and asked for his leg, for that his money was ready.   But the Jew avouched that the pawn was not profitable or of any worth, and he had thrown it away.   Then Faustus said that he must have it again, or the Jew must give him one of his own in lieu ; and the Jew was constrained to appease him by paying him yet another sixty dollars for his leg, nor saw that it was all deceit.

VII.

Faustus visited, among other puissant lords of that country where he lived, the Duke of Anhalt, whose lady being great with child coveted grapes in the month of January, whereas none were to be anywhere gotten; but Faustus, knowing her grace's mind, set a plate at one of the casements, and incontinently it was filled with all manner of fruit, as red and white grapes, pears, and apples, and he presented the same to the duchess, saying that they had come from a far place, where the summer was not yet ended : which caused the duke her husband to question Faustus concerning the difference of the seasons in various kingdoms, and was by his replies greatly contented and entertained.

And another time he raised for the same duke and duchess a strong castle, encompassed round with water on every side, and great rooms, in which guests sat at table with every sort of dainty dish and choice wine ; and in the courtyard were all kinds of strange beasts and land-fowl ; and Wagner, who was his servant, attended him, and laid the dishes and the cates ; and when the duke and duchess had admired all, suddenly the castle was wrapped in flames and consumed.

But when he was once more at Wittenberg, and had feasted all the students right nobly, he brought holly-wands, as many wands as there were students, and they all mounted thereon, and so to the Bishop of Salzburg's cellar, where they drank of his richest wines till the butler came, and they took their wands and vanished; and Faustus caught the butler by the hair as he went, and carried him to the top of a high tower, where he left him.

These and other sundry pastimes Faustus played, and it grew to be the nineteenth year ; and as he wox melancholy, thinking of the short time that remained to him, an old man, his neighbour, tried to persuade him to amend his life, and to repent his sins. To whom Faustus lent a not unwilling ear, and promised to consider his counsel.

But Lucifer sent Mephistopheles straightway to keep him in memory of his pledge, and made him sign again with his blood a scroll, which the Spirit bore away with him, and delivered it to Lucifer his master, which caused Faustus to forget the exhortations of his neighbour, and to fall back into his wicked course, and proceed therein more than before ; and that he might have greater pleasure during such time as was left to him, he bad his Spirit find him some of the fairest women in the whole world to be his concubines : and Mephistopheles did accordingly ; and there were two Netherlanders, one Hungarian, one Scot, two Walloon, and one Frank ; and they continued to sojourn with Faustus to the very last. Who at other sundry times had the fair Helena of Greece to be his paramour ; and once he shewed her to the students at Wittenberg : and she was attired in a most rich gown of purple velvet with costly embroidery ; her hair like the beaten gold hanging down to her hams, with amorous, coal-black eyes, a sweet and pleasant round face, cherry lips, a small mouth, and a neck like a swan ; and she gazed round her at the students while she stayed, and made them all so enamoured of her, that they prayed Faustus to let them see her again the next day. But he denied them.

VIII.

At length the four and twentieth year drew near to completion, and the Spirit appeared to Faustus, to command him to make preparation, for that against a certain day appointed the Devil his master would fetch him away. When he had departed, Faustus wox exceeding sorrowful, and sighed heavily, nor slept a wink. Whereupon Mephistopheles returned, and comforted him, saying: "Faustus, have better courage; for although thou partest with thy body, it is long unto the day of judgment; and even if thou shouldst live many thousand years, thou must die in the end. The Turks, the Jews, and many an unchristian emperor are in the same plight with thee; therefore be reassured; for the Devil, my master and theirs, hath promised that thou shalt not suffer the pains of the damned."

The Spirit lied, and spake not according to the Holy Scripture, nor did Faustus right entirely put trust in his words; and on the same day he summoned together the students of Wittenberg, his very friends and comrades, and addressed them at large on his wicked course of life, and how he had sold his body and soul to the Devil, and the hour drew near when he would be taken away from them. For four and twenty years he had yielded himself up to the lusts of his body, and had followed his stiff-necked and rebellious will; and now the close of all was at hand: that very night his hour-glass ran out. He prayed them all to forgive him any trespass he had committed against them, and to

live hereafter in the sight of God, beseeching Him
to deliver them from the temptation and deceit of
the Devil ; and he shewed them how he, miserable
sinner that he was! had fallen from God, had denied
baptism, the sacrament, and all righteousness ; and
how it was for them to war and strive continually
against the Devil by the grace of God and Jesus
Christ. Lastly, he solicited them to go to rest, and
not to fear if they should be aware of any noises in
the night ; and when he was no more with them,
they would find among his papers a record of all
things respecting his history, fully and truly
written.

One of the students hereupon said : " What led
you, friend Faustus, to conceal this matter from us
so long ? For we might, by the help of good
divines and the grace of God, have brought you
out of these toils, and freed you from the bondage
of Satan."

Faustus replied that he had often laboured to
return to the ways of truth and light, but that the
persuasion of the Devil was too potent, and "he
threatened me that, if I left his allegiance, he would
destroy me altogether, as this night he is like to do."

Then they entreated him not to give way too
much, and sought to teach him to pray, as thus :
"O Lord, have mercy on me, a miserable sinner!
And though I must give my body to the Devil,
yet preserve my soul to Thy service and honour!"
But he maintained that his sins were greater than
God could ever forgive ; and so they left him to go
to their chambers, but Faustus tarried in the hall
hard by. The students could not compose them-

selves to sleep, and lay awake, listening and fearful ; and presently, the hall door flying open, he was heard to cry in a smothered voice, *Murther ! murther !* and all was still.

But when, at daylight, the students went back into the hall, they found not Faustus, but his shattered and bloody remains scattered about, for the devil had dashed him against the walls ; and at last in the courtyard, on some horse-dung, they saw his body lying, fearfully and wonderfully mangled ; whereupon the masters and students who had witnessed these things obtained so much, that he was buried in the village near at hand.

Some went shortly after to his house, where they found his servant Wagner very heavy at heart ; and there was the whole History written by the hand of Faustus himself, as he had declared in his life. And the same night he appeared to Wagner, and disclosed to him many secrets, and where he had hidden much treasure.

FRIAR RUSH.

[*This is another of the stories founded on supernatural belief and agency, and was current in England in the early part of the reign of Elizabeth. It is mentioned in "Gammer Gurton's Needle," a celebrated comedy performed in* 1566, *in the following terms* (*Act* 3, *scene* 2)—

" HODGE.   *Saw ye never Friar Rush*
Painted on a cloth with a side-long cow's tail,
And crooked cloven feet, and many a hooked nail?
*For all the world (if I should judge) I should reckon him his
        brother:*
Look, even what Friar Rush had, the devil had such another."

Scot alludes to Rush in his " Discovery of Witchcraft," 1584, *and refers us to the narrative itself or to Wierus " De Præstigiis Dæmonum."*

It will be readily observed in the opening section of this romance that it differs materially in its structure and plot from the others which occur in the present collection, and that it personifies in Rush a spirit of immorality and corruption diffused among the Romish clergy abroad to procure their downfall. For this narrative is clearly of continental derivation, and its scenes are laid in that monastic life which had become toward the close of the sixteenth century almost a matter of tradition among our own ancestors. Yet the legend in its English habit has become naturalized here, nor did the early reader stay to inquire too nicely into the country of origin, where the particulars were of so popular a cast at once from their anti-papal tenor and their diverting and licentious complexion.

The work is of course a compilation, and exhibits matter common to other fictions, including an episode in " Friar Bacon" and the " History of the Three Friars of Berwick," where the woman discourages visitors to prevent the discovery of her amour with a monk.

The vision of devils, which the farmer beholds by stealth, and which leads to the dismissal of Rush from the priory after a process of exorcism, marks a certain undramatic and unreflecting inconsistency in the tale, and perhaps impairs the general effect. But these critical minutiæ were not much studied by the authors of ancient romantic compositions, whether for the stage or the closet.

" Friar Rush," although it appertains to the same necromantic cycle, is easily and broadly distinguishable from "Friar Bacon" in its texture and moral. While the latter is the product of the stealthy growth of myth round a real individual, Rush is a poetical or fanciful embodiment of an idea or principle, drawn into a connected narrative shape by the incorporation of apposite incidents, many of which are borrowed.

It may be unnecessary to point out the inconsistency of the story, as it stands, the imperfect observance of the attributes of the leading characters, and the want of dramatic harmony in the sequence of incidents. No one can fail to be struck and amused by the simplicity of the circumstances which attend the dismissal of Rush from the priory and his meeting with Lucifer ; and there is a slip in the construction of the story, where Rush seeks service with the husbandman or farmer, and his surprising celerity brings home the master earlier than ever.

It seems to be a series of anecdotes strung together without much regard to order, fitness, or proportion.

The investiture of the prior with the faculty of commanding the supernatural gifts of Rush, and at the same time of disarming and coercing him, and of casting the evil spirit out of the body of the young woman, forms a singular picture of the uncritical claim of the Church to control through prayer over the principle of evil as personified in Lucifer and Rush, even while it both profits and suffers by their miraculous endowments.]

I.

HERE is a pleasant history, how a devil named Rush came to a house of religious men to seek service there.

There was formerly, on the skirts of a great forest, a certain house and cloister of religion, which had been founded and built to maintain the service of Almighty God, and to pray daily for the souls of their benefactors and their own.

Which place, by reason of the great number of well-disposed persons who bestowed upon it their goods at their death for their souls' sake, grew mighty rich, and had gold and silver at will, so that the holy men that therein dedicated their lives to God lent themselves to riotous living and wanton ness, and omitted the services of the Church, spending their hours like beasts without reason, haunting harlots, and the goods which charitable people had given them wasting in unthriftiness and ribaldry, so that when the prince of devils and those who do his bidding and are his chief officers viewed and considered this misrule and abuse, they were well content, and sought to keep that holy brotherhood in the same course, which was to damnation.

Now of all these devils, the principal and most potent were Lucifer, Prince of Gluttony, Asmodeus, Prince of Lechery, and Beelzebub, Prince of Envy; who, with many other, assembled together, and after due conference chose one of their number to go and dwell among these religious men to promote their disorder, and keep them staunch in their wickedness and ungracious living.

So this devil assumed the likeness of an earthly creature, and went and placed himself at the gate of the house as a young man that sought service, and he wore a heavy countenance, betokening his poor estate and need of employment; and when the prior was coming out to go abroad he espied this young man, and asked him what he sought. The young man reverently answered and said: "I am a poor youth, that is out of service, and I stand in want of a master. And if so it be that you take me to be your servant, my lord, I will prove diligent, that all your convent shall be fain to keep me, and will do my uttermost to obtain your love and favour."

When the prior heard these words, he was moved with pity for the youth, and said to him: "Go into the kitchen to the cook, and acquaint him that I have sent thee; for my intent is that thou shalt there remain to do what thou canst, till something better befall."

Rush made lowly obeisance to the prior, and proceeded forth into the kitchen, where he in lowly manner greeted the master-cook, who, when he understood the matter, welcomed him kindly, and set him to do somewhat.

Then this devil, when he thus became under-cook in that house of religious men, rejoiced within himself, thinking of the part he should play among them, and of the discord and trouble he should breed in their midst.

In a few days' space came the prior into the kitchen, and found the young man there, to whom he said: "Where wast thou born? and what is thy name?"

The young man replied so: "I was born far hence, and my name is Rush."

The prior said, drawing him aside: "Rush, canst thou couple hounds together?"

"Yea, my lord," quoth he, "and more than that can I do; for I can couple men and women together, which is a rarer mystery; and, my lord, if your lordship so commanded, I could convey a fair young woman into your chamber, and bring her away in the morning, and no man should be privy thereto.   And all your counsels I would keep."

The prior, when he heard Rush speak after this wise, was a right glad man, and he said to him: "Rush, thou wilt become one of the most trusty of my servants.   Anon it may be that I shall find thee a message, the which thou canst do for me."

And after supper his lordship sent for Rush, and desired him to go on an errand for him to a fair gentlewoman, and to pray her to come to him.

"Let me alone, my lord," answered Rush; "I shall discharge this task to your full content."

Then he repaired to the gentlewoman's house, and with humble salutations greeted her, saying that he was sent by his master, the prior of a religious house there-by, to beseech her to shew kindness to him, and to go to him that very night, for that otherwise he should stand in peril of his life. And when the lady, whom Rush found sitting all alone, was apprised hereof, she declared that it were great pity indeed that my lord should die for her sake, and she would wait upon him incontinently, to do him what courtesy she could. So she and Rush departed together, and Rush brought her secretly to his master's chamber, where there was a table spread with choice viands and rich wine; and Rush did attendance upon the prior and the lady, whom after the repast he left, and the lady saved the Lord Prior's life.

The prior was overjoyed that he had such a good servant, and soon the other holy men, when they perceived that he was a fellow of such close counsel, gave him like commissions; and Rush laughed in his sleeve, seeing that they were so blind as not to know what he was, and thus to love and cherish him.

II.

It so chanced that Rush had occasion to stay abroad very late one night, and when he returned the master-cook chid him and beat him; and Rush wox wrath, and seizing the master-cook in his arms cast him into a kettle of boiling water that was upon the fire, and so left him there, while he went to fetch the gentlewoman for the prior from the town next adjoining.

When he returned certain of the friars came to him, and said how they had gone into the kitchen, and had found nobody stirring, and as they stood in debate by the fireside, one looked into the kettle, where he saw the master-cook seething, to his great wonderment.   Rush said that he had doubtless fallen into the kettle, and it was pity; and they all agreed to say no more of the master-cook, but to put Rush in his place.   So he acquitted himself therein marvellously well, and dressed their meat to their hearty content, mingling bacon with their pottage in Lent and Advent and on fast-days, so that it was exceeding savoury; and Rush proved a better cook than the one who cast himself into the kettle, and served these holy men seven years.

When the seventh year had come and passed, the prior called all the friars before him, and they held a council, and the prior said: "Rush has served us steadfastly a long time, and if it be your wills we will not remove him from the office which he now holdeth, but will advance him to be one of ourselves."   And they were well pleased, and so it was done.   The prior placed on Rush's shoulders a gown proper to his new estate, and Rush thanked him.   Yet he still remained master-cook of that house.

III.

But as he had fuller leisure than before, he occupied himself now and again, when his labour in the kitchen was ended for the day, with other affairs; and anon he set to making oaken truncheons, as many as there were brethren in the priory, and he sat at the gate fashioning them. Then when the other friars beheld him so do they marvelled in their minds, and demanded of him wherefore he made such.

To whom he answered: "Fair sirs, I get them ready putcase thieves should break into our house and seek to rob us, that we may have weapons to defend us withal; and if ye will come to me, when need is, ye shall have one each of you." And they heartily thanked him for his brotherly forethought.

Not long after it happened that a discord arose betwixt the prior and the sub-prior touching a certain harlot, whom both affected, and these two would have fought, but were abashed; and nevertheless the report got abroad that there was this difference, and some of the friars were for one, and others for the other; and they all wox strangely wrath, and went secretly, one by one, to Friar Rush their brother, and begged of him to let them have staves, each religious man one. Whereby it came to pass that the whole priory was provided therewith.

Friar Rush rejoiced inwardly, when he saw how the thing went, for he assured himself that there would be ere long a fray; and at the next midnight service, when they were all gathered in the church, and the prior arrived, as he was wont, last of all, his lordship saw the sub-prior, and his spirit was stirred up against him. So he sprang toward him suddenly, and dealt him a buffet, and the sub-prior struck him again; and the rest thereupon took sides, as their bent was, and out with their truncheons, and basted each other lustily with the same, till some were slain outright, and many were severely wounded and maimed. And Friar Rush, as soon as he perceived how the sport prospered, blew out the candles, and left them to grope about in the dark; and presently he brought out of the choir a heavy desk, and threw it in among them, to their further undoing and discomfiture.

Then, when he judged good, Friar Rush entered the church with a lighted candle in his hand, and cried: "Alack! sirs, how did you happen to fall out so among yourselves? Verily I see well that you do not regard your fair name nor the honour of your house. All folk hereabout will begin to say that ye be no honest, religious men, which I should be loth to hear; for I would not, if it were possible, suffer our holy place to come into such ill repute. Wherefore I pray you to let me intercede with you, and to do what best I may to make you friends together once again."

The friars thanked Friar Rush for his great charity and love, and shewed to him their bruises and wounds, for the which he expressed marvellous sorrow; and all their staves they brought back to him, which he assured them they could at any season have at need and commandment. To whom they shewed their indebtedness; and for a length of time none went abroad for shame's sake, for their sores were unhealed, and many were privily buried.

Friar Rush thought that he had done passing
well during such space as he had been among those
religious men, and he said to himself, "I will yet
achieve more in the way of making them worthy of
eternal fire ; and my name shall be famous at the
end of a thousand years."

IV.

My lord the prior, having a journey to make into
the country on some business of his, begged Rush
to get ready against the next morning one of his
waggons, and to see that the wheels and the axle-
tree were well greased. But Rush, feigning that
he so understood his master, took a great vessel of
tar, and tarred the waggon completely over ; and
when the prior would have mounted the waggon,
his clothes were all besmeared, and he demanded of
Rush what such a thing meant ; whereupon Rush
innocently told him that he thought those were his
commands ; and when the prior, seeing no remedy,
caused another waggon to be brought, and travelled
with Rush and the rest till they came to their inn
in the evening, the prior supped of the best, and
called for the best wine, but left none for Rush.

So Rush prayed the hostess to fill a bottle for
him and his fellows, and to put it in the reckoning,
and then a second, and a third ; and when the prior
asked for his reckoning, and saw the wine, Rush
told him that he and the others his servants had
drunk one bottle, and the second and third bottle
the horses had, for that they were so weary : and
the prior, albeit angry enough, said little, but Rush

never again accompanied his master after so be-
guiling him the second time.

But the prior then appointed Rush to be sexton
of the church, and it was his charge to ring the bell,
light the candles, and call the friars to prayers;
and his master enjoined him to count them, and to
note any that were absent. Now it happened in
no great space of time that they were all severally
presented to the prior, and they were very sore
and disdainful against Rush; but he heeded them
not, and he devised a sleight still further to bring
them into discredit. For, taking away the stairs of
the Dorter, he presently rang to matins, and the
friars hurried from their cells, and making for the
stairs, fell down one on the top of the other, and
one of them, that had a mighty big paunch, fared
the worst of all; and as they so fell, Rush, who sat
near the foot of the stairs, counted them, one, two,
three, four, and so on. They were aching in every
limb, especially the one with the great belly; but
they crawled into the church, and stayed there all
night, for they could not come to their cells again,
by reason that the stair was away. And when this
accident came to the knowledge of the prior, he
called Rush, and begged him to satisfy him touching
the same. To whom Rush shewed how the friars
had made such great haste to get to the chancel,
that their weight had broken the stair, and he that
had the greatest belly had the hardest fall. But
the prior shook his head, as though he questioned
Rush; and in effect he removed him from the
office of sexton from that time, and sent him back
to the kitchen.

V.

Friar Rush had oftentimes much leisure, and was wont to walk abroad at such seasons as his presence in the kitchen was not asked for, to divert himself, and make merry with pleasant company. One day he came to a village two or three miles away from the priory, and looking about him on each side he espied an ale-house, where sundry persons sat drinking and playing at cards. Rush made obeisance to them, and sat down among these good fellows, and drank with the rest, and anon joined them in their play.

He noted not the time as it passed, and at length it drew toward night. Then he remembered that there was nought provided for supper at home; and he rose suddenly, and paid for his drink, and departed. On his way back to the priory he saw a fat cow grazing in a field, and dividing it in twain, he left one half in the field, and the other he laid on his shoulder, and bore it to the house.

He quickly dressed the meat in two or three ways, and made thereof marvellously good broth, and all was ready at the appointed hour; and for that they all wist how late he had come home, and how a little before there was no fire in the kitchen, they gave him great praise for his despatch.

But the poor farmer, whose the cow was, going to seek it when it returned not home in the evening, found only half of it there, and the other clean gone, and so parted therefrom that he imagined not who could have done such a thing; for it was sundered as neither man nor beast could have sundered it.

A. L.   L

The farmer, returning home, lost his way, and darkness overtook him, so that he crept into a hollow tree, there to lie till the morning. He had not been there long, ere a strange company assembled near at hand, and began to enter into conference; and as he listened, he found to his amazement that they were devils who thus consulted together; and it seemed that the chief among them was called Lucifer, who summoned each of the others, that were his servants, one by one, to tell him what they had done for him and the good cause.

Then first of all Beelzebub said unto him : " Sir, I have sown dissension between two brothers, so that one hath slain the other."

"That is well done," quoth Lucifer; "thou shalt be well requited for thy travail."

Next he demanded of one named Incubus, what report he had to make of his good works.

"Sir," said he, "I have bred a war between two great lords; and they have met in battle, and many of their men have fallen in the fray."

"I commend thee heartily for thy loyalty to me," returned the master-devil; "thou shalt be well remembered. Norpell, what hast thou to say?"

"Master," he answered, "I have consorted with dicers and card-players, and have caused them to swear many great oaths; and I have parted man and wife, and made strife betwixt them, till the wife hath cut her husband's throat."

"Bravely done, Norpell," cried Lucifer; "thou art a trusty servant, and shalt have goodly recompense."

Next followed one called Rush, who recounted

to Lucifer all that he had achieved during such time as he had been in a certain priory ; and when he shewed him the greatness and rarity of his zeal, his master said to him : " Rush, if thou hast all these laudable acts truly accomplished, thou hast deserved of me better than any other. Now go, you and the rest, and prosper in your worthy enterprizes." And as the day began to break, the assembly vanished, and the farmer in the hollow tree, that had been nigh dead with fear, left his place and went home, resolving with himself the next morning to seek the Lord Prior, and apprise him of what he had seen and heard.

VI.

So accordingly he waited on the prior, this farmer, and desired to be admitted to his presence, for that he had a weighty errand.

" Sir," he said, when he saw the prior, " there hath happened to me this last night passed a great adventure."

" How so ? " inquired the prior.

" Sir," continued the farmer, " I had walked forth in the evening in quest of a cow, which returned not, as she was wont, after the day, and I found but one half of her, the other clean gone ; and then, as I set out on my way homeward, I missed the track, and took shelter in a hollow tree till the day should dawn. Lo! ere I had lain long therein, there appeared to my vision a strange concourse of creatures, whom I found to be devils, and of whom Lucifer was the chief ; and he held conference with the rest, and last of all with Rush, who acquainted him how he ruled you and your holy brethren, and made divisions among you, and so ordered your inclinations, that you might be damned, both body and soul."

When the husbandman had gone, the prior fell into a sad and contrite mood, and thought how he and the rest of that religious house had misdone in the sight of the Lord; and he called together his brethren, and opened to them the whole matter, telling them that this Rush was in verity a devil, and no earthly creature: whereat they were all grievously abashed and astonished, being heartily sorry that they had sinned in such manner against Almighty God by the motion and counsel of Rush, and they sank down on their knees and implored the Divine grace and pardon.

Then, at the prior's commandment, they assembled in the church, and went to prayer, and besought the Lord of His mercy; and in the midst of the prayers the Lord Prior went out, and to the kitchen, where he found Rush exceeding busy, whom he commanded to stand still, and conjuring him in the name of Almighty God and all the company of heaven, bad him transform himself into the likeness of a horse, and to abide at the gate, even at the very place where he first sought service, during his lordship's pleasure.

When the service was finished, they went to the gate, and found Rush there in the likeness of a horse; and they asked him wherefore he had at the beginning come to them and had tarried with them so long. To whom he replied, that he was sent thither to work them all the harm he might, and had he remained yet a while longer they would all have been damned.

Then they lifted up their hands and praised God that he had delivered them out of this peril; and when Rush prayed to be suffered to go, and promised not to come among them again, the prior gave him leave, and he disappeared; and ever after those religious men lived to the pleasure of Almighty God, and only to do Him honour.

VII.

His master Lucifer was troubled, because Rush was thus discharged from that house of religion; but he comforted him, saying, that he would anon surely meet with another service. And it happened that, as he walked in the country, he saw a husbandman, who worked in the fields, and he offered himself to his employment.

The husbandman told him that he should be fain to take him, but that he would fare ill with the goodwife, who brooked no man save him in the house. Rush answered, " Sir, let me alone; I shall see that thy dame is pleased with me." And so the husbandman took Rush home with him after the day's work done.

The goodwife scolded and fretted when she saw Rush, and understood the case; for she said that her husband was well able to compass alone all that he had to do, and they could not spare the charges of another. But Rush softened her anger, shewing that his hire was only for a time, and if so it was that his service was not welcome, he would depart. The woman said nothing more at that time, and spread supper ; and the goodman told Rush that he must be up betimes in the morning, for there was a long day's work before them.

But Rush rose early, and went to the field, and when his master came, bringing him his breakfast, there was nought left to do.

So they both returned, and when the goodwife saw what a profitable servant Rush was, she looked more pleasantly upon him. For the next day the farmer appointed twice as much for his man to fulfil, and Rush had come to the end of it all ere his master arrived with his breakfast; whereat his master greatly marvelled.

Now the goodwife loved well the parish priest, and as soon as her husband had departed the second time, this priest came to the house, and was well and lovingly entertained, so that one who had been by might have seen those two very busy, while the victual was making ready on the fire.

Rush, because he was a devil, knew hereof, and when he was with his master in the field, he said to him : "Sir, why be not your shoes better greased ? Is it not so that you have another pair lying under a great chest in your chamber ?"

"Yea, even so," answered the farmer.

"Then let me go home straightway that I may grease them for you against to-morrow."

So Rush returned to the house, merrily singing by the way ; and the goodwife, hearing the noise, looked out of the casement, and when she spied Rush, "Sir," quoth she to the parish priest, "it is so that you must hide yourself under the great chest among the old shoon, and I will cover you up, for our servant approacheth."

Rush entered the door, and went up into the chamber, saying to the goodwife, " My master bad me grease his old shoon by to-morrow"; and without more ado he put his hand in there, where the shoon lay, and felt the priest, whom he pulled forth by the heels, saying, " What doest thou here, thou rogue?" But the priest cried him mercy, and he let him go that time.

The husbandman and his servant went day by day to the field to work, and they both returned too early for the goodwife and her secret paramour. But one day, when the priest had again ventured to pay her a visit, Rush was seen coming, and she said, " Go into the stable, sir, even beneath the manger, and I shall lay a truss of straw upon thee."

But Rush, when she met him, demanding why he was back at home so soon again, would not be stayed, but declared that he must do his master's bidding, and clean out the stable. Which put that goodwife sorely in dread lest he should find the priest.

Rush took a fork, and shook the straw, and threw it about, till he came to the part where the priest lay, and because it was more weighty, he made a great ado, and raised it up with the fork, and carried it out of the stable, and cast it on the midden. Then, looking upon it, he espied the priest's gown, and feigned astonishment, and turned the heap over again, when out fell the priest. " What!" cried he, "art thou here a second time? Methinks I will

make an end of thee, false priest that thou art!"
But the religious man begged him to spare his life,
and let him go; and Rush consented, forasmuch
as the priest said that, if he found him there thereafter, he might do with him whatso he listed.

Nevertheless, so it fortuned that that priest,
because he loved the farmer's wife over-well, could
not restrain himself from seeking her company; and
at such time as the farmer and his man were abroad
he came once more, and they had not been in sweet
converse together very long when Rush appeared
suddenly, and the goodwife, wringing her hands,
scarce knew what to do.

But she presently bad that religious man haste
up into her upper chamber, and get into the cheese-
basket, which hung from the window.

"I am come, mistress," said Rush, "with my
master's privity to scour out your cheese-basket,
that is full of hairs, and very foul." And ascending
to the room above, he took a knife, and severed
the rope which held the cheese-basket, so that the
basket fell into a great pool of water beneath the
window. Then Rush fetched a horse out of the
stable, and tying the rope that had held the cheese-
basket to the horse's tail, drew it thrice or more
through the pond, and thus about the town, making
the folk wonder; and all this time he made as if he
wist nought of the priest being within, till he suddenly looked round, and, espying the priest, almost
dead with fright and sousing, cried out with a loud
voice, "Thou shalt not escape me now; lo! thy life
is lost." But the priest joined his hands together
in supplication, and offered Rush one hundred gold

pieces to release him : which Rush did, and giving
half to his master, bad him farewell, by reason that
he desired another service.

VIII.

Rush travelled far and wide, and passed from
one place to another, ere he could settle in any new
employment. But at length he came to a gentleman's house, where the master stood outside his
gate, and to him Rush said, vailing his bonnet, " Sir,
I am a poor young man, that has journeyed up and
down in quest of service, and none by any means
can I find."

" What canst thou do ?" asked the gentleman ;
" and what is thy name ?"

" I can do," the young man answered, "whatever
you bid me, and Rush I am called."

Then said the gentleman that he might tarry with
him ; and when he had been in that employment a
certain season, his master shewed him how he had,
above all things, in his mind how one might conjure
a spirit out of a woman's body.

" Why seek you, sir, so to do ?" his servant
demanded.

" I have a daughter," he replied, " who is a fair
young gentlewoman ; but she is sorely vexed in her
spirit, wherefore I conjecture that she hath a devil
within her."

" I counsel you, sir," Rush answered him, " to
proceed to a house of religion which is fifty miles
hence, wherein I was once a servant ; and the prior
thereof is a man very cunning in these things."

And the gentleman hearing these words, and because he was a person of great worship in that country, in place of going to the priory, prayed the Lord Prior of his goodness to repair unto him, to confer on a business which he had.

And when the Lord Prior understood the purpose of the gentleman, he made ready and went thither; and as soon as they had drunk and refreshed themselves together, the gentleman acquainted the prior with his great trouble. Then the prior asked him who had counselled him herein, and the gentleman said that it was a servant that he had, who was named Rush.

The prior commanded all to kneel down on their knees, and when they had so done he prayed to Almighty God to deliver that maiden from her vexation; and straightway a great devil flew out of her mouth, and she was whole. Her father was a glad man, and would have given the Lord Prior much gold for that he had done; but he refused it, saying: "Sir, I have a new church in building, and there sorely needeth lead for the roof thereof. I understand that this country is rich in lead; and if you will give me as much as will cover my church, my poor brethren and I will be your daily beadsmen for ever."

"But how shall the carriage be done?" asked the gentleman.

"Easily enough," answered the prior.

Then the gentleman brought him to a great heap of lead, and said to him, "Take whatever you need"; and the prior called to him Rush, charging him to carry enough for the roof of his church, who, once more taking the likeness of a horse, laid it on his neck, and was there in a quarter of an hour.

Then the prior transformed Rush into his own shape, and banished him for ever to a castle far away in the forest, whence he has not returned to this day.

FORTUNATUS.

[*The prevailing complexion of this rather well known fiction resembles that of several others which we have printed, as it follows the generic lines of all romantic literature of the same cast, and embraces adventures in the east of Europe and the rather indistinctly marked dominions of the Soldan. But in two leading respects, the Purse of Plenty and the Wishing Cap, "Fortunatus" has a special claim to our attention, and possesses peculiar characteristics or features. These ideas are evidently oriental inventions, and are in their spirit perfectly analogous to the numerous supernatural devices which form the salient and central element in the "Arabian Nights" and other popular story-books.*

In "Fortunatus," however, we readily discern a further novelty, and that is the inheritance by a second generation of the magical virtues of the Purse. It was a fairy grant for two lives. The Wishing Cap was acquired under different conditions, and was simply a talisman at the command of the wearer for the time being, provided that he had the key.

It is rather curious, in connexion with the visit which the hero is made to pay in this version at least to St. Patrick's Purgatory, that an account of that shrine was published just about the same time as the copy of "Fortunatus" which we have employed, that both are apparently unique, and that both want the whole of the prefatory matter and the title-page. Whether these two volumes proceeded from the same hand, we cannot say; the British Museum Catalogue describes the "Fortunatus" as a translation from the Dutch.

The introduction of the king of England's daughter, who bears the rather uninsular name of Agrippina, into the second portion of the romance as a prominent character follows the customary indifference on the part of early writers of fiction to historical verisimilitude. The disfigurement of a fair and high-born dame with goat's horns was a cruel and ungallant reprisal; but the wizard is not always to be reasoned withal. We are reminded of a scene in the "Merry Wives of Windsor"; but then Falstaff was not a youthful princess.]

I.

In the island of Cyprus there once lived a rich merchant, named Theodorus, who was a man of noble blood, and had inherited from his father a fair estate. But as he was rulingly addicted to the pleasures and vanities of the world, and spent his days in hunting, hawking, gaming, and costly entertainments, his good in no long time diminished, that he was reduced to great distress. Which his friends perceiving, they devised how his affairs might be brought back again to a flourishing condition, and likewise how his licentious manner of life might be restrained; and when they had fully conferred together, they resolved to counsel him to take a wife to himself.

Who gladly thereto assented, and they found the daughter of another wealthy merchant, Gratiana by name, to whom he opened his suit ; and these two were married in due time, and had a son, whom they baptized under the name of Fortunatus.

But his father, when he had espoused the daughter of this rich neighbour, and received in dowry much treasure, returned to his former course of living, and had quickly spent and wasted the whole of his wife's substance ; and when it was so that Fortunatus had grown up a comely youth, Theodorus, for that he had once more sunk into penury, in lieu of being gladdened by the thought of having such a child and heir, looked sorrowfully upon him, and even wept, when he was in his sight. Whereat Fortunatus was astonished and sorely grieved, because he deemed that he had offended his father.

But Theodorus said nay, and told him that he had displeased him in nothing, and that it was his poverty, which had ensued from his extravagances, which made him doubt that he should not be able to maintain him ; and Fortunatus therefore begged him not to be downcast on his behalf, for that he would take means to be no longer chargeable upon him.

One day the youth went to the sea-side, with his staff in his hand, and had not stood there long when the galley of the Earl of Flanders, who was returning from Jerusalem, put on shore for provisions ; and ere it departed, Fortunatus sought service at the earl's hands, and embarked with him on the ship for Venice.

The earl had been some time contracted to the

daughter of the Duke of Cleves, and was appointed
to wed her on his return ; and at Venice he bought
rich jewels and embroideries for his lady, wherein
Fortunatus, knowing the language of the merchants,
stood him in great stead, and mightily rose in the
earl's favour ; so that, when he landed in his own
country and bought horses for the wedding, he gave
the stranger next to his own the finest and most
sumptuous.

The kindness of the earl toward Fortunatus bred
great envy and despite in the minds of all the other
servants ; but he heeded them not, and in the jousts,
which were ordained to celebrate the nuptials of that
great lord, the Italian won one of the two jewels that
had been set apart for prizes for the two foremost in
the tilting, and one called Timothy gained the other.
Then the servants said that those two should enter
the barriers together, and both jewels to be to the
victor : who hoped that Timothy might overthrow
the stranger youth ; but it was far otherwise, for
Fortunatus won the day, to the great applause of
the spectators and admiration of his master, who
made him his chief chamberlain of his court.

The jealousy of the other servants lost all bounds,
when they saw how Fortunatus prospered, that had
so newly come among them ; and one of them at
length feigned a tale, how the earl, intending to
make war on another great lord, had a secret purpose to order it with all his officers whom he left
behind, that they might not wrong him by doing
violence to his young and beauteous lady ; and this
fellow persuaded Fortunatus that he was among
those who should be made eunuchs, and named

him who should do the work. Which so terrified
the young man that, without seeking further, or
staying to consider the likelihood of such a story,
he took leave, and fled from that land, to the great
sorrow of the same earl, when he was advised of
his departure. Nor wist the cause.

II.

Fortunatus made all the haste he could to escape
from Flanders, and came to Calais, where he found
an English ship bound for London, and sailed in it
thither. Knowing none, after a while he hired himself to a Florentine merchant in Lombard Street,
and by his diligence and pleasant manners gained
the love of his master and his whole household ; but
by reason of a robbery and murder which were committed in his master's house by another, he was like
to have been executed, had not some ladies, that
saw how comely a youth he was, interceded for him
with the king of England. Fortunatus therefore
left that country, and moved again over to France,
where he met with many strange and wonderful
adventures, and often went in peril of his life.

But that which was worthiest of note above all
was what happened to him as he was travelling from
Orleans to Paris. For he was passing through a
huge forest, when he suddenly became aware on
his right hand of a beautiful creature in female
habit, seated under a wide-spreading beech tree,
with a veil over her countenance. Who, when she
perceived his approach, rose, and stood in his path,
to his great content, since he had thought that in
that place had been nought but wild beasts.

He gazed steadfastly upon her, and mused in his mind whether she was a fairy or some phantom. But she, taking his hand, gently asked him whither he was going, and he told her, praying her of her company out of the wood. Whereupon she said, that she might in no wise accompany him, but that she would do more for him than any on earth could do.

"My name," quoth she, "is Fortune, and I hold commission from Him who made all things, and to whom by consequence all things are subject, to distribute six gifts, according as the stars from time to time direct and give leave : which are Wisdom, Health, Long Life, Beauty, Strength, and Riches. Now, even now, is the moment when you must choose, or the opportunity will be lost for an age."

Fortunatus was greatly astonished at these words, and secretly rejoiced at the happy tidings which Dame Fortune brake unto him ; and when he considered his great poverty and need of money, he chose of those six gifts the last. The lady therefore presented to him a Purse, which, in whatever country he was, would ever be filled with the money used there, both during his own life and the life of his sons, but no longer. And when he thanked her, she rebuked him, saying that it was her place to distribute these things, and that she was veiled, in that she might not see to whom she gave them ; but of the riches which he now possessed she exhorted him to lend some part to the poor.

Fortunatus heartily agreed to perform all that Dame Fortune enjoined unto him, and she led him out of the wood, and commanding him not to look

back, vanished.   Then he came to a road, and after
to an inn, where he had noble refreshment, and his
Purse answered all calls.   For he espied in a stable
rich trappings appurtenant to a horse and horse-
man, and asked of the landlord for whom they there
waited; and when he answered that they were there
for any one who would buy them at fifty gold
crowns, Fortunatus laid the money down, to the
landlord's amazement, seeing his mean apparel, and
took them away with him.

Presently he came to a place where an innkeeper
had three fine horses to sell, and he said that they
belonged to a merchant, and had been brought there
in hope to dispose of them for five hundred crowns
at the wedding of the Duke of Orleans to the
daughter of the king of Aragon, and the Earl Rodolph had bidden three hundred, but would give no
more.   "No matter for the price," quoth Fortunatus;
"let me see them."   And they took him where they
were, and he paid the money, and carried them
away.

Anon came the servants of Earl Rodolph, and
brought the 500 crowns ; but they were told that a
stranger had bought them, and when the earl heard
this, he caused. Fortunatus to be apprehended, and
brought before him.   To whom Fortunatus, questioned of him, replied that he had come honestly by
the money, and when the earl put him to the rack,
made confession that he had found 620 crowns in a
purse in a certain forest, and had cast away the
purse.   The earl asked him if he knew not that
the forest was his, and all that was therein ; and he
would have put him to death on the morrow, had

not many begged his life, and the countess's gentlewoman, who saw how well-favoured he was, in particular. And the earl at last sent him away, giving
him two crowns out to help him on his way.

Fortunatus hastened to leave that great lord's
jurisdiction, and was exceeding glad that he had still
his Purse with him ; and he next came to the city
of Angers, where a marriage was to be solemnized
betwixt the Duke of Brittany's daughter and the
Prince of Saxony ; and albeit he had good cause to
be wary in buying of horses, yet he presently purchased three others, with a costly equipage, and
hired two servants, and betook himself to the best
inn, where he abided the coming nuptials.

And when he had taken part in all the sports
and pastimes and masques and shows that were
arranged to do honour to the duke's daughter, and
had surprised all by his generosity and riches, Fortunatus, accompanied by a certain Irish gentleman
of his acquaintance, took ship for England once
more, and thence to Scotland and Ireland, where
the Irish gentleman sorely longed to see his family ;
and they visited St. Patrick's Purgatory, where
Fortunatus was well-nigh lost, his Purse notwithstanding : for that the Irish gentleman and he
penetrated into the cave, and could in no manner
find a passage out again by reason of the labyrinth,
till the abbot procured a guide ; and Fortunatus
richly requited the same, and the priests likewise,
and, so departing, they both sailed for Venice and
Constantinople.

In the city of the Great Turk, where festivities
were being held at that time, they put up at an

inn ; and when the host called for a reckoning,
Fortunatus kept his Purse under the table, lest any
should see it, and delivered the money to his friend,
who gave it to the landlord ; and Fortunatus, remembering his vow, demanded of him if it was
so that he knew any virgin who was marriageable,
and he was content to give her a portion.

Now the landlord was in his heart a thief, and
when he understood how great a store of money
the two gentlemen had, he came privily to their
chamber in the night, while they slept, and from
the purse of the Irish gentleman took fifty crowns ;
but because in the Purse of Fortunatus there
appeared to be nought, he cast it angrily under the
bed, where Fortunatus afterward found it, to his
mighty content. And ere long he met with a virgin,
upon whom at her marriage he bestowed four hundred gold crowns, and made all marvel at his riches ;
and his host once more applied himself to discover where these two gentlemen kept their money.
Whom, as he stole into their chamber in the darkness to tumble the clothes and see where the money
lay, the Irish gentleman, suddenly seizing his sword,
slew ; and the body they caused the servants, while
it was yet night, to carry into the court-yard, and
throw it into the well, saying that they had found
a thief in their chamber ; and in the early morning
they called for their horses, and paid their reckoning, and gave to each of the servants two ducats,
saying that they were sorry not to bid farewell to
the host, but would return shortly and thank him
for his courtesy. And because it was in the night-
time, they knew not that it was their master whom

they had cast into the well, but rejoiced at the bounty of the two gentlemen, who then set out, and after visiting many countries, and buying the richest merchandise and jewels wherever they came, at last embarked for Famagosta, where Fortunatus desired to see his parents.

He found that his father and mother were dead ; but he erected to them a noble monument, and built for himself a fair house, where he hired servants, bought a coach, and furnished himself with every necessary ; till the whole country began to wonder whence he got such vast sums of money, seeing that he left Cyprus so exceeding poor, and lived by no calling.

III.

Ere Fortunatus had dwelled long in Cyprus, he bought back the greatest part of his patrimony, which had been sold, and built a church and chantry, with houses and endowments for twelve priests, and he caused to be laid out gardens, parks, fountains, and fishponds ; and notwithstanding that he exercised no employment, he had jewels worth 100,000 crowns of gold, and seemed in no way poorer whatsoever he spent.

The king, seeing these things, and how all the nobles of the land vied with each other in doing honour to Fortunatus, thought that it was time that he sought a wife in marriage ; and he chose by the king's command one of the daughters of a great lord of his court, and she was called Cassandra, and she was the youngest.

Her two elder sisters felt much chagrin that

Fortunatus should have over-passed them; but he quieted them by giving them some of the jewels which he had bought at Venice and other places, and the remainder he distributed among the court, and offered some to the king and to the queen. And it came to pass, when the king would have the marriage celebrated in the court, that Fortunatus prayed his majesty to suffer it to be solemnized at his own house in Famagosta; and that for the cost thereof, with all the jousts and feasts and games and merriments, which his majesty might be pleased to command, he would be answerable, and in the lists would essay to shew his prowess before the king and the queen.

Fortunatus sent 2,000 crowns of gold by the Irish gentleman to Famagosta, and had all things prepared for the espousal; and he settled 8,000 on his wife, wherewith was bought to her use and dowry the county of Leghorn; and when the solemnities of the marriage were concluded, all the chief citizens of Famagosta were entertained for nine days together at the cost of Fortunatus, who, moreover, for the love which he bare to the Irish gentleman his many years' companion, gave him provision for his life in Cyprus. Who sent for his wife and family; but it unhappily fortuned so that, ere they could come to him, he died, being full in years.

IV.

Now when Fortunatus and Cassandra had been wedded for a certain space of time, and God did not bless them with offspring, they prayed to Him that they might have children as pledges of their affection ; and God heard their voice, and sent them two sons, who were baptized under the names of Ampedo and Andalosia.

Then, after a while, it entered into the thought of Fortunatus that he would once again travel abroad ; and when he had conquered the objections of his lady, who wept at the idea of losing his company so long, and who was all the more afraid that he resolved to go into heathen countries, where Christians were misliked and oftentimes slain, he hired a ship, and promising to return speedily to his wife, and giving her 10,000 crowns of gold for her expenses during his absence, he embarked with two servants and his Purse for Egypt.

Upon his arrival thither, he made a present to the Soldan twenty times richer than any had ever made before that time ; and the Soldan was marvellously well pleased, so that he greatly befriended him, and at his departure offered him letters to other kings, through whose lands he purposed to pass.   And at length he reached the court of Prester John, who had sixty-two kings subject him-to, and dwelled in a palace which glittered like gold.

Fortunatus, appearing to be a gentleman, was admitted by the officers at the gates, and was brought into the presence of Prester John, unto whom he gave more rich jewels, which the emperor gladly accepted, and caused Fortunatus to see all the treasures of his palace, of which he had never before beheld the like.   The walls were cased with silver, whereon were engraven stories of knights

and battles, and the achievements of former emperors; and the pillars which supported the hall
were of gilt cedar-wood.   At dinner Fortunatus sat
with the officers, for none but the princes of the
blood might sit with the emperor: and when all
were placed at the table, the bottles and glasses
began to dance; and when they ceased, presently
a tree full of fair oranges arose, and sundry black
men approached and gathered the fruit, whereupon
the tree vanished.   Next a stag, followed by a pack
of hounds in full cry, rushed in, and ran round the
wall twice or thrice, and disappeared; and then
several women in strange attire entered and played
upon the lute. All which caused Fortunatus to
muse how it came to pass; and one near him
whispered him in the ear that the emperor kept
necromancers, who performed these things for his
pleasure.

It came to the knowledge of these necromancers
that Fortunatus possessed a great store of gold,
and they raised their familiars by means of certain
charms to tell them who he was, and what was the
cause of his exceeding riches.   But the familiars
only knew that the stranger was a merchant of
Cyprus that had a secret mine, which could not be
exhausted during his whole life, and which they
were forbidden to reveal.   Then the necromancers
essayed through their wives, who were witches, to
visit the lodging of the stranger by night and bring
away such treasure as they might there find.   But
as they entered by the casement Fortunatus awoke,
by reason of the noise which they made, and wound-
ing one of them with his sword, the rest fled.

Yet he was so ill-contented with these and other arts to do him wrong and gain his Purse by sleight, that he suddenly left that place, and when he had visited the Holy Land, returned to Alexandria, where he was again nobly entertained by the Soldan.

Now, growing anxious to see his wife according to the promise which he had made to her ere his departure, he distributed largess among the servants, and then demanded of the Soldan permission to depart. But the Soldan, seeing what great riches Fortunatus owned, was loth that he should take ship before he had looked upon the treasures which himself possessed, lest in his own country he might vaunt that he exceeded in wealth the Soldan, that was the king of kings.

So he led him into his treasury, where in the first room were set out cloths of gold and rich tissues, jewels, rings, huge pearls, and other; and in the second an infinite store of money, whereof Fortunatus deemed that he had never beheld the like; and thus he said to him: "I have yet another thing to shew you, which is more wonderful than all these"; and he brought him, musing all the while what it could be, into a farther chamber, and pointed to an old Hat. "This," quoth he, "is the jewel which surpasses all others that I have."

Whereupon Fortunatus smiled, and said again to him, "Why, it is an old hat, and may be had for a small matter."

"Yea," answered him the Soldan; "if it were an old hat only, indeed, then were it not much. But if I should lose all my jewels, I might them renew; yet an' I lost this Hat, such another the world affords not."

Fortunatus wox anxious to know what the secret was of that rare jewel, and the Soldan continued :

" Since you are my friend, I will impart to you where its singular worth lies. Whoever puts on the Hat, which you here see, has but to wish, and he is forthwith in what place it pleaseth him to be. If I would join my nobles on hunting, I am with them in an instant, and back in my palace, as swift as thought. If I desire to be at the head of my armies, a hundred leagues away, it is the same. Therefore you perceive why I regard this above all my possessions as the most precious."

Fortunatus, when he heard this strange report, stood amazed, and privily considered how he might come by the Hat. " For," he pondered, " that and my Purse together were enough for the richest emperor in the world." And presently he inquired, if, looking at its rare properties, it were not weightier than any other. But the Soldan told him that, on the contrary, it was lighter ; " and," quoth he, " that you may satisfy yourself in this, set it on your head."

Fortunatus asked for nothing better, and putting on the Hat, wished himself aboard his ship in the harbour, and was there in an instant, and commanding his men to put on all sail, safely landed in Famagosta.

The Soldan was mightily discomfited by the loss of his wishing Hat, and despatched his fastest galley after the thief ; but it was of no avail. He vowed by all his gods that if he caught the spoiler, he would put him to the cruellest death that ever man died ; but the merchants of that place rejoiced in their hearts, for that they knew that Fortunatus would come no more to Alexandria to hurt their traffic.

V.

Fortunatus was thus the master of infinite riches and power, insomuch that the king of Cyprus chose rather to go to war with the Soldan than to deliver him up to him, or compel him to restore the wishing Hat ; and he was happy in the enjoyment of a faithful wife, and of two sons, now grown to man's estate.

But as in this world no one is perfectly contented, Fortunatus began, as he grew old, and he was toward threescore years, to reflect on the vanity of wealth, and even to wish that he had chosen, when his good fairy tendered him the choice, wisdom sooner than money. For he knew that his life was continually in peril, in case any should discover the secret, whether of the Purse or the Hat ; and to his wife, marking his melancholy and waning health, he opened the frame of his mind, and foretold the nearness of his end.

Then the father, being in his bed, sent for his two sons, and telling them how the case stood, blessed them ; and when he had so done, he revealed to them the extraordinary virtues of the Purse and the Hat, exhorting them in no wise to make known the same to any. And presently after he yielded up his spirit, and within a short while his wife died like-

wise ; so that their two sons, Ampedo and Andalocia,
were left alone.

Now, a sharp dispute arose between these two
brothers concerning the estate which their father
had left them.   Ampedo wished to keep it entire ;
but Andalocia coveted the Purse ; and after many
quarrelsome passages, that there might be no suit
between them, imperilling the discovery of their
secret, it was resolved that Andalocia should give
his brother from the Purse so many bags full of
money, with all the palaces and merchandize, and
other goods, and, to boot, the Hat ; and that he
should take the Purse for his share, returning to
his brother in six years' time, and returning it to
him, if he so willed it.

VI.

Andalocia shortly set out on his travels, and visited
the courts of many great kings and princes, of whom
all marvelled that he had such abundance of riches,
seeing how he was neither a king nor had any
employment in merchandize ; and some thought he
was a sorcerer or a priest disguised.

And it chanced, when Andalocia had come to
London, and had sumptuously entertained the king
and queen and their daughter, that Andalocia conceived a passion for that princess ; and the king
her father, wondering in his mind whence Andalocia
obtained all his money, set her to draw from him the
secret through the love which he bare to that maiden.
So the princess cozened him, to his great chagrin,
of his Purse, and he departed from that country in a
heavy mood.

His brother, when he returned home, upbraided
him with his folly, and said that it was a judgment
upon him for disobeying his father's command.   But
he fell in anon with a certain hermit, who taught him
the virtue of the apples which grew in the Holy
Garden, and stealing from his brother the wishing
Hat, transported himself again into England, where
the princess, the king of England's daughter, by eating of the apples, gat mighty horns, to the great
sorrow and amazement of all.

Hereupon Andalocia, disguising himself as a
physician, proposed to rid that great lady of this
strange enchantment, if she would be at the cost of
the remedy ; and while he administered to her certain drugs, and they remained in a chamber alone,
he took occasion to search for the Hat, which he
found under the bed, and the Purse near at hand ;
and, putting on the Hat, he bare her away from the
palace to a distant land, where he discovered himself, and reproached her with her perfidy.

He threatened to kill the princess ; but she implored his clemency, and he contented himself with
immuring her in a nunnery.   Then he proceeded to
Cyprus with his Hat and Purse, and was kindly welcomed by the king and by Ampedo ; and the king,
inflamed by the news that he had heard of the beauty
of the king of England's daughter, and knowing
that the horns came from enchantment, sent ambassadors to London to ask her in marriage, praying
Andalocia to remove the horns.   Whereto he agreed;
and they were wedded, the king of Cyprus and the
princess Agrippina.

The vast riches of Andalocia, which seemed to

have no end, and the more he spent to wax the greater, moved certain of the nobles about the court of Cyprus to envy.   Who wist not the property of that gift which he had, and hoped, if they should gain possession of all his goods, to be as he was ; and accordingly two of them, bolder than the rest, murthered him ; and his brother Ampedo, learning that he was dead, burned the Hat.

So the Purse, which was only to Fortunatus and his next heirs, parted with its virtue ; and the Hat, for which the Soldan of Babylon would have given untold gold to win it back, viewing it as the fairest jewel of his crown, perished for ever.

FEUDAL AND FOREST LEGENDS.

HEREWARD THE SAXON.

[Hereward the Saxon, the exile, or (as Kingsley puts it) the Wake, son of Leofric, a mythical Earl of Chester and Mercia, by Godiva, the heroine of the Coventry story, was undoubtedly an actual personage, and at the period immediately succeeding the Norman Conquest in 1066 *doubtless achieved somê, at least, of the feats of bravery and strength ascribed to him in the following monastic legend.*

We have only to reflect on the general complexion of ancient historical records which are not strictly documentary to become satisfied that a good deal of invention entered into the accounts of all such heroes of adventure, and we ought to be the less surprised that, as such fabulous material accumulated in the hands of compilers, biographies or series of exploits were amplified at pleasure, without much regard either to truth or propriety; and in these mediæval compositions we often find the prima stamina *of incidents introduced into works of later origin. At the same time, the reality and transactions of Hereward are established by several writers of early date and tolerable fidelity; and a chronicle of the twelfth century is indeed exclusively devoted to a commemoration of this Midland hero and Saxon champion.*

A. L.   177   N

The novel entitled "Hereward the Wake," in which Charles Kingsley has embodied the career of this extraordinary man, filling up the outline supplied by the chronicles from his own imagination, is neither better nor worse than the generality of such productions from an instructive point of view, and as a work of art is recommended by the insight and culture of the author. Such outputs of literary labour and skill are perhaps in a twofold aspect beneficial, since they inspire with a higher and purer taste many who would not be tempted to study the true text, and may lead a few here and there to inquire further.

Making all allowances for exaggerations and fable, these ancient "Gests," of which our collection embraces a few prominent examples, have their distinct value and function as collateral lights and indices, and cannot be ignored when the history of earlier England shall be finally written in the time to come. One salient feature must strike everybody, and that is the utter want of political consolidation at the period following the Norman conquest.

For the formation of a correct estimate of later fictions, a study and knowledge of such parent productions as the present and those which immediately succeed are absolutely necessary; from the dearth of real incidents or adventures to fill up an outline, or supply the semblance of a biography, the romancist naturally went to traditions, oral and otherwise, already in existence, and furnished his characters with exploits properly belonging to other and antecedent heroes. For instance, Robin Hood was undoubtedly a real individual; yet many of his recorded experiences are more likely than not to have been varied and localized versions of stories current before his, or at all events before the narrator's, time.

Hereward was not the Last of the English, *as Kingsley phrases it, but may be considered one of the last of the Saxon remonstrants in arms against the Norman interloper; and we may take exception, perhaps, to the term " Wake."*]

I.

WOULD you hear the marvellous adventures and glorious history of Hereward the Last of the Saxons, who was the son of Leofric, Earl of Chester and Mercia, and Lord of Coventry, by his wife the Lady Godiva ?

From his boyhood Hereward outshone all his fellows in spirit and strength, albeit in stature he was low. But he was stout of limb and broad at the shoulder and athwart the chest ; and knew no fear.

Round him, as he waxed somewhat in years toward manhood, he gathered companions like himself, wild, active, dauntless ; and his father the earl's rents and tolls he perforce collected to furnish himself and his friends with money ; and from many a dire peril his kinsfolk delivered the youth, who counted not his foes nor thought on the way out of danger and death.

At length, it happened that his father the earl shewed Edward the king how he could no longer brook the sojourn of Hereward in that country ; and the king commanded that he should depart the realm, who had only at this time eighteen years ; and there attended upon him in exile one of his father's serfs, namely, Martin with the Light Foot, and no other than he.

He repaired at first to the Scotish border, to the house of Gisebert of Ghent, his godfather; but because through his prowess in slaying a huge Norwegian bear, which none of the noble youths of the court of Gisebert durst engage, he drew upon him the envy of all, and went in hazard of his life, therefore he quitted that place, and reached the dominions of Alef of Cornwall.

This chieftain had a beautiful and only daughter, who secretly loved the son of the king of Ireland; but she was betrothed to a Cornish lord, one of her father's lieges, rather from dread, for that he was a man of might and following, than from inclination toward him on the part of Alef the chieftain.

That fair damsel discovered to Hereward her true mind, and leaned upon his counsel and comfort; and the Cornish lord, who looked upon the stranger with a mistrusting eye, lay in ambush for him, where he might chastise his insolence. But Hereward overcame and slew him, and because the Cornish men rose up against him, the Saxon fled, carrying letters from the lady to her lover the prince of Ireland; and he entered the service of the king, that prince's father, and performed many notable deeds of valour in his behoof.

But the daughter of Alef, that should have wedded the Cornish lord, was sought in marriage by another of that same country; and when the prince of Ireland sent messengers to Cornwall to ask her hand, they were cast into prison, and the nuptials were appointed to be shortly solemnized.

At the marriage feast the bride in her bridal array went round, attended by her maidens and a harper; and the harper sang to the strains of his harp, while one of the maidens served the cup in the name of the bride. And all joyfully took the cup from the maiden after the minstrel's song, save one who sat at the lowest table, with two or three his companions, that uncourteously refused it, and turned from the harper sternly away.

The bride approached the stranger, and tendered him the goblet with her own hand, and he took it, and gently saluted her; and as she went from him she threw a ring into his bosom unseen of any, and lifted her voice, praying all present to excuse the discourtesy of one unacquainted with their customs. For she, albeit his hair and visage were disguised, knew it to be Hereward who sat there; and tears trickled down her cheeks.

But the minstrel brawled nevertheless at the unknown guest, in that he had wronged his holy profession; until the visitor arose, and seizing the harp began to play upon it with the hand of a master, to the amazement of every one, while his companions joined him in chorus.

The new players were applauded by the whole party, and Alef the chieftain was content that one of such skill should have such reward as he might name, saving only his wife and his lands. But he was privily advised that the strangers were, maybe, Saxon spies; and all the doors were suddenly guarded, that none might pass out unchallenged.

Nevertheless Hereward and those that were with him had been forewarned by the princess their ally,

and had taken their way where they might lie in
wait for the wedding procession, as it wound along
the road, with the Irish messengers hand-bound, to
the castle of the bridegroom ; and at a convenient
opportunity they fell upon the Cornishmen, and slew
them, setting free the princess and the messengers.

Then he shewed unto the princess how he had
crossed the sea for her sake, and had stained his
skin and his hair, and how he had made a vow to
the king of Ireland, on the eve of his departure,
that he would accept nothing at a lady's hand, unless
it were offered by the princess herself. And she, on
her part, let him understand that at the feast she
at first surmised that it was he, and anon, ere she
threw him the ring, had it of certain knowledge.

Which noble lady was incontinently joined in
wedlock to her truelove, the prince of Ireland ;
and Hereward, when he had assisted at that auspicious ceremony, took his leave of them all, to
return to his own land. Unto whom tidings had
been brought of the death of his father, Earl
Leofric, and grievous harm done thereby to his
heritage and kindred.

II.

But the ships which were assigned by the king
of Ireland to convey Hereward, that was now Earl,
to England, were driven from their course by contrary winds, and made the coast of Flanders, where
the Englishmen were joyfully welcomed by the earl
of that province, for that they might by their valour
be helpful to him in his wars ; and when Hereward

had fought under the standard of the Earl of Flanders, and gained high renown, it chanced that he met with a fair Flemish maiden, named Torfrid, and presently wedded the same.

Yet, because he longed to set his foot again on his native soil, and was loth to put the life of that gentle lady in jeopardy, he prayed her to suffer him to take ship alone, and to abide patiently his return or news of his fortune. But she, as it was meet, demurred and wept; and in the end, accompanied by her and the two Siwards, the Red and the White, that were his kinsmen, and his servant Martin with the Light Foot, and other Saxons his sworn friends, he embarked for England, and landed in Lincolnshire, where, leaving his young wife in charge of the Siwards, he made all haste to gain his manor of Brunne. He arrived there on a calm evening with a single attendant; and both were lightly armed, for they had journeyed far afoot.

The strangers stopped before the entrance of a house in the village where dwelled a Saxon, one of Earl Leofric's dependents, and solicited shelter for the night. They were kindly received; but the faces of the inmates were sad and downcast, and to Hereward asking the occasion for their sorrow they replied that their lord, the Earl Leofric, was lately dead, and his estate had been given to a Norman, who was about to enter into possession. " Even yesterday," quoth they, " the invaders seized upon the house; and because Earl Leofric's young son slew two who would have dishonoured his mother, they killed the boy, and set his head over the doorway. O, that his elder brother, that is a wanderer in distant lands, were here, and these wretches would have their due!"

Hereward bit his lip, and said nothing; and when he and the other had partaken of the evening meal, all went to rest. But Hereward lay on his couch thoughtful and angry; and presently there burst on his ear the sounds of revelry and music in the near distance.

He sprang from his bed, roused one of the household, and found that it was the feast which was being held in his father's house to celebrate the succession of the Norman to the boy whom they had murdered. Arming himself, and bidding his companion do likewise, they cast long black cloaks about them, and hastened to the scene of noise and riot. First of all, Hereward took down his brother's head, reverently kissed it, and wrapped it in a cloth; and then the two placed themselves in the dark porch of the mansion, where they could oversee all that passed in the hall.

The Normans were scattered about round a blazing fire, stupefied with drink, and reclining on the bosoms of their women, while a minstrel was singing songs in reproach of the Saxon. One of the women prayed them to recollect that the boy who was dead had a brother, and if he were there, they might find things mightily different. The new Norman lord lifted his head when he heard these bold words, and approved what the minstrel had done, saying that Hereward durst not shew his face in England for fear of the gallows.

The minstrel thereupon wox louder in his scorn of the house of Earl Leofric, as his master's speech had given him warrant, and his insolence passed all bound, when a figure leaped out of the darkness, a Saxon sword gleamed for an instant in the air, and he dropped lifeless to the ground, cloven to the shoulder. Hereward rushed upon the merry-makers; and those who escaped from the hall were despatched at the door by Martin with the Light Foot. Not one remained alive; and the heads of the Norman seigneur and his fourteen associates were suspended over the doorway instead of that of their victim.

The Saxons kindled torches and set on fire the brushwood on the Brunnerwold as a signal to their adherents, and numbers flocked to Hereward's side; and amongst the rest Leofric the Mower, Leofric the Cunning, Widric the Black, and Widric the Heron, and the monks of Ely, with Thurstan their abbot, made cause with him against the invader.

The Earl of Warren with all his men was on the borders of the Marshes, and the Saxons withdrew into Ely. But an arrow from a Saxon bow laid the earl senseless on the ground, and he was taken away for dead; and because William the Norman chose his own countryman Thorold to be abbot of Peterborough, Hereward laid waste that town and burned it, all save the abbey-church, which he stripped of its treasures. For the Saxons and their Danish comrades, saith the story, going into the sacred building, clomb to the Holy Rood, and took thence the crown on Our Lord's head and the foot-stool that was at His feet, both of pure gold, and fetched down from the steeple the mantle that was of gold and silver, and two gold shrines, and of

silver nine.   Likewise they got at that time fifteen
great crosses, some of gold and some of silver, and
so much gold and silver besides, and money and
rich raiment, and books, that no man could reckon
their worth ; and the walls they left behind to
Thorold the Norman.

The Saxons and Danes, who had taken part in
this work to have security of the church, as they
said, shared all those things betwixt them ; and the
Danes thereupon departed out of England to their
own country.

The Earl of Warren, for that Hereward had
slain one of his blood, and had of late wounded the
same earl nigh unto death, bitterly grudged at these
passages of happy fortune for one on whom he only
looked as a thief and a homicide ; and he moved
the king, that was William the Norman, to put his
royal power in movement to destroy that insolent
rebel.

Unto whom the king at length assenting, siege
was laid to the Isle of Ely, and the Normans invested it on all sides ; and to the intent that their
horsemen and other might pass over the marshes
to the citadel and the town, William commanded
that a causeway of timber should be made to carry
across the soldiers on horse and on foot.

But because the ground was not steadfast and
firm, and the horsemen in their armour pressed
heavily on the timber-work, the causeway yielded
midway, and well-nigh all the soldiers on horse and
on foot perished in the marshes.

Whereat William the king was greatly abashed
and disheartened, and retired from the endeavour ;

and years passed before the fishermen ceased to drag up the horsemen in their rusted armour that fell at that season in seeking to reach Ely and take the Saxon abbot and his staunch ally Hereward, the ready and the strong.

Nay, William the Norman leaned to a peace with Hereward, whenas he saw how manful he was, and how good a friend so dread a foe might become; but he was restrained and dissuaded by the Earl of Warren and by Ivo Taillebois, Lord of Spalding, and other more.

Yet again the king essayed to make himself master of that stronghold in the marshes, and at another place, which was called by name Alreheche, he gathered together all the fishermen of that country, with their boats and tools, and built a second earth and timber dyke, whereby he might with his army gain the island, and prevail over the Saxons.

But among those who obeyed the call of our lord the king was one who laboured with the rest and earned his wage, and staying behind when all was done and ready till nightfall, set fire to the timber, that all was consumed; and it was Hereward that this accomplished; and thus our lord the king lost his pains and his hire.

III.

Meanwhile, the enemy environed Ely, and the king kept his court at Brandon, whence he could command the water-ways and be within reach of all. But food waxed scant alike in the royal camp and with those shut up in Ely, albeit the fishermen conveyed to the Saxons in their boats by stealth not a little ; and since the Saxons wist not what the king proposed, or how he fared, Hereward and the other chiefs assembling in council, it was resolved that a spy be sent to the court to learn what tidings he might ; and after conference had Hereward himself elected to go.

He cut his hair and beard short, and stained his features, and mounting Swallow his mare, a lean, ill-favoured beast, yet as swift as the winged creature whose name she bare, he set out unarmed and in mean attire.

He shortly met a potter, with whom when he had had a parley, and had taught him a lesson in courtesy with a stroke of his own staff, he bartered his wares for a penny, and made an exchange of clothes with the same, shewing him that, an' he should repair to Ely, my lord abbot would bestow upon him yet another penny in reward of his news.

Then proceeded the feigned potter to Brandon, and offered his merchandise to whomso would buy, and took his lodging as night drew on at the house of an ancient crone that was a Norman and dwelled therein with a companion. Whom the potter, that lay near them, listening heard discourse of what the lord of Spalding was next about to do ; for, seeing that no human force appeared to avail them against Hereward, the king and those about him had taken into their service a certain wise woman of Brandon and her associate, and were preparing to erect in the fens before the island a scaffold, whereon this wise woman and her attendant might upon the

Saxons exercise their skill in necromancy and witch-craft. Which was shortly to come to pass ; and those whom-with Hereward lodged were indeed they who should practise such arts on the enemy ; and only for that they deemed the potter ignorant of the Norman tongue, wherein they held debate, they let him, as he gave greater ear, understand the whole process.

Then, when he had heard all this matter to his singular content, the potter went forward to Bran-don, and cried his pots in the precincts of the king's court ; but the king was absent on hunting. The reeve came in on his affairs, and marking the stranger, sware that he had never yet seen a man who in his feature and bearing so favoured Here-ward the exile ; and thereupon many thronged round that they might judge what so famous a man was like, and they led him into the hall where the knights and gentlemen were. Of whom one asked him if he knew Hereward ? " Alas !" cried the potter, " only too well, lord. O, would that he were here, that I might be revenged upon him ! for he has robbed me of late of a cow and four sheep that were all my having in the world save my poor mare and these few pots to sustain a wife and two children.

When the hour for the evening meal approached, the potter shared the kitchen-men's table, and they ate, drank, and jested, till one offered to shave the potter's crown and make him monk. Which set the Saxon blood on fire, and the Norman was stretched on the earth. All fell upon the potter, and led him to the guard-room, where they brought

cords to bind him.   But he seized a sword in the
hands of a soldier, and slew all that stood in his
path ; and hastening where he had left his mare, he
leaped into the saddle and was gone.   For Swallow
flew as the wind, and he outstripped all his pursuers
save one, that followed his track even to Somer-
sham, which was in his own country.   Where the
potter accordingly drew rein, and turning the head
of his mare, disarmed the Norman, and bad him
play the part of messenger from Hereward the
Saxon to them at Brandon.

Hereward returned hastily to Ely, and shewed
what the policy of the king at present was ; and it
fell out as he had to the abbot and others made
report.   When the scaffold was raised amid the
marshes in front of the town, the wise woman and
her companion were set upon it on high, whence
they might be within view of the abbey and island ;
and the Normans lay hidden among the reeds and
underwood in parties, ready at command to advance
to the attack.   The king was in presence to hearten
them, and their numbers surpassed those that had
fought twice before against the outlaw.

The wise woman did her part according to her
cunning, and delivered curses upon Hereward and
the abbot, and all that were assisting to them, and
uttered spells and made strange gestures.   And once
she pronounced her sorceries, and twice : but ere
she could fulfil the enchantment which was at the
third time, the grass and thickets that surrounded
her and hid the Normans burst into flames at every
point ; the witch leaped from her seat and was
killed ; and Hereward and his men, springing from

ambush, first with their bows, and then with their swords, made that day more rueful for the besiegers than any before, so that the king, William the Norman, whose armour was pierced by a Saxon arrow, raised his camp, and concluded that if he could not take Ely by force of arms or by hunger, neverthemore could he by magic.

IV.

But it happened in the year of grace 1072, and in an unhappy hour for the Saxon cause, when the abbot and his monks began to grow weary of their too long enduring harass and incertitude, and doubted that their lands and treasure might be forfeited in the end to our lord the king by contumacy, that the abbot secretly treated with William the Norman, and admitted him into Ely. Whereby he hoped to have taken the person of Hereward. But Hereward had timely advice hereof, and with six trusty and stout comrades left the town and made for the Brunnerwold. Whereunto he came, and through each town and hamlet that he passed, drawing nearer to his own country and paternal inheritance, many joined him, till seven hundred armed men were under his banner. Our lord the king was an angry and a sad man when he thus saw his royal authority checked and disdained; and, understanding that the yielding up of Ely profited him but little, and that Hereward and his men were laying waste the lands of his Norman lieges and putting them to the sword, he made proclamation that the entire levies of the six Fenshires should

be called out on service under the Abbot of Peterborough and Ivo Taillebois, Lord of Spalding.

But Hereward, through his acquaintance with the
ground, and because he was secretly aided by the
common people, eluded every effort to draw him
into a general engagement, and at length in a sharp
skirmish in a wood, when the Saxons had thrown
the enemy off their guard by a feigned retreat,
Abbot Thorold and many other of the wealthy
Norman leaders were taken prisoners, and a great
number of the common folk slain.

Heavy ransoms were exacted from the abbot
and other chiefs.   Thirty thousand marks of silver
Thorold had to find ; and because he declared his
resolution to be revenged, and even offered the
goods of his church to any who should join him,
Hereward advanced to Peterborough, whence the
abbot fled at his approach, burned the town, and
despoiled the church of all its riches.

He took away all the gold and silver, and the
holy vessels, and the sacred garments, Hereward
the Saxon.   But, lo ! a vision appeared unto him
in a dream, commanding him to make restitution
of the same under pain of the displeasure of God
and the Holy Virgin ; and he restored those things,
as to do it was in him behoveful.

A generous enemy Hereward ; for he surprised
the good town of Stamford, coming upon it in the
night ; and the saying went that a great white
wolf, and spirits of the wood bearing enchanted
lights visible only to the Saxons, guided them on
their way.   But Hereward set the men of Stamford at freedom, and played toward their lord, Ivo

Taillebois, a noble part, and taught a lesson of forgiveness.

But, alas! when William the Norman saw how dread an enemy he was, and would be at one with him, and have him safeguarded to the court, Hereward forgot the duty which he owed to the sweet and brave lady, the Lady Torfrida, on whose wise and loyal counsel he had leaned in the hour of his adversity and trouble, and looked upon another one, the Lady Elfrida, beautiful, proud, rich of purse, and mistress of the ear of the court.

So in an evil moment Hereward put away Torfrida, the wife of his youth, and wedded that other, namely, the Norman widow Elfrida; and in verity he never prospered after. For whereas he had hoped to gain repose from his incessant watching and warfare, he had now neither quiet at home nor abroad.

For his enemies at the court of the Norman persuaded the king that Hereward meditated treason and high crimes against the peace of his grace and the realm; and it was so that he was delivered over to one Robert de Herepole, who conveyed him to the castle of Bedford, and threw him into chains, where he lay a whole year; but Robert de Herepole proved no unkind keeper, and those that nourished hatred toward Hereward grudged the gentleness of his captivity. So tidings came to the men of the marsh and the forest, who loved Hereward, and reverenced his estate, that he was about to be transported in charge of Robert de Herepole to the castle of Buckingham, where he might be more strictly kept by the Lord of

Spalding, his very foe ; and the Saxons lay in wait
for the guard that was appointed to attend Robert
and his prisoner from Bedford to Buckingham,
and rescued their beloved chieftain. Who, when
Hereward upheld him as one that had been good
master unto him, was spared, and was shortly
sent to William the Norman to plead truly for
Hereward, and set forth his case as it was.

Then William the Norman again admitted Hereward to his peace and restored unto him his lands.

Nevertheless, the peace of our lord the king
shielded not the Saxon chieftain from the treachery
of his enemies, and he had not Torfrida to advise
and to comfort him, nor had he at his side the
knights and others that had formerly fought and
conquered under his banner in many a glorious
fight.

The Normans assailed him on his very threshold,
and hovered round his dwelling ; and one day his
chaplain, whom he had set as watch while he ate,
to give warning of the approach of peril, feigned
slumber, and a force of Normans and Bretons surrounded the house and fell upon Hereward.

He seized a lance, a sword, and a shield, that
were by good fortune at hand, and faced his foes
like a wild boar. Fifteen of them lay at his feet ;
but his lance and sword were broken, and he had
nought but his shield for a weapon.

Four knights came behind him and buried their
spears in his back. Hereward dropped upon his
knees, but as he fell, he hurled his shield at Ralph
de Dol, a Breton knight, that advanced to despatch
him, and brought him lifeless to the ground.

Then he could no more accomplish, and sank never to rise again.

The noblest and most fearless spirit, and the strongest arm that were in the land were laid to rest for ever.

Four such men as Hereward the Saxon, and the Norman sway would have been overthrown.

FULKE FITZWARIN.

[*It is hardly disrespectful to the general reader to affirm that, while he has probably a very fair, if not a very accurate, knowledge of Robin Hood, he has none whatever of the personage whose name stands at the head of the present article. Yet it is not in the least degree too much to claim for Fulke Fitzwarin that in many leading respects his traditional fame and exploits furnished the material from which the story of the Barnsdale hero was built up; and it is curious and noteworthy that Fitzwarin was really a man of noble blood and extensive possessions during the period commonly assigned to Robin, namely, the reigns of Henry II., Richard I., John, and Henry III. (1160–1220).*

The founder of the noble and ancient family of Fitzwarren, or Fitzwarin, was Warin de Metz, cousin of the Duke of Brittany, who by his marriage with Melette of the White Laund, younger daughter of William Peveril of the Peak, and Lady of Whittington (by her father's surrender) and Alderbury, co. Salop, acquired those extensive and valuable possessions. By this lady he had several children, including Fulke his heir, the hero of our legend; and the line was carried down from him by a series of successors to a Fulke Fitz Warine, who, dying in

1429 *without issue, left his sister Elizabeth his heir.
Her daughter Thomasine, by her husband Richard
Hauckford, married Thomas Plantagenet, Duke of
Gloucester, sixth son of King Edward III. ; and, the
duke having no surviving issue, William Bourchier,
third son of William Earl of Ewe by Ann Plantagenet, his daughter, succeeded to the title, and was
summoned to Parliament* 1449–69 *as William Bourchier, knight, Baron of Fitzwarin. The Bourchiers
held this honour till* 1636, *when Edward Bourchier,
Earl of Bath, dying without male issue, his titles
fell into abeyance between his three daughters and
coheirs. The barony is at present in two moieties.*

But besides this dignity, we find that in 1342
William Fitzwarin, le Frère, *of the same stock,
was summoned to Parliament as " Willielmus filius
Warini," and that he was a Knight of the Garter.
He survived till* 1361, *and left issue ; yet neither he
nor his representatives received a further summons.*

*Fitzwarin, of whose romantic and surprising
adventures there is a nearly coeval account, entitled
by its proximity to the events to a more implicit cre-
dence than the " Little Gest," was unquestionably the
original type of this class of hero and legend ; and
we therefore felt that our volume would be very incomplete without a text of the interesting narrative.
Mr. Wright, it is proper to note, has pointed out
that the prose story among the Royal MSS. in the
British Museum is in all probability itself one degree
removed from the honour of being the original work ;
and that learned gentleman considers that it is a
paraphrase of an Anglo-Norman poem, no longer
known, on the subject. It is, however, apparently so*

true to its metrical source, that for our purpose it is equally serviceable.

It is also necessary to be aware that, although it is not so stated in the MS., Sir Fulke Fitzwarin, according to Mr. Wright, actually took up arms against King John in support of the baronial cause subsequently to the pacification of 1203 mentioned in the text, and was not finally reconciled to the Crown till the fourth Henry III. But, on the other hand, in Courthope's "Peerage," his death is placed ante 1195.

The expression in the MS., "plura ficta, præcipue de Fulcone quodam," may seem to impugn the historical veracity of the account in some particulars; and we have gone so far as to abstain from entering into all the details of foreign adventure, which have certainly struck me as not unfrequently being of the ben trovato type.

In many particulars of their lives and careers the two outlaws had little or nothing in common, and indeed the disloyalty and depredations of Fulke were limited to his personal animosity against his school- and playfellow King John. But at the same time he set the precedent followed by Robin a century or so later of helping and protecting the poor. Perhaps, in one leading respect, as being a fairly trustworthy report of the experiences of an old English baron, who spent the greater part of his life under the ban of the law, and who owed his inpunity in part to his own prowess and in part to the collusion of others, the story is unique; and there is also a subsidiary feature here which deserves to be noticed, namely, that his reputation was sufficient to tempt an adventurer in the north to personate him, and commit outrages in his name of which he was neither guilty nor capable. The passage where this fact is recorded is remarkably melodramatic and picturesque.

The "History of Fulke Fitzwarin," which has been printed entire in the old French, has tended to preserve a knowledge of this famous character and his relationship to his age; but in his case we have, so far as is at present ascertained, no series of popular ditties analogous to those which celebrate the achievements of Robin. This fact is chiefly significant of the neglect and oblivion into which the struggle maintained by the Shropshire baron against the Crown fell after his decease; while the reputation of the Yorkshire and Nottinghamshire hero was perpetuated by an espousal of popular rights and wrongs.

Robin Hood was a man of the people, sprung from them, and indissolubly identified with their wants and grievances. Fitzwarin, by far the greater man and more distinguished actor, merely carried on a species of guerilla warfare against John in a spirit of revenge and self-defence. Robin had no family ties; Fitzwarin was one of five brothers united together in arms by the alleged oppression of their sovereign.

The thread of the singular and eventful story will perhaps suffice to unfold the origin of Fitzwarin and the circumstances which led to his proscription. Like Robin, he was ultimately received back into royal favour; and in point of fact his connexions were so powerful, and the royal authority so comparatively weak, that he withstood the Crown under singular *advantages, and obtained at last an unqualified pardon. It will be observed that his range was far wider than that of his more generally known successor. For he not only haunted the Welsh border, which was the place of his nativity and the seat of his inheritance, but Kent, Windsor Forest and the New Forest, both far more extensive at that period than now, or even two centuries since, besides his occasional excursions abroad and two visits to the neighbourhood of London itself.*

The circumstance that Fitzwarin retired into private life some time before his death, and had a son of both his names, who fell in the battle of Lewes in 1264, prior to the composition even of the poem above mentioned, might have rendered us unusually cautious in receiving the account of the father's career, had it not been the case that the younger Fitzwarin lived in the king's peace, and was a loyal subject of the Crown, though in manliness of character worthy of his illustrious sire.

We judge from a passage near the end of the Royal MS. printed by Wright, that the brothers of Fulke, and perhaps himself, held property in Abingdon, which, on a grant of lands from the Earl Marshal at Ashdown in Sussex, they abandoned, and settled at Ashdown, founding the market town of Wanting with the right of a fair. It may be a clew to the personal appearance of Sir Fulke that his brother William is described, while he was the king's prisoner at Westminster, as a tall, stout, muscular man, with a long, black beard. Sir Fulke himself is indeed said in the history to have been, as a lad of eighteen, very handsome, strong, and tall.]

WHILE William the Norman reigned in England, among the great barons who served him in his wars, Payn Peverell, Lord of the Peak and the White Laund, with all the lands, chases, forests, and waste thereto appurtenant, was one of the most loyal and the most puissant; and when he died, because he had no heir, William Peverell, his sister's son, succeeded to all that fair heritage, and furthermore gat by conquest other lands, as all the land of Morlas as far as the water of Dee and Ellesmere. This William in the White Laund made a tower, which he named the White Tower, and dwelled in the same; and the town that grew round about it was called the White Town or Whittington; and yet other towns he built at Ellesmere and at Keyroc.

Now this William, again, had no heirs, yet he had two fair nieces: Elen, whom he wedded to Alan Fitz Flaeu, Lord of Oswestry, and gave her in dower all Morlas and Keyroc, and Melette, that was the younger and fairer; but no man pleased that great lady, for that she deemed none of her worthy.

Her uncle sought her, that he might know her full mind; and she said unto him, " Verily, sir, there is not a knight that I would take in the whole land for riches or estate, but he must be courteous, comely, and debonnair, and of his body the most valiant in all Christendom; and such will I have, and no other."

The Lord of the White Tower gave her assurance that he would essay his utmost to discover such a husband, and gave her in fee the White Tower and all belonging thereunto, that her hand might be

the more sought ; and she was thereafter named
Melette of the White Tower.

Then a tournament was proclaimed against the
feast of St. Michael the next ensuing, to be held at
the Castle of Peverell, for the love of Melette, and
whoever should be approved the best knight in all
the jousts by her allowance was to espouse her,
and enter upon her lands. The challenge was
dispersed through every country ; and at the
appointed season came to Peverell knights from
England, Scotland, France, and many another fair
region, even the king's son of Scotland, the
prince of Wales, and the dukes of Burgundy and
Brittany, and all clad in shining armour, with their
steeds in array of war, and their escutcheons and
devices. It was a noble spectacle to behold.

But albeit there was present at that time, for the
sake of that noble lady, Melette of the White
Tower, all the flower of chivalry, the honour of the
tournament remained on the first day with a knight
attired in red samit, who was all unknown, and
when the rest went to their inns, disappeared into
the forest nigh-hand. And on the second day he
entered the barriers again, and his colour was green
like the forest ; and as it had happened before, he
overcame all that challenged him, and, lastly, the
duke of Burgundy ; and when Melette of the White
Tower, who sat in a high place with her ladies,
viewing the contest, saw how matters went, she
called her page unto her, and commanded him to go
and deliver her glove to the Green Knight Adventurer, praying the same to be her champion.

Whereupon he once more withdrew, and now

returned accoutred in red, and did other deeds of marvellous prowess, that none might stand against him; and in the end judgment was taken that he was the winner of the prize. Then he disclosed himself to be Warin de Metz, cousin to the duke of Brittany, which duke had fully equipped him for the tournament; and Melette of the White Tower and Warin de Metz were joined in marriage, and had to them born, in the time ordained by God, a son, who was called Fulke fitz Warin.

Now inasmuch as Warin de Metz, the brave and gallant knight, grew in favour with King Henry, the second of that name, and was one of the most potent barons of that age, his son Fulke, when he came to boy's estate, was taught by the same master those things in learning that it was meet for him to know that gave instruction to the two young princes, Richard and John, the king's children, and the three were schoolfellows and playmates together; and when God called to him King Henry, and King Richard reigned in his room, Richard appointed Fulke Lord of the Marches of Wales. But it happened in the course of time that King John sat on the throne, and because he bare a secret grudge against Fulke Fitzwarin, since they had quarrelled in playing at chess in their nonage, he took from him this government and his lands that he had received in marriage, and bestowed them on Fulke's enemy, Morris Fitz Roger.

Besides Fulke, Warin de Metz had had four sons; and when King John wrought upon him this foul wrong, he repaired with his brethren to the court at Westminster, and renounced his allegiance in the very presence of the king, and with his cousin Baldwin de Hodnet and his said brethren, and their followers, left the city. The king sent certain knights in pursuit of them, by whom they were overtaken ; but the king's men were defeated, and Fulke was made an outlaw, and his estates forfeited to the king's use.

His father Warin de Metz and his mother Melette of the White Tower were dead ; and he hastened to his manor of Alderbury, gathered all that he could of his possessions, and with his four brethren and his two cousins, Audulf de Bracy and Baldwin de Hodnet, fled for the time to the court of his kinsman, the duke of Brittany. But at length, earnestly desiring to revisit his own country, Fulke secretly landed in England with his brethren and other companions, and travelling by night, while they lay by day in woods, reached the neighbour-hood of Whittington, where they set themselves to watch the doings of Morris Fitz Roger.

The news that so bold an outlaw had set foot on English ground soon reached the king, for a valet of Fitz Roger recognised him in the forest beside Whittington, and the king straightway appointed one hundred knights to seek for Fulke Fitzwarin, and take him wherever they might find him. But because Fulke and his kindred were allied by blood to some of the greatest in the realm, and many were, moreover, in dread of him, those that had this matter in charge were not over-zealous in their quest, and it was whispered that they might have found Fulke and the rest, an' they would, but feigned that they did not happen upon him.

One day as Fulke and his following were in the forest of Bradine, there came by ten merchants, with a rich convoy of goods, guarded by fourteen men-at-arms. John Fitzwarin was sent to ask them who they were, and whence they came, and begged them to repair to his lord in the wood to have speech with him. But one of the guard smote John Fitzwarin, whereupon the others appeared, and took the merchants and men-at-arms prisoners. Then it was understood that the merchandize belonged to the king, and that him-upon would fall the loss, an' it were taken them-from by force, for Fulke made it an ordinance to himself and to all that paid him obedience never to rob any but the king and his friends ; and so the merchants, when they had well satisfied him that the forfeit would not be theirs, but the king's, sent them away with a message of thanks to his grace for his goods.

King John was exceeding wrath at this insolency, and proclaimed Fulke a traitor to his crown, and that whoever should bring him in, dead or alive, should have a thousand pounds of silver and all his lands in England.

The outlaws privily removed into Kent, and Fulke, leaving his retinue in the forest, rode along the highway alone. He shortly met a man that carried on his head a chaplet of red roses, and he begged it of him ; and the fellow, saying that he was sparing of his goods who would not give such a thing at the request of a knight, handed him the chaplet, for which Fulke rewarded him with twenty sols.

But the man wist well who it was that he had

seen, and made haste to Canterbury, to tell the
news to some of the knights to whom was committed the duty of taking Fulke. Who raised the
country all round, and placed folk everywhere with
horns, to blow them if they saw the outlaw. Yet
Fulke knew nought hereof, until such time as he
heard one sound a horn ; and then all the watchers
drew together, and the outlaws gathered round their
chief, and there was a great fight, wherein the king's
people were beaten and slaughtered, and Fulke and
the rest rode away at full speed.

When they had left their pursuers far in the
distance, they dismounted and walked to an abbey,
where Fulke left his brethren and the rest, and, in
the guise of a monk, limping on one foot and sup-
porting himself on a staff, awaited the arrival of
the king's men. Who, shortly coming up, asked
him if it was so that he had seen any armed knights
pass that way. "Yea," he replied, "and may God
repay them the hurt they have done me ! Seven
of them on horse and fifteen afoot came along
even now, and because I could not, by reason that
I am so weak, move quickly enough, they threw
me down in passing over me, and well-nigh
wounded me to death." The king's men thanked
the old lame monk, and hurried away in chase, till
they were lost to view. But presently Fulke discerned eleven knights, well mounted on foreign
horses of price, approaching ; and as they came up
to him, their leader said in derision : "Look at this
great fat monk ! His belly, I warrant, would hold
two gallons."

Fulke's spirit rose within him, and suddenly

lifting his staff, he struck the speaker to the earth, and his companions, who had kept watch at the abbey gates, flew to his aid, seized and bound the knights, locked them up in the porter's lodge ; and, leaping on their horses, Fulke and his attendants drew not rein till they reached Huggeford, where Sir Walter de Huggeford, that was Fulke's kinsman, entertained them.

Now let us speak of a stranger adventure than all that befell him. When he had been with his company at Huggeford a certain space, came a secret messenger from Hubert le Botiler, Archbishop of Canterbury, praying him to wait upon his grace, as he had matters of great moment to confer with him upon.

So Fulke returned to Kent, and leaving the others in the forest, he and his brother William in the guise of merchants repaired to Canterbury, and to the primate's palace. His grace shewed Fulke how his brother Theobald le Botiler, that had espoused a very rich lady, and the most beautiful in all England, Dame Maud de Caus, was deceased, and how the king was seeking to win his widow to his mistress ; but she had taken sanctuary there, and was now beneath his roof. He said, " I pray you, good friend Fulke, and on my benediction command you, to take her to wife." And Fulke, seeing that she was good, and fair, and of honourable repute, and had in Ireland many strong castles and other possessions, after counsel with his brother William taken, assented ; and the union was privately solemnized by the archbishop himself within the palace. And after two days, Fulke, leaving his bride in sanctuary, proceeded to the forest, where Fulke made known to his brethren and friends what he had done : who made merry over the adventure, and in sport called him husband, demanding whether he had a mind to bring his fair lady to castle or to wood.

No sooner was he joined in wedlock to the sister-in-law of the archbishop, than he learned tidings which carried him incontinently to the north country. For a certain ribald knight of those parts, named Peter de Bruvile, under colour of being Fulke Fitz-warin, was sorely oppressing the honest people dwelling on the borders, and dishonouring Fulke's fair fame ; and in especial he understood that this Peter de Bruvile, with his troop, had broken the house of Robert Fitz-Sampson, that was a friend to Fulke and had done him many courtesies, and held the place, personating and discrediting him. For, let it be ever held in remembrance, Fulke was in arms only against the king, and no robber or murderer.

On the night then that he and his company reached the dwelling-place of Robert Fitz-Sampson, he bad the others stay behind in readiness, and clomb over the fence, where he heard sounds of mirth and revelry ; and looking by stealth through a casement, he beheld those caitiffs in the hall feasting and making merry, their visages masked, and Robert Fitz-Sampson and his lady, and their household, bound in one corner. He listened awhile, and the men addressed their chief as Sir Fulke, and the lady piteously cried out to him, saying, "Ah, Sir Fulke! for God's mercy, I never did you hurt, but have alway loved you to my power."

He heard no more, but rose to his feet, and all alone he went forward, sword in hand, crying, "Now, peace! I command you, all that be here present, and no one stir the least!" And he sware a great oath that if any amongst them should move, he would hew him into small pieces. So they were awe-stricken.

"Now," quoth he, "which of you causes himself to be called Fulke?"

"Sir," said Peter de Bruvile, "I am a knight, and am called Fulke."

"By God! Sir Fulke," exclaimed he, "rise up quickly and unbind this esquire and his lady, and the rest, and bind well in their room all your companions, or you shall be the first to lose your head."

Peter did as he was bidden; and when he had bound well all his crew, Fulke commanded him to cut off their heads, every each one; and so he did.

Then Fulke said to him: "You recreant knight, that cause yourself to be called by my name, you lie therein. I am Fulke, and that I shall make you speedily know, for I will requite you for procuring me the repute of a robber." And thereupon he smote his head off likewise.

And when he had accomplished all this, he called his companions, and they saw what had been done. And they presently sat together at supper, and communed on this strange accident and this deceit, which had so unjustly brought into disfavour the name of Fitzwarin; and Fulke saved Robert

Fitz-Sampson and his family and his treasure, that none was lost.

In the mean time, his lady, that was the primate's sister-in-law, had been delivered of a daughter in sanctuary, and had then repaired to Sir Walter de Huggeford; and she lay now at Huggeford and now at Alderbury, until King John, who had spies upon her, holding her in enmity by reason of her marriage, obliged her to take refuge in Shrewsbury, where, in the church of Our Lady, she gave birth to a second daughter; and so straitly was this unhappy lady watched, that when she was now again in travail, her child was born to her in a mean cottage on the mountains of Wales, and baptized in the Maiden's Well below; and the mother was so weak, that she was carried to the Grange at Caer-y-genant.

But Fulke, on his part, was more than ever restless, and the thought of Morris Fitz-Roger and his lost patrimony rankled in his bosom; and shortly after his visit to the north, and worthy chastisement of Peter de Bruvile and his crew, he resolved to make once more his way to Alderbury, where he lay with his comrades in the forest near the river-side, in a thick coppice, and was unseen of any. Who to John de Raunpaygne, one of the trustiest of his friends, thus spake:

"John, you know something of minstrelsy; dare you go to Whittington, and offer to play before Morris Fitz-Roger, to the intent that we may wise what he doeth?"

"Yea," answered John de Raunpaygne, and took a certain herb; and putting it into his mouth, his face swelled and grew discoloured, so that his own people scarce knew whether it were he or no. Then he donned such raiment as a poor man might wear, and took his instrument, and put a staff in his hand, and came to Whittington.

The porter led him in to Sir Morris, who asked him where he was born; and he replied, in the Marches of Scotland. He demanded of him what news he had.

"Sir," quoth he, "I know none, save of Sir Fulke Fitzwarin, that was slain of late, in committing a trespass in the house of Sir Robert Fitz-Sampson."

"Say you so?" quoth Sir Morris.

"Yea, truly," replied the minstrel; "all the folk of the country speak of it."

And Sir Morris was right fain of this good news, and gave the minstrel a cup of fine silver in reward.

John learned that Sir Morris would undertake next day a journey to Shrewsbury with a small company, and hastened back to his master with the tidings; and Fulke and certain of his band, placing themselves in the way, slew Sir Morris and all his knights that were with him. But when Sir Morris first espied Fulke, he knew him by his arms, and cried out, "Now I am assured that all minstrels are liars." Thus, notwithstanding, by so many fewer enemies had Fulke.

He gave the king no rest, and took side with Owen, prince of Wales, against him; and now that Sir Morris Fitz-Roger was dead, he re-entered into his patrimony, that had come to his house by Melette of the White Laund. But it so fortuned that in one of the battles that he had against the king's knights, Sir Audulf de Bracy was taken, and led to Shrewsbury, where the king was; and the king sware that he should be hanged.

John de Raunpaygne dyed his body and face as black as jet, attired himself richly, and with a tabor slung round his neck, rode on a fair palfrey to Shrewsbury.

When he was brought before the king's grace, the king asked him who he was and where he was born.

" Sir," quoth he, " I am an Ethiopian minstrel, born in Ethiopia."

" Are all the people in that land of your colour? " demanded his grace.

" Yea, my lord," John replied, " both men and women."

" What do they say in foreign lands of me, prythee? "

" Sir, they say truly that you are the most renowned king in all Christendom, and it is for that I am come to see you."

" Fair sir," quoth the king, " you are welcome."

" Sir my lord," returned John, " many thanks."

After the king had gone to rest, Sir Henry de Audeley, constable of Shrewsbury castle, desired to see the black minstrel, and summoned him to his chamber, where they made mirth with wine and melody, until Sir Henry suddenly said, " Go fetch Sir Audulf de Bracy, that he may have a good time, ere he dies on the morrow in the morning." And then they all discoursed together; and presently John sang a song that Sir Audulf was wont to sing,

and Sir Audulf gazed at him and knew him, but
made no sign. When Sir Henry called for the
cup, John sprang to his feet, and passed it to him,
but unseen threw thereinto a powder, which caused
all that partook of the drink to fall asleep ; and
each drank after Sir Henry save John and Sir
Audulf : who, when the rest were slumbering, tore
up the table linen, and descended through a casement to the river-side beneath, and escaped to
Whittington, where Fulke lay, and welcomed them
very joyfully.

When the king perceived that Fulke waxed so
powerful in Wales, he sent letters to Prince Owen,
who had wedded his sister Joan, and prayed him to
banish that felon from his court, or that, if so he
would deliver to him the body of Fulke, he would
restore him all his lands which his ancestors, the
kings of England, had at any time afore from his
lordship taken. Prince Owen shewed the letters to
his wife, who privately let Fulke understand that
her lord meditated coming to accord with the king.

Then Fulke sent his wife under charge of his
cousin Baldwin de Hodnet to Canterbury, and commended her to the care of the archbishop, her
brother-in-law, and with his four brothers, and Sir
Audulf de Bracy and John de Raunpaygne, all
armed, he repaired to the prince at Balaha.

"Sir," quoth he, "I have served you to my
power right loyally : but now one knows not in
whom to put trust, for you have received the king's
letters, whereof you have said to me nought ; and
in regard of the great promises that his grace
therein makes, you intend to betray me."

"Fulke," the prince replied, "remain with me; for indeed I had no thought of deserting you."

"Sir," Fulke returned once more, "I believe it full well, yet will I not in any wise stay here."

They quitted Wales accordingly, Fulke and his company, and journeyed till they came to Dover, where Baldwin de Hodnet advised them that he had left the Lady Maud in safe keeping with the archbishop at Canterbury; and then they put to sea, and landed in France.

The French king, that was named Philip, received the knights of England courteously, and they took part in certain jousts, which were at that time held in the fair city of Paris. The French knights bare themselves well, but the strangers overcame them at all points, and in especial Sir Fulke was marked of the king for his prowess. Of whom the king demanded his name, and he said, "Sir, I am called Sir Amis du Bois." Then King Philip asked him if he knew in England a knight named Sir Fulke Fitzwarin, and what his appearance and stature were, for his fame had spread widely abroad. Sir Fulke replied that he knew him well, and that he was much of his height; and King Philip was very gracious unto him and the other knights of England.

But when King John found that Sir Audulf de Bracy had been set free, and that Sir Fulke and his brothers had left England, and had gone to the court of his cousin, the king of France, he wrote letters to King Philip, urging him to drive Sir Fulke Fitzwarin from his realm. Then, for that he knew not that Sir Amis du Bois was verily Sir Fulke, he returned answer that he had no such knight in his land. But came Sir Fulke presently unto him, and craved liberty to go. The king asked him what more he needed to his full content; and Sir Fulke shewed him that he had news requiring him to return home.

Said the king, "Sir Amis du Bois, I think that you be Sir Fulke Fitzwarin!"

"Truly, my lord, it is so," quoth he.

King Philip said, "You shall dwell with me, and you shall have richer lands than ever you had in England."

But Sir Fulke excused himself, pleading that he was not worthy to receive lands of another that could not hold his own heritage; and he took leave of King Philip, he and his people, and came down to the sea, where he espied a ship, whereof he asked the mariner his name. He said that it was Mador, and that he was a Russian born.

"Mador," quoth Sir Fulke, "know you well how to carry folk from region to region in safety?"

Mador said, "Yea."

"Indeed," said Sir Fulke, "you have a perilous calling. Tell me now, what death did thy father die?"

"He was drowned in the sea," answered the other; "and so my grandfather, and his father, so far back as I can tell."

Sir Fulke deemed him bold to go to sea; and the mariner looked at him, and said again, "Where did thy father die, and thy grandfather, and his father, and the rest, prythee?"

"Verily," said Sir Fulke, "in their beds, I trow."

"Truly, sir," answered and said Mador, "since all your lineage so died, I marvel that you dare go to bed. But every creature, sir, will have that death that is destined for him."

Sir Fulke owned this to be true, and he caused Mador to build him a strong ship, and he hoisted his flag thereon; and they sailed along the coast of England till they met another ship, wherein were many knights, whereof one challenged them. Mador said that the ship was his; but the knight replied that he lied, for it carried the arms of Sir Fulke Fitzwarin, and commanded him to deliver up the body of that traitor. But Sir Fulke drew alongside the ship, and took all the treasure therein, and then let the sea enter, so that it sank. Onward thence they sailed, doing hurt to none save the king's ships, and came to Scotland, where they went on land to seek victuals.

They saw a boy tending sheep; and he led them into a cavern underground, and there left them, and went outside and blew a horn, that his servant on the mountain might hear him, quoth he, and bring food. The boy blew six moots, and returned; and presently entered six great and tall clowns and fierce, clad in coarse and filthy tabards, and each in his hand a great staff. Sir Fulke misliked their demeanour, but was silent. They went into an inner chamber, and anon they presented themselves in rich garments of scarlet and green and shoes of orfrey, and no king could be more magnificent; and they saluted Sir Fulke and his friends. Then was brought unto them an exceeding costly chessboard, with chessmen of gold and silver; and they invited the strangers to play. Each lost by turn, till it fell to Sir Fulke to have a game.

The fiercest of the clowns said to him, " Will you play ? "

" Nay," replied he.

" You must play or wrestle," quoth the clown.

" In good faith," replied the other, "there you lie, shepherd ; but I will play with you in the manner that I have learned." And he leaped up, and drew his sword, and he smote the heads of all the six clowns from their shoulders.

Thereupon he looked around and found a chamber, where an old woman sat with a horn in her hand, and often she tried to blow it, yet could not. Sir Fulke asked her what booted the horn, if she could not sound it. She said that if it were sounded, succour would come to her in abundance. He took the horn and passed thence into yet another chamber, where were seven damsels, very sumptuously attired, and working rich embroidery. They cast themselves on their knees, and sued for mercy. He lifted them up, and demanded who and whence they were.

One said : " I am the daughter of Aunflorreis of Orkney, and my lord dwelleth in Castle Bagot, in Orkney ; and it happened that as I and these other damsels, and certain knights of our acquaintance, took a boat on a time to solace ourselves on the sea, the seven sons of the old woman that you have seen came upon us in a ship, and slew our people, and seized us, and dishonoured our bodies. Whereupon we pray you to set us free."

And Sir Fulke took them to his ship, and all the

victuals, riches, and armour that he found in the cavern, with the haubergeon that he ever after prized above all other things to him pertaining, and would neither give nor sell to any. And when the ship was laden, he went again on land with his company, and blew the horn that the old woman had had in her keeping, and all the thieves of the country, two hundred or more, thronged toward them; and they slew them, that there were no thieves in that country afterward.

Sir Fulke left Scotland, and voyaged to many other lands, and saw great wonders, whereof the rarest was the dragon that ate human flesh and slept on a couch of fine gold, for his nature was so hot, and the nature of gold was to be cold; and this monster kept a fair damsel prisoner, that was daughter to the duke of Carthage. Whom Sir Fulke, after he had slain the dragon, restored to her father; and the duke was full glad, and offered her to him in marriage, with all his whole dukedom. But Sir Fulke refused, and sailed away toward England; and landing at Dover, where he left his ship, repaired to the forest of Windsor, where the king lay.

Now, Sir Fulke well knew that great forest, and when they came thereunto, they heard horns blow, whereby they judged that the king would hunt that day. Sir Fulke bad his company tarry behind, and very richly armed he rode alone to see what tidings he could gain of the king. For it entered into his thought to challenge the king for his dis-inheritance.

He presently met a charcoal-burner with a triblet

in his hand, and he changed clothes with him, and gave him ten besants to his pay, bidding him keep secrecy. He sat by his fire, blowing the embers, and drawing the wood together, when anon came up the king on foot, attended by three knights, for the rest were on the other side of the forest, who demanded of him if he had seen stag or roe. He said that he had seen a stag, and it had long horns, and if his grace pleased, he would lead him whither it had gone. The king and his knights, all afoot, followed the charcoal-burner until he came to a great thicket; and he prayed the king to wait, while he beat the thicket, and made the stag run his way.

Forth he sprang into the coppice, hastily gathered his following, and throwing aside the charcoal-burner's blouse, took the king and his attendants prisoners.

"Sir king," said he, "now I have you in my power; and such judgment will I exercise on you as you would on me, if you had taken me."

The king trembled with fear, and begged his life, which Sir Fulke only granted when his grace, in presence of his knights that were with him, swore to fulfil his covenant, restoring him all his heritage and goods whatsoever, and suffering him thereafter to dwell at home in peace with such security as he should think fit to require.

But as soon as the king had returned to Windsor, he went from his oath, and despatched a force of knights, under Sir James of Normandy, to take Sir Fulke wherever they could find him. John de Raunpaygne, Sir Fulke's trusty and well beloved friend, gave warning of their approach, and they set

upon them and slew all save Sir James of Normandy;
and Sir James of Normandy they bound and gagged,
and Sir Fulke changed armour with him, and the
rest clad themselves in the armour of the king's
men, and went to the king; and when they had
delivered to him Sir James of Normandy, whom he
deemed from his armour to be Sir Fulke, saluted
him, and took their leave.

The king was exceeding angry when he perceived
how he had been over-reached, and sent out a larger
troop of horsemen in pursuit of those outlaws, who,
being suddenly surprised, narrowly escaped capture ;
and Sir Fulke was sorely wounded, so that they
were fain to carry him away, and his brother
William remained a prisoner.

This was the gravest misadventure that had
hitherto befallen Sir Fulke, more especially since
he might not at that time rescue his brother, but
was taken on shipboard, and with his companions
visited many countries, acquiring great riches. Yet
he longed sore to return to England, and compass,
if he might, the deliverance of his brother, if he
were not already dead. And when they had again
set foot on their native soil, he and the rest, and
John de Raunpagyne, had found that William Fitzwarin was yet the king's prisoner, and lay at
Westminster, well guarded, they brought up their
ship as close as they could to the city, and in the
guise of mariners took means to deliver him, and
to take him to their ship, which set sail for Brittany.

There they spent half a year or more with Sir
Fulke's kinsfolk ; and Sir Fulke, still intent on
visiting the king with sharp reprisal for his treachery,

at the end of this time resolved that nothing should hinder him from landing once more in England; and he secretly came to the New Forest, which was to him right familiar, and the king hunted the boar in that forest with six knights, his attendants. The outlaws seized them all, carried them to their ship, and put out to sea. The king promised to grant Sir Fulke his peace, and to restore his castle of Whitington and all his lands to him, and to leave the six knights as hostages until the pardon was sealed. Which admitted to the king's peace Sir Fulke and his four brethren, and sundry others his companions in arms; and Sir Fulke and his three brethren submitted themselves to the king at Westminster, at his return from his duchy of Normandy, and were there received back into grace with much pomp, in the presence of the Earl Marshal of England, the Earl of Chester, and many other earls, barons, and clergy. Whereat Hubert de Botiler, archbishop of Canterbury, that had ever been good friend to Sir Fulke, unfeignedly rejoiced.

Sir Fulke came home at length to Whittington, where he found the Lady Maud his wife and their children, to his great joy, and they lived together in much honour; and their daughter Eva, when his wife Joan was dead, that was the daughter of the king of England, married the prince of Wales. But Sir Fulke, remembering him of his sins against God in the slaughter of many people, and other grave trespasses, built to the glory of Our Lady near Alderbury, in a wood on the Severn, the New Abbey, in which, in the fulness of time, he and his lady, the Lady Maud, were buried; and after him

his son, that was likewise named Fulke, remained
in the king's peace all his days, and was a valiant
knight in his service, that was, besides, by reason of
his broad domains and puissant kindred, a lord of
great weight and worship.

THE KING AND THE HERMIT.

[This, like the following article, is a fourteenth century minstrel's tale of the forest, but of a different structure and drift, and seems to pourtray some holy father, who dwelled in the silvan wilds with every outward appearance of poverty and asceticism, while he covertly appropriated the king's deer, and provided himself with plenty of good wine and ale. The scene of the interview is laid in the once vast forest of Sherwood in Nottinghamshire, where Edward has lost his way, and is separated from his companions in a hunting excursion.

The "King and the Hermit" is professedly derived by the reciter from an existing and probably longer text, which he terms " the romance," and to a copy of which we are at present unable to refer. The version which we possess is incomplete at the end, and not more than a single manuscript of it is known. It is exceedingly graphic and clever—unusually so for the period, and the writer was a person of no mean descriptive and humorous power. The manner in which the disguised king gradually draws out the hermit, and makes him reveal his poaching exploits, is remarkably dramatic and amusing ; and the casual preservation of the name of the hermit's boy-servant imparts to the whole an interesting verisimilitude.

In the portion which is unfortunately deficient the stalwart friar proceeded no doubt to court, and was well received. The king was apparently at Nottingham, the town more than once cited in the story; and thither his entertainer would of course repair. It must have been a curious meeting.

We perceive that the theatre of the present adventure was Sherwood; and the monarch concerned may be safely presumed to have been Edward the Second. It was during that prince's Nottinghamshire progress in 1323 that the circumstance may have occurred, and we have been consequently induced to consider this legend as allied to the Robin Hood series.

The winning affability of our kings where no political principle was directly involved, and where majesty was (as it were) on furlough, form the basis of numerous traditions and a fruitful theme for anecdote. The earlier incidents of this class illustrate in a very valuable and opportune manner certain traits which used to be considered beneath the cognisance of the historian.

It is observable, in the account of his mode of life which the hermit gives to his unknown visitor, that Sherwood Forest at all events was protected in the Plantagenet time by keepers and foresters, and that the friar was obliged to conduct his contraband operations after dusk.

This may serve in a measure to corroborate the authenticity of one or two of the Robin Hood stories, where affrays with the officers of the Crown are related; but these functionaries would, as a rule, exercise a sound discretion by giving Robin and his men a wide berth.

The reader of " Ivanhoe" will easily recognise the " King and the Hermit" as the foundation of an episode in that novel. The old fabliau, which we here reproduce for the first time in a legible shape, was originally inserted in a publication printed during Scott's lifetime, and in fact in 1812, just before the commencement of the Waverley series.]

JESUS that is King of heaven bring to a good end all such as follow the minstrel's calling, and tell passing strange adventures, gladdening the hearts of men, as they sit at meat, and drink the red wine!

I will sing of an accident that befell a certain king, if you will hearken unto me.

It happened in good Edward's time, that his grace went to Sherwood to solace himself with hunting the deer, and with raising the great hart among the coppices and on the moors.

And when the king's men had dispersed themselves about, and returned to his grace to report to him what they had seen, his grace asked them in manner following: "Fellows, where ye have been, in what places have ye seen most game?"

To whom they answered, sinking on knee: "Everywhere, east and west, lord, there is of game great plenty. Ere the sun go down, we can shew your grace two thousand head."

An old forester drew near, and, "Forsooth, lord," quoth he, "I saw under the greenwood tree a deer, and such large antlers as he bare I never of my days beheld before."

"Lo!" said our king, then, "I will grant unto

thee a royal pension to thy life's end, if so thou wilt
bring me that-to."

On the morrow, betimes, they set out, the king
and his men, with dogs and horses and trusty bows;
and to the greenwood are they bound; and when
they came thither, they spread their nets and their
gins, each archer standing by his tree, bow in hand.

Then they gave three blasts on the bugle-horns,
and uncoupled the hounds; and the hounds ran as
though they were mad, and started the game out of
the covers.

The king and his men followed with shouts and
blowing of horns through the forest, over hill and
dale, through thick and thin. The king rode on a
good horse; but the beast began to tire, for his grace
had been in the saddle from midday till evening:
and he fell behind the rest a little, to let his courser
breathe, till at last he was left alone, and knew not
where he was. And the night began to draw on.

The king thought within himself: " While there
is still light, it will be better to take shelter under
some tree; for if it grows dark, and I fall into a pit,
my horse and I were in evil case. I have heard
poor men call on St. Julian to lend them good
harbouring, and he has listened to their prayer.
St. Julian, as I am a true knight, send me grace this
same evening to meet with some abiding place!
Every year that I live I will make offering to yield
poor folk shelter for thy sake!"

Now not much farther had our king ridden, when
he became aware of a light in the distance, where
the wood waxed thinner; and as he approached, he
saw that it was some hermitage or chapel.

" Now, by St. Julian, good speed! Yonder I will go and beg a lodging."

A little wicket he soon perceived ; but it was fast, and he called out, that those within might hear his voice. And presently at the door of this dwelling in the forest stood a man, who by his mien and presence appeared to be a hermit ; and as he wended his way toward the gate where the stranger stood, he told his prayers on his beads. And when he saw the king, he said : " Sir, good even ! "

To whom the king replied : " Well met, Sir Friar. I beg thee to suffer me for this night to be thy guest ; for I have ridden far in the forest, and have lost my way, and it grows toward nightfall."

The hermit said : " Verily, for such a lord as thou art, my poor lodging is in no wise meet ; though sometimes, if it be a poor man that comes this way, and seeks refuge, I deny him not, lest he should take harm. I dwell here in the wilderness among the wild creatures, and sustain myself on roots or whatever I may get, as it is the will of the Lord."

The king answered and said : " I beseech thee, then, that thou wilt shew me at least the way to the nearest town, and ere a fortnight is passed thou shalt hear from me to thy advantage ; or, if thou canst not thyself go, that thou wilt suffer thy boy to lead me a mile or twain on the road, while it is yet twilight."

" By St. Mary," quoth the friar, " unless I deceive myself, little help gettest thou, sirrah, here."

Then said the king : " My dear friend, how far is it, pray you, to the town ? "

" Five miles," replied the friar ; " and a wild road

it is, by Our Lady! except ye have the day before
you."

" By God! hermit," cried the king, "with thee I
shall lodge to-night, or else I should come to some
mishap."

" Thou art a stout carl," said the hermit peevishly;
"yet if I were out of my hermit's weeds, I would
not be bearded by three of you. Well, I cannot
fight with you ; and if ye must come in, let it be
so, a' God's name, and ye must take even what ye
can get."

So the king put up his horse, and two handsful of
barley-straw he fetched out of some corner for him,
for the beast had had a hard day. The hermit
looked askance at him ; but the king took no heed,
and hewed some wood, and kindled a fire, and
seated himself down before it.

" Dear hermit, let me have some supper. The
sorrier the day, the merrier the night! By God!
if I were a hermit in this forest, when the king's
keepers had gone to rest, I would sally forth east
and west, with my good bow in my hand and my
arrows in a thong, and see what I could get to
gladden myself and my guests. What needeth the
king venison ? "

The hermit said to the king : " Good sir, prythee
tell me where thou livest ? "

" Sir," replied the other, " in the king's court I
have dwelled many a day ; and my lord rode on
hunting, as great lords use to do, and after a great
hart have we ridden from noon to eventide, and yet
he escaped away. All the day I have been out in
the forest, and I am foredone with weariness. I

pray thee give me to eat, and thou shalt not repent the service."

The hermit went away, and fetched bread and cheese and thin ale ; and the king took thereof, for he thought that other meat the hermit had none. Yet very shortly he had enough.

"Take it away," said the king ; "I shall requite thee ere long. Now, hermit, if I were in such a place as this, I should learn to shoot ; and when the king's keepers were well asleep, thou mightest get of the best. Though thou beest a friar, it were no reproach to thee to have a bow and arrows. Thou mightest shoot the wild deer, and no forester espy thee."

"If thou hast nothing better to tell me than this, forbear, sirrah," quoth the hermit then. "Why, were I taken in such a fact, I should be thrown into prison, and an' I could give no bail, should be bound hand and foot, and it would be a mercy if I were not hanged."

Then the king answered him so : "Were I in thy place, I should be astir o' nights, when I wist well that the king's foresters were a-bed. Now, come, hermit, as thou art a true man, if thou can'st handle a bow, make no secret of it to me ; for, by God! no man shall have it from me so long as I live. Come, hermit, if thou hast any venison, give me of the best."

The hermit said : "Men of high estate look jealously at my order, and would fain put me in prison, if so they might find that I busied myself with such things. It is our calling to spend our days in prayer and fasting, and to take no heed for our meat.   Many a time nought passes my lips but milk of the kine.   Warm thyself by the fire, and then get to sleep, and I will lay my cope over thee."

The friar eyed his visitor steadfastly, and considered in his mind, before he proceeded farther; and then he continued thus :

" Thou seemest a fellow something different from any that I have seen this long time in these parts. Let me see what can be done."

And he went to a chest, and drew forth two candles and lighted them, and set them on the table. The king marvelled after the words which the hermit had before spoken, but held his peace.

Presently the hermit fetched a cloth and spread it, and laid fine bread upon it, and baked venison ; and he bad him choose whether he would partake thereof, or have hot collops ; and he might have them salt or fresh, as it liked him best.

The king ate and laughed, and, " Well, hermit," cried he, " I might have had dry cheer had I not touched upon the shooting !   Now Christ save a friar that can furnish under the greenwood such good fare as this !   I swear the king himself is no better off than we, an' we might only come by some drink to wash it merrily down."

The hermit called his boy—William Allen was his name—and he said to him : " Go, and by the side of my bed thou wilt see a bundle of straw, and underneath there is a horn pot—God forbid that we should stint of it !   And when thou hast brought it, give our guest's horse corn and bread to eat. Return with despatch, and bring me my cup, and we will drink till dawn and have sport. I will see what sort of a fellow thou art."

The king was debonnaire enough, and answered : " Whatso thou wilt have me do, command me."

" When the wine comes, canst thou say *Fusty bandyas*? and I will make response, *Strike, pantnere*."

" Yea," quoth the king. But as soon as the boy entered with the flagon and the cups, the friar looked at the king, and the king was silent, for he had forgotten the words.

" Fie, man," said the hermit, " wilt thou take all night to learn them ? Say *Fusty bandyas*."

" *Fusty bandyas*," said the king.

" *Strike pantnere*," replied the hermit.

Then these two set to their wine, and jested together, and the boy filled their cups again and again. The king said : " For this good cheer I shall give thee reward, hermit ; it is the merriest carouse I have had this seven year."

" God bless us all !" quoth his host. " But, alas ! when thou comest again unto thy lord's hall, thou wilt forget the friar. Yet, perchance, if thou shouldest relate the adventure that thou hast had to-night among gentlemen where thou dwellest, there will be laughter and merry cheer ; and if thou wilt pay me another visit some night, I promise thee thou shalt not want a venison collop."

" Fear not," said the king ; " thou shalt not be forgotten. To-morrow, so soon as the day daws, we will go away together, and when we come unto the king's gate, they will not keep us long waiting, I trow. And trust me, hermit, the best that is to be had there shall be set before us two."

The hermit answered so,—

"I have been in the king's court, sir, ere now, and have had given to me to eat of a root, and have been kept loitering about half the day. Weenest thou that I am so pressed that I must hang my heels till I am called? I have neighbours here-about, whom-unto I send presents of the wild deer's flesh, and they let me have in return bread and ale, and so I live well enough."

"Hermit," said the king, "by my faith, I am well pleased with thee; thou art a bonny friar. I tell thee, man, if thou camest to the king's court on thy adventures, thou dost not know what may betide thee, ere thou goest thy way again. Though I be indifferently clad, I may make bold to go thither, and bring with me guests two or three; and no man shall say me nay, but I may do my pleasure."

"By Our Lady," said the hermit, "I trust that ye be a true man, if I came as ye say unto me. But for whom should I ask, prithee?"

"Jack Fletcher is my name; all men know me; and ye will find that I am a man of worship in the king's service."

The hermit, thus reassured, answered: "Come, then, Jack, into the chamber hard by, and I will shew thee something more."

The king followed the hermit into his bedroom, and spied about the hermit's bed many a broad arrow hanging. The hermit handed him a bow, and said unto him,—

"Jack, draw it up."

But the king could scarce bend the string.

"Sir," he said, "there is no archer that the king hath that can shoot with this."

Then the hermit took the bow, and placed in it an arrow of an ell long, and drew it to the head.

"Jack," said he, "there goes not the deer in the forest but that arrow should find it. Jack, since thou art a fletcher by craft, thou mightest now and again help me to a shaft or two."

The king answered that he would.

"Jack," said the hermit, "an I were sure that thou wast true, I could shew thee yet more still."

The king sware that he would never betray him, and the hermit took him into his larder, where were troughs filled with venison.

"Jack, how thinkest thou? While there is deer in this forest, now and then I may happen on some of the best; the king can have no better. Jack, if thou wilt, take some of my arrows, and we will try them in the morning."

They went back to their cups, and drank and talked till daybreak; and when they rose betimes, the friar said: "Jack, I will go with thee a mile or twain, to put thee in thy way."

"Much thanks," replied the king; "but last night, when we were together, you promised me that you would come some day to the king's court, and see what passes there."

"Certes," answered the friar, "I shall come, as I am true man, before to-morrow night."

The friar guided the king through unknown recesses of the forest, and brought him to a place which he knew, and then these two bad each other a warm farewell; and when the friar was out of sight, the king put his bugle to his lips, and sounded a loud blast, and his knights and lords, who had been scouring the forest in search of him, came up, and were rejoiced to see our lord the king once more, whom they had thought to be lost.

THE NUT-BROWN MAID.

[This delightful and exquisite piece, of which the antiquity is undoubted, appears to have been on sale as a broad-sheet in 1520, *and forms part of the miscellany known as "Arnold's Chronicle" (*1502*). But as it has no affinity with the remainder of the contents of that volume, it was probably reprinted there from a separate edition; so that it was, perhaps, a stall-ballad many years prior to the date above mentioned. It occurs among the earliest publications registered in the books of the Stationers' Company; and Captain Cox of Coventry, as Laneham lets us know in his Kenilworth letter, had it in* 1575.*

On a former occasion, the present writer ventured to draw attention to the similarity between it in point of tone and style and passages in Alexander Barclay's translation of the Eclogues of Æneas Sylvius Piccolomini, published about the same period. The pathos and purity of the narrative are at all events very striking, and almost defy a modern imitator. It is a sweet little idyl, commemorating the romantic courtship of a noble, under the disguise of a bourgeois, obliged to fly to the woods from the arm of justice, and a maiden, who claims to be a baron's daughter.

*It slightly reminds us of the " Lord of Burleigh";
and how far it excels it !*

*We have attempted to preserve as far as possible
the spirit and substance of the original, which presents the form of a dramatic interlocution more or less
founded on fact, and terminates in the triumph of
the heroine, whom the simple grace of the story has
made the lifelong friend of so many.   The composition almost stands by itself, by reason of its unusual
structure and its union of delicacy and beauty, so rare
at that remote date in our literary history.   It is introduced by a sort of process in which the two speakers
undertake to impersonate the characters represented.]*

RIGHT or wrong, men do ever complain of women,
saying that it is a labour in vain to seek their love,
for they will never requite the same.   For if a new
lover appear, straightway from their thoughts the
old one is a banished man.

Ah ! too true it is that often no trust is to be put
in them.   Yet in a case which I shall narrate to
you now you will see that they sometimes remain
steadfast and true.   Witness the Nut-brown Maid,
who, when her lover repaired unto her and made
his plaint to her to prove her, would not forsake
him, for she in her heart affected none other but
him alone.

Then let us discuss between us how the matter
befell.   Listen to the story of the Nut-brown Maid.
Now I will begin, and ye that be present, I pray ye
listen unto me, how she suffered, and what trial her
lover put upon her.   I am the knight, and in the
darkness I come as privily as I may, saying :

Alas ! it is so ; I am a banished man.

And I, to fulfil your desire, will do what I may

to shew that men to their shame accuse us women
without cause.   Therefore, my own sweetheart, say
unto me how it fareth with you, for in my mind I
love you alone.

It standeth thus.   A deed hath been done,
whereby great harm may come to me.   I trow that
I am destined to die a shameful death, or to flee
to the woods, and, with my good bow in my hands,
lead an outlaw's life.   Wherefore have I come to
thee, my own truelove, to bid thee a sad farewell ;
for I am bound to the thick forest, there to dwell
a banished man.

O Lord ! what availeth the happiness of the
world ?   The glory of a summer's day is quenched
before noon.   I hear thee say farewell.   Nay, nay ;
we are not so soon to depart.   Whither wilt thou
go ?   What hast thou done ?   All my cheer would
turn to sorrow, wert thou once away.   For of all
men I love only thee !

I can believe that for a little while thou wilt fret.
But in a day or twain thou wilt be comforted, and
indeed I pray thee not to lose thy labour by thinking on me.   For it is so, that I must hasten away
to the wood, a banished man, alone.

Now that thou hast unfolded to me how it is,
I shall speak to thee plainly my mind.   Since it
must be so, and thou hast not to choose but to the
forest to betake thee, I will not stay behind.   For
it shall never be said that to her lover the Nut-
brown Maid was untrue.   Make thee ready, then,
and thou shalt not tarry for me.   For of all men
there is none but thee whom I love.

O, think what will be said in court and city

by men and women of every degree, when it is
noised abroad that thou art gone! They will give
it out that thou hast escaped to the forest-side to
please thy wanton will, and that thou couldest no
longer abide without thy lover. Liever than thou
for me shouldest win an evil name, I will go, a
banished man, to the greenwood alone.

Though all should cry that I were at fault,
I would not waver, for the blame would rest with
them that sought to defame me. True love is
above shame, and I shall shew that they who would
not do as I, when thou art thus oppressed by
trouble, are recreants all. But not such the Nut-
brown Maid.

I avise thee to remember well how it be-
seemeth not a maiden to follow an outlaw into the
wood. For thou must carry his bow, and like a
thief be ever in dread of the law. Whereby much
wrong might to thee come. So let me, prithee,
go away, a banished man, alone.

As ye say, so it is, may-be. But love may lead
me to come afoot for thy sake, and help thee to
make a new home beneath the wood-shade. For,
if I have thy companionship, I ask no more. It
maketh my heart wax cold to think of parting from
thee, whom alone the Nut-brown Maid loveth.

An outlaw hath the hand of every man against
him. He may be taken and bound, and be hanged
on a tree, and become sport for the wind. And
what couldest thou do then? Thou couldest not
yield me succour. Thy bow would fall from thy
hand. O, let me pursue my way alone to the
forest, a banished man!

It doth not belong to womanhood, forsooth, to fight and to draw the bow. But if need pressed, I would even do what I might, and essay my most, as women have ere now, to serve and to save thee, whom only I love.

Yet hear me once more. I doubt if thou couldst bear the hardships of the forest life. Think of the thorny paths, the frost, the snow, the rain, the heat of summer and the winter's cold ; for whatever betide we must lodge under the green-wood, with no other roof over our heads than the poor thatch, and I know that thou wouldest soon wish that thou haddest not done this thing.

I have shared thy joys, and is it not meet that of thy griefs I should be partaker likewise ? Yet where thou art I cannot fare amiss. So let us haste to be gone. The Nut-brown Maid waits for thee.

Consider, when ye would dine there may be no victual to get, nor ale, nor wine. Consider, my sweetheart, thou wilt have no house but a bower of leaves and branches of the tree, and no bed to lie upon. O, thou art too tender to bear these things ; and I will depart and leave thee behind.

Such an archer as men say that thou art can-not fail to find meat among the wild deer, and the water of the brook will well suffice me for drink. Youth and health have we, and to sleep o' nights we may make shift as others do. So let us no longer delay.

Ah ! one other thing thou must do, ere with me thou canst go. Thou must cut thy hair, and let thy kirtle fall no lower than thy knee, so that thou mayest, if need be, bend thy bow the better against an enemy. But to-night woodward must I flee, and thou must have all prepared to set out before the dawn of the day.

I shall do for thee more than to womanhood pertains. I shall shorten my hair and my kirtle, as ye bid me. O my sweet mother, my heart bleeds for thee the most ; but, adieu! I must go whither fortune leads me. Thou art my guide and my refuge. Let us go ; the day beginneth to break.

Stay, stay ; thou shalt not go ; for methinks that whosoever it were that sought thee in love, thou wouldst accompany, belike, the same. The proverb says, " soon hot, soon cold" ; and this is true of a woman. Wherefore I shall let thee stay here, and seek the forest, there to dwell in solitude.

There is no need to use such speech to me. For thou knowest too well how hard I was to woo and win, and though my ancestors were noble, how I, a baron's daughter, stooped to love a squire.

A baron's child to beguile, O, it were an accursed deed ; and that she should mate with an outlaw, Almighty God forbid ! It were better for the poor squire to make for the forest alone, than to have it said that he had so foully betrayed thee.

Whatso hap, I shall never upbraid thee with such a thing ; but if thou goest, and so forsakest me, then shall I think that thou wast a traitor unto me, and I shall in no long space render up my breath.

If ye went, ye would rue. For I have already in the forest a maid fairer than thee, and because one would not endure the other, there should be strife, and I desire peace.

Even though that were so, my heart would still be thine, and to thy paramour I would be a hand-maid; nay, if thou haddest even a hundred, I would crave to be one among them.

My own dear heart, now hast thou well and fully approved thyself to be true and steadfast to me as never maid or wife was before. The case is not as I feigned it to be, when I sought to try thee. Pity indeed it were that such an one should suffer farther distress! Let it pass, whatever I said to thee when I began. I have done no trespass, nor is there need that I should to the greenwood go.

These tidings make me gladder than if I were crowned a queen. But, alas! I trust that ye are not playing with me, as ye did afore; for then my heart would break indeed.

Fear not; I tell thee truth: and as thou hast a baron to thy sire, understand that I, who shall presently go about to seek thee in marriage of thy father, had an earl, who is now with God, to mine, and that with all my broad lands in West-moreland I shall endow the Nut-brown Maid.

ROBIN HOOD.

[1. *In dealing with this ancient and favourite tradition, the editor has for the first time made use of such material only as appeared to him authentic, and has discarded all the more recent theatrical, May-day, and ballad-mongering superstructures on the original group and sequence of incident. Ritson and after him Gutch, in an even larger measure, have swollen the bulk of their respective publications by the indiscriminate admission of every scrap, good, bad and indifferent, bearing the name of the outlaw, where there was frequently no actual relationship to his personal history, and have consequently assisted in imparting an erroneous conception of the few known facts to the English reader. Ritson was by far the better critic of the two ; but the information at his disposal was still more imperfect than ours, and he laboured under the initial mistake of placing the hero of Barnsdale too early, and of attributing to him associates and exploits with whom and which he could have had nothing to do.*

The researches of the Rev. Joseph Hunter, and the critical labours of Thomas Wright and others, have contributed very importantly to rectify our view and estimate of this fine and imperishable episode ; and it is difficult to understand how any real service is done by persistence in exhibiting the few genuine remains, in this case, encumbered and disfigured by discordant literary interpolations and after-growths.

The true foundation for a narrative of the transmitted incidents in the career of Robin is the " Little Gest of Robin Hood," a piece too well known to require further description ; and there are certain auxiliary lights, which permit us to amplify the somewhat scanty record supplied by that precious relic, in the shape of a handful of separate ballads preserved in MS. and print. Such are the "Tale of Robin Hood" from the Cambridge MS., "Robin Hood and Guy of Gisborne," and "Robin Hood and the Potter." All these, especially the first-named, are very faulty and treacherous ; but the prose text which occurs below may be accepted as a careful and fairly complete embodiment of all that can be treated as of quasi-biographical value. Even this selected matter has required a great amount of rearrangement. In the original versions the sequence of events is often evidently erroneous and confused ; and, for instance, the epic of the "Knight," which forms the introductory scene in the "Little Gest," is improperly placed before those ballads which describe the earliest meeting between Robin and his two associates, Little John and the Curtal Friar.

The first portion of the ballad of the "Potter" is doubtless ancient and genuine ; but the central feature in the latter half is common to the anterior story of "Hereward the Saxon." The notion is borrowed by Peele, in his play of "Edward I." (1593) ; and in his case it was evidently a recollection of a ballad now no longer known in print, and by the merest accident transmitted to us in an unique MS.

Of " Guy of Gisborne" also it is difficult to doubt that there was, at one period, a printed text of very early date, since it is more likely that Dunbar, who died about 1515, *was indebted for his knowledge to a record in type rather than to a tradition or a MS. At present we merely know Guy from a single circumstance in his apparent employment by the sheriff of Yorkshire to capture Robin. But, according to Dunbar, he was himself a person of similar stamp, and possibly it was a case of setting a thief to catch a thief.*

A point which may be worth notice, by the way, although it is perhaps tolerably obvious, is that in the course of the following story, not only the sheriff of Nottinghamshire, but of Yorkshire, plays a part. In the ballad of " Guy of Gisborne," which lies in Barnsdale, Guy is in fact a scout, employed by the sheriff to track Robin, and obtain a clew to his whereabouts ; and of course the functionary for one county would have no jurisdiction in another.

In the interlude of the " Four Elements (1519)," *and again in Udall's translation of the Apophthegms of Erasmus* (1542), *is cited a piece entitled or commencing, " As Robin Hood in Barnsdale stood" ; this is not at present known as a separate broadsheet But it may well be identical with the tale of " Robin Hood and the Knight," with which the "Little Gest" opens, but which all the evidence conduces to refer to a later stage in the life of Robin.*

As regards the pieces affiliated on the legend, such as the "Noble Fisherman," the "Tinker," the "Shepherd," the "Forester," and others, while there appears to be no authority for associating them with Robin,

*they represent the ever-varying succession of adven-
tures and incidents to which the career of an outlaw
was open ; and we have in these stories circumstances
which, if they did not happen to him or his comrades,
may have befallen others similarly situated, with
whose names it would have been less profitable to con-
nect them. At the same time some apparently genuine
productions, like " Robin Hood and the Potter " and
" Robin Hood and Allen-a-Dale," are liable to the
suspicion of being partly indebted to existing traditions of earlier adventurers, Hereward the Saxon
and others ; and we apprehend the second part of
the " Potter "—a Barnsdale story—in Gutch, to be as
unauthentic as it is totally improbable, while " Robin
Hood's Golden Prize," though perhaps genuine, is, so
far as we can see, merely an altered text of the "Two
Black Monks" in the " Gest."*

*2. Hunter was, we believe, the earliest to fix with
a greater air of probability the period to which
Robin Hood belonged. Our older antiquaries had
been content, as a rule, to accept the ballad-mongers'
vague notion that he lived in the days of the Cru-
sades and Richard of the Lion Heart, and this loose
theory responded to the popular conceit that he was
as real a personage as Robin Goodfellow. He was
thought, again, by many to be an abstraction or type,
around which the professional caterers for the public
entertainment had collected a body of minstrelsy ;
and even his very name, which we now know to have
been usual enough, was regarded as open to doubt
and conjecture. Yet with all this scepticism there
was a certain circumstantiality, which went so far
as to confer on him a title, to provide him with a*

noble wife, and to bestow on his resting-place a dated epitaph.

In rejecting those portions of the Robin Hood ballads which we judge to be destitute of authority, and to be no more than literary compilations of a later period written for the stalls, we follow the example of the restorer, who removes the modern plaster from old cathedral walls, or him who, beneath a worthless mediæval text, brings to light a lost or rare classic. Even those pieces to which we have had recourse, such as the " Little Gest" and " Robin Hood and the Potter," while they are substantially of the highest curiosity and importance, were clearly the work of illiterate scribes ; and this is more predicable of the MSS. even than of the printed matter.

Mr. Hunter has exhibited a sketch of the outlaw's life, of which some portions will be found incorporated with the version which we print of the story. That accomplished and distinguished scholar arrives at the conclusion that Robin Hood was in the service of one of the dependents of the Earl of Lancaster— probably an archer—at the Battle of Boroughbridge, fought in March, 1323 ; and that subsequently to that disastrous event he with others sought refuge in the extensive woods in the neighbourhood of Wakefield, where persons of his name then lived, and to which he doubtless himself belonged. He was a man tolerably advanced in life at this time, and was married to one Matilda—not the Lord Fitzwalter's daughter, but an individual whose name occurs in a contemporary document. The Hoods, prior to the loss of the Lancastrian cause at Boroughbridge, appear to have been persons belonging to the yeoman class, and to have been well connected, especially if it be the case that they claimed near consanguinity with the De Stayntons, who were tenants under the Crown in capite *of the small Honours of Pontefract and Tick-hill, and of whom a female member, Elizabeth de Staynton, was prioress of Kirklees.*

3. The prevailing idea about Robin Hood is that he spent the whole of his adult life under the green-wood tree, and only retired to a nunnery when he needed in his last moments medical assistance and the services of a nurse. But such a view seems to be wholly inconsistent with the truth. Robin passed his youth and early manhood at or near Wakefield in peaceful obscurity with his family or his wife, and was already a middle-aged person when he sought the new home, where his worst enemy was "winter and rough weather." Nor is it to be supposed that he remained steadfast to one place during the period of his retirement from society. He shifted his quarters, as we know, from Barns-dale (near Wakefield) to Plumpton in the same county and to Sherwood in Nottinghamshire, either from the love of change or for greater security and concealment. For to his original delinquency as an adherent of the Earl of Lancaster or as the perpe-trator of some such act of violence as drove young Gamelyn and Adam Spencer to the wood in Chaucer's tale, he by his new course of life added that of a poacher and freebooter, and (above both) a despoiler of the hierarchy; and with the assistance of a small band of faithful confederates, which from time to time increased in number, he succeeded for a season not only in eluding pursuit, but in maintaining him-

self and his followers in comparative ease, and in relieving the needy.

The space occupied by the epic in its pure state and by the forest life of Robin is narrowed by Mr. Hunter to about twenty months. We are disposed to incur the risk of questioning such a view, inasmuch as the earliest glimpse gained of the hero finds him in possession of a limited retinue, it is true, but of a full treasury and of every evidence of power and prosperity, and the " Gest" expressly states that he led a life in the woods "two and twenty years"; nor is it for a moment to be taken for granted that the existing literary records are complete or consecutive. Our impression is that the Battle of Boroughbridge in 1323 occurred long subsequently to the adoption by Robin of a secluded and lawless existence, and that that event merely contributed to strengthen his resolution and to swell the ranks of his adherents. It goes without saying that Barnsdale, which we clearly apprehend to have been the first and for some time sole field of his activity, was under any supposition the haunt of dangerous characters before his day, and we can produce testimony to establish that in the last year of Edward I. that part of the road from Scotland to the north was notoriously and specially insecure.

It may not be altogether a futile speculation to inquire whether the exceptional precautions adopted to protect life and property in 1307 were directed against Robin Hood or against anterior and independent enemies to the king's peace, when taking back twenty-two years from 1325, the reputed date of his decease, brings us to 1303. But we owe, above that, a very respectful consideration for that well-known passage in the " Vision of William concerning Piers Ploughman," written by William Langland (who might have seen Robin) among the Malvern Hills about 1350, *where the author makes one of his characters say :*

" *I cannot perfectly my paternoster, as the priest it saith,*
  But I can rhymes of Robin Hood and Randal Earl of Chester."

And with these two lines before him we invite the reader to ask himself whether the allusion in the same breath, as it were, to an historical personage like the Earl of Chester and to the Yorkshire yeoman does not import something more than the transient experience of the forest and outlawry signified by Mr. Hunter's delimitation. Such a wide popular repute could scarcely have been acquired in those days of difficult communication in so brief a time as a year and a half or so in such a sphere of adventure. But it is worthy of particular remark that at a distance of only a quarter of a century from the date of his death he was already a hero of song; this helps to establish the authority of some of the traditional accounts and remains.

Not merely in the primâ facie *evidence furnished by the " Little Gest," where it speaks of the reception of the knight in the first fit or section, but in the precepts which the outlaw delivers to his subordinates for their guidance, we discern traces of lengthened standing and of former footprints in Nottinghamshire, with embittering recollections of its sheriff; and we can hardly avoid the conclusion altogether that Mr. Hunter has improperly curtailed the duration*

of the story, and that the mention in " Piers Ploughman" is due to achievements spread over a much
longer period.

4. *Under any circumstances whatever, Robin Hood
has accomplished the most signal triumph which has
ever fallen to the lot of an Englishman. By virtue
of unique attributes and under very extraordinary
conditions he has earned an imperishable name, one
which is part of our history and our birthright.*

Two centuries and a half after the composition of
" Piers Ploughman," a verse-writer of the reign of
James I.—Drayton in his " Polyolbion"—sings :

> " In this our spacious isle I think there is not one
> But he hath heard some talk of him and Little John;
> And to the end of time the tales shall ne'er be done
> Of Scarlock, George a Green, and Much the miller's son;
> Of Tuck the merry friar, which many a sermon made
> In praise of Robin Hood, his outlaws and their trade."

And here we are, at a distance of 550 years from
the epoch, with the ballad-hero constantly in our
thoughts and on our lips. He went to his grave
toward the close of Edward of Carnarvon's reign
without a suspicion that his country would care for
his reputation as dearly as for the memory of Magna
Charta, of which he was a practical exponent and
supporter. For in an age

> " When those may take who have the power,
> And those may keep who can,"

he upheld the poor man against the tyrannical or
usurious oppressor. He was a political heretic, and
in a sense a religious one, since he did not allow his
pious sentiments to blind him to the abuses of the
yet unreformed Church and the overbearing insolence

of the higher ecclesiastics. But his extraordinary fame came to him unsought, for had it not been for the ruin and proscription of his family and friends, he might have continued to the last a Wakefield yeoman, and have been buried with his fathers. The force of circumstances led him to retaliate for his outlawry by becoming a maker of history, and by inducing successive generations to exhaust their ingenuity in settling his personality and his period.

The nearness of many of the adventures of Robin Hood and his comrades to the Scotish border might account for the early popularity of the ballads in North Britain, and for the "Little Gest" being among the first productions of the parent Edinburgh press in 1508, apart from the sympathy of the countrymen of Wallace with the political principles held by Robin; for he was not so much an opponent of the Church as of the hierarchy, not so much of monarchical government as of feudal oppression and rapacity.

As it is, the edition of the "Little Gest" published in Scotland may or may not be anterior to that by Wynkyn de Worde. But it is quite possible that the latter printer executed one before his removal from Westminster to Fleet Street in 1502. So many of these more ancient typographical monuments have perished or at least so far failed to come to light, just as the Scotish edition of "Sir Eglamour of Artois" in 1508 at present takes precedence of the English-printed texts, and yet most probably was taken from one.

If in his political sentiments and principles Robin leaned in the direction of socialism, it must be re-

membered that it was a very different state of parties, of which he was a witness and contemporary, from that which at present has to reckon with the socialist as a problem and a danger. The Barnsdale outlaw saw before his eyes only two main orders or ranks of life, the patricians and plebeians. The great Middle Class, which has made England what it is, and which can alone maintain us in our position as a State, could be hardly yet said to exist as an active political factor ; and Robin laid down for himself the rule and maxim, not that all were equally entitled to share the national lands and wealth, but that the circumstances justified him in holding the balance between those who were too rich and those who were too poor. He was an unparliamentary redistributer.

The impotence of the civil authority in Robin's days is strongly exemplified by the impunity which our hero enjoyed during his term of sojourn in Barnsdale and elsewhere, and by the advantages which he gained in his occasional encounters with the municipal and even royal powers. The vast, uninclosed areas of woodland, the absence of an organized police, and the popular sympathy, had much to do with the success of the outlaw in evading detection and baffling pursuit.

5. We have spoken of the sophistication of the story by the later writers for the popular taste, where a perpetual demand for novelties created the necessity for changing the venue, and enlarging the true scope of the story. It is even easy to see how characters like the Pinner of Wakefield and Adam Bel were introduced into the idyllic drama as contemporaries and coadjutors of Robin ; they were both of the same neighbourhood and the same religion, and even an educated man such as the author of the " Polyolbion " unsuspectingly (unless it was by poetical licence) makes them members of the band.

It is not very surprising, however, to find in the literature of the seventeenth and eighteenth centuries such a lax and uncritical treatment of the subject, when we cannot peruse with care the compositions so much nearer the events described without detecting inconsistencies and oversights. The "Little Gest" itself, produced in the reign of Henry VII., asks re-editing, before it is capable of being used as part of a fairly chronological and authentic narrative.

The Robin Hood cycle of ballads presents the aspect of having furnished the parent-stock, whence the authors of all the other effusions of the kind, and primarily " Adam Bel," derived their inspiration and material. For several of these pieces outside the actual Barnsdale or Sherwood series possess a similarity of texture and treatment, and, although other parts of the country were densely wooded at that remote epoch, and afforded equal scope for the illustration of forest-life and scenery, it is noticeable that (with one or two exceptions) the whole of this family of legends is associated with the north of England and with Scotland. If we may compare small things with great, we are perhaps entitled to presume that out of the few incidents which the really ancient ballads in print or MS. embrace, the extensive collection in our hands gradually developed itself, just as the "Iliad" or the "Odyssey" may have grown to what we see them from slender prima stamina *or germs.*

The normal Robin Hood ballad, written for the meridian of the stalls, conveys the impression of having proceeded, if not from the same pen, from the same type of composer. It is couched in a trite and monotonous phraseology, neither in keeping with the topic nor with the period, and in some instances one is manifestly an evolution from another, with variations for the nonce.

Among the pieces inserted in their collections by Ritson and Gutch as possibly connected with this group, we confess that we discern nothing to the purpose. The story of "Robin and Gandelyn" is merely some passage in the careers of two foresters, who, like Robin Hood, were poachers of the king's deer ; and the name of one of the individuals has been wrongly given as Robin Lyth, because the stanzas commence with the words " Robin Lyth in greenwood bounden," the second word being not a proper noun, but a common verb, i.e. " lieth."

It is not our blame if the reader finds the legend, as we give it, shorn of some of its later excrescences. We have endeavoured to give careful consideration to all the ballads extant ; but we have found it imperative to reject a very sensible proportion as of no authority and as mere secondary structures ; and, after all, our chief fear is that we have been perhaps too indulgent to one or two pieces.

When we hear in the ballads of his removals from one place to another at a considerable distance, we must take into account the very restricted facilities for travelling in the fourteenth century and the aggravated difficulty which would present itself in the case of a man who was outside the pale of the law, and on whose head a price was not unfrequently set. Migrations from Yorkshire southward could only be accomplished by night or in disguise, and it was impracticable for the outlaws to transfer themselves to points many days' journey apart without great caution, and even then at serious risk, as they would be necessarily divided and liable to detection at halting-stages. We may, in fact, take it for granted that an exodus from Barnsdale or Sherwood was not undertaken before one of those retreats had grown untenable for the time.

It may strike some as one of those tasks which are better let alone, that of proving almost beyond doubt who Robin Hood was, when he flourished, and how prosaically his fortunes ended; it may be treated as a piece of indiscreet supererogation to tell how such a man, toward the close, failing in health and strength, accepted service under the Crown, and how, after a few months, he was compelled to seek medical or surgical aid in the priory, of which a relative was lady superior, and where he died from over-bleeding through the treachery, it is alleged, of Sir Roger of Doncaster, a priest, may-be, who had been one of his involuntary guests in Barnsdale formerly.

6. The history of this " Little Gest" seems to be that it was formed into a connected narrative out of a certain number of separate legends in MS. or in oral recollection by a north-countryman, who was conversant with the haunts of the outlaw on the outskirts of Wakefield and in the vicinage of the Watling Street, and who asserted his editorial pretensions by inserting here and there a few introductory or connecting stanzas. The narrative at the very outset represents the hero as harbouring a deadly resentment against the sheriff of Nottingham, so that at the point where the tale opens we are bound to infer that much has happened without leaving any vestige behind, and that the "Little Gest" is a garland, beginning abruptly, and plunging us in medias res. *But the starting-point of the adventures must surely have been in Barnsdale, not in Sherwood; and although Robin is usually considered a Nottinghamshire celebrity, whatever glory appertains to him is more properly a Yorkshire inheritance; for it was thence he sprang, and there, at Wakefield or in Barnsdale and Plumpton, that he spent the greater part of a not very prolonged life.*

The special interest and value of the "Little Gest" are manifold. It supplies us with items of information or portions of the epic nowhere else preserved, and not only shews the popular view of the subject, so far as it goes (for it is not exhaustive), nearly four hundred years ago, when oral tradition was capable of supplying a writer with a fairly genuine conception and report, but preserves, so far as the exigencies of metre and space allowed, the language of MSS. versions of still older date, to which the editor of the "Gest" had recourse, and of which fragmentary remains only at present survive. We also perceive that at the end of the fifteenth century the outlaw was associated with Nottingham, rather than with Barnsdale or Plumpton.

The editor of the "Gest" not unnaturally and not injudiciously (from his immediate point of view) placed the incident of the "Knight" in the foreground; but we see reason to differ from that

*arrangement, as the adventure was clearly one be-
longing to a more advanced epoch in our hero's career
as an outlaw.*

*The "Gest" is the sole attempt, which we are at
present aware of possessing, at a consecutive relation;
but it is, as may be readily perceived, imperfect in
many respects. "A Tale of Robin Hood," printed
by Gutch from the unique, but incomplete, Cambridge
MS., is simply the Nottingham episode, embracing
the capture of Robin and his heroic rescue by John.
It obviously appertains to the later period of the epic,
when Robin was a familiar figure at Nottingham
as well as at Wakefield, and when his renown,
moreover, had so strongly impressed the king, that
his uppermost thought, when he heard of his deten-
tion in the hands of the sheriff, was, not his punishment, but a supreme desire to see so famous a
character.*

*Robin's career appears to have commenced, as it
closed, in Yorkshire. The middle portion is chiefly
occupied by scenes laid at Nottingham or in Sherwood. There the closer proximity to an active
executive jurisdiction in the person of the sheriff
of Nottingham brought the outlaw most frequently
in peril of his liberty and life; and from the stress
which he is traditionally alleged to have laid on
unrelaxed hostility to the sheriff, we are probably
justified in concluding that there was some early
grudge in that quarter which Robin never forgave.*

*If we accept the view of Mr. Hunter in regard
to the chronology and habitat of Robin Hood as
broadly correct, we find ourselves in a position,
after the lapse of all the years between the first*

A. L. S

*quarter of the fourteenth and the last quarter of
the nineteenth century, to fix with remarkable exac-
titude the area and radius of his movements, so far
as the theatre of his earliest exploits is concerned
—Barnsdale and its environs. He lay, in fact,
within an easy distance of that portion of the
Watling Street which ran through Barnsdale, and
he relied for plunder on the travelling parties which
made this highway their route from Lincolnshire
to Yorkshire; and the deep forest on all sides
furnished to men familiar with every yard of
ground a secure ambush and concealment. The
compiler of the " Little Gest," or the author of the
ballad of the " Knight," even lets us understand that
the point on the Watling Street nearest to the outlaw's rude home in the forest was once known as
the " Sayles," although no such place is at present
distinguishable. The independent evidence of the
narrator imparts a strange reality to the incident
in the " Gest" where Little John and two others
are despatched by their master to look out for a
victim, who proves to be the distressed knight, and
to whom the outlaw, instead of robbing him, lends
a large sum of money to save his property from
forfeiture. It must have been something more than
an unintentional or unconscious coincidence, that the
monks are made to present themselves just at the
precise juncture when Robin has assisted a layman
to free himself from the clutches of the Church, and
can with a certain degree of consistency appropriate
the treasure found in the luggage of the ecclesiastics
to reimburse himself, so that my lord abbot is
virtually satisfied at the expense of his own order,*

and what is in excess is generously handed to the knight in return for his thoughtful present of bows and arrows.

We have mainly adhered to the sequence of events as it offers itself in the old account. But we must proceed to submit a conjecture, which strikes us as of sufficient force to justify adoption, that the meeting with the two monks and that with the knight have been transposed, as the possession of so large a sum as even four hundred gold crowns was unlikely, in the absence of some unusual piece of good fortune immediately precedent; and this may also help to explain the profusion of viands set before Sir Richard. The outlaws had had a good time.

We discern in Sir Richard at the Lee or (Al-Lee) a man of honourable character and unusually liberal sympathies, whose secular leaning was naturally more pronounced after his bitter experience of the cupidity and uncharitableness of the abbot of St. Mary's. He played a hazardous part in those days of clerical ascendency and despotism, and we are far from being perfectly acquainted with the duration and extent of his relations with Robin Hood, while of his ultimate fate we seem to be so far ignorant.

Mr. Hunter seems to create an unnecessary difficulty, in treating the episode of the "Knight" by concluding or presuming that his residence was in Yorkshire, where Robin and he first met. But he was then merely on his way to York to negotiate an extension of grace from the abbot of St. Mary's. After the repulse and pursuit of the outlaws at Nottingham on the occasion of the second archery meeting, Robin and his men take shelter in the castle of a knight, who is expressly said in the ballad-poem to be the same whom Robin had laid under such weighty obligations, and who evidently had a seat near Nottingham. The writer of the ballad calls it Utersdale, which may have been the name of the house or the locality. But Mr. Hunter thinks the ballad wrong, because a person of equestrian rank was not likely to possess two mansions in different counties. The fact is, that we do not know that he did; and the evidence is in favour of his abode being near Nottingham.

It is improbable that the yeomen had such familiar relations with two personages of the same rank. The "Little Gest," drawn up from still earlier records, pronounces the owner of the place near Nottingham to be identical with the recipient of Robin Hood's bounty. The king waits till he reaches that town, or at least that county, before he declares Sir Richard's estates under attainder. After his evacuation of his castle, the knight retires into Sherwood, and is there pardoned by Edward. The whole venue, *except the casual meeting in Barnsdale, is within a radius of Nottingham.*

7. There is another point dependent on this precise localization of a part of the tale. As early as 1307 *Barnsdale already enjoyed, we perceive, the repute of being a dangerous stage in the journey to the south; for we are told that when three dignitaries of the Scotish Church were on their way to Winchester under a royal escort, that escort differed from time to time according to circumstances, but when they arrived at Pontefract, on the confines of Barnsdale, it was raised to the maximum of twenty archers. The co-eval record says that this was "propter Barnsdale." But if a score of bowmen was accounted an adequate protection for such an exalted party, we naturally turn our thoughts to the force which Robin Hood is averred in ballad-lore to have had constantly at his command, and which could have readily overwhelmed the guard at its fullest strength. There is no difficulty in believing that the outlaws fluctuated in number according to circumstances or requirements; in the commencing sections of the "Little Gest" not more than four appear. To calculate by the score was at once a common practice and a common kind of hyperbole; and we must confess ourselves incredulous as to the existence of a body of one hundred and twenty or even one hundred and forty armed and desperate men, where their cardinal object and policy were to avoid notice, and to supply their deficiency in force by their tact, fidelity, and intimacy with the ground; nor should it be overlooked that they were principally persons of a rank superior to the common soldier. Nevertheless, on special occasions, it is quite possible that Robin Hood could rally together all the stout fellows within reach, and verify the five or seven score of song. As a rule, such a following might have proved a source of actual weakness, from its proneness to favour treason as well as publicity; and it is worth noting that throughout the story there is no hint of betrayal or disloyalty beyond one or two little brushes between Robin and his rather irascible lieutenant.*

One word more. The entry above quoted belongs to 1307, an early stage in the development of the machinery by which Robin set himself against the law; and we find that, later on, when the high cellarer of St. Mary's passed through Barnsdale, his escort was raised to fifty-two, and even that number was totally inadequate to protect him.

Our conclusion, upon the whole, is that the normal following of Robin limited itself to Little John and half a dozen others, and that when, upon information received, any remarkable emergency was expected, additional forces were collected by an understood and accepted principle of summons—not by bugle (for that was merely a rallying call), but by message. It is against probability, as it would have been against policy and prudence, that a large body of men, not amenable to the law, should have been constantly mustered in one spot or centre.

The situation of the outlaw in the woodland in those early days was of necessity less isolated than we may sometimes be apt to suppose. For his clothing, a portion of his diet, his tools and weapons, medical and surgical assistance, he was brought into periodical contact with the bordering towns or villages, of whose inhabitants he not seldom enjoyed the private sympathy; the present of bows and arrows from Sir Richard at the Lee was merely an exceptional windfall; and we see that Robin himself and John, if not others, ventured into Nottingham, and occasionally also into Wakefield, on urgent or special occasions. Robin had a wife, and possibly children, and some of his comrades may have been similarly placed; and in one instance we see that he proceeded to the county town to pay his devotions in the church of Our Lady there. As a Catholic, he naturally missed the services prescribed by his ritual; and the celebration of prayers or graces before meals by Friar Tuck or otherwise, if it was a reality, as affirmed in the "Gest," made indifferent amends for the privation.

We hear little, indeed, of the friar beyond the mention of his first encounter with Robin and accession to the party; and it is only by implication that we assign to him the function of priest-chaplain. He makes a more prominent figure in the plays and "Polyolbion"; he does not occur by name in the "Gest"; and it is possible that he did not long survive, or that he seceded.

The "Gest" makes Robin build a chapel in Barnsdale, which is not so unlikely; it may have been an inexpensive wooden structure, similar in appearance to many still visible in primitive localities; and the officiating priest, if not Tuck, was perhaps some not too fastidious priest at a modest stipend or a character of the type pourtrayed in the "King and the Hermit."

In more or less immediate connexion with this portion of the subject, it may be worth while to refer to a sermon of the fourteenth century, that is to say, just about the Robin Hood era, preached by a parson who has been robbed on the highway, and who makes his discourse an elogium on brigandage. He receives his property back, and a gold noble for his fee. The adventure may, of course, have no relationship; but the period accords, and the particulars are characteristic.

There is one aspect of the forest life of a proscribed character such as Robin Hood, which has never perhaps been much considered, and which *directly bears nevertheless on his day-by-day existence. What, in short, was the nature of the shelter which the woods could be made to afford, and, while it was sufficient to protect from the weather, could be without serious trouble replaced at different points? The hut or cabin of the keeper might be a permanent structure, however humble and limited; but the outlaw was not entitled to look for lengthened sufferance, and was at any moment liable to the seizure of his effects and the demolition of his retreat, even if he succeeded in eluding personally the officers of the sheriff or the soldiers of the king. The ideal picture of Robin and his merry comrades under the greenwood shade, regaling on venison and wine, and entertaining monarch and prelate, has often made us speculate on the scene in winter, in the drenching rain, in the deep snow, amid the wild hurricane—in the hour of sickness, and in the peril of death.*

From a casual allusion or so we collect that the outlaws stored their venison, wine, ale, and other provision, if not their habiliments, in caves, only known perhaps to themselves; after the accession of the sheriff of Nottingham's cook, they enjoyed the opportunity of having their food properly dressed; and for fresh water they resorted to the forest streams, or perchance (when they were in Barnsdale) to the well which still bears the outlaw's name, and is singled out by Mr. Hunter as probably a genuine link with Robin and his men.

We arrive at no definite authoritative clew on this point, since even in the early part of the "Little Gest," where Robin receives a guest at "the lodge door," the expression is merely that of the editor of

*the poem.   But the incidence of the case bespeaks
frequent removals and transfers, and consequently a
temporary and inexpensive description of refuge from
the weather, and storehouse for provisions and effects.
We have only to throw ourselves five or six centuries
back to realize in our mind's vision tens of thousands
of uninclosed acres, where small structures could
be placed out of the common track, and practically
invisible to the uninitiated.*

*Nor is even that process requisite, since at the
present moment, in the New Forest and elsewhere,
men conversant with all the intricacies of the denser
portions continue to reside years together in huts or
cabins constructed of timber and thatch; and such
persons become hardened to the weather, and enamoured of the freedom, till they are intolerant of
an ordinary roof.*

*A snake-catcher in this delightful region, who has
lived here on sufferance the best part of his life, has
an impediment in his utterance, which the local folk
ascribe to his parcel-snake mouth.*

*8. The densely afforested condition of England and
Scotland, both during and long after the mediæval
epoch, made possible a defiance of the law which
would now be scarcely maintainable for a day or a
week (as the case may be); and the strict and jealous
preservation of game, with the limited knowledge of
plantation, rendered silvan life, again, more secure
from the reluctance of the officers of the Crown to
destroy cover.   The forest folk-lore or romance,
which we possess, was, like everything else of the
kind, the product of favouring circumstances, which
can never recur.*

The men who ranged themselves round Robin, and shared his privations, enjoyments, and triumphs, were such as the Ridings of Yorkshire, and the north of England generally, are still capable of producing: long-backed, broad-shouldered, tall fellows, who were a match for all comers in muscle and pluck, and even "little" Much the Miller's son, was not improbably, if deficient in stature, compared to the rest, of the Rob Roy build. The men are yet on the ground; but the spirit and conditions have disappeared.

As regards Plumpton Park—when the "Gest" was written and printed, the residence and property of a family of the same name—it was in the Plantagenet time an open woodland and a royal chace, and doubtless originally formed part of the great forest of Knaresborough, of which the sole remaining trace is, we believe, the Stray at Harrogate, i.e. the Harrow Gate, or way, of that domain. The editor of the "Gest" terms it a park, because he knew it as such.

It should be borne in mind, in considering the removals of the outlaw and his followers from one point to another, even of the same part of the kingdom, that such changes were necessarily in their case accompanied by great risk and difficulty; and it is thereby safe and quite expedient to endeavour, as we have now for the first time done, to arrange in chronological order, so far as may be, the series of ballads and the contents of the "Gest," the result being a far more intelligible, and probably more accurate, view of the story.

After all, however, there must be much the same difference between the most realistic version now possible and the actual facts as there is between the sun and its photosphere.

But after his brief service at court, perhaps about the end of 1323 *or the beginning of* 1324, *it was to Barnsdale, not to Sherwood, that he retired to end his days. There was his true* patria, *his native place and air.*

The peculiar wildness and seclusion of this district in the fourteenth century, even in comparison with Sherwood, is exemplified by the apparent freedom from molestation which the outlaws there enjoyed. We do not hear of any incursions into it by the sheriff of the county, nor of any of those narrow escapes which Robin and his followers experienced in the Sherwood country.

Of the cause of his death, probably in the spring of 1325, *we get a meagre account; but it is nowhere stated that, looking at the not very lengthened interval between the reported failure of his health and that desperate enterprise for saving the life of Sir Richard at the Lee, the over-exertion was sufficient to impair the system of a man doubtless advanced beyond the prime of life.*

Of Simon Hood, presumably a relative, and a participator in the royal grace of 1323–4, *our cognisance is limited to the mention of his name as a recipient of pay as a valet or groom of the chamber. If he, which is almost certain, shared Robin's fortune in the woods, his name nowhere occurs in the ballads.*]

I.

LEND a courteous ear, gentlemen that be of free-born lineage, whilst I tell you of a good yeoman, whose name was Robin Hood. A proud outlaw he was, and a courteous.

In the famous town of Wakefield he was born and nurtured, a yeoman's son, in the days of Edward that was called Longshanks; and he grew up to man's estate there, and wedded a gentle wife, Matilda her name, and they lived in the king's peace many years.

But in the wars between our lord the king that now was, that is to say, Edward of Carnarvon, and his cousin the Earl of Lancaster, this Robert or Robin took arms for the earl; and when it was so that on the field of Boroughbridge, in the year of grace 1323, our lord the king took prisoner the said earl, and vanquished his men in battle, all such as fell not in the fight or were captives fled to the woods or over sea, and among the rest Robert or Robin Hood and Simon Hood and certain others sought refuge in Barnsdale beside Wakefield, a mighty forest and a fair.

Here they went to dwell beneath the greenwood, winter and summer, and set nought by the weather and by the law, namely, in Barnsdale on the Watling Street. Few they were in the first beginning. There were Robin, and Simon, and Much the Miller's son, and Little John, and William Scathlock, and Will Stutely, and Reynold, and Gilbert of the Wight [1] Hand, and Friar Tuck, all lusty men and true. But as the report went abroad of their free and merry life, and of the rich toll which they levied from abbot and baron and other of high degree, many came to them craving fellowship, or admitted

[1] Strong.

for their approved prowess with the bow and the
quarterstaff, and swelled the band, till it waxed right
numerous and strong, well furnished with arms and
goodly raiment. For food they wanted not; our
lord the king sold his deer to them best cheap; and
for venison that was over and above their need,
they were wont to barter other victual, and wine,
and provision of all sorts. So that Robin and those
that were with him lacked little truly, save their
homesteads and Holy Church.

Now you have heard tell that Robin was of the
yeomanry; but his comrades, one and all, were men
of the people. Albeit, however, they suffered a
common lot, and were bound together in brotherhood, they acknowledged Robin their master, and
were ruled by him in all things; and he prescribed
to them, at such time as they first gathered together
in the forest, the canons whereby they should be
governed in their dealings with the various conditions
of men and with women.

Verily Robin was a devout man, and sorrowed
more than all besides for that he might not, as his
former usage led him, pay worship to God, and His
Son, and Our Blessed Lady, where their churches
stood in the place of his up-bringing. Therefore he
sorely grieved; but no meat nor drink passed his
lips, nor was taken in his company, till three masses
had been said by the friar: one for the Father, one
for Christ Jesus, and one for the Holy Virgin whom
above all women Robin most loved and revered.

These, then, were the commandments which
Robin laid down for observance: "Look," quoth
he to Little John questioning him and saying on a

time, "Master, tell us what we are to do, whom we
are to take, whom to let go unharmed, whom to
succour." "Look," said Robin, "all of ye, that ye
do no hurt to any husbandman that tilleth with his
plough, nor to any yeoman that walketh in the
woods, nor to knight or squire that is a good fellow;
and I straitly charge you to lay no hand on any
woman, but to aid them all to your power for Our
dear Lady's sake and for St. Mary Magdalen's.
These bishops and these archbishops may ye beat,
and bind, and rob, and any such other that are
oppressors of the poor commons; and in especial
I commend to your attention, that ye never keep
him out of your minds, the proud high-sheriff of
Nottingham."

All of which ordinances, during such space of
time as Robin Hood lived and ruled in the parts
of Barnsdale and Plumpton, and of Sherwood in
Nottinghamshire, were held by his following to be
a law binding unto them; nor no king that ever
reigned in England received fuller and gladder
obedience than Robin, or was of greater worship in
Barnsdale and the borders thereof.

II.

Of all the brave and stalwart fellows who sware
allegiance to him, none loved him more dearly than
Little John, though, as you are presently to hear,
none was so wayward at seasons or so stiff-necked.
Yet he loved Robin again, and was loyal to the
heart's core.

How they first met was while our outlaws had
for a time, as their use was, removed from Barns-

dale to Sherwood; and Robin, one day in the morning, bidding his comrades hasten to him if they heard the notes of his bugle-horn borne in the wind, had wandered forth alone in quest of adventures.

He had not gone far when he encountered, at a narrow bridge over a forest stream, a stranger unarmed, save with a quarter-staff that he bare in his hand; and they met midway, nor would either yield ground. Robin drew back and bent his bow; but the stranger called him coward, for that he would assail a defenceless man.

Then Robin cast his bow aside, and stepping into the thicket, cut a good oaken cudgel, and returning to the bridge, " Now," quoth he, " we are more equal, and here we will fight till one of us is overcast into the water, and that shall determine the case."

The stranger was content, for he was passing tall and strong, and little doubted the issue, and after many a fierce blow surely enough Robin lost the day. He swam ashore, and drew himself to the bank by a thorn that overhung, and setting his horn to his lips, blew as he had aforehand given warning.

Greatly the stranger marvelled when he beheld the answer to the call.

" What has befallen, master," asked Will Stutely, "that thou art in such sorry plight ?"

" O, nothing," replied Robin; " only this fine fellow and I had a bout on the bridge, and he beat me, that I fell in."

" Is it so ?" they cried with one voice; " then he shall suffer likewise." And they seized the stranger in order to throw him into the brook.

But Robin commanded them to forbear, saying: "Touch not a hair of his head, comrades, for he is a stout fellow and a gallant. Prythee, friend, what is thy name?"

"I am called John Little," quoth the stranger.

"If thou wilt be one of us," answered Robin, "I will teach thee the use of the bow, and thou shalt want for nothing."

The stranger said: "Here is my hand; I will serve thee faithfully, and, I warrant, will play my part."

"His name shall be changed," cried Stutely, "and I will be his godfather. Let us prepare the christening feast under the greenwood tree, and baptize anew this pretty seven-foot babe."

The cloth was spread on the grass, and they brought venison and wine; and when they had eaten and drunk galore, Stutely spake in this wise: "This infant was called John Little; but for ever after to-day he shall be known as Little John." And they emptied their cups, and drank to the health of the new comer, till the woods rang again with their voices.

And this is how Robin Hood first found Little John, who proved staunch and trusty to the end, and loved his master in his heart as dearly as any; yet now and again they had passages betwixt them, not as on the bridge, but of words only, leaving no rancour nor bitterness, and being indeed, as the quarrels of sweethearts, the preamble to more fervent affection and loyalty.

Many have heard of the renowned Friar Tuck, that was of this band not the least, and that said grace and held mass under the forest shade, whereas no other parson nor any church was nigh-hand enough for resort ; and this was the manner wherein Robin and the friar became at the outset and beginning of acquaintance.

III.

In the summer days, when leaves are green, and flowers are fresh and gay, Robin and certain of his followers chanced to be in Barnsdale, and had good sport in killing the king's deer, and above them all Little John bare the bell, for that at five hundred feet he brought to earth a hart of grease.

"God's blessing on thee," cried Robin, "that made so noble a shot! By Our Lady, I would ride a hundred mile to see thy match, John."

Will Scathlock laughed. A loud laugh laughed he. "Master," he said, "there dwells in Fountain's Abbey a friar that will easily beat both him and thee. He can draw a good yew bow, that friar at Fountain's Dale, and better shoot in it than us every each one.

Robin sware a solemn oath, by the Holy Virgin he sware it, that no meat nor drink would he take till this goodly man he had seen with his eye. He put on his doublet, and his best hosen and shoon, and his mantle of Lincoln green, a cap of steel on his head, his sword and buckler by his side, and bow and arrows in hand ; and to Fountain's Dale he is gone.

And as he drew near to Fountain's Dale, no call had he farther to search, for the friar walked by the water-side, and well accoutred was he, and weaponed against need, with his cap of steel, and his broadsword, and his buckler.

Robin alighted down from his horse, and made him fast to a thorn, and as he came near unto that lusty friar, he called aloud unto him, saying, "Carry me over the water, friar, or thou shalt rue it."

The friar took up Robin on his shoulders, and bare him through the deep stream, till he reached the other bank.

"Now carry me in thy turn, thou fine fellow,' said the friar, "or at thy peril say nay." And Robin without a word did the like service for the friar.

The friar nimbly leapt off Robin's back, and Robin said to him once more : "Now say no say, thou curtal friar, but carry me over again."

Nought spake the friar, but suffered Robin to mount the second time ; and when in mid-stream they were, he cast him suddenly off.

"Now choose, my fine fellow," quoth he, "whether thou wilt sink or swim!"

They both swam to the bank, and Robin took his bow in his hand and let fly a shaft. But the friar fenced it off with his buckler of steel. "Shoot on, shoot on, thou fine fellow, a whole summer's day, and thy arrows I will catch as they come." And truly Robin spent all his stock, and harmed the friar no whit.

Then they took to sword and shield, and fought with might and main, till Robin began to slacken, and begged a boon. "I prythee," he said, "thou curtal friar, let me put my horn to my lips, and blow blasts three."

" Blow to thy heart's fullest content," said the friar. And presently came trooping over the lea Little John and many yeomen more, yea, half-a-hundred yeomen.

" Whose men are these ? " demanded the friar.

" They are mine," returned Robin. " What is that to thee ? "

" I beg a boon," said the friar, " the like that I granted thee. Let me put my fist to my mouth and whute thrice ? "

" Whute, friar," quoth Robin again ; " what is in a friar's whuting but should make me fain to hear it ? "

The friar set his fist to his lips, and thrice he whuted ; and incontinently there bounded over the sward of bandogs half-a-hundred. " Now," cried the friar, " there is for every man a dog save for thee, friend." But two of the dogs seized upon Robin, and tore his mantle from his back.

Little John took his good bow in his hand, and shortly half-a-score of the friar's dogs weltered in their gore.

" Take away thy dogs," shouted John, " or I will give both them and thee short shrift."

" A boon! a boon!" cried the friar. " Good fellow, hold thy hand, and thy master and I will agree, I warrant."

" Friar," said Robin, " if thou wilt forsake Fountain's Abbey and Fountain's Dale, and come with us, thou shalt be our chaplain, and every Sunday through the year thou shalt have a noble to thy fee, and I will give thee free living."

The friar said, " Yea," whom theretofore no man,

neither knight, lord, nor earl, had in seven years' space withstood ; and he was ever after of that merry company.

IV.

At another time, Robin, straying among the pleasant lawns of the forest, happened upon a lusty fellow that, with staff on shoulder, seemed to range in quest of the king's deer, whom Robin, desiring pastime, accosted, demanding what he sought, and holding him in hand that he was one of our king's keepers, to safeguard his deer.

" If thou art a keeper in this forest, with such a great commission, thou art bound to have other to succour thee, ere thou makest me, sirrah, to stand."

" Nay," returned Robin, " there is but I alone that shall such thing accomplish with the aid of a stout oaken staff from the thicket hard by. For seeing, good fellow, that thou hast not a bow nor a blade, I will, an' need be, fight with thee on equal conditions."

" My staff is eight foot long," quoth the stranger ; " get ye one the like of it."

Then these two set to work, since neither would yield, in right earnest, and it was so that, after a long bout and a sharp, Robin gave way.

" Good fellow," quoth he, " let us stay our hands and buffet each other in vain no more by my counsel. I prythee, what is thy name ? "

"Arthur Bland," replied the stranger ; " and I am a tanner in the town of Nottingham, whither if thou ever comest I will tan thy hide good cheap."

" Cease, good fellow, from such talk," Robin,

answering him, said. "My name is Robin Hood; and if thou wilt forsake thy calling and live with me in the free forest, thou shalt be welcomed by my faith, and shalt nothing lack."

"Take my hand as my pledge," said the tanner; "no man shall us depart. But say truly, if thou art Robin Hood, where is Little John, who is my near kinsman on my mother's side. Fain would I see him with eye."

Robin placed his horn to his lips, and blew once, and Little John came tripping down a green hill.

"What is the matter?" he cried; "master, I prythee tell. Why standest thou staff in hand? and who is this stranger? I doubt that all is not well."

"The tanner hath tanned my hide, John; but a bonny blade he is, and a master of his art, I warrant; and he saith that he is thy cousin, by Our Lady, man."

Then John, who had been at first about to challenge the tanner, whereas he thus understood that he was Arthur his kinsman, cast away his staff, and threw his arms about his neck; and those two brave fellows wept for joy.

Thus it was a glad and merry encounter in the end, and so in the choice of his comrades Robin was wont to let trial go before trust.

V.

Now, by reason of the many and grievous trespasses and felonies that these good yeomen committed against the peace of the realm, and of the hue and cry and horn-blow, and offer of reward thereupon ensuing, Robin and his fellows tarried not alway in one place, but removed themselves from Barnsdale to Sherwood, and back again to Barnsdale, and thence to Plumpton, that is beyond the forest of Knaresborough, so that men travelling with rich goods and store of money from the north through the midlands scarce knew which road to choose from fear of those outlaws, that regarded not king nor sheriff, and were both bold and subtle.

It befell on Whitsunday, early on a morning of May, that Robin and John and Much the Miller's son were in Sherwood together. "This is a merry morning," said Little John, "by Him that died on a tree ; a merrier man than I now am liveth not, I trow, in Christendom. Pluck up thy heart, master dear, and think how fair a season it is this Whitsunday morning."

"One thing," returned Robin, "breeds me pain, and it is that on so solemn a day I may not to my matins go. It is now a fortnight or more since I my Saviour saw. Verily I will go to Nottingham by the grace of Mary mild."

"Nay," brake in Much, "go not unaccompanied, but take twelve of us, well-weaponed, with thee, master."

"By my faith," said Robin, "I will not so ; but John shall be my bow-bearer, put-case I have need of it."

"Thou shalt carry thy own," John answering said ; "and I will carry mine ; and as we go along we will shoot for a penny under the wooded shade."

"I will not shoot for a penny, in sooth, John,

with thee, but for three," his master replied. And they set to their contention, till John had won of Robin five shillings to hose and shoon.

But when John claimed his winnings, Robin denied him, and gave him the lie, yea, smote him with his hand, that John waxed wroth, and pulled forth his sword.

" If thou wast not my master," he cried, "thou shouldest abi' it full sore. Get ye a man where ye will ; thy service I forswear."

So these two friends parted in anger, John back to the deep forest, and Robin to Nottingham ; and when Robin had entered into the town, he repaired into the church of Our Lady, and said his orisons, kneeling at the altar, and sundry worshippers saw him, and wist that it was Robin Hood, and marvelled, but said nought. Save only a certain monk, who—woe worth him !—carried the tidings to the sheriff, saying : " The king's felon is in Our Lady's church at the mass. He robbed me of a hundred pound, and I have him ever in my thought."

The gates of Nottingham were made fast, and the sheriff hied with an array of men to the church with their bills and staves.

"Alas ! alas !" muttered Robin, "now I miss Little John, forsooth do I."

But he drew his two-handed sword, and rushed into the thickest of the throng, and laid twelve of the sheriff's men at his feet, till it unhappily fortuned that, as he smote the sheriff himself on the head, the blade of his weapon brake, and he was fain to yield himself up.

Into a deep dungeon he was cast, and the monk

that had betrayed him set out to the king with letters from the sheriff, seeking our lord the king's pleasure, attended by a little page. Through Sherwood they rode, and ere they were on the skirts of the forest Little John and Much the Miller's son were by chance in a small house, where dwelled Much's own uncle. Now John and Much, who knew not what had happened, and had hoped that by the grace of Our Lady their master might be safe, espied them approaching, and went forth to meet them on the way.

John asked the monk what news, and the holy brother replied that he carried letters to our king from the sheriff of Nottingham, how a bold outlaw, called Robin Hood, was but yesterday taken, and lay at his grace's mercy.

"He robbed me and my fellow," quoth John, "of twenty mark, surely enough ; if he be taken, as ye say, forsooth we are not sorry."

"So did he me," said the monk, "of an hundred pound. I was the first to lay hands on him ; ye owe it to me that he goes no more at large."

"I pray God to give you thanks," replied John, "as we will do, when we may. We will even now go along with you, and bring you on your road safely. For Robin hath many a wild fellow belonging unto him, that, if they wist and came this way, would slay you of a certainty."

But when they had gone a certain distance into the wood, John and Much pulled the monk and the page from their horses, and John let the monk understand how grieved he was that the holy brother fell on his head.

The monk saw how the wind blew, and cried for mercy.

"He was my master, sirrah, that thou diddest betray," said John, sternly. "I warrant thou shalt never reach our king to tell him the tale." And he smote off the monk's head, and likewise the little page's, and buried them both.

Then they hastened with all the speed they could to our king where he lay, Little John and Much the Miller's son, and kneeled before his grace, presenting the letters of the sheriff. Our king demanded where was the monk that should have brought him these letters, and John shewed him how the holy brother had fallen sick and died on the journey.

Our king said : "There was never yeoman in England that I more longed to see." And he straightway caused to be delivered to John and Much his letters under his signet, commanding the sheriff to send Robin to him, and hold him harmless. Moreover, at their leave-taking, his grace gave them of his bounty twenty pound, and made them yeomen of the Crown.

They sped to Nottingham as quickly as they might, and shewed the king's letter under his signet to the sheriff, who doffed his hood to our king's seal, and demanded where the monk had become that had borne his message to our king.

Quoth John : "His grace took him so in favour, that he is now Abbot of Westminster by his grace's appointment."

Whereupon the sheriff made John and Much good cheer, and let them drink of the best with him.

And when all were gone to rest and asleep, because
John doubted what the king might do, he resorted
to the jail where his master lay. The jailor said
unto him, that Robin had broken prison, but John
shrewdly guessed that he spake not the verity,
and out with his sword, and forthwith despatched
him. Then he snatched the keys from his girdle,
and set Robin at large, and gave him a good sword
in his hand. Then, where the walls were lowest,
those yeomen clomb privily over, and made for the
forest.

"Master," quoth John, "see, now I have requited good for evil! Albeit thou diddest me
wrong, I have saved thee from the proud sheriff,
and so having done, farewell; for I go."

"Nay, it shall not be so, John," returned Robin,
taking his hand; "but for thy worthiness and love
I will yield thee my room, and thou shalt be in lieu
of me chief of Robin Hood and his men."

"Say no more, master," quoth John. "I crave
only the second place. We are friends again."

So ended the strife, and all the company was joyous enough: when they beheld Robin among them
whole and sound, yea, glad folk were they; and
under the greenwood tree, among the broad leaves,
they feasted together on pasties of the king's venison and the good red wine.

The sheriff of Nottingham made cry and proclamation for Robin, when he found that he had
been delivered from safe-keeping; for he doubted
that our king would displace him from his shrievalty
for so high a misdemeanour. But little he profited
by his pains; and so soon as our king understood

how Robin Hood was free, and how Little John had beguiled both the sheriff and himself the king's own grace, he wox exceeding wrath, and sware that, had it not been so that these yeomen had deceived them both alike, the sheriff should have been hanged high.

"I made them yeomen of my Crown," said our king, "and bestowed on them fee with my own hands. Forsooth, such a fellow as Little John hath not his like through all merry England. He is true to his master," quoth he; "by sweet St. John! he loveth him far better, I swear, than he doth me. Let it pass. So long as Robin Hood lives, he cannot forget how Little John brought him out of our castle of Nottingham."

VI.

During such time as Robin had tarried in Sherwood, there happened unto him many strange accidents besides; and, for example, on a certain day, as he, with John and Much, lay amid the coppice, in expectancy of some traveller passing thereby, lo! it was so that a gallant young fellow, yet with downcast mien, approached the place where they stood, as one that wandered he wist not whither.

So Robin bad them go forward, and greet him, praying him to come to their master, who thereupon, after fit salutation, demanded of the youth, if it chanced that he had ought by way of money in his purse, to aid poor men in their need.

"Nay, sirs," quoth he sorrowfully enough; "money have I none, save five shilling and a ring, that I have reserved against my wedding-day. I

was, forsooth, to have been joined in holy marriage
to a fair maiden ; but her folk have riven her me-
from, and my heart is near to breaking."

"What is thy name ? " asked Robin.

" I am called Allan à Dale," saith the youth.

"What wilt thou give me, Allan ?" quoth Robin
again, " to help thee to thy truelove ?"

"Neither gold have I, sir, nor fee," answered he ;
" but I will make oath upon the holy Bible to be
thy true servant my whole life during."

"When shall the wedding be kept, and where,
friend ?" the outlaw demanded.

"Marry, sir," replied Allan, with brighter cheer,
" at a church five short mile hence away."

Thereupon concluded Robin to aid young Allan
à Dale, and he said unto John and unto Much :
" I shall go thither, where the wedding is appointed, habited minstrel-wise ; and do you, with
some score of our fellows, follow me close, and be
at hand when my horn soundeth ; and do you, young
Allan, come with them along, and bring my bow."

So the outlaw spake, and forthwith he changed
his raiment, and was away ; and when he entered
the church, all were there assembled, and awaited
the bride and the bridegroom.

The priest, seeing Robin, prayed him to say
wherefore he came, and who he might be.

" A minstrel," Robin answered.

" I am right well content," quoth the holy min-
ister. "·Thou art the very man whom-for we
looked."

" It is well," said Robin ; " yet music get ye none
till the bride and her truelove I see."

Anon entered at the door the damsel, led by her father, and behind came the old and rich knight that she had been to the wrong of another bestowed upon.

The priest stood with his mass-book at the altar, and the wedding should have proceeded, when, to the amazement of all those present, the stranger-minstrel stepped forth, and forbad the rite.

"This is no match," he cried; "and since the bride is at hand, she shall choose her own mate."

Straightway he drew a bugle from under his coat, and blew thrice, and ere the priest and the rest of the company might ought resolve or do, four and twenty archers stood at the stranger-minstrel's side, and Allan à Dale was of them who delivered to Robin his bow, as he had charged him. There was no man in all that assembly who kenned not truly enough who the stranger was.

"Allan," he said, "this is thy truelove, and ere we go we will see thee wedded."

"They have not been asked thrice in the church," muttered the holy priest, "as the law of our land is."

But he was of Robin too afeard to grudge over-boldly, lest he should rue his hardihood.

Then Robin plucked off the priest's sack, and laid it on Little John; and John marched into the choir, and when he had asked the couple seven times, lest three might not suffice, he said: "Who giveth away this maid?"

"That do I," said Robin, "and he that seeks to take her from Allan à Dale, shall dearly abide it."

Joyfully those yeomen returned with Allan and

his dear to the forest, where they held the marriage feast; and so with much thankfulness and love the couple went their way to their own homestead, no man hindering them.

VII.

It happened afterward, because a hue and cry had gone out against him, that Robin forsook for a season the parts about Nottingham, and betook himself with Little John and the rest to Barnsdale once more; and on a certain morning in summer, where Robin slept in the wood, the woodwale sang so loud on a spray nigh-hand, that it awoke him: who to his comrades, joining him anon, said thus: "Last night, fellows, I had a dream, that two wight yeomen fought with me, and beat and bound me, and took my bow me-from withal, and by my faith, if I live, I will be avenged on them, John."

"Master," John answered and said, "dreams come and go like the wind upon the hill, that bloweth to-night and in the morning is hushed."

"Well, well," Robin replied, "thou shalt go with me, John, and the others shall stay behind within call, if need should be."

So these two donned their liveries of green, and took their bows, and forth into the forest they went their way. They shortly became aware of a stout yeoman that leaned against a tree. A sword and dagger were at his side, and he was clad in a leathern jerkin.

Now Little John prayed of his master that he

would suffer him to step forward and speak with the stranger; but Robin wox wroth, "for that," quoth he, "John set so little store by him," and was alway for leaving him behind; and such words grew betwixt them, that at length John departed, and left his master, who had threatened to break his bow athwart his crown.

Then, when he was alone, Robin advanced to the yeoman, and unto him said: "Good morrow, good fellow. By thy bow that thou carriest thou shouldest be a fair archer."

"I must speed on my way," returned the other, "while it is yet morning. I seek an outlaw called Robin Hood, and would liever meet with him than have forty pound in my purse."

"Let me be thy guide, good fellow," said Robin, "and I will take thee shortly to him. But first let us try our mastery under these trees so broad and green. We may chance to meet with Robin, ere we dream."

They cut two tall boughs from a briar, and set them up for a mark sixty rods each from other apart. Robin shot first by allowance, and missed by an inch; but the other came not near, albeit a good archer he was counted. The second time his arrow touched the garland; but Robin's clave both wands in twain.

"A blessing on thy heart! good fellow," cried the stranger. "Thou shootest as well as Robin Hood. Now, good fellow, tell me thy name."

"Nay," said Robin, "not till thou hast told me thine."

"I am called Guy of Gisborne," answered the

other, "and I hold a commission to take Robin Hood, wherever I can find him."

"My dwelling is in this wood," said Robin unto him again, "and I set by thee right nought. I am that Robin Hood of Barnsdale whom thou art appointed to take."

No sooner were the words out of his mouth, than his brown blade was in his hand, and those two fought to the death. Robin stumbled at a root, and fell, and his foe wounded him in the side. But he called on Our Dear Lady, and rose to his feet, and with a back-handed stroke Guy he hath slain. He smote his head from his body, and placed it on his bow's end, saying, "Thou hast paid a traitor's forfeit"; and he nicked Guy's visage, that none might know it, and changed garb with him; and with his bow and arrows, and horn, so that he wore his semblance in all things, he started in quest of John to let him understand the news, and make the peace with him again.

Now, Robin wist not that, after his parting from John, certain grave accidents had befallen him and sundry other of his company. For the sheriff of Yorkshire, with seven score men, had entered Barnsdale and had slain two of the yeomen, and gone nigh to take Scathlock, when John, drawing near, perceived how the matter was, and drawing an arrow to the head, shot William à Trent, one of the sheriff's men, that he never more stirred. But by misadventure John's bow brake, and he was straightway surrounded and taken, and fast bound to a tree.

A blithe man was the sheriff, whenas he saw how Little John was his prisoner, and he sware that he

should be shortly hanged, where he might be a
warning to all false traitors. "Be not so sure of
that," quoth John to himself; "for by Christ's help
I may yet go free."

"Hearken, hearken," cried the sheriff to his men;
"I hear good Guy's horn blow, and I warrant he
hath taken Robin Hood, or him slain; and lo! see
where yonder cometh that brave yeoman! Come
hither, come hither, good Guy, to me," quoth the
sheriff, "and ask what boon thou wilt."

"No boon I crave," returned Robin, "till I have
slain both master and man." And he sped in all
haste unto the tree where John was, under colour
of shriving him before his death; but the sheriff and
his men pressed closely after to stay him, for they
at last divined who it in truth was.

Robin cut the cords, and gave Guy's bow into
Little John's hands, and his sheaf of arrows, and
put his own horn to his lips; and the sheriff espying
the outlaws coming up, and John ready with his
bow, turned about and fled, carrying with him in his
breech one of John's feathered messengers.

So as Robin had formerly owed his life to John,
when he was close prisoner in the castle of Nottingham, now it was his gallantry and wit that brought
that yeoman safe out of the hands of the proud
sheriff, that would surely otherwise have shown him
scant grace; and these generous outlaws, namely
Robin and John, found, as in many a case before,
a soreness and severance the knitting up of a firmer
friendship.

VIII.

At another time yet, it was the Bishop of Hereford that was reported to Robin, as he lay in Barnsdale, to have it in his mind to cross the forest by the Watling Street, with his retinue ; and Robin enjoined upon his men who took that charge to slay a fat deer against the dinner-hour, for that he looked to have a bishop that day at his table, who would pay for his cheer as became so great a lord.

Robin and six of his fellows habited themselves like shepherds, and sat about the fire as the bishop came up. In lowly wise they saluted his good lordship, and to him asking they replied, "We are shepherds, that tend our sheep in this forest all the year round ; but to-day we make merry, and dine on the king's deer."

"You do well!" cried the bishop, his choler rising ; "you are honest fellows forsooth ! The king shall hear of it. Leave your fire and your fare, I bid ye, and come along with me."

"A pardon, a pardon ! I prythee, my lord," cried Robin ; "it ill becomes your lordship's cloth to take so many poor men's lives away."

But the bishop was deaf to entreaty, and would have had his guards seize the shepherds. Robin set his back against a tree, and from beneath his shepherd's smock drew out a bugle-horn. A loud blast made the woods echo, and ere the bishop had time to think, the shepherds had cast aside their garments, and where there had been six were sixty and more.

"Why blow you so lustily ?" asked Little John.

"O, John," answered his master, "here is a

bishop that will take us to our king, and grant us no pardon, will he not?"

"Off with his head," cried John, "and dig a hole in the earth for the varlet!"

"O, forgive me," quoth the bishop, changing his tune, "and let me go my way, good Robin."

"Nay, my lord, stay awhile; your dinner is dressed," answered the outlaw. "Let me assist your lordship." And he caused the bishop to dismount, and led him courteously by the hand to the spot where the repast was spread on the green sward.

They ate and drank, till it wox late, and the bishop and his folk lay under the trees on a harder couch than their habit was; and it happened in the morning, when it drew to the leave-taking, that Little John, by command of Robin, searched the bishop's mail, and found therein three hundred gold pieces. "Here is money enough," quoth he, "master, to pay for his lordship's lodging. It putteth me more in charity with him, by Our Lady! albeit I trow he loveth me but little."

Then the bishop and those that were with him went their way after many courteous salutations, and they thought in their hearts that they had done better, an' they had taken another road in lieu of the Watling Street, whereby such unforeseen discomfiture and loss were unto that great lord wrought.

IX.

Robin stood in Barnsdale, and leaned against a tree. By his side were John, Scathlock, and Much. Presently unto Robin spake John thus: "Master,

an' ye would give us the word that we might dine,
it were well."

"Nay," quoth Robin, "thereto I have no lust,
until I see some baron bold or other guest un-
bekenned, or some squire or some knight, that may
pay worthily for his cheer.   Take thy bows in
thy hands, good fellows, and leave me here; and
walk up to the Sayles, and so on to the Watling
Street.   Abide there until ye become aware of any
that may lighten the cost of our meal."

They went to the Sayles and to the Watling
Street; and they looked east and they looked west;
and no manner of man might they espy.   Yet at
last, as they cast their eyes down a by-way in Barnsdale, they perceived where a knight came riding
along.   Heavy was his bearing and little his pride
one foot was in the stirrup, and the other out.   His
hood hung over his eyes, and his garb was simple
enough : a sorrier man, forsooth, never rode in the
merry woods on a summer's day.

The yeomen approached him full courteously, and
Little John, because he knew that he was of knightly
degree, bending his knee at the saddlebows, wel
comed him to the forest-side.   "My master," quoth
he, "hath waited dinner for you these three hours
past."

"Who is your master?" the knight demanded.

'His name, sir, is Robin Hood."

"He is a good yeoman," the stranger returned
"whom-of I have heard much commendation
Albeit my purpose was to have dined to-day at
Blithe or at Doncaster, yet I consent with you three
to go unto your master.'

Then they went all together, and as he rode along the tears stole from his eyes, and coursed down his cheeks. They brought him to the place where their master tarried, who unto him said, as he doffed his head-gear, and beseemingly knelt: "Welcome art thou to me, sir knight! Truly I have expected thee these two hours."

"God thee save, good Robin," quoth the knight, "and all thy comrades so gallant and free!"

They sat to their dinner, and numbles of the deer, and water-fowl, and pheasant, with wine and bread in plenty, they had; and Robin bad the knight eat and drink, and spare not.

"Gramercy, Robin," said his guest, "such a fair meal have I not seen these three weeks. If ever I come again this way, I trust to give thee as good."

"By dear worthy God," cried Robin, "I am not so nice in the order of my diet. But since it was never the manner for a yeoman to pay for a knight's cheer, thou wilt clear the score, wilt thou not, ere thou goest hence?"

"I have nought in my purse," the stranger answered and said, "that I can proffer for shame."

"Tell me truth, sir," quoth Robin. "How much hast thou, all told?"

"Ten shilling and no more," said the other.

"An' so it be," said Robin, "not one penny do I touch, and an' thou needest more for thy occasions, I shall freely lend it thee."

Little John searched the knight's mail, and found indeed that he had sooth spoken; and thereupon Robin commanded them to bring wine of the best, and bad the knight drink to his content.

" Tell me now, knight," he presently said, "and I shall keep thy counsel right well : wert thou made a knight *malgré* thyself, or one of yeomanry? Hast thou been an unthrifty husband of thy substance, or an usurer, or a lecher?"

"None of these, by my faith, Robin, have I been," he protested; "for, God is my witness, an hundred winter herebefore my ancestors knights have been. I am called Sir Richard at the Lee. Within this two or three year, my neighbours well know that I could spend four hundred pound by the year. Now have I no goods save my children and my wife, till God amend my estate."

"How hast thou lost thy riches, then?" Robin demanded.

"By my not over-wise kindness. I had a son, forsooth, Robin, that should have been my heir, and whenas he had but twenty winters, jousted he with the best; and for that he slew on a time a knight of Lancashire, I was fain to lay my estate to pledge to save his life. To the Abbot of St. Mary's at York, Robin, my lands are in gage, and are forfeit, alas! unless so be the money be repaid within a short day. And whereas I have it not, I go to seek grace; and so, farewell, for the time draweth nigh."

"What is the sum?" Robin asked.

"Four hundred pound," said he.

"What, then, wilt thou do, put-case thou losest thy inheritance?"

"I shall cross the salt sea, Robin, and go to the Holy Land, where Christ our Saviour was quick and dead, and to the Mount of Calvary." And the tears once more started to his eyes.

" Hast thou no friends ? "

" Whenso I was rich of estate, Robin, yea, verily, had I store ; but now they shun me, and know me not."

" Pass the wine round," said Robin ; " the knight drinks not. Well, and hast thou neither any one who would be thy surety ? "

" By Him that died on a tree, none, save, maybe, Peter, Paul, and John."

" Cease thy jesting, knight, for by Him that made me, and shope both sun and moon," said Robin, " nought set I by such warrantise."

" None other have I," quoth he, " unless it be Our Dear Lady, that never yet failed me in my need."

" My dear worthy God, thou couldest have no better an one. John, go to my coffers, and tell truly four hundred pound."

And John went, as he was bidden, and Scathlock with him, and they brought the money to Robin, eighteen score pounds and upward.

Then Much spake grudgingly, whenas he saw so large a treasure about to go to Sir Richard at the Lee ; but John chid him, saying it was a good alms-deed to help so gentle a knight ; and withal he prayed Robin, if it were not meet to offer his guest a new livery, that he might appear before the lord abbot as became his condition.

" For ye have scarlet and green, master," said John. " There is many a merchant in England that hath not so rich a store."

And when Robin gave leave, he took his bow, and measured three ells of each colour, and at every ell he leapt.

"What devil's-kin draper is this?" muttered Much.

"By God Almighty," cried Scathlock, laughing, "he may give him all the better measure, since it costeth him so little."

But John marked them not ; and he prevailed on Robin, who was nothing loth, to find him a new gray courser, and a new saddle.

"What dost thou give the knight thyself, John?" Robin inquired.

"Even a pair of gilt spurs, master," he answering said, "that he may pray for all this company."

"To-morrow," said Sir Richard at the Lee, "I must be at St. Mary's to redeem my lands, or they go from me for ever. When shall be my day, Robin?"

"This day twelvemonth in this place," the yeoman replied ; "and I lend thee John to keep thee company to York as thy servant, and to aid thee to his power, because it were shame that a knight should go unattended."

The knight set out from Barnsdale, blessing Robin Hood and his men for the best friends that could to him have befallen ; and with John at his side pricked forward on his way to the abbey of Our Blessed Lady, merrier in heart than he had weened ever more to be ; for in his mail he carried the freedom of his fair lands and his children's heritage.

X.

The Lord Abbot sat in high state at St. Mary's at York, and with him were the high cellarer and the chief justiciary of England, and the sheriff of Yorkshire, that were partakers, all of them, in the venture whereby on failure of his day Sir Richard at the Lee, that gentle knight, lost his lands at Utersdale for aye.

The high abbot remembered them all, who were there present, how this day twelvemonth the knight of Utersdale had borrowed of him four hundred pound, and laid his lands in pledge; and that if he came not soon to redeem them, he should suffer disherison.

"It is full early," said the prior; "the day has much to run. I had liever lay down a hundred pound than take away too lightly the knight's belongings. He is may-be beyond sea, and cannot reach England in just time. I wis he may be suffering great hardship; and it were sore pity to deal too strictly with him, and too sternly use our power."

"Thou art ever in my beard," quoth the high abbot, "by God and by St. Richard!"

"He is dead or hanged, doubtless," said the high cellarer, "and we shall have anon four hundred pounds more to spend by the year."

"He will not come yet, I dare well undertake," said the chief justiciary.

Meanwhile, Sir Richard at the Lee and Little John had ridden well, until they came to the abbey of Our Lady at York, and ere they drew within sight of the gates, that gentle knight threw off his upper habit, and clothed himself in poor weeds, and Little John in like manner; and when they knocked at the gates, the porter opened to them, and shewed them how the lord abbot, with many more of high degree, were at their meat.

They descended from their horses, and the porter said : "Lead them into the stable, where they may have whereof to eat, and rest, till ye have for them again need."

"By God that died on a tree," quoth John, "they go not thither by my counsel." And whileas the knight, whose valet for the nonce he was at this time, was brought into the hall, John stayed behind with the horses and the mail wherein the money lay, that they had carried there-withal.

The knight went forth into the hall, where they sat at table, and kneeled down, and in lowly wise saluted the high abbot and all there assembled.

"Sir abbot," said the knight, "I am here to keep my day."

"Thou hast brought with thee the four hundred pound, hast thou not?"

"Not one penny," quoth the knight.

"Thou art a shrewd debtor," cried the abbot. "Sir justice, it is well; I drink to thee!—What doest thou here, then, sirrah, that thou art before me without the money?"

"I am here, sir abbot, to pray your good lordship of a longer day," he said, and yet knelt.

"The time has come and gone, and thy lands have passed from thee," said the high abbot.

The knight besought the chief justiciary, and like-wise the sheriff, and once again the high abbot, that he would lend a merciful ear unto him, and unto the lord abbot : " I will be thy true servant, my lord," quoth he, " till I have well gotten the four hundred pound," and to him still denying : " But I have my land again, full dearly it shall be bought. It is good, lords, to assay a friend, ere a man have of him need."

The lord abbot looked upon that gentle knight full angerly, and bad him quit the hall, calling him a false knight. But he shewed the lord abbot that he spake not truly, for he had never been other than true ; and then he rose to his feet, and to the lord abbot he said : " To suffer a knight to kneel so long is scant courtesy. I have been in many a tourney and many a fight, and have ever stood in the front."

" Sir abbot," said the chief justiciary, " what wilt thou give over and above, that the knight may sign a release ? Else dare I to swear that never shall ye hold your land in quiet."

" An hundred pound more I will give," said the high abbot.

" Give him two," said the chief justiciary.

" Forbear your reckonings, my lords," said the knight, more firmly. " Not one, nor two hundred, nor a thousand, should serve ; I will not have, for heir to my lands, abbot, justice, or friar."

They all sat marvelling what he might signify, and conferred together. But the knight started to the door of the hall, and returned straightway, bearing in both his hands a bag ; to the board where they sat he advanced, and loosening the cords, he shook out four hundred pound.

"Here is the gold, sir abbot," he cried, "that thou diddest lend to me on my lands. Haddest thou been more courteous, thou mightest have had something to boot."

They had all laid down their knives and spoons, and ate and drank no more.

"Sir abbot, and all the others that I see," said the knight, "ye have your money again, agree among you, as ye may; and since my day I have kept, I shall take back my land, whatever ye may do."

He marched straight out of the hall a proud and jocund man, and found Little John in the court awaiting him; and they took horse, and went their way; and whenso they had lost sight of York, they donned again their gayer raiment, and proceeded on their road together, until John took leave of that gentle knight to go unto Nottingham, and Sir Richard at the Lee drew not rein until he came to his own gates at his house in Utersdale in the forest.

"Welcome, my lord," said his wife, "albeit lost is all our good."

"Nay, madam," he replied, "not so; be of better cheer, and pray for Robin Hood, that his soul may enter into bliss; for without his bounty we had been beggars for a certainty. As I went by the way, madam, I met that excellent yeoman, and he lent unto me the money, wherewith I have freed our lands."

XI.

It happened that, while Little John yet attended on the knight, there came a report of a shooting that was to be held at Nottingham, and because the knight had no longer occasion for a valet, and was in haste to be at home, John and he parted with friendly greetings ; one to repair to the archery, the other to his house in Utersdale.

The bowmen, who answered to the proclamation of the sheriff of Nottingham, were archers good and true ; but the stranger, whom no man knew, alway cleft the wand. Quoth the sheriff : " By Him that died on a tree, this is the best archer that I ever saw withal." And presently he accosted John, saying thus unto him : " Tell me now, wight young man, what thy name is, where thou wast born, and where is thy present dwelling ? "

" In Holderness, sir, I was born," John answered unto him, " and I am called Reynold Greenleaf, when I am at home."

" Say to me, then, Reynold, wilt thou live with me ? I will give thee to wage twenty marks by the year."

" If so be," quoth John, " I may get leave from my master that is, I am well content to hire myself for the twelvemonth, sir." And John feigned that he got leave, and abode with the sheriff. Yet nevertheless he loved him not, and thought alway, even from the first, how he might beguile him.

" So help me, God ! " he said in his heart, " I shall prove unto him the shrewdest servant that ever he had."

It chanced on a certain Wednesday, that the sheriff went betimes on hunting, and left John at home a-bed ; and John rose not till it was passed noon, and was a-hungered. Therefore he went to the steward, and prayed him that he would give him to dine.

" It is all too long for Greenleaf," quoth he, " to fast."

But the steward churlishly denied him, saying that he must tarry until such time as the sheriff returned ; and the butler started to the door of the buttery and shut fast the same, lest John might gain an entrance.

John at a blow struck the butler to the earth, that a hundred winters would not have seen him stir again, and spurned open the door with his foot. A goodly livery of ale and wine he there procured, and repaired unto the cook, demanding victual. But he up and smote John, and cried : " Thou art a fine fellow truly to take hire in a household, and dine at thy own pleasure."

John drew his sword, and the cook snatched another nigh-hand ; and for a whole hour they fought together, those twain, and neither harmed other.

" I make my vow to God," said John, " thou art one of the best swordsmen, as thou art one of the stoutest fellows, that I ever with my eyes saw. An' thou couldest shoot in a bow as well, I would take thee to the greenwood with me, and thou shouldest have twenty mark by the year to thy fee and two liveries."

" Put up thy sword, Greenleaf," said he ; " we are in accord."

And the cook went and fetched numbles of the doe, and bread, and wine ; and when they had eaten and drunk to their content, and had sworn

fealty each to other, John made him privy to his
true name, and whither they were appointed to go ;
but ere they departed, they went, treading on eggs,
and brake the sheriff's chest, wherefrom they took
three hundred pound and more, besides much silver
plate in vessels, masers and spoons, and forsooth
left nought.

When they were to Sherwood come, John became aware of Robin Hood, where he lay with
certain of his yeomen, and courteously greeted him
and them.

"What tidings from Nottingham, John, prythee ?"
asked Robin ; " and who is this good yeoman thou
hast brought thee-with ? "

" The sheriff," said John, " sendeth thee his
heartiest commendations, and by his cook, this fine
fellow here, presenteth thee with all his silver, and
three hundred pound to boot."

" I swear by my faith," said Robin, in glee, " it
was never with his goodwill that all this came to
me."

Then John shewed his master how the sheriff
was even then on hunting in the forest some five
miles thence away, and he prayed him to gather his
men together, and he would let him see fair sport ;
and for that Robin trusted John, he agreed, inquir-
ing no more.

John, then, yet remaining in the habit that he
wore in the sheriff's service, hied as quickly as he
might (for it drew toward the afternoon), until he
espied the sheriff and his men, where they were on
hunting with hound and horn ; and he did him
courtesy, and kneeled him-before.

"Where hast thou been, Reynold?" the sheriff said, "that I see thee here?"

"I have been in the forest, master dear," quoth he, "and so fair a sight saw I, that I could not rest until I had you thereof advised : a great hart, and with him seven score deer, and their antlers were so large and strong, that I feared to shoot, lest they should me slay."

The sheriff desired to be led where the herd might be viewed, and they rode, he and Reynold, and the rest, till suddenly they came in sight of Robin and his comrades.

"Behold the herd, master," cried John, "and there is the master-hart!"

"Thou hast betrayed me, Reynold, woe worth thee!"

"Thou art to blame, sir," quoth John, "that I was mis-served of my dinner."

"Come, sheriff," said Robin, "let us sit to meat." And they gave the sheriff place ; but when he saw his silver vessels on the board, he wox heavy, and ate not ; for now he perceived well the whole case, how the cook and Greenleaf had wrought together, and robbed him of his treasure. "Be of better cheer, sheriff," Robin said again ; "thy life is granted unto thee by the grace of Robin Hood." And when it grew toward the night, Robin bad John and the others to prepare for rest, and prayed the sheriff to do likewise.

Now, it was the summer season, and those yeomen were wont to doff their hosen and shoon, and their kirtles, and wrap themselves in their mantles.

"Make thyself blithe, sheriff," said Robin; "for this is our order in the forest."

"It is harder than anchorite or friar," returned the other; "for all the gold in Christendom I would not stay here long."

"Nay, twelve months, sir, thou shalt abide with me," Robin answered, "and I will teach thee to be an outlaw."

"Sooner smite off my head," cried the sheriff, "and I will hold thee harmless."

"An' thou must indeed go, sheriff," said Robin, "swear unto me on this sword that thou wilt never thy whole life during do scathe to me or mine, but be good friend to us, and helpful to thy best power."

The sheriff sware as he was enjoined, and was suffered to go his way in peace; and he thought that while he was a living man he would never set foot in Sherwood more.

XII.

Now, after these occurrents at Nottingham and in the broad forest of Sherwood, whereby the sheriff of Nottingham was so humbled and so strangely cosened of his good, Robin thought fit to remove himself from that part for a while, and returned with John and the others, who attended him at all times, to Barnsdale; and one day, as these yeomen stood together by the Watling Street, they were aware of a man that sold pots, who along the way came in his cart briskly and merrily, as one who dreaded nor brooked no hindrance.

"See the proud potter, where he cometh," said

Robin. "He has passed here oft before, and never a penny of toll hath he paid."

"I met him at Wentbridge," quoth John, "and worse luck befall him for it; he dealt me a stroke that I shall never of my life forget. I lay forty shilling I will let him have it back to-day. There is scarce a man among us all that will make him stand."

"Here is forty shilling," returned Robin, "and more, and ye will, that I will bring him to yield me a pledge."

A yeoman kept the stake; and away started Robin, and laid his hand on the potter's rein.

"Fellow," said the potter, shortly, "what is thy will?"

"Three year and more, potter," said Robin unto him, "thou hast haunted this road, and thou wast never so courteous a man as one penny of toll to pay."

"What is thy name, fellow? Who of me asketh toll?"

"Robin Hood is my name," he replied; "some pledge thou shalt leave behind thee."

"Pledge I not have," quoth the other, "nor toll I not pay. Thy hands off my horse, or thou shalt rue it, by my faith."

From his cart he leapt, and thereout he took a two-handed staff. Robin drew his sword.

"Let my horse be," cried the potter, and Robin and he set at each other, while John and the rest watched hard by under a tree, and laughed at the passages betwixt those twain.

John said to his fellows: "Yond potter will

hold his ground, mark ye." And almost ere he had spoken, he, with a deft downward blow, struck the buckler out of Robin's hand, and laid him on the sward.

The others ran up to help their master, and raised him to his feet, and John said : " Who has won the wager now ? Shall I have thy forty shillings, master, or shalt thou have mine ? "

" O," quoth Robin, " if they were a hundred, they are yours."

" Scant courtesy it seemeth," then said the potter, "whenas a poor man goeth on the way to follow his craft, to let him, as ye have me done."

" By my troth, thou art right," Robin said; " that is good yeomanry ; and if so be thou camest hereby every day, never more shalt thou be questioned but in hearty fellowship."

XIII.

The day was at hand when the knight of Utersdale was under covenant to render himself in Barnsdale, and restore to Robin the four hundred pound that so happily redeemed his lands from pawn.

Robin stood in the forest, and with him were John, Scathlock, and Much the Miller's son.

" Shall we go to our nuncheon, master ?" asked John, for it was mid-day.

" Nay," said Robin ; " I doubt that Our Lady is wrath with me, that she sendeth me not my money."

" Have no fear," John replied, "the sun has some way to go ere it set, and I dare answer for the knight, that he is trusty and true."

"Take thy bow in thy hand, John," quoth his master, "and let Scathlock and Much bear thee company, and go up to the Watling Street. Thou mayest by chance alight on some one, be he a messenger from Our Lady or a man that can make us mirth, or a needy yeoman that I might bestead."

Not well pleased was John to go longer fasting, yet he girt on his sword, and they all sallied forth to do as their master had commanded them, and presently they descried a right royal equipage, as it came by the way. Two black monks went before, each on a fair palfrey, and after them followed seven sumpter-mules well-laden, and men-at-arms fifty and two. No bishop rode more proudly in progress.

"I lay my life," cried John, plucking up his heart again, "that these holy men have brought us our pay. Make ready your bows, my brethren, and fear not. There are but three of us, all told; yet our master will give us a sorry welcome, an' we bring not these guests to dine with him this day."

"Stay, churlish monks," John cried, "or you are dead. Full wrath ye have made our master, that stays fasting for you."

"Who is your master?" demanded the foremost monk.

"Robin Hood."

"He is a strong thief, whom-of heard I ever yet no good."

"He is a yeoman of the forest," said John, "and he has bidden you both to dine with him yonder where he lies."

But Much let fly a bolt at one of those holy men, and he fell to the earth; and of those fifty men and two that were set as a guard over the sumpters, all, save a little page and one other, fled out of view.

They led the other monk, that was truly the high cellarer of St. Mary's at York, to the lodge-door, and Robin did off his hood, but the cellarer lacked the like courtesy.

" He is a churl," said John.

" No matter," said Robin. " How many had he with him ? "

" Fifty-two and another monk, that we left on the ground."

" Let the horn sound," said Robin, "that we may have company befitting, put-case they should return."

The high cellarer, after he had washed, sat to dinner, and drank of the best, and Robin and John served him right dutifully, till, when all was done, Robin shewed him how he had lent, it was a twelvemonth, a little money to Sir Richard at the Lee, so that he might acquit himself of a debt to St. Mary's. The high cellarer sware that he wist nought of such a matter ; but Robin held that because he was an officer of the abbey, he must be the messenger sent to keep the day, and for that he was so true to the time he yielded him great thanks. The high cellarer made a vow, that he had but twenty marks in his mail.

" If it be so," quoth Robin, "thou mayest even keep them, and I will lend thee more an' need be."

John spread his mantle on the ground, and out of the cellarer's coffers he took eight hundred pieces, and more. " The abbey," said he, " hath doubled our venture."

"Monk," said Robin, in high glee, "Our Lady is the truest woman whom-of I ever heard tell. By dear worthy God, an' I had searched all England through, I could not have placed my money to more profitable usance. Fill of the best wine, John ; let the cellarer drink, ere he go."

But the cellarer said, "Nay," and put spurs to his palfrey, as to go.

"Whither are ye bound, sir?" asked Robin.

"To certain manors in this country," he answered, "whereas our reeves do us wrong."

"Greet well your abbot from me," said Robin, "and your prior also, and pray them well every day to send us such a guest."

XIV.

In the meantime the knight of Utersdale came not, and seemed like to break his day. But about three hours after noon, as Robin and John and certain others yet lingered on the scene, rode Sir Richard at the Lee in sight, attended by his following ; and as he drew near, he alighted from his palfrey, and bent his knee to Robin.

"God save thee, good Robin Hood, and all this company," quoth he.

"Rise, gentle knight," said Robin ; "right welcome art thou to me. And, I pray you, what taketh you so late to the greenwood?"

"It was my duty, good Robin," he answered ; "but I shall tell you, that I was kept at a wrestling, whereby I passed, namely, at Wentbridge, and holp a poor yeoman, whom they would have wronged else."

"'Fore God, thereof give I thee thanks, knight; he that aids poor yeomen is my friend."

"Have here, Robin," proceeded the knight, "four hundred pound that I borrowed, and twenty marks for the courtesy."

"Nay," Robin answered; "Our Lady by her cellarer hath already satisfied me; and if I should take it twice, it were a shame indeed. But truly, knight, thou art welcome; and what import these bows and arrows, so fair and fine, that thou hast brought thee-with?"

"A poor gift to thee, Robin."

Robin took them in good part, and then he told the knight all the story about the high cellarer; and over their supper well they laughed.

"And hast thou gotten thy lands securely back into thy hands?" the yeoman demanded.

"Ay, at length; but the abbey laboured shrewdly to dispossess me, and sent messengers to London to make suit to our king thereupon; and the high cellarer himself was to have gone thither to moot farther therein, and was only by thee stayed from his purpose."

"He let me understand differently," quoth Robin, "and he was a false monk. What was the wrestling at Wentbridge, knight, whereat thou didst so courteously intervene?"

The knight shewed how there published a wrestling for a prize to the winner of a pair of gloves, a gold ring, and a pipe of wine, and how a stranger yeoman won it; but they denied him his right, and would have slain him forsooth, had he, the knight and his retinue, not ridden into the throng, and for the sake of Robin Hood defended that yeoman, and caused to be delivered unto him the trophies of the day. " And I gave him," added he, " five marks for his wine, that it might be broached, drink who would."

Robin was right glad ; and because the knight was not rich, and had spent of his substance not a little in coming thither so accompanied, and in furnishing a hundred bows and the like number of sheaves of arrows, all of the best, his heart opened, and he said to John, as the knight made ready to go before the gloaming : " Fetch me four hundred pound of the cellarer's treasure that he left behind."

Then when John had brought the money, he turned to Sir Richard at the Lee, and said: " Thou wilt keep thy four hundred pound, knight, and four hundred other I count out to thee for thy bows and thy arrows; and if thou ever standest in requirement of more, let me have thy news.   But my counsel to thee is, for the time to come be a better husband of thy store."

So they parted for awhile, Sir Richard at the Lee and Robin Hood ; and Robin holp him to mount his palfrey, and bad him heartily well to fare.

XV.

Still a short while the yeomen tarried in Barnsdale ; but anon came tidings of a noble shooting at Nottingham beside the forest under the greenwood shade, whereto all the bowmen of the north were bidden, if they listed, to repair, and the prize to the best archer was a silver arrow feathered with gold.

Now, Robin, remembering well that the sheriff

of Nottingham had plighted to him his faith to do him and his evermore no scath, and wishful, besides, to prove his mastery at the pair of butts, called certain of the trustiest of his fellows unto him, and opened unto them his desire to go to Nottingham to the shooting.

Little John, Will Scathlock, Little Much, Gilbert with the strong hand, Reynold, and one other, together six, he chose to enter the barriers him-with. The rest he commanded to be in readiness, lest the sheriff should prove false. And against the day it was so, that they all removed to Sherwood, each to fulfil his part.

The sheriff stood by the butts, and the fourth in order among the marksmen was Robin himself. All the others shot well and with good approval ; but Robin won the arrow, and received it right courteously.

Presently arose a hue and cry, that it was Robin that was there, and the horns were blown amain. The outlaws stood together, and bent their bows ; and those who were behind wist well enough what had befallen, when the sound of their master's bugle brake upon their ears.

Loudly reproached Robin the sheriff with his treason, and sware that the next time he would ask a different pledge than that he had taken from him in the forest, when his life was at his mercy ; and as the yeomen fell back, they sent a cloud of arrows among the sheriff's men, and many a soul perished. But John was wounded in the knee, and could scarce stir, and he prayed his master, sooner than let him fall into the hands of the sheriff, to despatch

him for the love of God and for all his passed
service.

" Not for all the gold in England, John," quoth
his master.

" Ay, so say I too," cried Much.   And he bent
down, and took John on his back, and bare him
along ; and as they ever continued to retreat, now
and again he set him down, and sent an arrow from
his bow on its errand.   And so, by little and little,
through the wound of John staying them somewhat,
they left the sheriff's men behind, and a goodly
number dead ; and while the most part dispersed
themselves in the forest, Robin and John, and a
certain few other, arrived in fine at the castle of Sir
Richard at the Lee at Utersdale in the forest,
walled and double-fossed.

The yeomen had no sooner entered the gates
than they were made once more fast ; and the good
knight and his lady welcomed Robin and his fellows
to their house, the knight saying that than Robin
he loved no man in the world more dearly ; and with
them they remained a certain space at bed and
board.

The whole country the sheriff raised by cry and
by horn, and laid siege to the knight's house, commanding him to surrender unto him the king's
enemy ; but he would not by any means, until he
saw the king's writ, and the sheriff had it not, nor
could so strong a place, held by these good archers,
gain into his hands.

But shortly arrived our king's letters out of
Staffordshire where his grace was in progress, shewing that within a fortnight he should be in Notting-

ham, and charging the sheriff against such time to
muster levies, for his mind was to take that outlaw,
that he should no more set him at nought, and be
lord of the north country in his room.

Robin bad adieu to the knight at the end of
twelve days, and right courteously he had been
entertained, with John, and Much, and Scathlock,
and Gilbert of the strong hand, and Reynold, and
returned to Sherwood ; and that gentle knight, not
deeming that the sheriff of Nottingham set spies
upon him and catchpolls, as he was hawking on
horseback at the riverside one morn, was suddenly
taken prisoner by an ambush, and carried toward
Nottingham bound to his steed.

The lady his wife rode as fast as she might to
Robin in the forest, and shewed him the sorry
chance, praying him for the love of Our Lady to
aid them once again.   Robin doubted that he should
not overtake the sheriff's men until they were well
into Nottingham, and the sheriff was like to hold
the knight with all his power ; for shortly our king
was looked for, and of men he had enough by
our king's ordinance.   But Robin, because time
so pressed, summoned every yeoman within bugle's
reach, and enjoined them, as they loved him, to
render themselves in Nottingham town, ere the
bridges were drawn and the gates were shut.

Over hedge and over ditch these yeomen made
their way, Robin at their head, a goodly company
with their bows on their shoulders and their broad-
swords at their sides, and they came to their journey's end ere the sheriff could order the bridges to
be drawn up and the gates to be sparred.

The sheriff was in the street to receive his prisoner, and was aghast when he beheld that strong array of yeomen, with Robin Hood, in the rear.

" Hold, sheriff," cried Robin ; " what news hast thou of our king ? By dear worthy God ! I have not walked so hard this seven year, and I trow it is not for thy good."

He bent his bow and shot the sheriff dead, and speeding up to him, where he lay in his blood, smote his head from his body.

" Lie there, traitor," he cried ; " whilst thou wast alive, thou wast false to me and other." And then he sprang to the knight, where he lay bound, and ungirthed him, and gave him a weapon ; and all the yeomen, sword in hand, formed themselves in array, and drove the sheriff's levies before them.

" Leave thy horse behind thee, knight," said Robin at length, " and come back with me to Sherwood, until we have devised means how to obtain grace from Edward our comely king."

XVI.

Now, our lord the king, namely, Edward that was called of Carnarvon, having come into the northern parts in the month of April, in the year of grace 1323, and in the seventeenth year of his reign, visited in due course York, Holderness, and all the country about Doncaster and Thorne. In the month of August he passed much time in the Forest of Pickering. Part of September his grace spent at Whorlton Castle and in the neighbourhood of Richmond and Jervaulx Abbey ; and on the

twenty-second of the month he was at Haywra
Park in the Forest of Knaresborough, where he
saw how sorely he had been despoiled of his deer,
whereof he could meet with scarce any of great horn.
Then his grace moved by way of Skipton into
Lancashire, and on the fourth October rested at
Ightershill Park by Clitheroe. Thence he removed
to Blackburn, Holand, and Kirkby, and on the
twenty-third he was at Liverpool. Upon the
Mersey he took ship, and visited Ince and the
Castle of Hilton, and on the third of November,
journeying by the monastery of Vale Royal, Sand-
bach, Newcastle-under-Lyme, Croxden, Langford,
and Dale Abbey, he arrived on the ninth at his
town of Nottingham, where he purposed to abide
a fortnight or thereabout, so that he might make
inquisition into affairs and into the condition of his
Forest of Sherwood.

The good people of Nottingham well knew our
comely king, who had formerly made progress in
that country, and had been in residence at New-
stead and at Clipstone. But it was a sad story
which he heard, when he came thither at this
present, of the death of the sheriff by the hand of
Robin Hood, and of the treason of Sir Richard at
the Lee.

Our king declared forfeit unto him the lands of
that knight, and sware an oath, that whoever
should bring unto him the head of so great a felon
should receive them freely at his hands under his
seal. But an old courtier, that waited on the king,
let him understand that his grace's act would be
void and of none effect, for that so long as Robin

Hood lived no man would be suffered by him to enter into possession of the estate of Utersdale, and prayed his highness not to grant it to any one who was dear to his grace, for that his life would be little worth.

In the meantime, Robin and his men followed their accustomed employment and usage, and freely killed the king's deer ; nor could the king come to a knowledge by what means he might take that yeoman, or have sight of him.

Then up and spake a forester, who was near his grace, and said after this manner : " If ye will see Robin Hood, ye must do as I ye counsel. Take five of your best knights, and go down to yonder abbey ; put on monk's weeds ; and I will be your guide. I will lay my head that I will show you that yeoman shortly."

The king assented, and clad himself like some abbot, with a cowl, and a broad hat, and stiff boots ; and they all set out on horseback for the forest, the king singing, as he went, *The convent was clothed in gray.*

They had not gone a mile within the wood, ere they met with that good yeoman, and Little John, and Sir Richard at the Lee, and certain few others with him. Robin started to the abbot's side, and grasped his bridle-rein.

" Sir abbot," quoth he, "a while ye must here abide. We are yeomen of this forest, and live by the king's deer ; other shift have we none. Ye have churches and rents, and gold in store ; for Saint Charity, give us of your plenty."

" Good friend," said the abbot, answering him,

" I have lain at Nottingham a fortnight with the king's grace, and have spent all my substance save forty pound."

" Sir abbot," quoth Robin again, "if it be so, spare us half, and keep the rest for thine own occasions." And the abbot did so, and Robin delivered the money to his fellows, that they might share it among them.

" Gramercy," said the abbot, "for thy courtesy ; and Edward our king greeteth thee well by me, and biddeth thee come to Nottingham to wait upon him." And the abbot took from his pocket the broad signet, to which Robin straightway bent his knee.

" I love no man in all the world so well as I do my king," quoth he ; " welcome be my lord's seal and thou, for that thou bearest it. Sir abbot, because thou art so good a messenger, thou shalt be my guest, and all that are with thee, under my trysting tree."

Robin sounded his bugle, and seven score archers answered shortly to the call, and made their obeisance to their master.

The king was moved by the sight, and said himself-to : " By St. Austin, his men are more at his bidding than my men are at mine." And when they had feasted well on the fat venison, and fair white bread, and red wine, and Robin and John had ended their service on the abbot, Robin spake unto him, saying, that he would have him now see what sort of life they led in the forest, that he might make report unto the king, whenas he met with his grace.

Under the linden they set up butts at good distance and the rose garland, and whoever shot not therewithin lost his bow and arrows, and received a buffet to boot on his bare head. No grace was shown to any. Robin, John, Gilbert with the wight hand, and Scathlock, shot wonderly well ; but the last time Robin missed the garland. " Sir abbot," said he, " I deliver thee my arrow, and thou shalt give me my due."

" It belongeth not to my order," said the abbot ; but because Robin would not have it otherwise, he folded back his sleeve and dealt the outlaw such a blow that he fell well-nigh.

" I make my vow to God," cried Robin, "thou art a stalwart friar, there is pith in thine arm. Thou shouldest shoot well in a bow, thou ! "

And then, because Robin, and that gentle knight, and other, had privily known from the first who the abbot truly was, and because the forester that had counselled our king was indeed a secret messenger from Robin, they looked wistfully at him for a moment, and forthwith sank on their knees at his feet, and all those wild outlaws, when they beheld them so do, did in like sort.

" We pray you," said Robin, " of your royal mercy to my men and to me, and to this gentle knight, Sir Richard at the Lee."

" For you, I grant your petition," said our king, "if so you will leave the greenwood and your now kind of life, and if you will serve me in my court."

" Content am I, liege lord," said Robin, " to come into your service, with certain of my men, and see what it is."

" Hast thou any coats of Lincoln green, that thou canst provide me and my knights that are in my company withal, ere we return to Nottingham ? "

And Robin furnished our king and his five knights with that they required, and then they all repaired together townward again ; but Sir Richard at the Lee was not of the number, for our king had not yet declared his mind him-upon.

Robin rode by the side of the king, and they both bare bows in their hands, and shot pluck-buffet ; and now Robin won, and spared not the king, and now the king had his turn. But his grace allowed Robin the better archer.

The good folk of Nottingham fled amain, when they erst espied so rare a gathering, all in Lincoln green, with their weapons bent ; and they thought that his grace had fallen in the forest, and that none in all the town would be left alive. The king laughed, and made himself seen, and there was great rejoicing and much good cheer ; and in the end our king lent an ear to the suit of Robin Hood on behalf of Sir Richard at the Lee, and recalled what he had done to his hurt, and assoiled him.

XVII.

Our king removed from Nottingham to Duffield Frith, and rested at Ravensdale Park, and thence after a time he proceeded unto Kenilworth, to spend the feast of Christmas, while Robin Hood prepared to enter upon his strange new life, as he had made covenant with his grace, and was appointed by the same to be a valet of his chamber.

Fifteen months Robin remained in that office, and not seldom lost his daily wage, for that he kept not the court, but strayed away, none knew whither; and at the end of five quarters or so, when it drew toward Christmas of the year of grace 1324, he fell sick, and importuned our king that he might be suffered to return to Barnsdale, where he had made a little chapel of St. Mary Magdalen, and sorely desired to abide till he was called by God aside.

"My lord king," he said, "I yearn to behold Barnsdale once more, ere I die. I was erewhile a good archer, one of the best in merry England; but my strength is well-nigh fore-done, and I have no lust to my food, nor sleep not."

When he came to Barnsdale, it was a winter's evening, yet he heard the notes of the birds and saw the dun deer; and when a great hart bounded by in the short distance, he sent an arrow, which brought it to earth. Then he knew that he had not lost his cunning, and was glad. Presently, when he blew his horn, some of his old companions came to him: Little John, Scathlock, and other; for they had had secret tidings of his return.

They all sorrowed at heart; for they perceived well that their master was ill at ease, and that his vigour of body had departed from him,

He tarried too long in the forest to seek again the court for dread of the anger of our king. But he shewed his comrades how he deemed it best to proceed to Kirklees Priory, and pray the prioress, that was his kinswoman, to have him let blood, put-case it might bestead him.

Now, the prioress had a paramour, that was Sir

Roger of Doncaster, a holy brother, and he entertained no goodwill toward Robin Hood ; and when it was so that Robin was let blood, this Sir Roger procured false play, whereby the strength of that yeoman ebbed away, and he died, who would have more worthily come by his end, sword in hand, beneath the greenwood tree. But thus it was ordered ; and he had, when he left the forest to wait upon the king, been a dweller in the woods, and an outlaw, as the story saith, twenty years and two.

ADAM BEL.

[*Having thus dealt with the Saxon legends of the kind and the Robin Hood group, with the "King and the Hermit," we come to the ballad-epic of "Adam Bel, Clym of the Clough, and William of Cloudesley," which is to be regarded as a most interesting, though perhaps the latest picture of old forest-life remaining to us in this class of composition.*

The writer is unknown, and the first edition yet recovered is dated 1536. *It is evident that in forming the narrative there was an eye to productions of the same tenour already in existence, and since no ancient MS. copy is at present known to be extant, he may have partly relied on then surviving north-country oral tradition, as where (in the black-letter impression) he employs the words " as I heard say"; but we cannot tell whether he was aware that, as Mr. Hunter first pointed out in modern days, one Adam Bel was living in the time of Henry IV., and was the recipient of an annuity out of the fee-farm of Clipston, in Sherwood, Notts.*

At any rate, Bel, if not the two others, was a noted character at the end of the fifteenth or beginning of the following century, and possibly brought a career as an outlaw to a close, as Robin

Hood had done, by receiving the royal pardon and a pension.

The former circumstance may have been borrowed from the earlier incident of the queen's intercession for the burghers of Calais, where it is more appropriate.

The author of "Adam Bel" has naturally and necessarily selected a particular passage in the career of that outlaw and his two associates for treatment and preservation. We do not know how long the little band continued to defy the law, out of the pale and protection of which they had placed themselves; but the term was most probably still briefer than that of the proscription of the hero of Barnsdale and Sherwood; and it should be received into account that their original offence apparently limited itself to poaching, and the case was not aggravated within the royal knowledge by homicide and sacrilege until it had become too late to retract.

We can admire at our leisure the discrepancy between the king's estimation of the value of his deer and that of the lives of his lieges. The slaughter at Carlisle was doubtless exaggerated; but his grace's emotion was in any case mild, and it was promptly diverted and extinguished by an archery-match.

The old narrative presents the not uncommon defect of developing the plot imperfectly and obscurely, and it is essential to a clear comprehension of the sequence of events to amplify and transpose here and there, just as, on the other hand, it becomes imperative to curtail, from time to time, where there is unserviceable redundancy.

The opening of the tale recalls to mind that of

" *Guy of Gisborne*," *and the episode of the apple is of course much older than this, and seems indeed to have existed in German folk-lore before the days of Tell.*

The present story is, in fact, of a composite texture, with the names of three notorious characters to recommend it to notice. Of the real history of Bel and his comrades it is impossible to say how much we learn here or how little. His friends and himself had, according to the romancist, forfeited their lives by deer-stealing, not, like Gamelyn in Chaucer, by manslaughter, nor should we be too sanguine of the identity of the person mentioned in the record as a pensioner, uncommon as the double name may be; for the Adam Bel of song was a Cumbrian hero, playing his part on ground still more northerly than Robin Hood; to him Carlisle stood in the place of Nottingham, and we are transported from Sherwood or Barnsdale to Inglewood, a vast tract of woodland once stretching from Carlisle to Penrith.

One feature in "Adam Bel" peculiarly appeals to our sympathy and admiration, and it is the dramatic prominence given to Alice, the noble and tender wife of Cloudesley; for in the Robin Hood epic there is really no female character, Marian being a later creation, and Robin's own wife never appearing in the genuine remains.]

I.

MERRY and joyous it is in the green forest, when the leaves are full and broad, to walk beneath its breezy shade, and hearken to the wild birds' song.

It is of three good yeomen of the north country
that I seek at present to tell you all : Adam Bel,
Clym of the Clough, and William of Cloudesley.
Archers of approved skill were they, and outlawed
for venison ; and in the town of Carlisle, where they
dwelled, they sware brotherhood, and to the forest
betook them. Whereof twain were single men ;
but Cloudesley had taken unto him a wife, and with
moist eyes he brake from fair Alice, and the children clasped to his knee, to lead a strange new
life in Inglewood with his two comrades, their
hand against every man, and every man against
them.

So they made such shift as they could, and
passed their days amid the forest glades and lawns,
sustaining themselves on the king's venison and
the water of the brook ; and ever and again a little
boy, who had served Cloudesley as his swineherd,
was sent to him privily, and brought him and the
others victuals and raiment, and news withal.

Till, after a certain space of time, Cloudesley
waxed homesick, thinking often on his young wife
Alice and his sweet little ones, whom he had left
behind him ; and he said to the others, that he would
fain make his way to Carlisle, to gladden his eyes
with the sight of them all once more. For Alice,
while she caused the little swineherd to pass to and
fro with meat for the foresters, held it unwise to
charge the boy with any message, praying Cloudesley
to come unto her, seeing that she was so straitly
observed.

Then said Adam Bel to him : " Ye go not,
brother, by mine advice ; for if ye be marked, and

the justice take ye, your life is even at an end. Stay, prythee, where ye are, and be content."

But Cloudesley replied : " Nay, wend thither I must ; and if so I return not to you and Clym by noon, ye may augur that I am taken or slain."

And when his brethren saw that they might nowise prevail upon him they said no more, and he departed on his way as it grew toward evening.

With a light step and an anxious heart he sped along till he came to the gates of Carlisle, and he passed in thereat disguised, that no man might discern who he was ; and he paused not till he was at his own window, and called on Alice his wife to undo the door, for it was her own William who stood without.

Then when the joy of the meeting had a little abated, fair Alice gazed at him pensively, and said : " William, it is so, that this house has been watched and beset for you this half-year or more."

But he replied to her : " Now I am here, bring me to eat and to drink, and let us make good cheer while we may."

Now there was an old wife in the chimney-corner, that Cloudesley had harboured for charity's sake some seven years, and that had not of long time set foot on ground. This shrewd and cursed crone, albeit she had eaten his bread so long, seized her occasion, and crept privily to the sheriff, where he lived, and warned him that that very night William the outlaw had by stealth come into the town, and was even now securely at home, where they might have him.

The sheriff caused the bell to be rung, and the

justice and the sheriff getting their men together, they soon encompassed the house round about on every side. Then Cloudesley made all the doors fast, and took his sword and buckler and bow, and with his three children and fair Alice his wife mounted the stair to an upper chamber, where he imagined that he might withstand them all ; and by his side his true wedded wife held a poleaxe in her hand.

Cloudesley bent his bow, and the arrow shivered in two against the justice's breastplate. " Beshrew the varlet," muttered Cloudesley, "that dressed thee in that coat ; if it had not been thicker than mine, thou haddest not spoken more."

" Yield, Cloudesley," cried the justice, "and give up thy arms."

" A curse light on him," cried Alice, " who lendeth us such counsel ! "

And they kept them all at a distance, for Cloudesley was at the window with his bow ready bent, and none durst break the doors, so true an archer was he.

" Set fire on the house, since there is no other way," shouted the sheriff ; and they did as he bad, and the flames quickly rose. Cloudesley opened a back window, and let down his wife and his children, and said to the sheriff, " For Christ's love, hurt them not, but wreak all your ire on me." And he kept his bow busy till all his arrows were spent and the fire nigh burned his bowstring in twain.

" This is a coward's death," he exclaimed, " and liever had I fall sword in hand than thus." And he cast down his bow, and taking his sword and buckler, leaped down among the throng, and smote them on every side, till only by hurling doors and windows at him could they make prisoner that stout and bold yeoman.

Then they bound him hand and foot, and led him to prison, and the justice commanded that he should be hanged the next morning, and that the gates should be shut, so that none might enter thereat. For the justice doubted that Adam Bel and Clym of the Clough might gain tidings of their fellow, and might essay to rescue him from the gallows.

"Not Adam Bel, nor Clym, nor all the devils in hell," quoth the justice, "shall save thee from the rope this time."

Early in the morning, a pair of new gallows was erected in the market-place, nigh the pillory, and the gates of Carlisle were locked.

Now Alice, seeing no other remedy, had that same night that Cloudesley was taken despatched with all speed to Inglewood the little swineherd, who crept out unobserved through a crevice in the wall after dusk, and lost not a moment in finding the two foresters, where they lay under the greenwood shade.

"Too long, too long," cried he, "tarry ye here, ye good yeomen. Cloudesley is taken, and to-morrow betimes he shall be hanged on a new gallows in the market-place."

"He might have dwelled with us in peace," said Adam Bel, "as I prayed him heartily to do, and now here is a shrewd pass." And he took his bow in his hand, and a buck that bounded by was stretched suddenly on the ground. "That will serve us for

our breakfast," he said, " ere we go. Fetch me my
arrow again, boy ; for we shall have need enough."

Now when these yeomen had eaten their meal
hastily, they girded on their swords, and took their
bows and arrows and bucklers, and sped on their
way, for time pressed, and it was a fair May morning when they reached the gates of Carlisle.

II.

" We must devise some sleight," said Clym of the
Clough, " to get in. Let us say that we are messengers from the king."

" I have a fair letter," quoth the other ; "we will
declare that we have the king's signet ; the porter
is, I warrant, no clerk."

They beat hard at the door, and when the porter
heard that they had the king's seal, he unlocked the
gate, and let them enter.

" Now we are in," whispered Adam Bel ; " but,
by Heaven ! I do not know how we shall make our
way out again."

" Let us seize the keys," whispered Clym.

They beckoned the porter to them, and wrang his
neck, and cast his body into a corner. " Now, am
I porter in his room," cried Adam, " the worst that
they have had here in Carlisle this hundred year."
And without more ado they hastened to the market-
place, placing themselves where they might not be
noted. They espied the gallows, and the justice
with his inquest, that had adjudged Cloudesley to
die, and Cloudesley hard by in a cart, bound hand
and foot, with a rope round his neck.

The justice called a boy, and promised him the

outlaw's clothes, if he would dig his grave against the time for despatch.   Cloudesley cast his eye aside, where his two brethren stood, and he said to the justice : " Such wonders have happened ere now as that a man who diggeth a grave for another lieth in it himself."

But the justice answered and said : "Ah! thou talkest proudly.   I will hang thee, fellow, with my own hand."

Scarce had the words fallen from him, when an arrow pierced his breast, and a second the sheriff's ; the rest began to scatter, and Adam, running up to the cart, loosed Cloudesley, who wrenched an axe from a man near him.   There was a panic ; the bells were rung backward, the out-horns were blown, and the mayor with a strong force behind him arrived with their bills and their swords.

The foresters, when they saw them, were dismayed by their numbers, and retreated toward the gate ; and when they could no longer use their bows, they cut down all that came near with their swords, till at last they reached the gate, and unlocked it ; and when they were without, Adam Bel threw the keys at the heads of the mayor's men, and cried : " I give up my office.   Prythee, elect a new porter."   And they waited not to see what further befell, but took their way back to Inglewood, where Cloudesley found fair Alice and his children three, that had thought him dead ; and there was great rejoicing among them all, and they feasted to their heart's ease.

Then, when those three bold foresters, with Alice and her children three, had supped merrily together, and they had rested somewhat after that notable work at Carlisle, quoth Cloudesley to the others: "Brethren mine, let us even go straightway to London to our king to seek his grace, ere the tidings come to his ear, how the justice and sheriff be slain, with many more ; and Alice and two of my children shall repair to a nunnery hereby, and my eldest son I shall take with me."

So, when they came to London, they sought our lord the king, pushing bluffly past the porter at the palace-gate and the usher, and all, who pressed after them in a body to know what they would have ; and they said that they had travelled far to obtain from the king a charter of peace.

When they were brought into the presence of our lord the king, they fell on their kness, as the law of the land was, and each held up his hand ; and they said : "Lord, we beseech thee to grant us grace, for we have slain your highness's deer."

"What are your names ?" asked our lord the king.

"Adam Bel, Clym of the Clough, and William of Cloudesley."

"Ah ! be ye those thieves," returned our lord the king, "that men have reported so oft to me ? Gramercy, sirs, I shall see well that ye be hanged without more ado."

"We pray your highness," said they again, "that you will suffer us to leave you with our arms in our hands till we are out of this place, and we will seek no farther grace."

"You talk rather proudly," quoth our king. "Nay, nay ; ye shall be of a surety hanged all three."

Now the queen, hearing the news of these archers having made so long a journey to see her lord the king, came to him, praying him, as he had made promise to her on her marriage to grant the first boon she should ask, to yield unto her the lives of those three yeomen ; and the king, albeit he was wroth that she should have begged so mean a thing when she might have had market-towns, castles, and forests to her use and pleasure, said unto her : "I depart not, madam, from my word ; they are yours."

"My lord," she said, "much thanks.   I undertake that they shall become to your grace good men and true.   But, prythee, speak a word to them, that they may know your bounty to them."

"You are pardoned, fellows," our lord the king said thereupon.   "Go now, wash and sit to meat."

A crafty man was William of Cloudesley, who thought of fair Alice and his sweet children, and wist well that the men of Carlisle would send messengers to London without delay to apprise our lord the king of what had there befallen ; and, certes, scarcely were those three yeomen assoiled by our lady the queen's favour, when, as they sat at meat in the king's kitchen, there came a post from the north country to disclose the whole thing as it was.

The messengers kneeled, and presented their letters, saying, "Lord, your officers of Carlisle in the north country greet you well."   And when our lord the king brake the seal, he was a sad man ; for he found that those three yeomen, to whom he had granted grace, and leave to wash and eat at his board, had slain three hundred and more, with the justice and the sheriff, and the mayor and many other, and had ravaged his parks, and killed his deer, and by all that country were held in dread.

"Take away the meat," cried the king; "I can touch no more. What archers be these, that can do such feats with their bows? Marry, I have none such. Methinks I will see them shoot." And his grace commanded that his bowmen and the queen's should forthwith hold a meeting, and set up butts. Whereto Adam Bel, Clym of the Clough, and William of Cloudesley were summoned to come.

They all took their turns, and the king's bowmen, and the queen's, put out their whole strength and skill before those three yeomen of the north country; but those three yeomen carried everything; and there was much marvelling at such archery.

But William of Cloudesley spake and said: "Gramercy, I hold him no archer that shooteth at such wide butts."

"What wouldest thou, then?" demanded the king.

"Such a butt, lord," he answered, "as men use in my country."

And the king gave him leave that he should shew his meaning.

Then Cloudesley took two hazel wands in his hand, and set them up two hundred paces apart, and he said to the king: "Whoso cleaveth them both in twain, I hold him an archer indeed."

No man that was with the king raised his voice or made a sign, but all were still and silent; and the king said : " There is none here who can do such a thing."

" I shall try, then," cried Cloudesley, stepping forward suddenly ; and fixing a bearing arrow in his bow, he drew it to the head, and split both the wands in two.

" Thou art the best archer," exclaimed the king, delightedly, " that I ever beheld."

" Wait a moment, lord," said Cloudesley, " and I will shew your grace even more. Here is my little son, seven years old ; dear enough to his mother and to me he is. Grieved in our hearts were we if any misadventure should befall him ; yet, lo ! I will bind him to a stake, and place an apple on his head, and at sixscore paces I will cut the apple in two."

None believed that even Cloudesley had the courage and steadfastness to achieve such a deed. But he called his son to him, and fastened him with his back toward him, lest he might wince, to a post, and the apple was laid upon the child's head, and sixscore paces were measured out. Cloudesley stood motionless for an instant, not a breath was heard throughout all that meeting, and many prayed for the yeoman, that God would protect him in his task, and some wept. He drew out a broad shaft, fixed it in his good bow, and the next moment the apple had fallen from the child's head, and not a hair was stirred.

" God forbid ! " cried the king, " that thou shouldest shoot at me ! I perceive how my officers in Carlisle sped so ill when they had such a foe. But I have tried thee sorely, William, and thou art an exceeding good archer. I give thee eighteen-pence a day, and thy clothing, and make thee a gentleman and chief forester of my north country ; and thy brethren twain shall be yeomen of my chamber. Thy little son, whom thou so lovest, I will place in my wine-cellar, and when he cometh to man's estate, he shall be farther preferred."

So said the king ; and our lady the queen commanded that Alice should be brought to London to the court, and should be set over her nursery.

So fared those three yeomen excellently well through the mastery of William of Cloudesley and the gracious offices of our lady the queen ; and when they had gone on pilgrimage to Rome to our holy father the pope, to obtain remission of their sins against God, they returned to their own land, and lived ever after in ease and worship.

ROMANTIC LEGENDS.

CHEVY CHACE.

(End of Fourteenth Century.)

[*The circumstances connected with this historical incident, so far as they can be ascertained, are set forth at considerable length in the editions of Percy's " Reliques." The object which we had in introducing this and one or two more of the ballads into the present series was to enable the reader to compare the rude metrical version with a prose rendering true to the substance and sense, and unfettered by rhyme. In the ballad form this and other narratives suffer very seriously from the necessity of compliance with the laws of metre, however faulty the distribution into lines and stanzas may be; and every one must see that, while the observance of the arrangement entails redundancy and obscurity, the language employed by the scribe is destitute of critical authority and philological value.*

In giving a place therefore to " Chevy Chace" and the " Battle of Otterburn" in a prose book intended for general readers, the object has been to present two famous episodes of ancient border-life more intelligibly, without sacrificing the heroic spirit, which breathes throughout. It is only to be lamented that in two such cases we have not purer and more contemporary texts as our guides, and have to depend

*on MSS. copies not far in point of slovenly illiteracy
from the Percy folio.*]

THE Percy came forth out of Northumberland, and
he hath made a vow to God, that within the third
day he will hunt in the Cheviot Hills *malgré*
Douglas and all his men, and the fattest harts in
all that country will bear with him away.

He came forth out of Bamborough with fifteen
hundred archers so bold, that from three shires were
chosen, and on a Monday morn began the making
in readiness on the Cheviot for the chase. That
day's hunting may rue the child that is unborn.

The drivers beat the covers for the game, and
the greyhounds were let loose, and on a Monday
against noon a hundred fat harts lay dead.

Then they blew a moot, as they stood on the
ground in the long grass, to call together the hunters
and the bowmen, and the Percy came to see the
quartering of the deer.

Quoth he : "The Douglas promised to meet me
here this day, to hinder my hunting, if he might.
But I doubted that he would fail me, by God! as
he has done."

But then spake a squire of Northumberland,
saying that he saw where the Douglas came toward
them with his folk, that were twenty hundred spearmen, the like whereof were not in Christendom ;
spears, bills, and swords they carried : men bold of
heart and strong of arm.

"Leave off the quartering of the deer," cried the
Percy, "and stand well to your good bows ; for
never since ye were born stood ye in worse need,

never since ye left your mothers, were ye in so perilous case."

The doughty Douglas rode in front of his men, and his armour glittered in the morning light like the glowing ember. A bolder child than he was never sprang from a woman.

"Tell me what men ye are," quoth he, "or whose, and where ye got leave to hunt on the Cheviot in my despite."

"We shall not to thee say," answered him the Percy, "what men we be, nor whose; but we will hunt here at our will, thee and thine notwithstanding. The fattest harts that ran in Cheviot have we slain, and to bear them home it is our intent."

The Douglas said: "By my troth that must cost the life of one of us two this day; yet to kill all these guiltless men were great pity. Now, Percy, thou art a great lord, and I in my own country am called by the name of earl. Let our following stand aside, and do we betwixt us the battle."

"Christ's curse light on his head," said the Percy then, "who thereto saith nay. There is no man in England, Scotland, or France, that was born of woman, but I dare meet him in lawful fray."

But up and spake a Northumbrian squire, Richard Witherington was his name: "It shall never be said in southern England, nor told to king Henry, for shame's sake, albeit I be a poor squire, and ye be great lords both, that I saw my captain fight, and looked idly on. But while I can hold my weapon, I will fight heart and hand."

His voice prevailed, and the battle opened; and seven score spearmen of the Scotish host fell to

the English bows. The Douglas came on, parting
his men in three, and took the English on every
side, and many a brave of Percy's liegemen was
pierced by the Scotish spears.

The Englishmen put away their bows, and drew
their blades ; and they hewed down many of their
foes, cleaving through helmet, gauntlet, and rich mail.

But at length the Percy and the Douglas met
face to face, and fought, till they sweated, with
swords of Milan steel, and till the blood spouted
out their basenets like rain.

"Hold, Percy," cried the Douglas, "and I will
bring thee to James, our Scotish king, who shall
bestow on thee an earl's fee, and thou shalt be quit
of any ransom, for thou art of all the men that ever
I met in fight the valiantest."

"Nay," answered the Percy to him, "did not I
say to thee before, that to no man of a woman born
would I yield ?"

Then, as they thus spake together, sped an arrow
from a mighty bow, and it hath stricken the Douglas
to the heart, that the only words he could say were,
"Fight on, while ye may," and he was no more.

Then Percy leaned on his sword, and saw the
Douglas die ; and taking his hand, quoth he : "Woe
is me! To have saved thee I would have pledged
my broad lands for three years' space, for a better
man and a braver was not in all the north country."

With that a Scotish knight, Sir Hugh the
Montgomery, that saw how the Douglas had fallen,
rode at his best speed through the battle, and staying not till he came where the Percy stood, pierced
him through the body.

But an archer of Northumberland set an arrow in his bow, a cloth-yard long, and drawing it to the very head, slew Sir Hugh the Montgomery straightway thereupon ; and the shaft was so true that the swan's feathers were dyed with the red heart's blood.

Now the Scotish and Englishmen returned to the fight, and when the bell rang for evensong the battle yet went on, went on by the light of the moon, till many could scarce stand on their feet ; and of the fifteen hundred archers of England, and of the twenty hundred spearmen of Scotland, only fifty of each side went home to tell the tale.

There fell with the Lord Percy Sir John of Haggerston, Sir Roger Hartley, Sir William Heron, Sir George Lovell, Sir Ralph Rokeby, and Richard Witherington, the brave squire of Northumberland, that when both his legs were cut off, fought on his knees.

There fell with Douglas, Sir Hugh the Montgomery, Sir David Liddell, Sir Charles Murray, and Sir Hugh Maxwell.

On the morrow they brought biers of birch and hazel to carry away the dead to Christian burial, and widows came to seek their husbands that had fallen ; and there was like mourning in Teviotdale and on the English side for that day's work.

Tidings came to Edinborough, to James the Scotish king, that Douglas, Lieutenant of his Marches, was slain in the Cheviots ; and he wrang his hands, and said : " Alas ! all Scotland through shall I never find such another captain as he was that is dead ! "

Tidings came to fair London, to our king, that the Lord Percy, Lieutenant of the Marches, lay dead within the Cheviot Hills, and he said : "God have mercy on his soul, good Lord, if it be His will! And albeit I have a hundred captains as good as he, for his death, an' I live, will I have requital."

Our noble king sware an oath, and kept his faith as a prince of renown, and in the Battle of Homeldondown six and thirty Scotish knights fell in one day ; and so the Lord Percy was avenged.

THE BATTLE OF OTTERBURN.

(*End of Fourteenth Century.*)

[*We have mentioned the reason for inserting a prose version of this stirring tale, which, in fact, forms a companion and sequel to the last. Mr. Robert White's monograph on the subject, published in* 1857, *should be consulted by those desirous of becoming acquainted with the whole of the details. That writer, who enjoyed the fullest advantage of local knowledge and sympathy, assigns the battle to* 1388, *and supposes that it was fought in the full of the moon in August. The Scotish force is variously estimated, but Mr. White arrived at the conclusion that the Earl of Douglas brought into the field* 6,600 *men, horse and foot.*

There seems to be little doubt that in this fight, as well as that within the Scotish border, the Scots were entitled to claim the victory. Chevy Chace was rather a border raid; Otterburn may be regarded as a battle. But the difficulty attendant on verification in all matters of this kind at so remote a date ought to admonish us to make an allowance for exaggeration and misstatement, due to ignorance or prejudice.

The true and exact relationship between the two productions forms, in fact, a subject of great difficulty, and there is some serious confusion, which it might be impossible to disentangle with available material. The two ballads evidently refer to two actual incidents in successive order : Chevy Chace, a deadly skirmish, and Otterburn, which was subsequently fought between much larger forces on both sides.

But several of the same names and particulars are common to both engagements, while the conclusion in the Otterburn narrative importantly varies. Popular literary composers were apt to employ their subject-matter rather arbitrarily and loosely, and fidelity to history was of secondary consequence to recitative effect. Neither of the stories seems to be extant in a contemporary text.

A nearly parallel case of two variant accounts of an historical event presents itself in the prose and metrical versions of Flodden Field, the former by an unknown writer, the latter by Skelton ; and a particularly curious point of resemblance is that in the prose report the Scotish king is stated to have been slain, while in the poem he is correctly described as a prisoner. So in " Chevy Chace" Percy falls ; but in the "Otterburn" ballad the hero is taken and exchanged for Sir Hugh the Montgomery.]

I.

IT befell about the Lammas-tide, when the husbandman wins his hay, that the doughty Douglas prepared to cross the English border to harry the land of the foe with fire and sword. All that rode that day may rue the riding.

The Earl of Fife, the Scotish king's son, sailed across Solway, and entered in by way of Carlisle. The rest came over Ottercap hill, and down by

Rodeley Crag to Green Layton, rousing many a stag as they went.

The Scots fell suddenly on Northumberland, and burnt many a town and village, for the English had not wist of their purpose ; and when they had burnt Northumberland and all Bamboroughshire they said that they would ride to Newcastle.

So, on the morrow, when the day dawed, they raised their standard, and to Newcastle took their way, where Sir Henry Percy was, that kept the marches and Berwick-on-the-Tweed.

And when they were under the walls of Newcastle, they challenged Sir Henry Percy to the fight, and they let him wit that they had harried and burnt Northumberland and Bamboroughshire, and spoiled his fair inheritance.

Sir Henry Percy stood on the walls, and cried to Douglas : " It sorely grieveth me if ye have harried and burnt Northumberland ; but an' ye have wasted Bamboroughshire ye have done me great trespass, and therefore one of us shall surely die."

" Where shall I bide you ? " replied Douglas, " or where shall we meet ?   At Otterburn nigh the Watling Street, ye shall have good lodging.   There ye shall find the roe, the plover, and the pheasant to do you pleasure."

" I am content," quoth Sir Harry Percy ; " ye shall not stay there long ere I come to you."

And these two valiant men pledged their troth one to the other, there at Otterburn, nigh the Watling Street, to meet shortly ; and Sir Harry Percy gave the Scots a pipe of wine over the walls, that they might pledge themselves therein.

Then the Douglas turned back homeward, and pitched his standard at Otterburn on a Wednesday ; and he bad his men seek pasture for their geldings.

Now a Scotish man that had been set to watch hied him full fast to the pavilion of the Douglas, and warned him that he espied afar off the English host drawing toward them with seven standards. But the Douglas deemed it a tale, for he thought that the Percy would never dare to look on his colours, since, when he was at Newcastle all the men the Percy led could not stand up against him.

The Douglas stepped out of his pavilion, and when he beheld the English, as they drew nearer, he saw that it was no play, and ordered his men to get ready, and chose those whom he judged meet to set over the rest.

To his uncle the Earl of Menteth and to the Earl of Huntly he gave the van, and to the Earl of Buchan the rear ; and with them were the laird of Swinton, Sir David Scott, Sir Walter Stuart, and Sir John Haggerston. And the laird of Johnston and the laird of Maxwell remained near the Douglas, who had under arms on that day betwixt six and seven thousand men, all told.

II.

The Percy drew near to the Douglas, and cried with a loud voice that whereas he had burnt Northumberland, and had wrought him great wrong, one of them should die.

" Lo ! " returned the Douglas, proudly, " I have twenty to thy one, as thou mayest see."

The Percy alighted from his steed, and all his

men did likewise, and they let their steeds go to seek pasture, and prepared to fight a-foot; and the Scots exceeded the English, saith the history, fivefold.

But when the battle was about to begin, there came a knight with letters for Sir Harry Percy, saying that his father, which was the noble Earl of Northumberland, desired with the Lord of Greystoke to see the fight, if he might tarry their coming, which was speedy.

Quoth the Percy again: "Go to my father, and say thou sawest me not; for my troth is plighted to yonder Scotish knight, and his to me, that we shall fight on this very ground where we stand: and if I failed I might be called coward, and my manhood questioned, than which I had liever die the worst death."

Then he dismissed the messenger of the earl, and commanded the minstrels to play, and the archers to let fly their arrows. "Let every man," said the Percy, "think on his own truelove, and commit himself to the Trinity; and for me I vow to heaven I flee not."

The Douglas standard floated on high, so that all might see it, with its Bloody Heart and Three Stars. And on the English side the Percy shewed the White Lion with the three Luces and the Silver Crescent. The Scots called on St. Andrew, and the Englishmen on St. George, Our Lady's knight.

The two hosts met, and fought fiercely and stoutly, and there was great slaughter on one side and the other. Two knights with closed visors encountered and clashed together, till the sweat and the blood poured together from their basenets.

" Yield thee ! " cried the Douglas, " or thou wilt
be slain.   For I see by thy bright basenet that thou
art some man of worship, and by thy burnished sword
that thou art an earl or else a knight."

" By my faith," answered the other, " and thou
art right, yet will I never surrender to thee while I
may stand."

Then the Douglas knew that it was no other
than the Percy who was opposed to him, and they
renewed the battle, and smote each other, till they
sweated, and their helms and armour were broken
and dented ; till at length the Percy with his sword
sharp and long struck the Douglas to the heart.

Still they fought the whole day into the night,
till the Percy was taken prisoner.   And of the Scots
all save eighteen, saith the chronicle, and of the
English, save five hundred, fell.   And besides Sir
James the Douglas, were slain on that side the
Earl of Menteth, Sir David Scott, Sir Walter
Stuart, Sir John of Haggerston, Sir Charles
Murray, and Sir Hugh Maxwell.   And Sir Hugh
the Montgomery was taken, and was after exchanged
against Sir Harry Percy.

There lay dead of the followers of the Percy,
Sir John Fitzhugh, Sir James Harbottle, and the
gentle Sir George Lovell.

They brought biers of the birch and the hazel
tree, and fetched away the dead on the morrow,
and widows came to claim their husbands that had
yielded up their lives in that fight.

Now let us for the Percy pray to Jesus most of
might, that He may bring him to everlasting bliss for
his knightly gentleness !

CAULINE.

AN IRISH STORY.

(*Fourteenth Century.*)

[*Here we have from the folio MS. of Bishop Percy, an incorrect and illiterate authority, but in many cases our sole resource, a legend of Irish origin, or of which, at least, the scene is laid in that country. That was our inducement to select it as the third specimen of a metrical narrative of this class reduced into modern prose from a barbarous and corrupt poetical text. Percy has enlarged and sophisticated the particulars, and has followed the precedent of Shakespear in his "Hamlet" of making the event tragic. But, while this might have been preferable, it is necessary for us to follow the old ballad, such as it is, and to marry the hero and heroine after a series of vicissitudes and narrow escapes. The incident in the folio MS. of the lion and the false steward reads, however, like a clumsy interpolation.*]

THERE once on a time dwelled in Ireland, far across the sea, a bonny king, and with that king a young and comely knight, who was called Sir Cauline.

Now this king had a daughter of unparalleled beauty, whom many a prince and noble would fain have wedded ; but Sir Cauline loved her best of all.

Yet durst he not speak his mind to that maiden; and his passion, nursed up in secret, fretted him the more, till he wox sick, and could not leave his bed.

After mass, the king was wont to dine, and when the wine had to be served, he said: " Where is Sir Cauline, that commonly attendeth at the board to serve me with wine?"

" Sir," replied a knight that stood by, " Sir Cauline sore aileth, and unless some leech may tend him, belike he will die."

The king was grieved at these tidings, and commanded them to fetch his daughter, who was a right cunning leech, and to take him of the venison and the bread and the red wine; for he, too, loved Sir Cauline, and loth was that he should be in jeopardy of his life.

Then, when the lady Christabel was so bidden of her father the king, she hied straightway to the chamber where that knight lay, attended by her maidens, and she left her maidens at the door, and entered in, and asked him how he fared.

" Ah! lady," he said, " sick indeed am I."

" Now rise for shame, sir," quoth she; " for the tale goes in my father's hall, that you are dying for the love of Christabel."

" Fair lady, it is indeed for thy love that I pine. If thou wert to requite my passion, I should be whole again."

To whom she answered: " Sir knight, I am a king's daughter and my father's heir, and, alas! I can give thee no hope of espousing me."

Then Sir Cauline replied: " Thou art a king's

daughter truly, and such as I can never be thy peer. But let me do some valiant enterprize better to deserve thy hand."

The lady Christabel said : " I am content ; yet, O ! if any mishap should befall thee, it would be a sorrow to me for ever. Lo ! on the Eldridge downs I enjoin thee to watch all night till cockcrow. The Eldridge Knight lieth there in wait for all who come that way, and never yet has man returned alive from the encounter with that fell heathen. For he is a giant, and unless Heaven bestead thee, thou art lost."

" On the Eldridge hills, lady, for thy fair sake I will wander, and will either bring you a thorn that groweth there as a token, or never see thee more."

The Lady Christabel returned to her chamber with her maidens, and Sir Cauline incontinently sprang from his couch, and to the Eldridge hills rode, there to tarry till daybreak. Up and down he roamed without beholding any one, and at last midnight arrived, and the moon rose. Presently his ear caught the sound of a bugle across the moors, and he soon espied a warrior of fierce mien approaching him on horseback, a lady at his side holding the bridle.

" Fly, or thou diest," cried the stranger.

" I shall not fly," returned Sir Cauline ; " for I fear thee not, since thou art no Christian knight."

They pricked their horses, and ran at each other, spear in hand, and both stood their ground, yet were their weapons shivered to atoms. Then they drew their swords, and met in close combat, till helmet and hauberk, mail and shield, were well nigh hewn to pieces. The Eldridge knight held his own ;

for he was a doughty wight, and had never yet met his match. But Sir Cauline was not to be daunted, and by a backward stroke he suddenly smote off the right hand of his foe, who sank on the ground, faint from the ebbing of blood.

Then Sir Cauline lifted his sword above his head, and sware by the Holy Rood that that caitiff should die. But the lady, who had been standing near, and had seen all the fray, came and supplicated Sir Cauline that, for the sake of the maiden whom he loved best, he would spare her lord's life. "For the love of the maiden that is to you most dear, strikc not, I beseech ; and whatever you command, my lord shall perform." Then Sir Cauline made the Eldridge knight swear on that very spot where they stood that he would believe in Christ, that he would never visit Eldridge again, and that he would renounce warfare till his dying day. Then the Eldridge knight was suffered to remount his horse, and he and his lady have gone to their castle.

Sir Cauline took up the bloody hand, on which were five rings of gold of foes that the Eldridge knight had slain in combat, and his sword as hard as a flint ; and homeward wended he, impatient to see the lady Christabel.

Down he sank on his knee, when he was admitted to her and said : "Lady, I have been on the Eldridge hills, and these tokens have I borne away."

She welcomed him, and commended his valour.

"O lady, I am thy own true knight, ready to obey thy behests, and hopeful to obtain thy love." He paused, for he could utter no more.

The lady Christabel blushed deeply, and sighed, as she rejoined : "Alas! sir, how may such a thing be, seeing that my degree is so high ?"

The knight appeared to be downcast at these words, and she continued : " But since thou hast approved thyself so nobly in my service, I will promise thee, if I cannot wed thee, I will wed none other."

Then she held out her lily-white hand to him, and he kissed it ; and the tears started from his eyes. She bad him depart, and keep his own counsel, lest her father should kill them both ; and from that day forth the king's daughter, the lady Christabel, loved that brave and good knight, Sir Cauline, and oftentimes they met and secretly conversed together.

Now, it happened one day, that as these lovers were in an arbour together, the king, walking out in the evening to take the air, passed the place where they were. Lo! an angry man was he, and what vengeance did he not vow on Sir Cauline! Into a deep dungeon the knight was cast, and the lady Christabel was consigned to a lonely tower, where she endured grievous suspense as to her lover, whom the king threatened to hang and draw.

But the queen happily befriended Sir Cauline, and she prevailed on her husband to spare his life, and banish him from the land. " But," he declared, " if ever that false traitor, madam, sets his foot again in my kingdom, a foul death shall be his lot." So that gentle knight departed out of the realm, more sorrowful at quitting the lady Christabel than if he had been adjudged to die, and she, the lady

Christabel, released from durance, vowed perpetual chastity, and refused the suit of many a king and many a duke, and many a lord of high degree, till her father, seeing how melancholy she had grown, proclaimed a tournament to amuse his daughter, and distract her from her sadness.

There came to it lords and knights from many a far country to break a spear in honour of the lady Christabel, and many a lady was there, fair in feature and rich in apparel, yet none that equalled Christabel even in her unjoyous mood.   The knights vied with each other in daring and valour for the honour of the ladies whom they loved and of the lady Christabel, the king's daughter ; but each day a stranger, whom none knew, bare away the prize.

Black was his acton, black his hauberk and his shield.   None wist whence he came, or whither he went when the jousting was done ; and it fortuned on the fourth day that a horrible giant, preceded by a dwarf, who carried on his shoulder five heads, presented himself, and challenged any knight present to enter the lists with him.   He was the cousin of the Eldridge knight, this giant, and came to avenge him.

The dwarf said : " My master may only be appeased in one way.   Give him thy daughter, O king, and he will depart ; or thy castle shall be burned, and thy head shall be added to those which I carry, unless thou canst find a champion able to cope with him."

The king heard these words, and looked round the lists ; but never a knight stirred a foot.   Then the king said : " Is there not a knight among you all will fight for my daughter and me? Whoever will vanquish this grim paynim shall be my heir, and shall have fair Christabel to his wife."

Still no one rose; for when they viewed that loathly giant, their hearts quaked within them. All woe-begone was the lady Christabel, when she perceived that no help was near; and she thought of Cauline, and the tears gushed from her eyes.

Then started to his feet the stranger knight, and said that for the lady Christabel's sake he would give battle to the giant, if she would lend him the Eldridge sword.

"Fetch forth the Eldridge sword," exclaimed the king, with alacrity. "Courteous knight, we give you great thanks; my daughter shall be your guerdon."

The Black Knight grasped the sword, which the lady delivered to him, and entered the lists. The giant was impatient to begin.

"Ah!" murmured the lady Christabel, "that this were my own true knight!"

They fought for a season amid breathless silence and with all eyes fixed on them. The king knew that his realm and his daughter hung on the issue. The lady Christabel scarce dared she to turn her eyes on the spectacle, nor could not bear to look away. Thrice the cousin of the Eldridge knight smote the stranger with his sword, and at the third stroke he sank on his knees. It was a parlous moment; the lady Christabel shrieked; and all gave up the Black Knight as lost, when he, summoning his remaining strength, regained his feet, and plunging his sword into the foe, pierced him to the heart.

Loud and prolonged were the shouts which

greeted the giant's fall. The lady Christabel thanked Christ that He had freed her from such a husband. But the king and those about him hastened toward the Black Knight, in order to see how he fared, and to tender him their joyful congratulations. Alas! they found him in a dead swoon, weltering in his blood.

The king called his daughter to essay her craft in leechdom ; " for," said he, " I would rather lose half my lands than that this courteous knight should die."

The lady Christabel no sooner drew near to try her skill, than she cried, " It is my life—my lord," and fainted away.

Sir Cauline indeed it was, who had returned from banishment at all hazards to attend the tournament. He opened his eyes, and gradually recovered his consciousness ; and the king's daughter, the lady Christabel, staunched his wounds, and sweetly ministered to him.

And when his strength had a little returned, the king told him that he would give him broad lands in reward.

" Take your lands, sir," said he ; " you promised me your daughter to my wife."

And the king answered, " Let it be so." And Sir Cauline and the lady Christabel were married with great pomp, and after the king's death Sir Cauline reigned in his stead. For sons the old king had none.

THE KING AND THE TANNER.

[*This racy little tale may be classed among the* fabliaux, *and is in its original form of very great antiquity. Although the name of Edward IV. is usually coupled with it, it is more probable that the personage who actually met with the adventure, if the relation is founded on fact, was the second Edward. In his "Popular Poetry of England," 1864, the present writer collected all the information relative to this episode and production with which he was able to meet, and pointed to it and other relics of a cognate character as forming a class by themselves, and as having probably owed their existence in an English dress to various foreign and oriental models. The earliest imitators of anecdotes found in the literature of other countries were apt to be the most tolerable; their followers, in the constant search for something novel, did not hesitate to commit anachronisms and incongruities, and to change the personality of the story without regard to historical or dramatic fitness.*

A broad line of distinction should be drawn between the original, or at least older, versions of these stories and those which emanated from the later ballad-writers, who never studied the costume of the period with which they were dealing, nor concerned themselves with anything beyond the production of a marketable commodity.

It is to be remarked, that the closing passage only infers the actual knowledge on the part of the tanner of the rank of his companions, although in an antecedent place, where the royal retinue salutes the king, the tanner is made to suspect the truth.]

As our comely king Edward once rode with certain of his lords on hunting in Warwickshire, at such time as his grace made his progress in those parts, he fell in with a tanner of Daventry in a quaint array. The fellow was jogging along on horseback, some distance in front, and no other saddle had he than the black cow-hides, with the horns hanging down on either side, which he carried to his tan-yard to be tanned.

Our king chuckled at the sight, and thought that he would have some sport. He bad his men keep behind, and he would go on, and ask the tanner some questions to engage him in talk. "Wait here," said our king, "and you shall hear presently how I have sped."

He pricked his steed and drew up by the tanner's side.

"Sir, God thee save!" quoth our king.

"Good day," quoth the tanner.

"Good fellow," said our king, "one thing I thee pray : to Drayton-Basset I would ride ; which is the road?"

"That I can tell thee," replied the other, "where I sit. When thou comest to the gallow-tree, turn to the left hand."

"Thank you very much, fellow," said our king. "I will beg the Lord Basset to requite thee for thy

courtesy.   But, good fellow, I pray thee accompany
me to Drayton-Basset, wilt thou not, eh ? "

" Nay, by my faith," cried the tanner, " I were a
fool if I did.   I am in as great haste to get to the
end of my journey as thou art of thine.   Ride on,
and find thy way ; thy horse is better than the one
I have."

The tanner paused and looked at our king, and
presently he said to him : " What sort of a man
art thou, now ? "

" A wanderer about," responded our king, " in
many a country."

" Ah ! " cried the tanner, archly, " I had a brother
who followed that kind of trade, and he came to
an ill end."

Our king smiled, but only said : " Tanner, I prythee ride with me a mile."

" What the devil ! " replied the tanner.   " Art
thou out of thy wits ?   I must get home to my
dinner.   I have had nothing to eat."

" Good fellow," said our king, " trouble not thyself about thy meat ; thou shalt have enough to-
night, I warrant thee, if thou wilt eat."

The tanner looked hard at him, and then he said
scornfully : " By Christ's passion, I trow I have more
money in my purse than thou hast in thine.   Dost
thou think I am going to be out o' night ?   By
God ! I was never out o' night since I was born."

He heard sounds behind him, the tanner did, and
cast his eyes back, and the cow-hides began to slip
down ; for he was aware of the king's men, who
came riding up at full speed.

" This is a thief," thought the tanner ; " and he

and his fellows will have my horse, my hides, and my money." He judged it wise to dissemble.

"For fellowship, then," he said to our king, "I will ride with thee; if we meet again, thou must do as much for me."

"God-a-mercy!" said our king, "I shall pray the Lord Basset to thank thee anon. Now," quoth he, "thou ridest hereabout pretty much. What news hast thou for me?"

"No news," quoth the tanner, as they rode side by side, "save that of all the goods that be, cow-hides are the costliest."

"One thing tell me," said our king (for the rest had not yet come up); "what dost thou hear tell of the Lord Basset in this part?"

"I know him not," answered the other; "I have little enough to do him-with; he doth not buy of me the leather wherewithal to clout his shoon."

"I love thee well," said our king; "one thing more tell me now. Thou hast heard his servants speaking of him. What do they say?"

"Ay, by God!" said the tanner, "that I can resolve thee. They know him well, and say he is a good man."

So they rode together and talked till the Lord Basset and the rest overtook them, and, dismounting, fell on their knees.

"Alack!" thought the tanner, "this must be the king; and surely I shall be hanged on a high gallows, that all men may me see."

He quaked for very dread, and would have stolen away while the others were in converse. But our king kept his eye upon him, and presently he said:

"Good fellow, thou must abide here with me, for thou and I are going on hunting together."

So the tanner had no choice but to ride on, and when the party came to the king's chace, our king said : "Fellow, what shall I do ? My horse stands so high. Good friend, let us exchange. Have thou my horse, and I will take thine."

The tanner dismounted, and cast down his hides, and up gat the king. The tanner laid his hides, for that he would not lose them, over the king's saddle, and off he galloped after our king, for fear he should steal his horse.

But our king's horse, catching a glimpse of the black cow-hides, weened he had the Devil on his back, and flew like the wind. He lacked no spurs. Our king was intent on following the deer ; but he looked aside and saw how it went with the tanner, and he feared lest harm should befall him ; and anon the tanner's head struck the bough of an oak, and down he fell sprawling on the ground.

Our king laughed and said : "Tanner, thou rodest too fast. By St. John ! such another horse-man saw I never. By St. James ! I could not help laughing, wert thou my own mother."

"I beshrew the son," said the tanner ruefully, "who could make sport of his mother so."

When the chace was concluded, our king changed horses again, and each had his own, whereof the tanner was glad.

"God-a-mercy!" said our king, "if I can do ought for thee after this day's adventure, trust to me. I will be thy friend for ever."

"God-a-mercy !" said the tanner, "thou seemest

a good fellow; if we meet in Daventry, I will give thee to drink."

"By my troth!" said our king, "if I meet thee in Lichfield, I will do for thee as much."

So they went on talking merrily till they came to Drayton-Basset, and there the tanner knew certainly that it was our king with whom he had fortuned to meet; and our king commanded that a hundred shillings should be given to him to recompense him for the damage to his head and his black cow-hides after his parlous ride on our king's horse.

And so our king and the tanner of Daventry parted good friends at last.

THE SQUIRE OF LOW DEGREE.

(*Fifteenth Century.*)

[*This is not a mere brief sketch, or more or less fragmentary account of a single incident, but an elaborate and artistically constructed story of English origin, although the scene is laid elsewhere. It aspires to the dignity of a romance of chivalry, and of those which we possess it would be difficult indeed to specify one more richly descriptive, so unusually dramatic and varied, and so full of curious illustrative detail. The anonymous author has avoided the common error of making his work too tedious by prolixity and dull interlocutions; his enumeration of birds, trees, and dishes, and the particulars into which he enters about architecture, furniture, and costume, abound with interest for the student under many aspects.*

The descriptions of natural history and scenery betray the employment of foreign material, inasmuch as English arboriculture was, even in the sixteenth century, in a very imperfect state of development; and from the allusions to certain heroes of chivalry or romance, as Sir Gawayn and Sir Guy, Lybius Disconus (Le Beau Inconnu), *and the giant Colbrand, it is manifest that its composition was posterior in date to the works in which their exploits are celebrated.*

The steward, who is introduced as a foil to the hero of the piece, is to be distinguished from the cognominal character in the " Heir of Linne," the " Lord of Lorn," and elsewhere, as he was evidently the high steward of the kingdom, or grand seneschal, like the officer of state in Scotland in whom the reigning house of Stuart originated, and who survives in the Prince of Wales for the time being.

The weakest and least satisfactory part is the attempt at tragic pathos, where the king's daughter mistakes the corpse of the false steward for that of her lover, and pays it funeral honours. This misconception is more flattering to the lady's virtue than to her instinctive discernment. But here, as well as elsewhere in the narrative, the writer has lost the thread, and is guilty of some amount of confusion, which it has been judged desirable to remove by a slight reconstruction of the text.

Attention need scarcely be directed to the scene where the king's daughter issues from her chamber " as naked as she was born " in search of the squire. This expression, or " belly-naked," was formerly considered imperative to signify a complete state of nudity, since a person was termed naked *if he or she was destitute of the upper clothing, and was reduced to the shirt or chemise. Numerous examples of this might be adduced from our early literature.*

We have left this and two other passages, where the steward alleges to the king that, had it not been for his presence, the squire would have lain with the princess, and the king repeats the conversation to his daughter, because they are characteristic of the masculine frankness of the old time, and are survivals

of the language employed in the mediæval fabliaux,
*and in such works as the "Book of the Knight of
the Tower."*]

A SQUIRE of low degree loved the king's daughter.
He was a man for whom every one had a kind
word, for he was courteous and debonnair, and he
was marshal of the royal hall, who set the king's
guests in the order which they should keep when
they met together to dine or to feast.

Now all marked how, whatever he did to conceal
it, this squire grew more and more oppressed by
melancholy, and none knew what the occasion and
reason of the same were; but it was for that this
squire secretly loved the king's only daughter and
heir, namely, the king of Hungary. Not a soul
wist how well he loved her. He had privily nursed
his passion for that lady seven years, and not a whit
nigher was he yet to a fulfilment of his dreams.

Oftentimes he wandered out of the king's hall,
or out of his own chamber into the palace garden,
where the birds were singing upon the trees, as if
it might be that they sought by their sweet melody
to assuage his distress and brighten his cheer;
and he was wont to seat himself in an arbour, hard
by that princess's window-casement, and make his
lament to the creatures of the air.

"O, that I were rich!" he cried, "or high-born—
nay, or a king's son, that I might be worthy of that
dear lady! O, that I could do some enterprize to
deserve her hand, like Sir Gawayn or Sir Guy of
Warwick! Then should no man win her from
me."

But it was of no avail, for he was poor and unknown, and only the marshal of the king her father's hall ; and one day it happened that he was in the arbour, just below the lady's casement, when he was so troubled in spirit, that he lifted up his voice in piteous wise, and at length sank down in a swoon.

In her oriel, fair with painted glass, the king's daughter stood ; and when she heard the sound of that squire's voice, as he thus bemoaned his fate, she removed one of the ivory pins wherewith the casements of the oriel were made fast, and threw the casement wide open.

The sun was clearly shining through the rich glass windows, and upon the garden, and upon the arbour, and that lady saw the squire, as he lay on the ground, and said unto him : " Sir, why lamentest thou in this manner night and day ? I prythee discover to me the cause, and, an' I may without reproach, I will seek to lighten thy sorrow."

The squire rose to his feet, and knelt on one knee, and answered so : " Lady, my grief, be avised, so it please you, is all for the love of you. Seven years have I kept my secret, and I know that you are of such high lineage that I cannot hope to gain your hand. But a word from you might be to me a comfort and a joy, and if, as I sorely doubt, you deny me, I will forsake this land, and my kith and kin, and go as a pilgrim into foreign countries, using my spear as a staff, and beg my bread, where Christ Jesus was born and crucified ; nor no other mistress, to my life's end, will I have ! Therefore, sweet lady, by Him that died on Good Friday for us all, and harrowed hell, I beseech you to speak truly to me, and let me not be deceived."

Then the king's daughter replied to him, as she stood in the sunlight in the painted oriel above the arbour: "Squire, thou shalt have my love; but thou must make no man privy thereto, and thou must go forth and serve my royal father in his wars and cast away thy brooding over thy fate ; and thus all may peradventure be well hereafter. But I warn thee against my father's steward, for he hath an evil tongue, and misliketh thee ; and if he betrays thee to the king, thou must suffer the law, whereof I should be sorely ill-content. To deserve my love, thou art to engage in deeds of chivalry and perilous adventures across the seas, in Lombardy and at Rhodes. And I straitly charge thee that thou must fight at Rhodes three Good Fridays ; and if thou so doest, thou art worthy to wear thy spurs, and thou shalt get a shield of blue, in token of thy loyalty, with vine leaves festooned, and a white baudrick, and a red cross, and all other things to knighthood appurtenant. And thou art to go everywhere, with six yeomen upon thee attending, and for thy cost I will give thee a thousand pounds, so that thou mayest lack for nought ; for it is not enough to say, "Go, and fear not"; a man of worship must have wherewithal he may maintain his quality and estate ; and thou wilt return and present thyself to the king my father as a knight that hath (like Sir Guy or the Comely Unknown, as I have read in the Book of Arthur) ever upheld the right, and is worthy to seek in the way of marriage his daughter and heir. Therefore, sir, go thy way, and God prosper thee ! Seven years I shall await

thy coming back, and shall remain in my solitary
maidenhood!"

So the squire joyfully departed, and prepared to
take his leave of the king and the queen, and all
the court, that he might speed on his journey; for he
was impatient to begin to deserve the love and the
hand of that great lady, who would make him, for
that she was her father's heir, king of that country,
when the old king should die.

Now, while the squire thus discoursed with the
king's daughter, the steward was hard by, and they
wist it not, and every word that fell from their lips
he heard well; and he began to devise in his mind
how he might best make the case known to the king
his master, and cross that squire, of whom he was
full jealous, for he also loved that lady, and longed
to gain her for his wife, that he might reign in that
country after the king that now was. And it was
of this false steward that the lady bad the squire
beware, lest he might come to a knowledge of their
intent, and denounce him to her father.

The squire yet did service in the hall, until such
time as it was convenient to depart, and by his
gentleness and courtesy took all hearts; and the
king looked upon him, as he knelt to tender him
the dishes, and thought within himself that he was
the seemliest man he had ever viewed.

But the steward, at the first occasion, sought his
master, and opened to him the matter, leaving
nothing untold, and saying how the princess had
made promise to him thus and thus, and, "Sir,"
quoth he, "had they not espied me at last, I ween
verily they would have lain together."

The king refused to believe the tale, for he said to the steward that the squire had served him in his hall his whole life, and he could not be guilty of so foul a deed, nor did he think that his daughter would consent thereto; for he might come to win that lady in wedlock, since many men rise from lowly station to high degree, nay, to a crown, by valour, or by good fortune, or by marriage; and he warned the steward not to defame the squire, for that, if he found that he bare false witness against him, he would cast him into prison, and a shameful death he should die.

Then the steward stood firm in what he had declared, and said that he would lose his life if it were not as he had avouched. "Sir," quoth he, "if you will grant unto me certain armed men, I will take this squire to-night in the princess's chamber and bring him to you."

"Steward," the king replied, "you shall have as many as you desire. Be in readiness against he comes, but be not seen; for I command you in nowise to hinder him, if he merely speak with the lady my daughter, yea, if he even kiss her. But if he do offer to break her chamber, shew yourself incontinently, and take him in my name, and hold him, till you know my pleasure."

The steward answered that he would fulfil what the king bad him; and anon the hour for dinner came, and then all assembled in the hall, the king and his court. Now, when the squire had, as he was wont, served the king on his knee, he departed, and coming again knelt down, craving leave to pass the sea, that he might enact deeds of chivalry in divers

countries, and become a true knight. And the king
assented to his prayer, and promised him gold and
men to bear him company, saying that he trusted
he would ever remain loyal to him, as he had heretofore done.

Now, when the squire and his companions had
taken their departure, and had reached a certain
village a mile away, the squire sorely longed once
again to speak with his dear lady, the king's daughter. So, leaving the rest, he hastened back alone,
and entered the postern-gate, and approached the
tower where the princess lodged ; and as he went
along he noted how men hung about him as they
would watch him. But he did not yet know that
the steward had played false ; and when he came
to the chamber of the king's daughter, " Thy door,"
he cried, " undo ; for I am beset round about with
spies. O, undo thy door, my betrothed ! "

The king's daughter slept ; and when at length
the sound of a voice outside awoke her, she took it
to be some rude trespasser on her privacy, for she
knew her truelove to be far away. But when she
demanded who it was, and the voice answered, "Undo thy door, it is thy own squire, who cometh once
more to bid thee adieu," she opened the door, and
kindly greeted him, and again exhorted the squire
to comport himself so, that her royal father might,
on his return from the wars, see fit to wed them
straight one to the other. Then he saluted her
tenderly, and took his leave.

Now, meanwhile, the steward was lying in wait
for that squire, as he issued forth from the princess's
chamber, and at a convenient point they encompassed

and attacked him, thirty and four all told. The squire laid some of them dead at his feet, and then, after a fierce combat, nearly severed the steward's head from his body. But he was outnumbered, and taken captive ; and they stripped him of his surcoat, and arrayed in it the dead steward, whom they left at that lady's door, when they had slashed his face, so that none might know that it was not the squire.

Then they took him before the king, and the king commanded that he should be cast into a deep dungeon ; and so it was done. But it happened shortly after that, that the king himself privily went to the prison, and said to the squire : "I am content that thou shouldest go forth, and cross the sea, and approve thyself a true knight in the eyes of all men ; and when thou dost return, it may be that thou shalt yet wed my daughter. But I charge thee, go secretly, and let no man weet thy counsel."

And the king at that time had knowledge how the steward's guard had wrought a deceit on his daughter, and had stripped the surcoat from the squire, to put it on the dead body of their master.

The squire was fain enough, and the king gave him of his own treasure all that he needed ; and he went on his way, and performed many valiant acts in Tuscany, Lombardy, Portugal, and Spain, and made his offering at the Holy Sepulchre, as his lady had enjoined upon him.

Now, it happened that, when the king's daughter undid the door of her chamber, and stood forth there, as she rose from her bed, as naked as she was born, she beheld the body of the false steward ;

but because it was arrayed in the squire's garment, and his visage was disfigured, she took it to be indeed her own true lord, and threw herself down upon the corpse, and bitterly wept. But presently, lest any should come upon her at unawares, she lifted the body up, and took it and laid it in a secret place, where none should surmise, and anointed and embalmed it, inclosing it in a sweet-smelling coffin ; and she set it at her bed's head, and every night and every morning she kissed it and prayed by it. This she did seven years together, and kept her counsel, and none wist wherefore she mourned so long. But her royal father feared lest such sorrow might bring her to her end, and he sought to yield her diversion by hawking, hunting, and fishing, if he might prevail on her to accompany him. But she prayed him not to persuade her, for she listed not to turn to any such things, for she mourned for one, no man should know whom. Yet her father the king guessed well how the case stood, and said nevertheless not a word to her.

At last after seven years, the squire, who had become the flower of chivalry, bad farewell to the strange lands which he had visited, and returned secretly to his own country, that none was privy to his return save the king only ; and the king was overjoyed to see him again, and after a while commanded him to abide in his own house, till he the king had avised himself of what his daughter's mind was, and had communed with her.

So the king repaired to the tower where his daughter's chamber lay, and when he came near, he heard her lamentations, albeit seven years had come and gone since the squire, as she thought, was slain by the false steward ; and when he had listened for a season, he came to the door, and desired that it might be opened to him.

"O father," quoth she, "thou hast heard all that I spake !"

"Daughter," he said, "grieve no longer. Thou art to be wedded to a king."

Then he unfolded to her the story. How the steward had accused the squire of unknightly discourtesy toward her, and had held him in hand, that had he the steward not been by, the squire would have lain with her ; and how after, when the squire, her own truelove, had slain the steward, and was fain to yield to force of numbers, and was taken, the body of the steward, wrapped in her lord's surcoat, was laid at her chamber door to beguile her ; then again how, when they who were with the steward brought the squire to prison, he the king had with his own hand privily enlarged him, and sent him across the sea to seek his fortune, and he repeated : "And now, daughter, weep not, for thou shalt espouse a king, or may-be an emperor."

The king's daughter replied, that she cared not to wed any man, seeing that her own truelove was dead ; and as she uttered these words, she fell into a swoon.

The king her father raised her up, and bare her in his arms, breathing into her ear as they went along : "Thy sweetheart liveth, and is here, lady. He hath been in foreign lands, and hath won much renown. I shall make him knight, and one of my great lords, and after me he shall wear the crown."

" O, why, then," asked she, "if thou diddest know all this, diddest thou not discover it to me? But if the squire be truly here, let me see him."

Then when she was brought where he was, and she perceived that he was whole in limb and health, she uttered a loud cry, and again fainted away.

The squire caught her in his arms, and kissed her over and over again, till she rallied, and became sensible of her unexpected happiness. Her father the king spake unto her and said: "Daughter, have herewithal thy own truelove, and let no one seek to depart you two, under pain of God's displeasure." And he drew her tenderly toward him, and kissed her once, twice, and thrice.

The country was full of rejoicing at the glad tidings of the safety of the squire, and his forthcoming nuptials with the king's daughter. There was banqueting, music, and minstrelsy; and the king gave order, that all the chivalry of Hungary should be summoned to honour the marriage of the squire and his lady with a tournament, and jousts, and merry-making; and the story says that the festivities lasted forty days.

At the end whereof the king called his twelve councillors unto him, and his son, the squire of low degree, and his daughter whom that squire had espoused, and in the midst of them all he yielded up the crown, and made the squire king in his room, and all did him homage.

THE HEIR OF LINNE.

[*This charming tale conveys the burden of many a true story of the olden time, with the exception that it involves a more auspicious conclusion than was generally accorded to the actors of such parts in real life. Experience is here allowed to prevail, and the prodigal, reinstated in his patrimony by his father's goodness and foresight, remains steadfast to his resolution never to compromise his honour again.*

The earliest known version of the "Heir of Linne" is a very defective one in the Percy folio MS., written late in the reign of Charles II. by some illiterate scribe, who has mangled everything which he touched.

In the episode of the Knight *in the Robin Hood ballads, we meet with an incident of a somewhat cognate character, except that there the estate is mortgaged to the Church, and through the instrumentality of the outlaw is not only redeemed from foreclosure, but, as it eventually happens, with money taken from two ecclesiastics passing through Barnsdale just after the departure of Sir Richard at the Lee with the loan to enable him to keep his day at York.*

Here it is the treacherous steward, who strips the heir of his estate by offering him, under pressure of poverty arising from his improvidence, a sum

of ready money for the property; and the happy
denouement, *by which the lord, or laird, wins back
his own, is principally remarkable for the purely
casual occurrence of the opportunity, so far as we
are enabled to judge, for re-entrance and the slight-
ness of the effort made by the steward to hold his
ground.*

*Nevertheless, it is a pretty illustration of a phase
of bygone English and Scotish life, when such things
were constantly happening without the fortunate intervention of the romancist to lend them a dramatic
development.*

*Early Scotish landowners were in many cases
recipients of a scanty rent-roll, with much paid in
kind, even when the estate was territorially considerable. The hero in the present instance carried in
a couple of bags or so the redemption-money of his
property, perhaps a few hundred pounds of the currency of the period.*

*Unless the narrative which we have used is corrupt
or imperfect in that place, a curious point of old
Scotish custom seems to peep out, where the principal
person of the little drama, when he has received a
pittance from one of the company in the hall, sits
down with the rest, as we take it, and drinks wine,
as if some payment were a necessary prelude, and
the* bouche *or table were maintained by a common
fund.*]

Of all the lords in fair Scotland one was the unthrifty Heir of Linne ; and of him is my song.

His father and mother were dead, and he was
the head of his clan.   Long time he resorted to the

cards and the dice ; and at his table good fellows sat, and made merry, and drank the clear wine. None that would play and drink was unwelcome to him.

In whose coffers at last the red gold waxed scant enough, and he wist not where to go to seek money, wherewith he might continue in his folly.

To whom came John of the Scales, his steward, and thus spake he : "An', Lord of Linne, thou doest stand in need of the red gold, I will gladly bestead thee. Nay, wilt thou not sell to me for broad money in hand thy father's lands ? "

The Heir of Linne was in his hall in the midst of the other lords his very friends, and John of the Scales spake to him these words aside, and they gladdened his heart.

For he perceived how the money he should get thereby the which would pay the cost of many a feast and many a bout ; and thereto he saw no end.

Therefore he assented to the surrender of the fair estate that he had received down from his father, albeit the price which the steward in his deceit offered was unjust.

" I agree," quoth he, " John o' the Scales, to sell thee my land ; here take it to thee."

" I draw you to record, lords all," cried John o' the Scales, "and a God's penny, lo! I cast to the Heir of Linne."

He went away, and shortly he came again, and counted out the gold upon the board ; to the last piece he counted it out. And then he said : " The gold is thine, the land is mine ; and now I am the lord of Linne."

" Here is money enough," said the Heir of Linne, "for many a day to come, to keep me and mine in merry sort." And he drank and he diced, and he played the wanton, with all his company. Till it happened in three quarters of a year that his store, which he had received from John o' the Scales, shrank to nought, so that he had but three pennies all told left to him, and his friends forsook him, every each one, till he was left alone.

" Now, well-a-day," he sorrowfully cried, "whenas I was the lord of Linne, I lacked nothing, and had gold and fee; but now I have sold my lands so broad, I must fain go to Edinborough to beg my bread."

To whom, asking alms, some gave, and some not, and others bad him to the foul fiend go; and, quoth they, "an' we should hang any thief, we would even begin with thee."

So he sojourned in Edinborough it was three quarters of a year, and he waxed exceeding melancholy. "Well-a-day, and woe is me!" he said. "Now that I have parted with my land, every man is against me; but whenas I was the lord of Linne, I lived passing well, as my father, God be with him! did before me during his whole life."

He stood pensive and sad, the Heir of Linne; and money had he none. But he bethought him suddenly of a paper, that his father had left with him, and had commanded that, unless he were in extreme need, he should in no wise open the same.

" Now, by my troth," said the Heir of Linne, " I may well do it; for never was I yet pressed so sore."

He sought out the paper, and read it, and it

enjoined him to repair to a lodge in the forest, where he should find in a secret place a key, and in the thickness of the wall, where no man might surmise, three chests, two filled with gold and one with silver; and his father, that was the lord of Linne before him, forgave him his trespasses against God, and him, and the world, and once more set him free.

The unthrifty Heir of Linne wept with joy at the happy tidings; and whenas he had privily resorted to the lodge, and found the treasure, as his father had truly set out, to his infinite pleasure and solace, then he filled certain bags therewith, and made all speed to gain the house of John o' the Scales.

He laid his bags in a corner, saying forsooth to the serving-men that they held bread given of charitable folk to his asking, and went into the hall, where three lords sat at a board in a row, and the middle one was John o' the Scales, for he was lord of Linne, and the lady of Linne, his wife, sat hard by.

Then spake the Heir of Linne to her, praying her of her courtesy that she would bestow upon him one penny, for that he was exceeding poor.

But the dame answered and said: "Christ's curse light on my head, if I give thee ought, as thou art an unthrifty loon."

Then a good fellow, that sat near John o' the Scales, "Have thou here," quoth he, "thou Heir of Linne. I will lend thee forty pence, for that thou wast in thy time kind of heart, and other forty to them, if need be."

The Heir of Linne gave him great thanks, and waxed wroth with John o' the Scales, for that, seeing he had gotten his land so good cheap, he would not even an alms-penny afford unto him in his necessity.

Said John o' the Scales: "Certes, a fair price I paid thee for thy land, and thou shalt have it back better cheap by an hundred pound, an' thou wilt."

John o' the Scales wist not of the matter that has been said of the chests of gold and silver, which the careful father of the Heir of Linne had put away to be a saving grace in the hour of extremity, and he deemed that he might safely challenge him to the bargain.

But the Heir of Linne drew from his pouch a God's penny and cried with a loud voice, "I hold you to record, lords." And he presently fetched the bags, and lo! they were filled, in place of bread, with the red gold; and he counted out the pieces on the board.

He counted the pieces on the board, and never a piece was wanting; and he said: "The gold is thine, the land is mine; and I am once more the lord of Linne."

"Have you here, you good fellow, that lately lent me forty pence: lo! I give you forty pounds therefore, and make you keeper of my forests and my chaces."

Quoth John o' the Scales his wife: "Alas! this is a shrewd turn. Yesterday I was the lady of Linne. To-day I am but Joan o' the Scales."

Quoth the lord of Linne: "If ever again I put my land in jeopardy, Christ's curse light on my head!"

ROSWAL AND LILIAN.

[*This is a story of Italian, or at least foreign, origin, which first presents itself in a Scotish garb at a period long posterior to that to which it appertains by its costume and character. The close and cordial relations, which subsisted between Scotland and the Continent at an early date and down to the time of Mary Stuart, favoured the transmission of fiction and folk-lore thither from France and Italy. The author of the romance of "Sir Eger" opens the scene in Bealm or Beaum, down to much later times an important province of France, but never a separate kingdom.*

The story only exists at present in a late seventeenth century version (1663); but the wholesale destruction of ancient Scotish popular literature permits us to suspect that we have lost the prior editions, more especially as a production entitled the "Lord of Lorn," which is formed from it, was already current, even in England, in the reign of Elizabeth, and is included in Bishop Percy's folio MS., unless, of course, it should be the case that the altered tale preceded the original in order of publication in this country.

"Roswal and Lilian," however, most probably dates back to a period anterior to 1580, *when the* "Lord of Lorn" *was first licensed at Stationers'*

Hall, and, like many other favourite compositions, may have passed through a series of impressions without leaving a vestige behind; since these of 1663 *and* 1679 *seem to survive in solitary copies.*

It is curious that Field in his "Amends for Ladies," written in the reign of James I., employs a "Lord of Lorn" as a synonym for a prodigal, whereas that story offers in its present shape no ground for the allusion. The passage in the play may indicate the existence at one time of an early printed copy of the tale of the Heir of Linne, the Scotish prodigal—a character, by the way, sufficiently exceptional to merit commemoration—and Lorn *for* Linne *may be the dramatist's slip.*

The rifacimento *under the title of the " Lord of Lorn" in the Percy MS. is deplorably corrupt, and in every respect inferior to the Scotish text; and the black-letter copies in the Pepys and Roxburghe collections exhibit still further debasement and a still wider departure from the true legend.*

The incident of the horses and armour may have been borrowed from the romance of " Robert the Devil," in one of its varied forms; but there is the remarkable peculiarity in the present fiction, that the temporary possession of the chargers and trappings of the three knights confers on Roswal the gifts or qualifications of their true owners. This appears to be an unusual form of delegation.

The notion of the gray and green armour was perhaps suggested by the stories of "Sir Eger, Sir Grime, and Sir Grey-Steel," and "Sir Gawayne and the Green Knight."

On the whole, "Roswal and Lilian" may be pro-

*nounced an interesting little novel, and fairly
dramatic in its structure and plot.*]

I.

THERE was once in the realm of Naples a worthy
king, that was nevertheless somewhat distrustful and
overbearing in his conditions. Who by his queen
had an only son, called Roswal, a paragon of beauty
and valour.

Now this worthy king had in his council three
knights, and because they gainsaid his authority he
cast them into a deep dungeon beneath his palace,
there to be their lives during; and of that dungeon he kept the key by day and by night.

Young Roswal, who lay in a chamber over the
prison, heard the groans of these ill-fated men, and
it stirred him to compassion when he thought how
stern and hopeless a doom was theirs; and one
night, while his father the king slept, he came
privily in, and taking the key from beneath his
pillow, set free those three gallant knights, and
restored the key again to its place unmarked.

The gaoler marvelled when, in the morning, he
went to take his prisoners their scanty meal, and
found the dungeon empty; and when he had reported to the king this strange accident, the king
waxed exceeding wrath, and swore by the rood that
whoso had done that deed should die the death; yet,
inasmuch as none had had the key, as it seemed, all
held it to be some miracle whereby those three
knights were thus enlarged.

Till young Roswal came to the king his father,
and made open confession that it was he who had

perpetrated the act ; and thereupon, for that the
king was hard of heart, and brooked not at all that
insolency, the fair young prince was adjudged to
die, nor might the tears of his mother, nor a regard
for the youth of the guilty one, effect more than a
change from death to banishment.

Attended by the high steward of the kingdom,
and furnished with every royal appointment, he set
out for the court of the king of Beaune, to whom
his father gave him letters, making known who he
was, and praying him of his courtesy to entertain
him for a season.

But the steward, noting well that Roswal was
richly provided with money and jewels, and considering that they were both of years to answer to
the king's letters, thought within himself that he
might do well to despateh the prince on the way,
and whereas the king of Beaune knew not the heir
of Naples, counterfeit that unhappy boy in his
presence.

Nevertheless, in the event, he slew not Roswal,
whom he yet bound to secrecy, and stripped of all
that he had, his princely clothing, his jewels, his
money, and his letters, and left naked and hungry
by the wayside ; and he spurred his steed, and came
to the court of Beaune, where he was received with
all honour beseeming the letters that he bore in his
hand.

For the king of Beaune, when he saw how the
friendship of the king of Naples might be profitable
unto him, was mighty content at the visit of his son,
and joyfully assented to his suit, when the prince
that was indeed the false steward, sought after a

while the hand of Lilian, the king's daughter ; and when the contract of marriage was signed between the ambassadors of these two kings, the day was fixed for the solemnities, and a tournament was proclaimed in honour of the bride.

II.

Let us leave the false steward, and speak of young Roswal, whom he would have drowned in a brook, as he stooped to drink, in the journey from Naples, but desisted only because the youth sware upon his honour never to reveal the secret, and surrendered to the steward his treasure and letters, with all that he had.

He wandered he wist not where, when the false steward had gone, and came to a poor cottage, where a kind woman received him, and lent him food and shelter.   To whom, seeking his birth and name, he answered and said, " I come from a far country, and my name is *Disaware*."

The good wife, perceiving how debonnair he was, and how in feature and disposition he favoured her own son, sent him to the same school, and thought to rear them together as brethren ; and Roswal, that had been well nurtured, moved the schoolmaster to wonder, for that he knew more than he did, and his learning did not reach to the instruction of the strange youth in any science that the boy kenned not already well enough.

It came to pass that the high steward of Beaune, understanding these rare qualities, took Disaware for his page, and carried him to court, where the eye of Lilian the princess observed him; and in process of time, while the prince of Naples, that was truly the false steward, was already affianced to her, this royal maiden grew privily enamoured of the page, and less and less in conceit of him who was appointed in due time to be her spouse.

But all the while, who Disaware was, and whence he came, she knew not, nor would he break his vow to the wicked steward of his father the king. And as the time for the tournament approached, which was to endure three days, Disaware became melancholy and absorbed, and the princess urged him to make her privy to the cause of his discontent, and asked why he should not let his name stand among the jousters. But he resolved her nought, and as touching the tournament he was not expert in such exercises. The nearer it drew to the day he waxed the sadder, and on the morning of the tilting he rose with the dawn, and repaired to the forest with his dogs on hunting. For he could not bear the sorrow that his secret passion for Lilian the princess bred in his mind.

Yet he had no heart to follow the chace, and rode listlessly about, when he was suddenly accosted by a venerable figure in the likeness of a knight, who led by the bridle a white charger, carrying at the saddle-bow a suit of white armour.

He was the more amazed when the figure stood before him, and addressed him in these words: "Prince, don this harness, and mount this horse, and so clad resort to the tournament. At thy return thou wilt find me here. I will hunt the deer with thy hounds, and present unto thee the game."

Disaware, not presuming to question or disobey
so lofty a summons, armed himself, leaped into the
saddle, and entered the lists, where he overcame all
foes without breaking his own spear, and at last,
preparing to charge the prince of Naples, that was
the false steward, and seeing him motionless with
fear and astonishment, checked his steed in mid-
career, and vanished from sight.

The king of Beaune and all present were transported with wonder and admiration of the prowess of
the White Knight, and the king vowed that he would
make him an earl, an' he knew who he was. But
Disaware had returned to the forest, and unarmed
himself, and when they repaired to the palace, he
was already in the hall, laden with the fruits of the
chace.

III.

Lilian the princess was angry because Disaware,
in place of doing his enterprize for her honour in
the tournament, contented himself with the humbler
trophies of the forest ; and while she spake at large
of the valour of the White Knight, she besought and
enjoined him to attend the second day's tournament,
and signalise his valour for her sake. He bowed,
but gave that gentle lady no pledge ; and he mused
whether he should again meet with a like adventure
in the forest, and who the stranger could be that
had so befriended him, and called him by his princely
title. Nor did he deem him a mortal, but rather
some spirit of the woods.

A second knight, clad like the former, met Disaware on the following day, leading a gray horse,

charged with a suit of gray armour, and greeted him
in like manner as the first knight had done ; and the
prince of Naples, that was in verity the false steward,
not seeing the White Knight, rejoiced at his coming
triumph in the tilt. But the Gray Knight, chal-
lenging him, laid him senseless on the ground, and
then engaged all the others there present, and when
he had vanquished them by turn, disappeared as
before.

Lilian the princess was, among the rest, greatly
astonished by these feats of chivalry, yet she
imagined, when she viewed the Gray Knight, as he
fought in the lists, that he something resembled her
own Disaware. But when she hastened back to the
palace, Disaware had just returned from hunting,
and of all the doings in the tournament wist nought.

On the third day, not the White Knight nor the
Gray, but one mounted on a bay steed, clad in green
armour, with a red shield and a golden helmet,
defied all comers, and threw the false steward that
he was wounded nigh to death ; and when all was
done, he cast, as he rode past her place, a gold ring
into the lap of Lilian the princess, and so vanished.

Now, when he returned a third time to the forest
to restore his horse and armour, he was met, to his
great amazement and joy, by the three knights that
he had delivered from prison, and were the cause of
his exile from the court of his father the king ; and
they shewed him that, because he had so suffered for
their sakes, therefore they had done him this good
office, and would yet do more, to the intent that the
false steward might not fulfil his wedding with
Lilian the princess.

IV.

Now as the season for the nuptials approached, Lilian the princess had been filled with despair, and wist not what she should do; but she at length made confession to her father, the king of Beaune, that she loved not the prince of Naples, and that her heart was entirely set on Disaware, whom she believed to be fully as noble by his birth as the prince. Her tears and prayers were bootless, however; and that gentle lady was married in the church to the prince of Naples, who was the false steward; and after the celebration of the marriage, the bride and the bridegroom sat in the hall on the daïs, side by side, to receive the guests as they passed before them, and saluted them, to do them worship.

There was a great throng to wish them God-speed ere they departed; and among the others three strangers, magnificently clad, appeared, and did reverence to the king and to Lilian the princess, but the prince of Naples they marked not. Then the king demanded of them wherefore they marked not the prince, that was his daughter's wedded husband; and they answered and said that they perceived not the prince. At which answer the king and all that were there present wondered; but anon entered the hall Disaware, to whom the knights drew near and made obeisance, falling on their knees and kissing his hand.

This strange spectacle struck the assembly speechless. The false steward was persuaded that all his misdeeds and deceit were on the eve of discovery:

and in fact the three knights that had paid homage to their lawful prince proceeded to unfold the whole story, while Roswal, that kept no longer his feigned name, and yet had not broken his vow, acknowledged all his obligations to his benefactors.

The false steward was straightway hanged, and the true Roswal was united to Lilian the princess. The feast lasted twenty days, and the prince of Naples gave largess to the minstrels ere he and his dear lady, whom he had so hardly won, went their way back to Naples to his father's kingdom. He approved himself good lord to all those who had served him in adversity : the good wife and her son, and the schoolmaster, and the good steward, who promoted him to be his page. They were richly requited, and, as the story saith, the boy with whom he learned his book died a bishop.

After the death of his father and of the father of Lilian, the prince Roswal became king of Naples and Beaune ; and when God called him at length away, of his three sons, the eldest was king of Naples, the second king of Beaune, and the third pope of Rome ; and his two daughters married the king of France and the prince of Apulia.

THE BLIND BEGGAR OF BETHNAL GREEN.

[*We have ranged this famous tradition among those connected with foreign adventure, because the hero won his fame, and the story owes its interest in the climax, to the military achievements of the English in France. We are entitled to infer and believe that the narrative was in existence either as a prose chap-book or a ballad before* 1600, *when John Day and others produced a drama on the subject in three parts, but without using the text, as we at all events now possess it; nor is there any reference in the Stationers' Register to the publication of the work at an early date; so that the play was perhaps founded on oral hearsay, and the title conferred on it when it was put into print, long after its production, in preference to that of " Thomas Strowd," the name of the Norfolk yeoman, who is made quite as prominent a character in the performance as the Beggar himself.*

*In the play of " George à Green, the Pinner of Wakefield" (*1599), *the Earl of Kendal, who is made to aspire to the crown, bears the name of Henry Montfort.*

It is evident that we have this legend transmitted to us in a singularly corrupt and degraded state, and Bishop Percy and others have bestowed upon it a fair share of their cobbling ingenuity. The accepted accounts in prose and verse were probably founded on some old tradition of the mysterious preservation and survival of the son of Simon de Montfort after the battle of Evesham. But it is the work of some ballad-monger, who has supplied the deficiencies in the plot from his own not very opulent fancy; and we have of course no alternative but an acquiescence in the slender salvage of time, and in the popular view of the subject so far back as the reign of Elizabeth.

The prose chap-book seems to exist only in very late impressions, and differs in some respects from the metrical tale. It attempts to supply certain biographical details, which are elsewhere deficient, and more fully explains the origin of the wealth accumulated by the hero of the legend.

But it seems to be remarkable that of so romantic an episode we have received from earlier writers no credible record, and have to rely on a meagre outline in doggerel rhyme or prose.]

I.

In former days, when the rose of England eclipsed the lilies of France, and true English valour made that nation bow to us, among other brave gallants that went over to try their fortune was one Mont-fort, a person well descended, and who was not to be turned from his purpose either by the entreaties of friends or the tears of a kind and beautiful wife, so naturally was he inclined to war and so greedy of fame.

So, taking his lady, who would by no means stay

behind, and who accompanied him in man's attire, he, with many hundreds more, crossed to Calais, and engaged in all the battles and skirmishes that arose between the French and English, and was more than once saved from capture by the courage of his wife, till it chanced in a great fight that Montfort fell, and was left for dead among the slain.

But his wife, since he returned not in the evening to their home, sought him out on the field of battle, and there found him by the aid of the moon's light almost at the last gasp. Whom this noble lady raised gently up, and bore to a shepherd's cottage, where she dressed his wounds, and by administering cordials and by carefully tending him she brought him back to life, to his great amazement and her unspeakable joy.

Unhappily, through a blow which he had received, his eyesight was lost, and he was condemned to endure blindness during the whole remainder of his days. With such money as she had left, however, his wife took him back to England, where, after a perilous voyage, they arrived, and settled at Bethnal Green, which is beside London.

While Montfort was abroad in the wars of France his parents died, and his kindred had taken and wasted much of his patrimony; and because they deemed, as indeed they hoped, him dead, they looked coldly and shrewdly upon him when he sought alms at their hands. Whereupon Montfort, because he was blind, and could follow no craft, resolved to live by begging of charitable people, while his goodwife plied her spinning-wheel; and he awakened in the breasts of many well-disposed passengers a lively interest in the strange and stirring scenes that he had witnessed in France, and gat much money thereby. Yet none wist who he was nor whence descended ; and he was commonly called the Blind Beggar of Bethnal Green.

II.

This Montfort, in his rambles, shortly contracted acquaintance with others who pursued a like industry, and one day he came home, seeking his way with his staff, as he was wont, and told his wife that he had been bidden as a guest to a certain house in White-chapel, which was a beggars' hospital or home ; and when he went there, accompanied by the faithful partner of all his joys and sorrows, they were something at first abashed, for that all those present wore such gay clothes and made so merry. He, however, that of all the rest had specially bidden them stood forward, and made them both welcome, and prayed them to share their good cheer, which they were accustomed to make on that their yearly meeting ; and at their departure they chose Montfort to be one of them, and presented him with a dog and a bell, which he found ever after, so long as he exercised that calling, very serviceable to him in his travels.

His success in the begging trade waxed so great by reason of the greater curiosity that people entertained about his strange fortune, that he no longer remained content with frequenting Bethnal Green and White-chapel, but went up to London, where he never returned without plenty of coin in his pouch,

till he and his good wife exchanged a bed of straw
for one of down, and began to live more freely ; and
in due time it happened that God blessed them with
a daughter, whom they baptized under the name of
Elizabeth,

Montfort resolved, his employment as a beggar
notwithstanding, that their child should be educated
in all arts and accomplishments becoming her birth,
of which none yet knew the secret ; and pretty
Bessy, for so she grew to be called by virtue of her
beauty, gradually excelled in music, singing, dancing,
and all other matters all the virgins of that neighbourhood of what degree soever. Whose envy was
thereby moved toward her, that they mocked her
in the street, and asked what a beggar's child should
do with so much learning. But Bessy bore their
cruel taunts meekly, and only reproved them by
saying that, if they had been born as she was, they
would not have wished to be so evil intreated.

Albeit Montfort thus caused his daughter to be
instructed in all the sciences befitting a woman to
know, he did not refuse her suit when she fell on
her knees one day and begged his blessing and
leave to seek her fortune. Yet she had gone no
farther than Romford in Essex when, frequenting
an inn there to get refreshment, the mistress looked
kindly upon her, and hearing her history, and that
she was of honest parents, persuaded her to abide
with her, and take service, telling her that she
should be to her as a daughter rather than a servant.

III.

This accident brought unlooked for fruit, for a great multitude of persons resorted to that house, where Bessy the beggar's daughter lay, and certain courted her in the way of marriage. To all of whom she pleaded the meanness of her birth and the inequality of fortune. But in especial she was sought by four, to wit, her master's son, a London merchant, a gentleman of fair estate, and a knight; and they offered her rings and rich jewels to prevail upon her, which she refused, praying them of their courtesy to spare the blushes of an innocent maid.

This backwardness still further inflamed their desire to possess and enjoy her; and then she resolved, in order to make trial of their constancy, to enter upon a further discovery of her parentage.

So, when she had on a certain day asked those four to be present together to enable her to choose truly which she would have to her spouse, she spake as follows: " My parents, worthy sirs, live at Bethnal Green. My father is a beggar, who is led, for that he is blind, by a dog and a bell; and my mother plies her spinning-wheel. Without their consent cannot I wed no man."

These words struck the inn-keeper's son, the merchant, and the gentleman dumb; and they found cause to excuse themselves, leaving the maid alone with the knight. Who shewed her how the others had courted her for her beauty and youth, yet when they heard her low birth eschewed her, and proved untrue; while he, being possessed of a good fortune, loved her for her excellent qualities, and was ready straightway to make her the mistress of all that he owned.

Nevertheless, Bessy refused to accept his hand until such time as he had seen her parents, and obtained their agreement to the marriage. But she acquainted him with her favourable feeling toward him, whom from the beginning she had secretly preferred to all the rest.

IV.

It was accordingly agreed that Bessy should ride behind the knight to Bethnal Green ; but they had scarcely started on their way when the knight's uncle, with many of his friends, came to the inn to inquire for him, and, finding that he had departed with the beggar's daughter, pursued and overtook them hard by Montfort's little house on the Green.

The knight's uncle was loth that he should marry below his degree, and some of those that were with him coveted the hand of Bessy for themselves ; so that there was a sharp skirmish outside the house, which Montfort hearing, came to learn what it signified.

Then, when he understood that pretty Bessy was without, and that a knight had brought her thither to gain his consent to their marriage, he waxed wroth at the tumult which they raised at his door, and advancing toward the knight's uncle said to him so : " Sir, I cannot see you, for I am blind ; but I hear more than is customary among civil people, nor is my daughter so mean that she should be thus accosted and affronted on my own threshold.

A. L.   D D

Wherefore I pray you, sir, desist from your brawling, or I may seek you out with my staff. I have known the day when a taller fellow than you durst not rouse me. If your kinsmen or you do not hold my child a fit match for you, even let her alone. In beauty and good breeding she is not much wanting ; and, as for money, her father is ready to drop angels with any man for her. So mark me, sir."

The old beggar's speech confounded the knight's uncle, who nevertheless sent for his bag of gold that he had with him by his servant ; and when he gat it, out from under rags and old shoes fetched Montfort two coney-skins crammed with coins. Then they began to drop their money, angel for angel ; but the knight's uncle shortly yielded the palm to the beggar, for his store was spent, and Montfort had plenty left.

" I think you have the philosopher's stone, good sir," quoth the other, " or keep a familiar to bring you treasure from the Golden Mountains. But I withdraw my objection to the marriage of my nephew, and the sooner they go to church the better."

The knight's uncle was in truth afeard lest the knowledge of the beggar's riches should rob his kinsman of so great a prize, and the other suitors were mad enough to miss Bessy, as soon as they understood that she was to be wedded to the knight.

The old beggar spared no cost to make the ceremony sumptuous and becoming the dignity of the husband of his pretty Bessy ; and a rich feast was appointed, with music and dancing and all kinds of merriment ; and the bride was dressed in the choicest stuffs, and wore the most splendid jewels that could be bought against gold.

At the banquet the guests drank to the health and happiness of the knight and his lady; and while they were all assembled there, and merry over their cups, the old beggar rose from his seat, and craved the attention of as many as were present to what he had to tell them. Whereupon, amid a deep silence, he described to them his illustrious descent from that Simon de Montfort who had been one of the most powerful barons in England, his own exploits in the wars of France, his wonderful rescue from death on the field of battle, and his resort, when he came back to his own country, to a beggar's life at Bethnal Green.

When he sat down, after he had recounted these things, the company loudly applauded all that had fallen from him; and the knight and his friends were overjoyed to find that Bessy, as she had Simon de Montfort to her grandsire, not only surpassed her husband in fortune, but at least equalled him in birth.

WHITTINGTON.

(1350–1424.)

[*This tale is one of the series which every literature creates and possesses with the twofold object of
supplying the immediate demand for novelties, and
of providing historical personages of more or less
remote date and antecedents with a biography. The
most familiar example of this mode of treatment is
the romantic particulars which used to pass current
for incidents in the life of Shakespear, even after
critics had abandoned in despair the attempt to throw
much real light on his career. We cannot wonder
therefore that, in the case of a man who died in the
first half of the fifteenth century, and whose transactions were chiefly recorded in unpublished civic
muniments, we encounter a puzzling mosaic of myth
and truth, which on analysis is shown to contain a
very small residuum of trustworthy matter.*

*We may take it as established that Sir Richard
Whittington was the son of Sir William Whittington,
member of an ancient family in Gloucestershire, and
dame Joan his wife, and that he was born in London
in or about* 1350. *He married Alice, daughter of
Hugh Fitzwarren. In* 1379 *we find him contribut-
ing to a City loan, and ten years later giving surety
to the chamberlain for* £10 *toward a fund for the*

defence of London. He was successively common-councilman for Coleman Street, and alderman for Broad Street, Ward.

In 1393, *being then on the court of aldermen, he was chosen to be one of the sheriffs of London ; and at nearly the same time he became a member of the Mercers' Company, incorporated by Richard II. in the year just named, not improbably through his or his father's agency. By letters patent of June 8th,* 1397, *on the death of Adam Bamme in office, he was appointed by the king Lord Mayor of London* ad *interim, and at the ensuing Michaelmas was formally elected by the City for the next year. In* 1406 *and* 1419 *he again served the office, proceeding on the last occasion to Westminster to be approved and admitted by the Barons of the Exchequer. In* 1415 *he formed one of the civic procession which went on foot to Westminster to return thanks for the victory at Agincourt.*

In 1393 *Whittington was probably already a wealthy and influential man, and we have it on undoubted authority that he was patronised both by Richard II. (deposed in* 1399) *and his uncle Thomas of Woodstock, Duke of Gloucester, Lord High Constable of England (murdered in* 1397). *It was toward the close of his long and useful life that he formed the design of perpetuating his name by certain monumental works. In* 11 *Henry IV.* (1409–10) *we find him receiving the royal leave for the foundation in St. Michael's Paternoster in the Reóle or Royal, of his hospital or* Domus Dei *for thirteen poor men, who were to pray for his good estate and that of his family and friends ; and in the following year the corporation gave him the ground for his College. Stow, in one place, states that he began to build the library of the Greyfriars in 1421 at a cost of £400; but it seems to be doubtful whether he lived to complete all his grand projects of improvement and goodness. For he died in the beginning of the year 1423, his will being proved in March, and his four executors appear to have at all events finished the College, and to have paid for the repairs of St. Bartholomew's Hospital and Guildhall. It was in his last mayoralty that he reopened Ludgate as a debtors' prison, in compassionate regard for reputable citizens, whose health was endangered by the noisome state of Newgate; and where the old historian of London speaks of him having built Newgate, we are surely to understand its restoration or reconstruction on an improved model.*

Whittington was buried in the church of St. John the Baptist, or St. John upon Walbrook, and his remains were twice disturbed: first, for the sake of ascertaining whether some great treasure was not originally deposited in his tomb; and, secondly, to encase the bones in a more secure and becoming manner.

The professional occupation of Whittington as a mercer, perhaps in succession to his father, was almost unquestionably the source of his manifest opulence; and it has been suggested that the cat story, which was in existence before his time, arose from an imperfect apprehension of the import of the word achat *or* acat, *the term then commonly employed in French for the sale of merchandize or mercantile transactions. The mere circumstance that Whit-*

tington's father was a knight bespeaks him a person of some consideration and standing, and the reference to Richard II. and the Duke of Gloucester in connexion with the younger Whittington's benefactions may shew that the family rendered financial assistance to the Crown, and obtained some equivalent.

But it must strike any one, who reflects for an instant, as a strange caprice of fortune that in the commonly accepted accounts of Whittington we hear of many things which he never did, with an altogether false conception of his origin, and, granted the premises that he rose from a very low station to power and riches, are left very imperfectly informed of his philanthropic munificence and exemplary nobility of character. In him the Gild of Mercers had and have their most illustrious member and one of the most important contributors to their aggrandisement.

The earliest allusion to Whittington in our literature appears to be a story of a dream which he had after the foundation of his college, and which is preserved in a jest-book of 1526. It is not worth repeating, and down to the reign of Elizabeth, when Stow published his Survey and Annals, nothing beyond a vague legendary impression of the man prevailed. Stow explicitly refers to the conditions attendant on admission into the almshouses, and Heywood the dramatist, about the same time, in the "First Part of Queen Elizabeth's Troubles (1605)," repeats Stow's account almost in so many words. Yet in the face of this evidence a play was produced, in which the anonymous author founded his plot on Whittington's low birth and great fortune, and down to the present instant the favourite notion is that which is fostered by the chap-book and the pantomime. The striking antithesis was not to be lightly surrendered.

Let us see that Whittington constitutes a rare type of legend. We can understand the super-structure or incrustation of fable on the genuine histories, such as they may be, of the gods and heroes of antiquity, of prehistoric kings, of great warriors in the age of chivalry, of early navigators and explorers, of students of literature and science in illiterate and unscientific times, and of enemies of the Church in various ways; but here we are confronted with a sober London merchant of the Plantagenet period, for the leading events of whose beneficent life we have fairly reliable data, and whose memory is preserved in the popular mind by a nursery tale, barely entitled to serious discussion. It was the usual incidence of Eastern romance to accomplish results by a coup de main; *it suited the dreamy, despotic, and inert Oriental temperament. The Arabian inventor would not have succeeded so well if he had depicted fortunes acquired by life-long industry; and even we in the West cherish this sort of imaginative illusion, when it is brought home to us, when it is affiliated on a veritable alderman and mayor of London, on some actual and breathing merchant-prince, a practical man of business, a bene-factor of his species. He must owe all that he had and was to wedges of Barbary gold, earned for him by a cat!*

The chap-book to which we have above referred, and which has been employed in the following account, adopts the view of the hero already laid before the

*public in a play no longer known, although the writer
quotes Fabian, Harding, and Stow, and, in fact, pads
his little book freely with matter not directly relevant
to Whittington from the annalists of London.   At
the same time Heywood, in a drama printed in 1605,
and acted earlier, repudiates the fiction as to Whittington's origin, and follows Stow.*

*Every family must have a beginning.   There is a
possibility that we have to go a generation back in
quest of the poor boy who attained riches and spurs
by his commercial enterprize, and that it was really
Sir William Whittington whose birth was humble,
while it does not follow that the cat legend might
appertain to him any more than to his son, the
Whittington of history.   The confusion between him
and his father is rendered more plausible by the
absence of the name of the latter in any list of civic
officers and proceedings.   He may have been merely
a prosperous, self-raised merchant.]*

I.

RICHARD WHITTINGTON was so obscurely bred that
he could scarce say who his parents were; and
being well-nigh starved in the country, it appears
that he came up to London, where he expected to
meet with greater charity.

He was ashamed to beg, and the thought of
stealing he abhorred; and during two days he
wandered about the streets, gazing on the shops,
with next to nought to eat.

At length he waxed so faint, that he seated
himself on a bench beside a merchant's gateway in

Leadenhall Street, and had not rested there long when the merchant himself, going forth for his occasions into the city, looked on him, and, not knowing his hard case, demanded why he loitered there sooner than busy himself with earning his living in some lawful vocation ; and he threatened him with the stocks or the whipping-post.

But Whittington made legs to his worship, and shewed how it stood with him, saying that there was no employment, how mean and poor soever, that he would not take, if it should offer. The merchant, thereupon eyeing him more favourably, called to one of his servants, and desired him to give the youth victual such as the house afforded, and on his return he would have further speech with him.   And the servant did so.

While the merchant, then, was absent at the exchange in Lombard Street, Whittington sat by the fire in the kitchen to warm himself (for it was the winter season), and plenty of good food being presently brought, he fed like a farmer, and the colour returned into his cheeks ; so that when the merchant's daughter, learning that a new visitor had arrived, came into the place where he was, she was greatly taken by his fair looks and by his honest answers to the questions she put to him concerning the country whence he had travelled up.

The dinner hour arrived, and Master Fitzwarren (for this was the merchant's name) brought home one or two friends to partake of his good cheer ; and the servants' table was also set out, at which Whittington was prayed to sit, albeit he had so newly broken his fast ; for all liked his company well, some being pleased with his country speech, and others entertained by his simplicity.

II.

Now when Master Fitzwarren's guests had departed, and he and his daughter remained alone, she commended his charity in that he had befriended the poor fellow that now sat in the kitchen. To whom : "God-a-mercy ! daughter," quoth he, "right glad am I that thou hast remembered me thereof : for I commanded my servants to care for him, and I marvel if they have so done."

His daughter answered and said : "Father, I even bad them let him stay dinner, nor dismiss him, till you could have conference with him."

Master Fitzwarren rose, and with his daughter passed into the hall, where they called Whittington to them. Whose address was so lowly and modest, that he enlisted in his favour that gentle lady, the merchant's daughter ; and in the end he was admitted into the household to do what labour was enjoined to him, and to have bed and board, and clothing.

Wages he had as yet none ; yet with a penny, that some kind man gave him for a service, he bought a young cat, which he made his companion ; and it had the leaving of his plate, and slept in the same garret with its master.

The merchant was accustomed from time to time to adventure ships upon the sea to distant lands with merchandize and goods ; and it entered into his practice (for he was a generous man) to suffer all his household and servants to put in somewhat ;

and now it was the case that a ship was in course of fitting out for a long voyage, and all had license to join to their power.

Only Whittington, albeit Master Fitzwarren gave him leave, had nought to send ; and when his kind mistress, the merchant's daughter, made offer to lend him money out of her purse, her father replied, saying that each must give out of his own proper chattels. So he prayed Whittington to consider well if he had anything his very own which he might put to hazard, for the *Unicorn* was lying at Blackwall, and was ready to set sail.

Whittington could only offer his cat, and loth enough he was to part with so dear a playmate ; yet, because he was urged, he let it go, and right glad the captain was of it, for it destroyed the rats and mice wherewith the ship abounded, and which damaged the cargo and other commodities.

III.

Meanwhile, it happened that Whittington and the kitchenmaid at Master Fitzwarren's proved no good friends, and she so evil-intreated him, because he was too honest to plunder, that at last he could bear his life no longer, and, gathering up the few clothes he had, ran away. He ran toward Bun-Hill, and it being All Hallows' Day, the bells of Bow Church began to ring, and they were, as it seemed to him, tuned to this ditty :

> " Turn again, Whittington,
> Lord Mayor of London :
> Turn again, Whittington,
> Lord Mayor of London ! "

This made a deep impression on his mind, and because it was so early, that he might return ere the family had risen, he resolved to go back, and found everything as he had left it, and none cognizant of his departure and flight.

Let us leave Whittington, who grew to be beloved of all, save the shrewd kitchen-wench, and speak of what befell the *Unicorn*, which, driven by contrary winds, was enforced to land on the shores of Barbary, where no Englishman had ever traded before ; and the Moors, when they perceived such an unwonted sight, hastened down in great numbers, and bought all the rich goods which Master Fitzwarren had despatched by his factor ; and the king of that country, when he understood the matter, sent for the Englishmen, and likewise purchased from them, and bad them to a great feast.

The custom was among this people, which were not Christians, but heathens, worshipping Mahomet, to sit at meat, not round a table as our use is, but on a carpet, like tailors on a shop-board ; and when the viands were spread, and all were prepared to partake of the good cheer, a swarm of rats and mice settled upon the dishes and consumed everything, to the meat on the trenchers of the king and the queen.

This spectacle annoyed the Englishmen, and the king to their asking replied that he would gladly give half the revenues of his dominion, if he might be quit of this terrible visitation, since he could not lay down his head on his pillow at night, unless a watch were set to guard him from destruction.

The factor thereupon made known to the king

that, it being so, they had a strange beast on board their ship which would speedily rid the kingdom of this plague ; and his grace said that he would lade the vessel with gold, silver, and pearls to have so rare a treasure. The Englishmen doubted if they might spare the beast from the ship, for that, while they slept, it kept the vermin from their merchandize and their diet.

All the more the king desired to see and possess such a blessing ; and at last the Englishmen went and fetched the cat, which, when the dishes that had been devoured were renewed, and the rats and mice again made their entrance, no sooner shewed itself, and seized on such as were nighest, but they all fled, and were seen no more.

Greatly the king and the nobility rejoiced when they had witnessed this sport, and vowed that the hunting of the lion was not comparable with it ; and because the cat looked to have kittens, which would in short time people the whole realm, the king made it so, that the price of the cat by far exceeded all the other lading of the ship.

When they had set sail from Barbary, and safely arrived at Blackwall once again, Master Fitzwarren, when he learned what fortune poor Whittington had met withal, sent for him when he was scouring the pots in the kitchen ; and whereas he at first excused himself, saying that his shoes were soiled, and the floor of the parlour but newly rubbed, to the repeated calls of the merchant he in the end answered, and presented himself before Master Fitzwarren, with whom were his daughter, the factor of the ship, and her pilot.

Whereupon to Whittington making humble obeisance as before, the good merchant spake graciously and heartily, saluting him by the title of Master Whittington ; and he caused chairs to be brought, and placed Master Whittington by his side. But he, moved by this strange exaltation, wept, and asked the meaning thereof. To whom his master replied, that he was now a better and richer man than himself, and exhibited to him the prodigious wealth that he had gotten through his cat in such unlooked for sort.

IV.

Master Whittington bestowed of his exceeding great substance on the factor, and all others that had shown him courtesy ; and when he was sumptuously clothed, and went in all things like a gentleman, the merchant's daughter, that before had pitied him, began to cast an eye upon him, as upon one whom she would fain have for a suitor, and to her father's singular content, who designed a match betwixt these two.

Now it was not long ere Master Whittington sought that lady, his kind mistress when he was poor and hungry, in marriage ; and Master Fitzwarren spared no cost at the wedding, whereto were bidden the lord mayor and aldermen, and all the chief merchants of the city of London, and shortly after he was pricked for sheriff, and acquitted himself in that office with infinite credit.

At length, that the words which the bells of Bow Church had rung out might be fulfilled, in the one and twentieth year of king Richard the Second,

Master Whittington was chosen mayor, and was knighted by the king's grace. During the term of whose mayoralty there arose great discord and trouble in England, and grievous pride and riotous excess in living by reason, as it was deemed, of the singular growth of commerce with foreign countries through Sir Richard Whittington and other merchants his very friends encouraging strange new fashions and vain wantonness in diet.

Which Sir Richard Whittington was four times mayor of London, and as in his life he founded divers noble charities in remembrance of the gratitude that he owed to Almighty God for having raised him, so mean a creature, to so great a fortune and dignity, so his executors by his ordinance after his death continued that good work for the souls' health of the said Sir Richard and dame Alice his wife.

THE PINNER OF WAKEFIELD.

[*The present is a north-country story, and seems
to have a certain measure of support from tradition,
though the exact period when the hero flourished is
not at present to be ascertained. We find the subject
popular enough to induce an Elizabethan theatrical
manager to accept and produce a play embodying the
tale, and this performance was repeatedly placed
upon the stage about 1594. The drama was printed
in 1599, and was probably founded in part on the
prose fiction, of which numerous editions must have
appeared prior to the date of any now extant; but at
the same time, as a comparison will establish, the
playwright has by no means implicitly followed the
thread of the narrative, as here given, and even
places the events in the reign of one of the Edwards.*

*There is almost to a certainty no authority or pre-
tence whatever for assigning the Pinner or Pound-
Keeper of Wakefield to the same epoch as Robin
Hood. The two celebrities were perhaps fellow
townsmen, but doubtless at a considerable interval,
and the social grade of Robin and his political par-
tizanship have conferred on him a more catholic and
enduring fame than that of the jolly Pinder, who,
reduced to his historical dimensions, was little more
than a lusty Yorkshire worthy of the fifteenth or*

sixteenth century, wholly irresponsible for many of the achievements with which he is credited by his biographers and the playwright.

The " History of George à Green " is, we fear, no more than an entertaining medley, or hotch-potch, in which chronology and truth are pitilessly immolated at the shrine of the book-vending Moloch. We have to resign ourselves to the task of presenting the series of adventures much as they are related, but with a four-lined caution to all whom it may concern that they must take the account for what it is worth, its uncritical and heterogeneous character forming a common incidence of such compilations, when readers knew little of remote persons and events, and the literary fraternity was not much better informed.

The romance, besides being unfaithful to history, is so confused and inconsequential in its arrangement, that it has been found an unusually difficult and irksome task to throw the incidents into an intelligible form and order.

Perhaps, after all, its main curiosity may be as a sample of the facility with which, given a central figure, the remorseless author overturned all the unities for the momentary effect, just as "Ivanhoe" on the modern stage is an illiterate jumble of incongruous elements ; indeed the discursive story of the Pinder in its original shape is the prototype of our historical novel with its equal disregard of documents and matter of fact.]

I.

IN the days of King Henry the Second, when England was torn by intestine discord, and families were so divided against each other, that father and son, and brother and brother, were oftentimes opposed, there lived in the town of Wakefield one Geoffrey à Green, a rich farmer, that in the wars was adverse to the king, and lost his inheritance; and dying, left one only son of tender age, namely, George à Green.

This young fellow, because his father had forfeited to the king all his goods and lands, was brought up hardly, and save that in the parish school he learned to read and write, he was an indifferent scholar, and more studied the advancement of his bodily strength, which soon gained him renown among his equals and neighbours thereabout. More especially since he began by giving his schoolmaster, that brooked not his high spirit and insolency, a fall, which went nigh to cripple him; so that George left his lessons and broke up school.

For some time he lay idle, nor knew not what calling to choose to his best liking; and whereas a friend counselled him to resort to a famous astrologer that dwelled at Halifax, and for forty pence divined the future of every man, George sought his house. But for that this wise man was then busied with discovering who had done him an ill turn, and could not, George kept his money, holding him no seer that could not attend upon his own needs.

Nevertheless George, lacking employment, and growing in the love of all in that township, was shortly invited without any suit on his part to take the place of Pound-keeper or Pinder; and albeit there were many others who would have fain competed with him, all voices were for George by reason of his crying need of some livelihood and his excellent qualities.

But he desired that merit should decide the choice sooner than favour ; and when he proposed that all such as stood for the pindership should meet on Wakefield Green on a given day after evensong, and join in a match at quarterstaff, the prize to the winner being the office that lay vacant, all agreed ; and when the time came, George played the part of champion, and the rest were defendants.

The meeting on the green was to all comers : bakers, butchers, tinkers, every one ; and each challenge was given in its turn to the music of the bagpipes, and a throng of gentlefolks from far and near attended to see the sport.   As soon as George had laid one low, another appeared in his place, like Hercules and the hydra ; but when he had disposed of some twenty of them, and still appeared as fresh as a daisy and ready for more, the rest perceived the vanity of further trial, and by universal consent the prize was awarded to George.

This victory gained him a great name over all that country, and made many a fair damsel gaze upon him favourably that had been a witness to that evening's doings.   But in especial his prowess was marked by the paragon of beauty in the northern parts, Beatrice, the daughter of justice Grymes ; and the Pinder, that had long known her for a great lady, yet far above him in reach, espied her betwixt the bouts in the ring, and figured to himself that her smiles and her glances as she looked toward him, meant no harm.

II.

Now when God took to Himself the king of England, that was Henry the Second, and Richard the First, named Cœur-de-Lion, reigned in his room, this Richard, going to the Holy Land to defend the cross and sepulchre of Jesus Christ from the heathens, left his realm in charge of the Bishop of Ely. Whose covetousness and overbearing, together with the disloyalty of Prince John, the king's brother, bred sore discontent, insomuch that under the Earl of Kendal a host gathered itself together to defend the rights of the people.

This army consumed much provision and substance, and sent into the shires messengers to require subsidies in money and food; and one Mannering came into the northern parts, and namely to Wakefield, to solicit the bailiff and justices of that township to grant him under his commission, sealed with three seals, a contribution to the cause. He stood covered before the bench, as representing the Earl of Kendal; and when they had heard the nature of his suit, and hesitated to deny him or to grant him that he prayed, he waxed mighty insolent, and overawed the magistrates, so that they began to lean to yielding to him.

At this juncture the Pinder, stepping forth from the body of the court, where the justices sat, craved liberty to answer the earl's messenger in the behalf of his neighbours and townsmen; and when they had given him liberty, he at first demanded by what title Mannering stood covered in that presence, and when the messenger answered not, he plucked the bonnet from his head, and threw it to a distance.

Quoth Mannering : " How darest thou offer this violence to me, who come armed with such a commission ? "

The Pinder begged him to shew that to him. Which, the permission of the justices granted, he perused, and then, as though he would have kissed it in reverence, tore it, keeping only the three seals wherewith it was sealed. Mannering began to stamp and storm ; but George took him by the collar, and shook him, saying that he would soon cool his choleric blood ; whereupon pointing his dagger at the messenger's breast, he made him swallow the seals, one after the other, and then quaff a draught of ale to wash them well down. " For," cried the Pinder, "it shall never be said that a messenger was sent by such great personages to the town of Wakefield, and that none made him drink."

Mannering perceiving no remedy, and feeling the wax tickle his throat, drank supernaculum. "Now," said George, " commend me to thy master and the rest, and make known to them that the Pinder of Wakefield, albeit he has torn their commission, has yet sent them back their seals by their servant."

So he, departing in secret ire, went in quest of the Earl of Kendal, whom, with others, he found at the house of justice Grymes, and already incensed by the flout which the same Pinder had offered to a spy sent out to gain secret information how Sandon Castle might be brought into the possession of the rebels.

For George, happening to meet with this spy, that knew him not, shewed him how he was accustomed to sell corn to the garrison, and was well

known of them, and so agreed with the same for
a rich reward to convey him in a sack into the
castle, as he were a bushel of corn ; and in the
night-time he should leave his concealment, and
open the gates to the Earl of Kendal's men.   But
when the spy had entered the sack, the Pinder
made it fast with a strong cord, and cast him over
his shoulder, and took him, and hoisted him up on
the tree before the castle-green, where the Musgraves, who kept the castle for the king, might
easily see him, with the scroll on his breast setting
forth his treason and who put him there.

Which when Sir William Musgrave and his son
perceived from the walls of the castle, greatly raised
the Pinder in their conceit.

III.

Meanwhile, as George à Green grew more and
more famous throughout all the north country, the
fair Beatrice, justice Grymes' daughter, who had
been courted in vain by lords and knights, and had
had even the Earl of Kendal among the suitors for
her hand, was more and more enamoured of him,
and his exploits, with which the whole kingdom
began to ring, kindled in her breast a violent desire
to see him or to write to him ; and the Pinder, on
his part, waxed melancholy by reason of his passion
for that lady, and the thought of the great distance
between them in birth and fortune.   So, when it
came to pass that George sent a letter by his boy
to Beatrice, and she returned a gracious answer by
the same messenger, the Pinder was a joyful man
indeed.

Then when certain other letters had passed between these two lovers, and Beatrice was so straitly watched by her father, that she might not meet the Pinder, they devised a plot, whereby the Pinder's boy, whose name was Willy, was admitted to the chamber of Beatrice in the guise of a sempstress' maid, that had laces and the like to sell. Who, changing clothes with the lady, remained in the place, and braved her father's anger, when he should discover the cheat, while the other took flight, and tarried not till she came to the spot appointed for the meeting with George.

It happened about this time that Maid Marian, that was the Lord Fitzwalter's daughter, and sojourned with Robin Hood beneath the broad shade in king Richard's forest of Sherwood, grew pensive and dejected, and so strangely bare herself that Robin, who was in very truth the noble Robert, the banished Earl of Huntingdon, deemed it in his secret thought to be for that this fair may was importuned by Prince John, the king's own brother, to hearken to his love. But when he asked her, she said Nay, but that it was because the fame of George à Green for valour and Beatrice his paramour for beauty threatened to outshine theirs; and she had a sore longing that she might accompany him to Wakefield town, and challenge those two to a trial, so that it might be known and allowed of all which was the valianter, he Robin or George à Green, and the fairer, she Marian or George's Beatrice.

To whom Robin yielded compliance, and he, with Little John, Scathlock, and the Friar, set out accordingly, in company with Marian; and their other weapons those outlaws left behind, and carried only their quarter-staves on their necks, as the custom of the country was; and they drew not breath until they came to the cornfields that neighbour upon Wakefield, and crossed them, bearing down the corn. Whom the Pinder, that was abroad thereabout with his Beatrice, shortly noting, sharply accosted, as one who was privileged by his office to warn trespassers in the growing season. But who the strangers were, he yet knew not, for they had not their bows, nor wore their forest livery.

Beatrice intreated him not to be over-bold, since there were four to one; but George, seeing such wrong done, was not to be held back, and taking his staff from his shoulder, barred their way, demanding recompense. The strangers answered and said, that the satisfaction was for him to seek. " Marry, sirs, and so it shall be," quoth the Pinder; " and as you are true men, come not upon me all at a time."

It was a sorry spectacle for those two virgins to view, when the lusty Pinder engaged one by one Robin and his merry men. Scathlock and Little John he soon laid at his feet. The Friar approached, and poised his staff by way of entrance. " O," cried George, " I must refuse nothing to the Church," and placed him where his two comrades were.

Then began the fiercest part of the fray; for the Pinder and Robin set at each other like lions, and Marian made no doubt that George had at last found his match. But the Pinder proved too much

even for him ; and he had to beg him, after such a
bout as had rarely been witnessed in these parts, to
hold his hand, and then discovered who he was.

To whom the victorious Pinder courteously addressed himself, saying that, after king Richard, he
was the man whom he most honoured ; and he
craved pardon of Maid Marian, praying Beatrice
to do likewise ; and those two comely mays embraced and kissed each other, Marian declaring
Beatrice to be the glory of the northern parts.

IV.

While these events were taking place, king
Richard, having left the Holy Land, returned to his
own kingdom, and sorely grieved to learn what
tumults and rebellions and great abuses had been
committed during his absence.   But it was a mighty
solace to his grace to receive at the hands of the
Musgraves the arch-rebel Armstrong, and anon by
the hands of justice Grymes the Earl of Kendal,
Lord Bonville, and Sir Nicholas Mannering, who
were brought before him, and delivered as prisoners,
in the name of George à Green, that by stratagem
had newly taken the same.   And by cause that the
Earl of Kendal had been encouraged in his disloyalty by a prophecy that the king would one day
vail his bonnet to him in the city of London, Richard
uncovered himself before him in mockery thereof,
and said unto him, " My lord, you are welcome to
London."

The king's grace, hearing the fame of George à
Green so widely and loudly bruited, resolved, so

soon as his affairs afforded him leisure, to make a
progress into the north country with the Earl of
Leicester and with Musgrave, disguised as plain
yeomen ; and it chanced that they arrived at the good
town of Bradford on Trail-staff day, when the sturdy
shoemakers are licensed by ancient use to come out,
and make all comers vail their quarterstaves. Now,
when those three seeming yeomen carried their
staves on their necks, as not knowing the custom,
certain shoemakers rudely beat them to the ground ;
and to the yeomen demanding why this was done,
they replied that they had had the right time out
of mind, and that it was to them and their heirs for
ever.

Wherefore one of the three that was the king
axed them where was their patent. "We have
none," quoth they, "nor want it ; for staff-end-law
suffices us." And the yeomen, because they feared
discovery, trailed their staves, to avoid a fray. But
Robin Hood and Maid Marian, and George à Green
and Beatrice, and the rest, coming up, and the shoemakers summoning them in like fashion, that was
a different matter, for Robin and George and their
men set upon the shoemakers, and the whole town
was shortly astir ; but the shoemakers reckoned
without their host, and were fain to cry mercy, saying
that they felt it to be no dishonour or disparage-
ment to be beaten by such renowned men as Robin
and the Pinder.

Then followed the drinking and pledging of healths,
and the first was to good king Richard, and George
gave it, and Robin, as the next best man in the
company, pledged it ; and the bowl was then passed

round to the shoemakers. Only the three yeomen
that trailed their staves were excepted out of it, by
reason that they were, quoth George, unworthy to
drink to so brave a king. The second health was
to Robin, and the third was to have been to George,
when the three yeomen, casting aside their disguise,
stepped forward, and the Earl of Leicester craved
leave to let king Richard follow next in order.

Hereupon all fell on their knees; but the king
raised them by turn, and first to Robin he said:
" Rise, Robert Earl of Huntingdon. I restore thee
thy lands, wrongfully taken from thee by my brother
and my lieutenant the bishop of Ely, and bestow on
thee the hand of thy Matilda, the lord Fitzwalter's
daughter."

Next his grace called for George à Green, and
after that he had lustily commended his loyalty and
prowess, desired him to kneel, that he might make
him knight. But George humbly prayed that he
might be suffered to remain, as his father had been
before him, a yeoman; and then the king, assenting,
gave him in requital of his worthy services to the
crown of England the moiety of his royal right in
the good town of Kendal and all his title in chief
to the good town of Bradford, to stand, he and his
heirs, in the place of the king for ever.

Unto whom anon, as these passages were so
happily proceeding, came justice Grymes, to cast
himself at his prince's feet, and beg worthy punishment for him that had stolen his daughter, and left a
boy in her room. But when he understood what the
king's pleasure was in respect of George à Green,
the justice suffered himself to be persuaded, and to

offer no hinderance to the marriage of Beatrice his heiress to the Pinder of Wakefield, whom Richard of the Lion Heart had so enriched, that he might forsake his office, and who had generously refused to be higher in dignity than his father Geoffrey à Green, albeit in wealth and in authority he became by royal bounty one of the greatest lords in his own country.

THOMAS HICKATHRIFT.

[*This tale appears to be destitute of any hidden moral, and, so far as is at present discoverable, is of no great antiquity, an edition of the seventeenth century being the earliest which has been seen, and no references to it occurring in earlier books. It is certainly a piece of pleasant melodramatic extravagance, of which the gentle reader is invited to credit just as much as he thinks fit. The narrative opens by laying the adventures in a fairly remote era, and preserves an unvarying uniformity in bringing Tom triumphant out of every exploit. The hint for this kind of romantic hyberbole came to us from Germany through French channels, the language and literature of the Fatherland being very sparingly studied and understood in England down to comparatively recent days.*

All these narrations of prodigious bodily prowess appear to be recollections, as it were, of the myth of the Grecian Heracles. They had become common and popular in early foreign literature, and had grown to the pitch of burlesque extravagance when Cervantes ridiculed them in his "Quixote." "Hickathrift" is a product more germane to the British soil.

The incident toward the close, where the giant lands in England, mounted on a dragon, and with a

*retinue of bears and lions, reads like some confused
or figurative account of an early invasion defeated
and crushed. The details are too scanty to enable
us to judge; but the localization of the tale in the
Fen country may render it worth mentioning that
that was one of the last Saxon strongholds after
the Norman Conquest, and forms the theatre of
many of the daring exploits of Hereward the son of
Leofric and Godiva.*

*Of course the selection of a scene or site in these
cases is apt to be arbitrary. Even the legend of Jack
the Giant-killer, which is usually associated with
Cornwall, is made in the earliest known copy a
north-country story, carrying, perhaps, in either con-
tingency the political and social moral which the
present writer has pointed out in his " Studies in
Jocular Literature."]*

I.

IN the reign of William the Conqueror there lived
in the Isle of Ely, in Cambridgeshire, an honest
labourer, named Thomas Hickathrift. He was a
stout fellow, and could in a day do the work of two
ordinary men.

As he had an only son, he called him after himself, and sent him to school. But Tom would learn
nothing. God called the old man aside, and his
widow tried hard to maintain her boy ; but his chief
delight was to sit in the chimney-corner, and he ate
as much as five grown up men. At ten years old
he was six feet high, and three feet across, with a
hand like a shoulder of mutton, and everything else
proportionable.

Tom's mother, being so poor, begged of a rich farmer, her near neighbour, a truss of straw, to help her somewhat in her housekeeping, and when the farmer said she might take what she would, she, returning home, begged her son to fetch it, since she had leave gotten. But he said to her nay, unless she first should borrow him a cart rope. Which to humour him she accordingly did.

He thereupon repaired to the farm, and found the farmer and two men threshing. The farmer bad him help himself.

Tom laid down the rope, and began to pile up the straw upon it, till he had got together by computation about 2,000 lbs. weight; and they jeered him which saw him so do, and said what a fool was he, whereas he could not carry the tithe thereof home. But Tom tied up the straw, and threw it over his shoulder as if it had been an hundredweight, to the great admiration of all.

Now, as his singular strength began to be known, and his mother was a poor woman, every one declared it to be a shame that he should stay idle at home when there was plenty for such a hand to do; and Tom was sought by all around by reason of the speed with which he despatched the tasks that were appointed him. For when a man came to him, and asked him to bring a tree home for him, and Tom and four others went after it, his companions essayed to draw the tree into the cart by pulleys, and could not stir it; but Tom lifted the tree up, laid it on end, and put it into the cart.

"There," quoth he, "see what a man can do!"

"Marry!" they replied, "that is true enough."

And as they returned through the forest, they met a woodman, of whom Tom begged a stick to light his mother's fire; and when he had leave, he took a tree larger than that in the cart, and marched home with it on his shoulder faster than the six horses could bring the other.

Yet, albeit Tom was so strong, that his strength equalled that of twenty common men, he was very gentle and tractable, and loved young company; and he took pleasure in going to fairs and the like to see sports and diversions.

Upon a time he went to a wake, where many young men were met together, to wrestle, play with cudgels, throw the hammer, and other pastimes; and Tom watched those that threw the hammer a certain while, till he came forward, and asked if he might try his skill. Then he told them to stand aside, and he would see how far he could send it; whereat some mocked him, as he was not known for a player. But he raised it to feel the weight thereof, and then hurled it into a river five or six furlongs away, to their utter amazement.

He presently after joined the wrestlers; and though in very truth he knew nought of that science, he threw all by turn, some over his head, and others to a distance, yet as gently as he might; and at last none would enter the ring with him, deeming that he was some spirit.

II.

It happened that a brewer of Lynn, wanting a servant to carry beer to the Marsh and to Wisbeach, and hearing such a report of Tom, sent for him, and hired him, fitting him out with a new suit of clothes from top to toe.

Tom proved a good and faithful servant, and did more work in a day than any other in three; and the brewer shortly made him his chief helper, and trusted him to go alone with the beer-cart. But he warned him from the beginning which road he should take to Wisbeach, since a monstrous giant kept part of the Marsh in those days, and made the other road, albeit the shorter, exceeding perilous to travellers and other.

Tom, however, was in mighty good case with the plenty of food and strong ale that he gat from the brewer, and after a while he waxed impatient of the longer way, and privily resolved to go by the shorter at all hazards.

When he arrived at a certain point in the journey, he flang open a gate, which led through the Marsh in the neighbourhood of the giant's cave; and the giant, espying Tom mounted on his cart, cried out to him with a mighty great voice, like a lion, to know by what authority he came through his land, and he pointed to the row of heads that hung from the trees, saying that his should shortly hang higher than the rest.

But Tom defied him; and while this giant hastened to his cave to fetch his club, Tom turned his cart upside down, and gat ready the axle-tree and wheel for his sword and buckler.

The giant was astonished to see what Tom had done, and said to him that he had a twig which would make short work of his axle-tree and wheel, and him ; and indeed his club was as thick as a mill-post. But he had more than his match in Tom, who laid on him with his axle-tree till the giant, being fat and unwieldy, lost breath, and Tom brought him to the ground. Then, cutting off his head, he entered his cave, where he found large store of gold and silver, and so returned home.

His master greatly marvelled when he saw the giant's head and all the money, and the whole country was overjoyed to be quit of the giant ; so that by common consent Tom pulled down the monster's dwelling, and built himself a house on the same spot, with a park thereabout, and through the giant's treasure, which he kept, he became rich, and instead of being called Tom was known thenceforth as Master Hickathrift.

III.

When he had thus become a great man, and his fame had grown throughout the whole land, Master Hickathrift, as he was now named, did not leave altogether his old pursuits, but oftentimes diverted himself with merry passages and gallant exploits. At one time he met certain football players, and when they had given him liberty to try his strength, he kicked the ball so that none ever saw it more ; and at another, when four highwaymen, meeting him unattended, would have had his money, he slew of them two, making the rest fly, and took from them a mail wherein were two hundred pieces of gold.

Only once Master Hickathrift fortuned to meet with a man that made him stand, and it was a tinker of that country, who was a stout fellow, and at cudgel-play expert above measure ; and these two met, and challenged each the other ; and Master Hickathrift, because he had no weapon with him, took the bar of a gate hard by, and the tinker had his quarter-staff. But albeit Master Hickathrift stinted not of his blows, and even once smote his foe with such a mighty stroke that he reeled and fell, in the end he had to yield, and confess that the tinker had the best of it. Whom Master Hicka-thrift, in no wise bearing malice toward him, took home and kindly entertained ; and they were fast friends from that time forward.

Soon after a great rebellion arose in the Isle of Ely, wherein 2,000 persons or upward were actors, and the sheriff took refuge in the house of Master Hickathrift, praying him of his counsel and aid, whom he had long known for a valiant and loyal man; and Master Hickathrift undertook, in company with the tinker his brother (for so he called him), to do what he could. Accordingly these two set out, with the sheriff as their guide, and rode till they came where the rebels were assembled together.

Master Hickathrift demanded why they troubled the sheriff; and their answer was, that their will was their law, whereby they would be governed. To whom Master Hickathrift: "And these are our weapons, whereby you shall be destroyed." And he and the tinker laid about them with their clubs, till they had killed or put to flight the whole army of rioters. It was a world to see how they fought! The tinker smote off the head of a man with his club, that it flew fourteen yards, and killed the chief leader of the rising ; and Master Hickathrift, when he was tired of using his weapon, laid hold of a lusty, raw-boned miller, and hit with him right and left, to the general wonderment of beholders.

The great services of Master Hickathrift and the tinker were reported to the king, who sent for them, and in the presence of his nobility thanked them, saying that if he had an army of 20,000 such, he might enact deeds worthy of Alexander ; and he bad Master Hickathrift kneel, who rose incontinently Sir Thomas Hickathrift, while to Henry Nonsuch the tinker was awarded a pension of £40 a year.

IV.

His mother being now dead, Sir Thomas Hicka-thrift turned his thoughts to marriage, and wooed a rich young widow in Cambridge. It happened that a young spark in that city likewise affected her, and did all he could to outstrip his rival, till at last he met him by chance, and challenged him. Sir Thomas had no weapon, and the other with his sword counted on soon despatching him. But his adversary parried the first blow with his arm, and suddenly wheeling behind him, gave him such a kick as carried him up, as he had been a crow, to the roof of a thatched house by, and thence into a fish-pond, from which he was dragged by a shep-herd. Then this fellow hired ruffians to lie in ambush for him, and endeavoured to compass in many ways Sir Thomas's death ; but at length the marriage was celebrated with great pomp and rejoicing, and the king again sent for Sir Thomas, who went up to court with his bride, and was received with much honour. Whom, for that a monstrous giant, riding on a fiery dragon, and accompanied by fierce lions and bears, had landed in the Isle of Thanet, and threatened to destroy all his majesty's lieges there, his majesty made straightway governor of that island ; and it happened that Sir Thomas and his brother the tinker, whom he summoned to join him in this emergence, quickly rid the place of the said giant and all that came in his train, to the infinite pleasure and relief of all, seeing that he was the fearfullest that had ever been seen. His head was like the root of an oak tree, his hair hung down like snakes, his beard resembled rusty wire, and he had one eye in the middle of his forehead as big as a barber's basin.

When all these brave actions had been performed, and the Isle was free from danger, Sir Thomas besought the king that he might return home ; and he spent the remainder of his days with his lady in great content.

THE KING AND THE NORTHERN
MAN.

[*We have admitted this as the concluding item in
the series of anecdotes in which a royal personage is
made to play a prominent part, because it differs in
its character and structure, to some extent, from the
others, being the work of a professed and known
pamphleteer of the reigns of James I. and Charles I.,
Martin Parker, author of that celebrated ballad,
" When the King enjoys his Own again." Here it is
a north-country lawyer, who has robbed a young man
of his inheritance in Northumberland, and the latter
undertakes the journey up to London to procure redress. He finds his majesty, at length, at Windsor,
playing bowls in his shirt, obtains his suit, is feasted
by the courtiers and made drunk, and finally returns
with the royal letter enjoining the lawyer to pay him
£100. The production is probably a concocted myth;
but it points to what was doubtless a not unfrequent
abuse, and is entertainingly written.*]

THERE was a man who had had handed over to him
from his father in Northumberland, in a dale, a fair
estate in land. The old man kept in his time a
good house in the country, and staved the wolf from
the door; and it was the king's land which he held,

and twenty shillings a year he paid to our lord the king therefore.

In due course, then, the father died, and the eldest son succeeded to him, paying the same rent. A wife and bairns and an aged mother had he to keep by his labour; yet well enough he might have thriven withal, but a crafty lawyer, who collected the rents for our lord the king, and who had a farm just adjoining this one, cast a grudging eye on the poor man's estate, and thought within himself how he might compass his downfall.

So he went to this husbandman on a time, and said to him : " Thy lease has expired. The king wins no credit from such fellows as thee. Thou must depart. The world is before thee."

The poor man prayed him to be good master unto him, and to grant him a continuance of his lease, and he would give him forty shillings. But the crafty lawyer declared that not even forty pounds would satisfy him, for he must yield up his farm to him, and lie at his courtesy.

" I have a wife and bairns," said the poor man ; " I cannot do so. Thou seemest a good fellow. Leave me free in my land, and I will give thee five marks."

The lawyer refused to hearken unto the husbandman, and threatened to dispossess him and his from their holding; and the neighbours privily held counsel with the poor northern man, and spurred him on to laying his case before the king himself.

He was nearly distracted, and scarce knew what to do. But at last he asked his old mother's blessing on his knees, and took leave of his wife and bairns, and fetched out his bob-tailed dog, saying unto him, "And thou sall gang wi' me to the king." His jerkin was of gray, and his bonnet was blue; and he carried a good staff in his hand, and he and his bob-tailed dog forth went on their way.

Hardly a mile and a bit had he walked from the town when he met one of his neighbours, and begged of him how far it might be to the king's court, for thitherward, quoth he, he was bound, as fast as he could hie. The other said that he was sorry for him; it was a matter of nine or ten days' journey to the king.

"Alack!" cried the poor husbandman, "had I wist it had been so far to him, I would ne'er have gone out of the town, and had liever spent some silver at home."

They trudged along, he and his dog, and little had they to eat, and hard was their lodging. Many and many a day passed, and mile after mile was left behind, ere they spied the steeples of churches and the house-tops as thick together as could be.

"There is no cheap land hereabout," thought the husbandman.

But when he came unto London city, and inquired for the king, they told him that he was at Whitehall. So thither accordingly he repaired, and as he went along he was amazed at the fine dresses of the folks whom he met in the streets. "Good God!" he cried, "if a man had a thousand pound, he might come to the end of it here."

He went to a tavern and gat his supper, and then went to bed. But he lay so long the next morning, that the court had removed to Windsor.

" Ye ha' lain too long, man," said his host. "The court is gone to Windsor; it is farther to walk by twenty mile."

" Curses upon it!" exclaimed the countryman. " I should ha' known better. The king had wind of my being here, and has gone out of my way."

" Tush, tush!" said the landlord, "think not he fled for you. But make the best of your way to Windsor; the king will pay your charges."

So to Windsor he went, with his staff on his shoulder and his bob-tailed dog at his heel; and although the gates of the castle stood wide open, he laid on them with his staff till the whole place echoed with the blows.

A porter appeared, and asked him whether he was mad, and what he wanted.

" Why, I am a tenant of the king, and must speak with him," said the poor northern man.

" There are plenty here," answered him the porter, " who can deliver a message for thee."

" There is not a knave among ye to whom I will unbosom what I have to tell," quoth the other. " I were told, ere I left home, I should not get my suit for nought; here's a penny for thee."

" Thanks," said the porter; " I'll fetch a nobleman to thee, to hear what thou hast to say."

The porter told the nobleman that a clown was at the gate; no such strange fellow had been seen there this seven year, and he called them all knaves that the king kept, and was exceeding liberal in his rewards, for he had bestowed on him a whole single penny, if he might be let in.

The nobleman desired the porter to admit the

stranger; and when the porter returned he told the poor northern man to leave his staff behind the door, and to let his dog lie in the courtyard.

"A pretty cur thou hast brought with thee!" said the porter. "I'll warrant, if the king see him, he will want to keep him for himself."

"I'll be hanged," said the poor northern man, "if I go to the king without my staff and my dog; there may be fellows hanging about that, for lack of money, will pick my purse."

"Yea," replied the porter; "I reckon you should go well armed, for you do not know what may happen."

"Let him in with his dog and his staff," said a courtier advancing; and the stranger bobbed and ducked, and thought it might have been the king. "If ye be sir king," quoth he, "as I verily trow ye are, ye're the goodliest man that ever I see. So many jingle-jangles about a fellow's neck I never beheld in my days afore."

The courtier told him that he was not the king, though he had a fine coat, and the other said: "If ye be not he, help me to the speech of him, and I'll give ye a groat."

The courtier went to the king, and let him understand what kind of a man was outside and demanded audience of him, and dubbed all rogues or worse that were in the place; and the king desired that he should be admitted with his staff and dog, and when the game of bowls was over which the king was playing, he would hear what he had to say.

So the courtier fetched the poor northern man, who followed him with his staff in his hand, and his bob-tailed dog at his heel, through all the courts and rooms and ante-rooms, and he wondered why the king left them all empty instead of filling them with corn and hay, and he looked up to the painted ceilings, and stumbled over something, and fell sprawling on the ground.

At last they came within sight of the alley where the king and his friends were playing at bowls ; and the king had taken off his doublet, and was in his shirt, the weather was so hot.

"Lo," said the courtier, "the king is yonder, fellow ; he'll speak with thee anon."

"What!" said the stranger, "he in his shirt ? Why, he is an unthrift, that hath spent his money and pawned his coat ! I mislike this bowling, that hath undone our king. Beshrew me, if that fellow in yon gay clothes hath not won his coin and his doublet of him."

But when the courtier approached the king, he made obeisance to him, and the poor northern man then knew that he was indeed him whom he had sought from so far ; and when the king gave him leave, he shewed him the whole case.

"Where is your lease, man ?" asked the king.

"Here be it, sir," replied the poor farmer, "if you can read."

"Why, what if I cannot ?" returned our king.

"I have a son, seven year old, who can read it as fast as thou canst run on the highway."

The king took the lease, and when he had read it, then he said to the poor northern man : "I warrant thee, thou haddest not forfeited it, though thou hat felled five ash trees more."

"Ay, ay," quoth the other, "none of your warrants for me. He that is at me about this cares nought for your warrants or mine."

"He shall have an injunction," said the king, "to restrain him from troubling thee, fellow."

"What sort of a thing be that?" asked the stranger.

"Why," answered his grace, "it is a letter that I will cause to be written to him."

"O!" said the stranger, "keep it to yourself: I could ha' got one written a long way cheaper in my own country."

"It is an attachment," said our king, "till he pay thee a hundred pounds, good fellow; and thou canst call on all thy neighbours to take part with thee."

"I see that you are fond of writing," said the stranger.

"I see," said our king, smiling, "that thou art hard of belief."

"Well," said the poor northern man, "for thy pains, I give thee a shilling."

"I'll have none of thy shilling," said our king. But the fellow threw it, so that it fell inside his shirt, next to his skin.

"Beshrew thee!" said our king, "dost thou not see I am hot with bowling? Thy shilling strikes cold to me."

Then our king, when he wearied a little of this talk, sent for twenty pound, and said unto the poor northern man: "Here, fellow, is for thy charges up and down."

And the poor northern man took the gold wonderingly, thinking to himself, that if he had known the king had so much, he would have kept his shilling in his purse.

"Farewell, good fellow," said our king, then; "and see if the lawyer do not obey our command, when he has our letter delivered unto him."

The courtiers gave him a good dinner, and, taking him to the wine-cellar, made him drunk; and when he had come to himself, away he started on his journey home, staff in hand, his dog and he.

The lawyer met him in the street on the Monday morning after his return, and cried, "Well, you are a stranger indeed!" And then he told him where he had been, and the lawyer asked him why they could not have settled the dispute in a neighbourly way. So the poor northern man shewed him how he was no match for the like of him, nor were his neighbours; and he had got a letter from the king for him.

Now the king's letter was to command that the lawyer should be seized, and put into the stocks till he had paid the poor northern man one hundred pounds; and when the lawyer said that the letter was good, and that he would go home and fetch the money, the neighbours took him and bound him, and till the poor northern man was satisfied there he stayed. And the poor northern man was commended for his good courage; and he saw well, that the letter of our lord the king had more virtue than if he had got one written for him better cheap in his own country.

DESCRIPTIVE AND HUMOROUS
LEGENDS.

JOHN ADROYNS.

[We include with satisfaction this capital dramatic narrative, probably founded on an actual occurrence within the knowledge of the writer, and forming one of a series of tales belonging to the first quarter of the sixteenth century. The preservation of such interesting and illustrative relics, where they belong to the humorous class, and have no religious or political aspect, is as accidental as it is fortunate and important, since they shed a remarkable light on our social habits and employments, and render more possible a correct acquaintance with the conditions of our ancestors in former times. In foreign literature, and to some extent in English translations of continental stories, we find an abundance of material of this character; but there is a singular paucity of tales which, like the present and others which we have selected, are purely indigenous in their origin and costume. The conduct of the adventure in which John Adroyns is the foremost figure is managed with the same skill and judgment which mark other specimens of the same kind of composition about this period, and there must have been one or more persons of unusual literary ability concerned in producing such racy and permanently valuable relations, especially if we look at the low general level of popular writing during the Tudor era.

A. L.   449   G G

*We have elsewhere [1] furnished some grounds for
believing that Sir Thomas More and John Heywood
employed their pens in inditing some of the items in
the "Hundred Merry Tales" (1526), and that More
observed in such a case an advised incognito, as we
conclude that he did when the original impression
appeared without any name of the " Serjeant" (or
Tipstaff) " that would learn to be a friar."*

*" John Adroyns," " The Miller and the Tailor,"
" The Maltman of Colebrook," and certain others,
derive an enhanced value from the circumstance
that they are under no obligation to external sources,
but genuine homebred facetiæ, and moreover of a
high order of merit.   They also offer the interesting
consideration to us, that they are from their structure of a dramatic cast, and are not dissimilar from
those slight plots which constitute the ground-work
of Heywood's clever and diverting interludes.]*

IT fortuned that in a market town in the county of
Suffolk there was a stage play, in which one named
John Adroyns, who dwelled in another village two
miles thence, played the Devil ; and when the play
was over, this John Adroyns departed in the evening
from the town where the play had been acted to go
home to his own house.   But as he had brought no
change of dress with him, he had to walk to the
next village in the raiment which he had worn on
the stage ; and on the way he passed by a rabbit-
warren belonging to a gentleman of the village

---

[1] *Introduction to a Reprint of A Hundred Merry Tales*, 1526,
folio, 1887.

where he lived. At which very time it happened that the priest of a neighbouring church, with two or three other unthrifts, had brought with them a horse, a net, and a ferret, to catch rabbits ; and when the ferret had been loosed, and was in the earth, and the net covered the hole of the burrow, close by the path which John Adroyns had to take, the priest and his companions suddenly became aware of the said John attired in the Devil's apparel. Knowing that they were on an evil errand, and thinking it to be the Devil indeed, they all ran away. John, it being dark, perceived not the net, and stumbling over it fell down, so that he nearly brake his neck.

But when he had a little come to himself, he saw that it was a net to catch rabbits, and he guessed that they fled for fear of him ; and when he looked farther, he spied a horse, laden with coneys, tethered to a bush, and so he took the net, and leaping on the horse's back with the coneys hanging down on either side of him, rode to the house of the gentleman who owned the warren, counting on thanks for his service.

When he came to the place, he knocked at one of the gates, and one of the gentleman's servants asked who was there, and forthwith opened the gate ; and as soon as he set eyes on John in the devil's raiment, he was terrified, and put to the door again, going to his master, to whom he vowed that the devil was at the door, and would have admittance. The gentleman despatched a second man to see what it was ; and he, not daring to open the gate, demanded in a loud voice who was outside.

John Adroyns answered as loudly back : " Tell thy
master that I must needs have speech with him, ere
I go."

This second fellow, when he heard that answer,
likewise imagining that it was the Devil, returned
to his master, and assured him that it was the Devil
indeed there, and that he must speak with him
before he departed.   The gentleman began to grow
a little frightened, and called his steward, whom he
enjoined to bring him sure word who was at the
gate.

This steward, who was the wisest of the gentleman's servants, thinking that he would so best see
who was outside, came to the gate, and peeped
through the chinks here and there ; and he saw
that it was the Devil sitting, on a horse, with coneys
hanging down about him.   Then came he in great
haste and dread to his master, and said : " By God's
body, it is the Devil himself that is at the gate,
sitting upon a horse laden with souls ; and by likelihood he is only waiting for yours to be gone."

This gentleman, marvellously abashed, sent for
his chaplain, and said to him, " Let the holy candle
be lighted, and fetch holy water " ; and they all went
to the gate, and the chaplain said, " In the name
of the Father, the Son, and the Holy Ghost, I
command and charge thee to tell me wherefore thou
camest hither."

This John in the Devil's apparel, seeing them
conjure in such manner, said : " Nay, fear me not,
for I am a good Devil ; I am John Adroyns, your
neighbour in this village, that acted the Devil in the
play.   I bring your master a dozen or two of his

own coneys, with their horse and net that would have stolen them, whom I caused for fear to flee."

When they heard him thus speak, they knew his voice, and opened the gate and let him in; and there was a right good laugh over the whole matter.

THE MILLER AND THE TAILOR.

*[The subjoined story is from the same source as
" John Adroyns" and the " Maltman of Colebrook,"
and is at once more elaborate and more dramatic.
It is in our estimation one of the drollest and best-
sustained narrations of the kind in our language.
The plot is slightly involved, but it is managed and
developed with rare skill and felicity. The treatment of this and other narrations and pleasantries
in the " Hundred Merry Tales" (1526), tends to
corroborate the notion which we broached in 1887,
that Sir Thomas More had a share in compiling the
volume, which combines with unusual literary merit
a singular freedom from grossness, and was evidently
under the inspiration of some masculine intellect with
a precocious sense of humour and a descriptive faculty
at that time almost unique. Like the preceding
relation, the particulars here found were by no means
improbably derived from an actual fact, although
the writer doubtless permitted himself more or less
license in the way of romantic embellishment.]*

THERE was a certain rich farmer in a village, who
marvellously loved nuts, and planted trees of filberts
and other nuts in his orchard, which through his
whole life he cared for well ; and when he died
it appeared that his executors were to engage to

bury with him in the grave a bag of nuts under pain of losing their executorship. So these executors did as they were bidden.

It so happened that on the very night after the burial a miller in a white coat came to the dead man's garden to steal a bag of nuts; and as he went along he met with a tailor in a black coat, an unthrifty fellow, and discovered to him his scheme. The tailor confessed in his turn that that same night he planned stealing a sheep. It was determined between them that each should effect his purpose, and that they should meet, later on, in the church porch, the one who came first to tarry for the other.

The miller gathered his nuts, and was the first to reach the porch; and while he waited for the tailor, he sat down and cracked nuts. It being about nine o'clock, the sexton came to ring the curfew; and when he looked, and saw a man in the porch dressed in white and cracking nuts, he weened that it was the farmer risen from his grave, cracking the nuts that had been buried along with him, and sped home in all haste and told a cripple, who lived in the same house what he had beheld. This cripple, when he heard the sexton so speak, reproved him, and said that, were it in his power to go to the place, he would conjure the spirit. "By my faith, if thou art not afraid, I will carry thee on my back," said the sexton. And the sexton took the cripple on his back, and brought him to the churchyard; whereupon the miller in the porch, seeing one approach with something on his back, and weening it had been the tailor with the sheep, rose up, and came toward them, saying, " Is he fat ? Is he fat ? " The sexton, hearing these words, cast down the cripple, and said, " Fat or lean, take him as he is," and vanished ; and the cripple by miracle was made whole, and ran as fast as the sexton, or faster.

The miller, perceiving that there were two, and that one ran from the other, thought that one was the owner of the sheep and had espied the tailor stealing it ; and lest somebody might have seen him steal the nuts out of the orchard, he left the shells behind him, and hied home to his mill. Presently came the tailor with the sheep on his back to seek him, as it had been arranged ; and when he saw nought but nutshells, he concluded, as was indeed the truth, that the miller had gone home. So, throwing his sheep once more over his shoulder, he walked toward the mill.

Meanwhile the sexton, when he ran away, went not to his own house, but to the parish priest, to whom he shewed how the spirit of the dead man was seated in the church porch eating nuts ; and they both proceeded back together to the place, that the priest might conjure the spirit. The priest put on his stole and surplice, and took holy water with him ; and as they went along, the tailor with the white sheep on his back met them, and in the dusk, taking the priest in his white surplice to be the miller in his white coat, shouted to him, " By God ! I have him ! I have him ! " meaning the sheep which he had stolen.

But the priest, seeing the tailor all in black and a white thing on his shoulder, imagined it to be the devil bearing away the spirit of the man that had just been buried, and ran away at full speed, the sexton following at his heels. The tailor judged that the two had been following him to take him for stealing the sheep, and thought that the miller might have got into trouble for stealing the nuts. So he went on toward the mill, to see if he could be of any use to the miller, and to hear what news.

When he rapped at the mill-door, the miller called out, "Who is there?" The tailor answered and said, "By God! I have caught one of them, and made him sure, and tied him fast by the legs." Then the miller feared that the tailor had been taken and secured by the constable, and that he had now come to fetch him away for stealing the nuts; wherefore he ran out at a back-door as fast as ever he could. The tailor heard the door open, and going to the other side of the mill saw the miller posting off; and for a few moments he stood musing there with his sheep on his back.

The parish priest and the sexton, who had been hiding near the mill for fear of the spirit of the dead man, presently caught sight of the black tailor and the white sheep again, and fled in dismay, and the priest, not knowing the ground, leapt into a ditch, where the mud almost reached his chin. Then the tailor, perceiving that the miller ran one way and the sexton another, and that the priest cried for assistance, and supposing that it was the constable, who had come at last to arrest him, cast down the sheep, and also disappeared.

Thus each man suffered misfortune, because some had done what was wrong and others what was foolish, and all were afraid without cause ; and a good deal was owing to the time when it happened, for it was in the night that all this strange game of errors was played.

THE MALTMAN OF COLEBROOK.

[This is a story of the earlier part of the reign of Henry VIII., and is not improbably founded on truth. It is of remarkable interest, from the local descriptions of spots in the city of London and the suburbs, and from the skilful manner in which the incidents are worked out to their tragical climax. The foot of the modern passenger treads on the ground where the scenes of this dramatic adventure are laid, and his eye can identify the precise points where the successive stages of the tale occurred ; and yet how totally all is changed ! There is no lack of " beguilers" among us in the present day ; but altered conditions lead them to set about their business differently. When the unhappy individual depicted in this tradition flourished, there were comparatively few buildings between Cornhill and Knightsbridge, which constitute the two limits of the episode ; there was no police, no lights, no made roads. Within living recollection, the stream crossing the highway at what is now Albert Gate was still open ; it was that into which the maltman, in the final scene, jumps to rescue the supposed treasure, which a traveller has let fall a moment before his arrival, and which proves to be a bag of stones. On the other hand, the passages from one thoroughfare to another in the city which favoured the deception with the capons remain to this

*hour a familiar feature in the same neighbourhood,
if they are not even known by the same names.*]

A CERTAIN maltman of Colebrook, who was a very
covetous fellow, and whose only pleasure was in
getting money, came on a time to London to sell
his malt, bringing with him four capons; and when
he had sold his malt, and put the money, which was
four or five pounds, into a little purse tied to his
coat, he went about the streets to sell his capons.

An artful adventurer, that was a dice-player and
a spendthrift, had watched the maltman, and had
devised a scheme by which he imagined that he
might cozen him either out of his capons or his
money; and so he came up to the maltman, as he
carried his capons about, and asked him how much
he would take for them. He told him the price of
these capons, and when the other knew the price
thereof, he bad him go with him to his master, and
he would see that he had money for the capons.
The maltman agreed to this; and when they reached
the Cardinal's Hat in Lombard Street, his companion took the capons from him, and prayed him
to wait at the door, while he entered, and shewed
his master the capons, and he would bring him the
money for them immediately. The man, when he
had thus got the capons, walked into the seeming
house, and passed out at the other end into Cornhill.

The maltman tarried there a good time, and at
length he inquired of one of the servants belonging to the Cardinal's Hat what had become of the
fellow who had borrowed the capons to shew to
his master.

" Marry," replied the tapster, " I cannot tell thee. There is neither master nor man in that house ; it is a common thoroughfare, and goeth into Cornhill. Be sure he has gone off with your capons."

The maltman, hearing these words, ran through the passage into Cornhill, and asked every one for a fellow in a tawny coat that bare capons in his hand. But no man could satisfy him where the fellow was who had taken his capons, and the maltman made his way back to his inn, sad at heart, intending to get his horse and return homeward.

Meanwhile, the fellow who had stolen the capons had changed his clothes, and donned a fur gown ; and coming to the maltman, who sat on horseback, preparing to depart, said to him : " My good man, I thought I heard thee inquire just now for one in a tawny coat that had stolen from thee four capons. If thou wilt bestow on me a quart of wine, I shall bring thee to a place where he sitteth drinking with others, and hath the capons in his hand."

The maltman, judging the newcomer to be an honest man, consented to pay for the wine, and accompanied him to the Dagger in Cheap. Then he said to the maltman : " Get down from thy horse, and go to the other end of this long passage, and there thou wilt see if it be not as I have told thee ; and I will hold thy horse till thou comest again."

The maltman, full of hope that he should regain his capons, dismounted and went in, leaving his horse with the fellow in the fur gown ; and as soon as he had gone, the other led the horse away to his own lodgings. But the folk inside the house, when the

maltman demanded of them where the fellow with
the capons was, knew nought of any such man ;
and so he returned to the door in search of his
horse.   But neither his horse nor the man in a fur
gown was to be seen.   Some told him that they had
noted such an one, and others had not cast eyes
on him ; but nobody could say which way he had
gone.   So he retraced his footsteps to his inn, more
downcast than he was before ; and his host counselled him that he should put no trust in any one in
London, and that the best thing for him to do was
to get home.   So, with a heavy heart, the maltman
bent his steps once more toward Colebrook.

The rogue, who had all this time hovered about
the inn, heard tell that the maltman was going back
to his dwelling place, and disguising himself like an
apprentice, and throwing over his shoulder a bag
full of stones, made all haste to Charing Cross,
where he waited for the maltman ; and when the
maltman came up, this apprentice accosted him,
seeking to know whither he was bound.

Quoth he, " For Colebrook."

" Marry," quoth the other, " right glad am I
thereof ; for I must go to Brentford, to carry to my
master the money I have in my bag, and I would
fain have company."

The maltman, having in his pouch the price of
his malt, was also well content, and so they journeyed together a while.

At last, the apprentice outwalked the other a
little, and as they approached Knightsbridge, he
laid down his burden on the parapet of the bridge,
and seated himself beside it, to wait for the malt-

man.   And when the maltman had almost come up
to him, he let his bag fall over the bridge into the
water, and starting up, cried out and said : " Alas !
I have let my bag drop into the water, and there
is forty pound therein.   If thou wilt wade into
the stream, and get it for me again, I shall give
thee twelve pence for thy labour."

This maltman, sorry for the apprentice's loss, and
well content to earn the twelve pence, plucked off
his coat, shirt, and hose, and waded into the water
in quest of the bag.   In the meantime, the apprentice snatched up the clothes, with the purse which
was tied to the coat, leaped over the hedge, and
ran as hard as he could toward Westminster.
When the maltman at last recovered the bag, which
had fallen into deep water, and came back to
the bridge, there was nor apprentice nor clothes.
He had lost his garments and his money ; and when
he opened the bag, and found therein nought but
stones, he became like a madman, and ran, naked
as he was, toward London, exclaiming : " Alas !
alas !   Help ! help ! or I shall be stolen.   For my
capons are stolen, my horse is stolen, my money
and clothes are stolen, and I shall be stolen myself."

And he ran about the streets of London naked,
crying, " I shall be stolen ! I shall be stolen ! "
And his reason forsook him, and he died miserably.

THE MILLER OF ABINGDON.

(*Fifteenth Century.*)

[*The miller has a sort of literature of his own.
Even before the time of Chaucer, the followers of this
trade were renowned in early fable and song for
their gallantry and roguery. The Miller of Trump-
ington, in the Reeve's Tale, is, of course, the best
known member of the fraternity, and our great poet
has done full justice to the subject and the character.
The scene of that story is still, or was not many years
ago, known as " The Old Mills " ; but the parent*
fabliau *was French.*

*The plot of the " Miller of Abingdon" is free and
droll enough—in truth, thoroughly Chaucerian, and
if some should deem it a little too much so, we shall
not be surprised.   But it is characteristic of the
period for which it was written, and affords a highly
pictorial and vivid insight into an English interior
of the class of person with which it deals ; and in
point of construction it betrays the workmanship of
no ordinary hand.   As in the case of a passage in
the " Squire of Low Degree," we must not enter too
nicely into the question of female discernment, where
the two scholars are accepted in lieu of Jenkyn and
the miller.*

*In the case of a transfer of scene for the nonce,
it may be immaterial to note that the miller in this*

story was doubtless the servant of the Abbot of Abingdon, to whose fraternity the mill and its appurtenances at that time belonged.]

In the town of Abingdon there formerly dwelled a widow, that had two sons. These young fellows went to school at Cambridge, which lay five miles distant ; little learning enough they gat, and all that they had to keep them at bed and board, and to clothe them withal, their poor mother gave, for other means of nurture had they none.

Seven years kept she these lads at school, and then she said to them, that the times were so hard and dear that she could do no more for them. Her sons bad her to be of good cheer, for, quoth they, we will go up and down the country, and make our suit to kind people, and all will go well. So they started on their travels, and throve so well, that they brought back to the good old woman, ere many days were over, a bushel or two of wheat. Full glad was she at this sight ; but they lost no time, and, borrowing a neighbour's horse, took it to the mill to be ground.

A jolly fellow was the miller of Abingdon, and he had a fair daughter, with a charming face and figure. Jenkyn, the town-clerk, loved her right well, did he.

Now, this miller was a shrewd man, and of every one's corn which came to him, the blame was not his if he did not take pretty heavy toll. The two poor scholars knew with what sort of a customer they had to deal, and arranged to watch him closely while their corn was being ground, in order that none might be lost ; and they even let him under-

A. L.   H H

stand that they could not afford to let any go astray, so precious to them it was.

The miller, who well comprehended what this their drift was, was at first rather perplexed, when he saw how wary the youths were, and wondered how he should circumvent them. A happy thought came into his head. He took his little son aside, and said to him so : " Boy, loose these fellows' horse privily, and lead him into our back-yard, ere the meal be ready. I will be even with them yet."

The little boy did as he was bidden, and when the sack was filled up one of the youngsters heaved it on his shoulders, and down they went, both of them, to lay it on the horse's neck, and so return home. But when they reached the door, and looked out, no horse was there.

" Alas ! alas !" they cried, "we are undone ; our horse has run away."

" By God !" exclaimed the miller, holding up his hands, " then see you him no more ; for some thief spied him out, and has made away with him."

One scholar said to his companion, " Let us go in search of him, you one way and I another."

But so afeard were they lest the miller should purloin some of their meal while they were away, that they tied the sack up tightly, and set a seal on it. When they had at last set out the miller laughed heartily to himself, and sware many a good oath, that if he might get none of their corn he would help himself to their meal.

His daughter came to the mill, to bring him his dinner, and he brake unto her the whole case. He related to her how two scholars had come on horseback from Abingdon to have a measure of corn ground, "and they gave me a hint," quoth he, "that they would not have me steal any of it."

The girl smiled.

" But, daughter," he continued, "fetch me a white sheet, prythee, and we will see what can be done."

So she did ; and they two placed the sheet on the floor, and shook the sack lustily over it, so that a good bit of the meal escaped through, and yet the sack was whole. They shook the sack, and beat it, till they had got a fair peck for their pains. The miller bad his daughter take up the sheet, and when she had, he held a bag, into which she emptied the loose flour.

"And now, daughter," he said, "go home with that to your mother, and tell her the news."

And so the maiden did.

Meanwhile the scholars, after wandering about the whole day, could get no intelligence of their horse, and they thought that the best thing to be done was to return to the mill, and carry the sack by turn to Abingdon as best they might.

The miller was sorely afflicted by the news which they brought, and was as greatly astonished as they were at the strange disappearance of the animal. They told him, however, that they thought the wisest course would be to put up for the night at his house, if he would kindly lodge them, and resume their search in the morning. " For," said they, " it will never do to shew ourselves in Abingdon without the horse."

" By God !" cried the miller, "that gladly will I, sirs, and you shall sup to your full content."

"We will pay you your price, whatever it be," they rejoined, somewhat proudly.

So, presently going to fetch the sack, where they had left it, one of them lifted it up to see how heavy it was.

"By St. John!" cried he, "that fellow has helped himself, I will wager a crown."

"Nay, nay," put in the other; "look, the sack is unbroken."

They said no more, and, carrying the sack between them, the scholars accompanied the miller to his house.

The miller's wife welcomed them, and his daughter too, and they asked them to sit round the fire, while the supper was being gotten ready. They soon set to their meal, and there was good ale, with which they wet their mouths well; but one of the brothers could not keep his eyes off the miller's daughter, and he privily trod on her foot, whereat she blushed, and turned her face from him away.

The supper over, says the miller to his daughter, "Get ready a bed for these scholars, and make it comfortable, that they may sleep till day." Turning to them, "And if so be you hear any noise in the night you may suppose it is my man, who is at work up town; when he comes in the dog will bark."

Now the person whom the miller meant was Jenkyn, the lover of his daughter; and they all slept in the same loft, and Jenkyn had one bed, and the miller and his wife a second, and the maiden her own, being the third. The two scholars lay in a room just adjoining, and they had to pass to it through the other; and as they passed their eyes fell on a cake, which the girl had made for Jenkyn, against the time he came. But little they guessed it was from their flour.

An accident, however, detained Jenkyn in town that night. He had to go to a fair by daybreak the next morning, and so he had no choice but to sleep at Abingdon.

The two brethren lay in bed, talking each to other in a whisper. One said to the other : " By God and by St. Michael ! I cannot settle to sleep from thinking of that girl. I should like ever so much to contrive some means of finding my way to her."

" O, that is nonsense," his brother said. " I am thinking of our horse, that we borrowed, and, by Jesus, that us so dearly bought ! I would we might come by him again."

But the other prayed him to lie still while he got up and tried the door. He opened it very quietly, and a low voice inside murmured, " Jenkyn, are you there ? "

" Yea, forsooth," rejoined the scholar, in an under-tone ; and in he went.

The room was dark, and he did not know his way about, and, instead of making for the bed, he bruised his shin against a form, which made him groan.

" Why, Jenkyn," said the voice again, "you ought to be able to manage better than that by this time." And by the sound he was guided to the right point, though he could not help laughing in his sleeve at the damsel's mistake.

When they had been together some little time, she told him all about the two scholars, who had come to her father's mill on the Monday morning with their çorn, and how the miller had treated their horse, in order to have his will of the meal, and how when the horse could not be found they arranged to sleep at the miller's, and were in the next room. The scholar, whom she took to be Jenkyn, laughed at the tale, and said, " That was cleverly managed, my darling." And so they fell asleep.

The miller's wife had occasion to rise, and although she was so familiar with the place, it was a spacious apartment where they all lay, and she at first went astray ; but presently she knew that she had found her husband's bed, because at the foot there was a child's cradle, and when her hand touched the cradle, she was sure that she was in the right track ; for she was not aware that the other scholar had artfully shifted the cradle while she still slept, and laid it by the side of his own couch. She lifted up the coverlid unsuspectingly, and lay down by the scholar. The miller was as sound as a rock.

The fellow that feigned himself to be Jenkyn knew better than to wait for daylight, and he said to the miller's daughter : " My dear, I must dress myself, for I have to attend a fair the very first thing in the morning."

" Buy me, sweeting," she whispered, " cloth for a new gown, and I will give you the money when I see you."

" By Jesus !" he replied, " I have but three shillings ; that will not be enough."

She put her hand out of bed, and gave him out of a money box thirty shillings, and the cake also, which, quoth she, she had made expressly for him. The scholar wished her good day ; for, as he told her, his master would expect him by cockcrow, and went away merrily with his money and his cake.

But he thought that, as he passed his brother's bed, he would let him understand what good fortune he had had ; and groping in the dark till he came to the one without the cradle, he roused the miller out of his sleep, and unfolded the whole story, even to the concealment of the horse in the mill-yard.

The miller started up, and there was a fine fray, in the course of which the miller had his head broken, and the scholar escaped. He rejoined his brother ; they hastened to the mill, recovered their horse, threw the sack of flour on his back, and made the best of their way home with their thirty shillings, their cake, and their meal. They gave back the horse to their neighbour, and repaired to Cambridge, by their mother's advice, to be out of the miller's way. But he kept his bed many a long day through the buffeting which he had got on that ever-to-be-remembered night, while his daughter found that she had given her love, her savings, and the cake to the wrong man.

The two scholars prospered well. They had their lodging and entertainment for nothing ; the flour of which the miller had cozened them was restored to them with interest ; and the money which was to buy the miller's daughter a new gown at the fair served to gladden the heart of the poor widow.

The saying goes that the miller was never allowed to forget how he had once been outwitted by two striplings from Cambridge.

THE FRIAR WHO TOLD THE THREE
CHILDREN'S FORTUNES.

[This short moral apologue is taken from an English story-book of 1526. *It occurs there with others of equal excellence, all belonging to a period just before the Reformation, when greater license was permissible in speaking and writing about the clergy, and when the science of medicine had developed into a profession for laymen, who already enjoyed the invidious distinction of counting in their ranks many incapable practitioners. The same criticism is applicable to the law, which has thus, as we perceive, been in possession of its unhappy notoriety since the days of Lyttelton, and before Francis Bacon was born. Nor does the friar in the tale spare his own order, that of the Mendicants presumably, unless we are to infer that it was a sly hit on the part of one brotherhood against another. The reference to the study of chiromancy, or palmistry, is rather early for English literature.]*

THERE was a friar who was in the habit of frequenting, in the exercise of his duties, a certain village where lived a very rich man, of whom he had never yet been able to get the value of a halfpenny. He thought, however, he would still go on trying his best; and it happened one day, as he came into the village, that he saw the man's wife standing at the door of their house. But when the woman perceived the friar coming, she ran in and told her children, if the friar inquired for her, to say she was not at home.

The friar, of course, had seen her going in, and suspected the cause; so he came up to the house, and asked the children if their mother was at home. They, as they had been bidden, answered, Nay. Still he stood there, and gazed first at one of the children, and then at another. Presently he beckoned the eldest to him, and asked him to let him see his hand. "Ah!" said he, loud enough for the mother to overhear him, "what sad things are in store for thee, poor child!" Then he looked at the palm of the second, and exclaimed, "Alas! this poor boy's future is still darker than his little brother's." Lastly, he took the hand of the youngest child, and let it fall from him again, saying, "And thy lot is the hardest of all!" And when he had uttered these words, he turned away to go.

But the mother, who had been listening at the back, rushed out, and implored him to stop, and not leave them so soon; and first of all she spread the table with her best fare, and invited him to help himself. When he had done, she begged he would explain to her what he meant just now by saying that all her children had gloomy prospects before them. He hesitated at first; but, upon being pressed, he said: "The first shall be a beggar; the second shall be a thief; the third shall be an assassin." The poor mother was distracted; but the friar begged her to be comforted, for, said he,

" I think, mistress, I know a remedy." She asked him eagerly what that was. Then he said to her : " Make the one that is to be a beggar a friar ; the one that is destined to become a thief, an attorney ; and the last, that will grow up to be a murderer, make him a physician."

THE SERJEANT TURNED FRIAR.

[*We have below a droll little account of an un-happy device adopted by a serjeant or sheriff's officer to arrest a man who had involved himself in debt, and was keeping out of the way on the pretence of illness. It proceeded from the pen of no less a personage than Sir Thomas More, and was origi-nally printed about 1520 as a separate pamphlet. It is included among More's works in the collected folio edition of 1557.*

The production is a mere trifle, and may be said to disarm criticism. It was probably a pleasantry, which either occurred to the illustrious author or was founded on fact. The disguised tipstaff was punished, perhaps, severely enough, but fraudulent impersonation was usually requited in those days with a visit to the pillory.]

THE adventure which you are now about to hear shews very clearly how wise those are who attend to their own affairs, and who do not flatter them-selves that they can play some part which is strange and new to them without running a great risk of misfortune.

What can a hosier know of the shoemaker's craft, a smith of painting, or a draper of teaching boys their lessons ? Is it likely that a man-servant who has done nothing but wait at table and attend to the wine-cellar will succeed as a cutler, or that one who has been brought up to the law will make money by turning merchant, or that a merchant will speed well if he becomes his own lawyer ? A hatter might as soon turn philosopher, or a pedlar theologian.

Now, listen to a case where this very sort of thing happened. A man, who all his life had tried to save up money, died, and left his property to a son, who was so unlike his father, that if he had had three hundred pounds bequeathed to him, instead of one hundred, it would not have sufficed to meet his extravagant tastes.

One hundred good pounds in gold nobles had this youth ; and so afeard was he lest, if he invested it in merchandise, some rogue should beguile him of it, that he kept it himself. First of all, he laid it in a crock, where no man might espy it ; but the crock soon appeared to him to be too large, and he laid it up in a cup. The cup pleased him for a time only, and then the safest place of all struck him to be to lodge what remained inside his person.

In short, he gradually squandered every shilling of his inheritance ; and when he had no more of his own, he began to borrow money and goods of others without repaying any one, since all went in luxury and riot. He lived merrily, kept agreeable company, and made people say that some were born under lucky stars. By little and little his purse grew thin, and his credit failed ; and a friend, who pitied him, took him into his house, when he had

pawned his coat for bread, and lay under a hedge
for shelter.   Under the roof of this kind protector
our prodigal lay for some time so sick in body, as it
was reported, that by no means might he stir abroad;
and a certain merchant, to whom he was a debtor,
went to a serjeant to ask him in what manner he
should proceed in order to secure this man, and
gain his money.

The serjeant said: "Do not disquiet yourself;
leave it to me."

"Ah!" answered the merchant, "but he lies
close; he will not come out."

"I have had great experience in these affairs; I
will arrest him, and then you need not care.   Let
me be baked, if I fail!"

So the two parted; and the serjeant bethought
him how he should compass the matter.   "He is
sick," said he to himself; "he lacks spiritual
counsel.   It is well remembered!   I will change
raiment with a holy friar of my acquaintance, and
I will seek speech of him under that colour."

He lost no time in seeking his friend, who lent
him his attire; and as he paraded before the mirror,
and rehearsed the part which he was going to play,
he flattered himself that he was clean perfect.   Off
then started he to execute his mission in God's
name, and when he came to the house he knocked
softly at the door.

A damsel presently opened it, to whom said the
pretended friar: "God speed, fair maid!   Such a
man (naming him) lodgeth here, doth he not?"

"And what if he doth?" retorted she.

"O, no harm, my good damsel.   It does not

pertain to my order to hurt any ; but with him fain would I speak."

" By my faith, sir," quoth she, " he aileth so ye are not like to have sight of him to-day."

Quoth he : " Fair maid, yet this much I pray you would do. Go to him, and say that an Austin friar would confer with him for his soul's sake."

" That will I," she replied. " Wait you here, father, till I come down again."

The maiden went up, and broke to the man the news, as she had been told ; and he, nothing mistrusting, desired her to return, and conduct the friar to his room, where they might converse together.

The friar ascended to the chamber where the sick man lay, and when he saw him he greeted him with all becoming gestures and expressions. The sick man offered him his hand, and he grasped it with religious fervour.

Said he : " You are in trouble, sir, I understand."

" Yes ; matters have gone better with me than they do just now," he answered.

" Be of good cheer, sir," said the friar ; " all shall be well with you anon. God will direct everything for the best ; and so dismiss all sad thoughts, and take counsel with me. But while we converse, let this maiden leave us."

The girl descended again, and the sick man observed : " Now, holy father, let me hear straightway what happy tidings you have for me."

But the friar, as soon as they were left alone, whipped out his mace, and said : " I arrest thee ; you are in my power, and shall not escape for all the money the mayor has in his purse. Get up, and come along."

The sick man, astounded and furious, raised himself in bed, and dealt the false friar a blow which felled him to the ground. He was afraid that he had slain the man, and out of bed he jumped, and raised him on his feet, and rubbed him till he shewed signs of animation. Then presently he recovered himself, and grappled with his prisoner; and they tugged and lugged at each other, and tare each other's hair, and at last both sprawled together on the floor, and rolled over and over, kicking and tumbling, like pigs in a poke.

Hearing the noise, the maid and her mother rushed upstairs; and when they espied the two fellows struggling and bleeding on the ground, they came to the succour of their lodger. The girl pulled the friar's hood over his face, and belaboured him soundly, as he lay prostrate, with a battledore; while the wife basted him with her distaff till he was distracted with pain. Then they dragged him along the landing, and threw him between them down the staircase, saying: "Adieu, good sir, adieu! Pray commend us to the mayor."

The serjeant crawled away as best he could, and went home to have his sores dressed. "Ill luck betide him," he muttered, as he went, "who occasioned me to play the friar!"

THE MONK OF LEICESTER

WHO WAS FOUR TIMES SLAIN AND ONCE HANGED.

(*Sixteenth Century.*)

[*This well-sustained and amusing story is an English version of the "Sexton of Cluny," and bears some resemblance to the old romantic ballad of "Earl Richard" and to adventures which occur in the "Arabian Nights" and the "Gesta Romanorum." The incident of propping up the corpse against a door is adopted in the "Second Maiden's Tragedy," and in Marlowe's "Rich Jew of Malta." The present writer, in his introduction to the metrical legend in his "Early Popular Poetry"* (1864), *has pointed out other analogues and imitations of the original French* fabliau. *The localization of the story was a common expedient, where old wares were served up again for the nonce.*]

In the olden time, there was in the good town of Leicester a monastery of great renown; and among all the holy brethren who belonged to it there was none who could compare with Dan Hugh.

Dan Hugh was young, and he was lusty, and for a fair woman he was ever on the watch. Now there was in this town a tailor, who had been married seven year or more to a good and comely wife; and when Dan Hugh was wont to pass that way, and to behold her, he conceived a passion for this woman, and wondered when he should be so fortunate as to find her alone, that he might have speech with her; and he thought that, if he could find an opportunity of addressing her, he should succeed in his suit.

One day it happened that he found her by herself, and he came at once to the point.

"Fair creature," said he, "unless you agree to love me, I cannot live."

"O sir," replied she, "I have a good husband."

"Say me not nay," he pursued; "I must love thee, whatever it cost me."

"If it needs must be so," quoth the woman, "come to me to-morrow, for my husband rideth out of town, and so we may enjoy each other's society; and if ye come not, it is your fault. But," she added, "if I prove kind to you, Dan Hugh, what present will you make me?"

"Twenty nobles," quoth he.

"That is good," quoth she.

And so they kissed each other and parted.

The tailor returned home in the evening as usual, and his wife disclosed to him all that had occurred.

"Why, wife," he cried, "would you wrong me?"

"Nay, nay," she cried; "I will keep true to you, forsooth, and get the money for us into the bargain. Just before it is time for him to arrive, I shall lock you in the chest in our room, and when I call you must come."

So when five o'clock struck, Dan Hugh, punctual to the minute, knocked at the door and was admitted. He locked the tailor's wife in his arms, and kissed her; and then he asked her if her husband was out of the way.

"Yea," she said, "and he cometh not back till the afternoon."

Dan Hugh took her in his arms, and would have dallied with her, but she loosed herself saying, "For shame, let go; first, I must have the twenty nobles which you promised me." And after some hesitation, when he saw that she was firm, he pulled out a purse and threw it into her lap. Then he thought that it was all right, and he drew her toward him once more. "Nay, nay," she exclaimed, "let me put the money in the chest, and then I shall feel more easy."

She went to the chest, leaving the monk on the tiptoe of expectation, and when she opened it to put in the nobles, out leapt the tailor. Without giving their visitor time to collect himself, he dealt him a blow on the head which stretched him lifeless on the floor. Thus was Dan Hugh first slain.

"Alack, husband!" cried his wife, "is he dead indeed? What can be done?"

"You must give me your good counsel," said the tailor, "so that we may get rid of this false priest."

And when the woman had thought a little she said: "Let us wait till the shades of evening have fallen, and then you must carry him and set him against one of the walls of the abbey, and go your way." And so the tailor did.

Now the abbot, hearing that Dan Hugh had gone out, marvelled where he could be when he failed to return at the due hour, and he was wrath with him, and sent one of his servants to look everywhere for the missing brother. The messenger searched high and low, and at length he perceived Dan Hugh standing by the wall. So he went up to him, and spake thus : "Dan Hugh, I have been seeking you, and wondering where you were." Dan Hugh did not stir.

"Sir," proceeded the abbot's man, "you must come to my lord straightway, or you will be in disgrace." But Dan Hugh did not utter a word.

Then the abbot's man deemed it best to go to his master, and report to him what he had found. Quoth he : "Sir, Dan Hugh stands stock upright by the wall, and never a word will he speak to me, but he stareth upon me, like one that lacketh grace."

"Is it so ?" demanded the abbot ; "get me a staff, and I will see whether I can make him speak."

Then they went back together, and the abbot cried : "Why dost thou neglect thy holy service thus, fellow ? come hither, with a vengeance !"

But never a whit did Hugh heed the bidding.

"Rogue !" exclaimed the abbot, "will you not come ? Beshrew me, I will give you a rap on your head which will make you wake up." And he smote Hugh with his staff, and brought him to the ground. So was he a second time slain.

"My lord," said the abbot's man, "see what you have done ! Dan Hugh is dead. You will be suspended from your place."

"What is to be done, then ?" quoth the abbot.

"What reward will your lordship give me if I help you out of this dilemma ?" asked his man.

"Forty shillings shall be yours, my good fellow,' said the abbot.

"He loved a tailor's wife in the town passing

well; I shall, as soon as it is dark, take the body and prop it up against the man's door, so that it may be supposed that the husband killed him, for he is angry enough with him, that is so."

The abbot's man did as he had engaged, and ran home as fast as he could, when he had left the body at the tailor's door. The tailor and his wife were very anxious about the affair, lest it should be found who had taken the priest's life; and as they lay in bed, the tailor dreamed that Dan Hugh came back, and stood by their door. "Good Lord! man," cried his wife contemptuously, "are ye afraid of a corpse? Methought that ye slew him."

Thereupon, notwithstanding, the tailor rose and went to the door with a poleaxe in his hand; and when he opened it he beheld the monk hard by, and he was in sore trepidation lest Dan Hugh had returned to take revenge. "Wife,' he called out, "he is here; I am a dead man unless I strike first." And he lifted his weapon and struck Dan Hugh heavily on the head, so that he dropped down like a stone. And this was the third time.

"Alas! wife," said the tailor, "this caitiff will be our undoing. How are we to get rid of him?"

"Wait till after midnight," said she, "and then put him into a sack and carry him to the mill-dam, and cast him in."

The tailor took this advice, and marched toward the mill-dam with Dan Hugh on his shoulder; but as he drew near the place, he saw two thieves also bearing a sack, and when they perceived the tailor, they took him to be the miller returning home, and let their load drop, and ran away. The tailor found that the other sack contained bacon stolen from the mill, and he took it up, threw it over his back, and made the best of his way home, leaving Dan Hugh behind. The two thieves, when the tailor had gone, returned in search of their bacon, and seeing the sack with the monk inside, mistook it in the dark for their own, and trudged merrily back to the place where they lived.

One of them said to his wife : " Ope that sack, wife, and see what we have brought. It is good bacon, and we will make fine cheer."

And when the woman undid the sack, no bacon, but the dead monk, was inside. " Merciful Heaven!" she ejaculated, " have ye slain Dan Hugh then ? Well, ye will be hanged for certain, if it is discovered."

" Nay, dame," said they ; " it is the false miller who did it." And they went forthwith and took the sack back to the mill, and hung it up in the place from which they had stolen the bacon.

When the miller's wife rose in the morning, she went to the larder to cut some bacon for breakfast, and was aghast when she perceived the monk hanging from the hook, and the bacon gone. " Well," she cried, " he has got his due, that is certain. This is the devil's work ; he slew him for robbing us of our winter's store ! "

" Hush! wife," interposed the miller, making his appearance ; " the chief thing is to consider how we shall dispose of him."

The woman had a device ready at hand. " Sir," said she, " in a field hard by my lord abbot hath a horse grazing. Let us wait till nightfall, and set the monk upon his back, fast-bound, with a pole under his arm, as though he would joust; and the horse knoweth his way well to the abbey, and to-morrow, early in the morning, when the abbot sallieth forth on his mare to look after his workmen, he will meet the monk on his horse, and there will be sport."

The miller did as his wife counselled, and led the horse by the bridle till it came in sight of the abbot on his mare, and when the horse saw the mare, the miller let go the bridle, and off gallopped Dan Hugh, tilting straight at the abbot.

"Help! help!" exclaimed his lordship, "for the love of the saints! for I see Dan Hugh will be avenged. Alas! I am a dead man!" And with that he jumped off his mare and ran for his life. His servants came up, and with their clubs and staves beat Dan Hugh unmercifully, till at last he fell off, and was lifted up dead. And this was the fourth time, and the last, for now they buried him. And so our story ends.

A SELECT LIST OF WORKS OR EDITIONS

BY

WILLIAM CAREW HAZLITT

OF THE INNER TEMPLE

CHRONOLOGICALLY ARRANGED

1860–1891

---

1. **History of the Venetian Republic:** its Rise, its Greatness, and its Civilization. With Maps and Illustrations. 4 vols. 8vo. *Smith, Elder & Co.* 1860.
   A new edition, entirely recast, with important additions, in 3 vols., crown 8vo, is in readiness for the press.

2. **Old English Jest-Books, 1525–1639.** Edited with Introductions and Notes. Facsimiles. 3 vols. 12mo. 1864.

3. **Remains of the Early Popular Poetry of England.** With Introductions and Notes. 4 vols. 12mo. Woodcuts. 1864–66.

4. **Handbook to the Early Popular, Poetical, and Dramatic Literature of Great Britain.** Demy 8vo. 1867. Pp. 714, in two columns.

5. **Bibliographical Collections and Notes.** 1867–76. Medium 8vo. 1876.
   This volume comprises a full description of about 6,000 Early English books from the books themselves. It is a sequel and companion to No. 4. See also Nos. 6–9 *infra.*
   " There never was a more accurate and painstaking bibliographer than Mr. Hazlitt, nor is there any bibliography of English literature which can compete with his works. I have found from personal experience that they are absolutely necessary to the English collector."—BERNARD QUARITCH.
   These and the three following items are the result of more than thirty years' continuous labour, during which the author doubtless has had submitted to his notice more English book-rarities than any other bibliophile in Europe. There are several thousands of articles in this work, which may be regarded as an appendix to the bibliographical account of early English literature.

6. **Bibliographical Collections and Notes.** SECOND SERIES. 1876–82. Medium 8vo. 1882.
   Uniform with First Series. About 10,000 titles on the same principle as before.
   " I very respectfully, yet with cordial pleasure, submit to such sections of the educated and reading English community in the United Queendom, the States of America, and elsewhere, as feel an interest in that early literature, which ought to be dear to the entire English-speaking race, a *Third* and *Final* Series of my *Bibliographical Collections and Notes,* forming (with my Handbook), the fourth volume of my achievement in this province of research.
   " The objection to the multiplication of alphabets by the sectional treatment, which I have adopted since the appearance of the Handbook in 1867, is a very valid objection indeed from the point of view of the consulter. But as this has been, and remains, a labour of love, and as the cost of production was a grave problem, I simply had no alternative ; and to the suggestion which I offered in a prior introduction, that, after all, these serial volumes might be regarded in the same light as so many catalogues of public or private collections, I have now the gratifying announcement to add, that a complete Index to the Handbook and the three Series of Collections and Notes is in preparation by Mr. Gray of Cambridge, who has most generously volunteered to do the work, and will form a separate volume, to be published by Mr. Quaritch, when it is completed.
   " I have incorporated (generally with additions and corrections) in my volumes by degrees nearly the whole of the Bibliotheca Anglo-Poetica, Corser's Collectanea (excepting, of course, the lengthy and elaborate extracts and annotations), the British Museum Catalogue of Early English Books to 1640, the Typographical Antiquities of Ames, Herbert, and Dibdin, the Chatsworth, Huth, Ashburnham, and other private cabinets, and the various publications of Haslewood, Park, Utterston, and Collier.
   " Since the Second Series came from the press in 1882, several large private libraries have been dispersed under the hammer, and all the articles previously overlooked by me have been duly taken up into my pages. I may enumerate, for example's sake, the celebrated collections of the

Earl of Jersey, the Earl of Gosford, Mr. James Crossley of Manchester, Mr. Payne Collier, the Duke of Marlborough, Mr. Hartley, Mr. N. P. Simes of Horsham, Sir Richard Colt Hoare, Mr. Michael Wodhull, Sir Thomas Phillips Phillips-Hill, the Rev. J. Fuller Russell, Mr. Henry Pyne, and Professor Solly."—*Preface to Second Series.*

"Mr. W. C. Hazlitt's second series of *Bibliographical Collections and Notes* (Quaritch) is the result of many years' searches among rare books, tracts, ballads, and broadsides by a man whose speciality is bibliography, and who has thus produced a volume of high value. If any one will read through the fifty-four closely printed columns relating to Charles I., or the ten and a half columns given to 'London' from 1541 to 1794, and recollect that these are only a supplement to twelve columns in Hazlitt's *Handbook* and five and a half in his first *Collections*, he will get an idea of the work involved in this book. Other like entries are 'James I.,' 'Ireland,' 'France,' 'England,' 'Elizabeth,' 'Scotland' (which has twenty-one and a half columns), and so on. As to the curiosity and rarity of the works that Mr. Hazlitt has catalogued, any one who has been for even twenty or thirty years among old books will acknowledge that the strangers to him are far more numerous than the acquaintances and friends. This second series of *Collections* will add to Mr. Hazlitt's well-earned reputation as a bibliographer, and should be in every real library through the English-speaking world. The only thing we desiderate in it is more of his welcome marks and names, B.M., Britwell, Lambeth, etc., to show where all the books approaching rarity are. The service that these have done in Mr. Hazlitt's former books to editors for the Early English Text, New Shakespear, Spenser, Hunterian, and other societies, has been so great that we hope he will always say where he has seen the rare books that he makes entries of."— *Academy, August 26th,* 1882.

7. **Bibliographical Collections and Notes.** A THIRD AND FINAL SERIES. 1886. 8vo.

Uniform with the First and Second Series. This volume contains upwards of 3,000 Articles.

"Mr. Hazlitt has done much work during the last thirty years, and some of it has been bitterly attacked ; but we venture to think that the debt of gratitude which all students of Old English literature owe to him for his bibliographical collections must remain in the most enduring opinion of his labours. We would bid all readers who care for the books of the past read the practical, manly, and comprehensive introduction prefixed to this volume. It forms one of the best pleas for the study of English literature which we know ; and coming close upon the important speech of Mr. John Morley, it takes up a phase of the subject not yet adequately recognised. The academic side has been put by Mr. Morley, the practical by Mr. Hazlitt : 'The England in which we dwell is one with the England which lies behind us. So far as the period which I comprehend goes, it is one country and one race ; and I do not think that we should precipitately and unkindly spurn the literature which our foregoers left to us and to our descendants for ever, because it may at first sight strike us as irrelevant to our present wants and feelings. . . . The considerer of modern opinions and customs is too little addicted to retrospection. He seems to be too shy of profiting on the one hand by the counsels or suggestions, on the other by the mistakes, of the men who have crossed the unpassable line, who have dealt with the topics and problems with which we have to deal.' These are stirring and sensible words, and we should much like to see them more widely distributed than the limited issue of this volume will allow.

"It is impossible, in a short notice such as we can only give, to do justice to the contents of this work. The titles of every book or tract are given in full, having been transcribed by Mr. Hazlitt himself ; and there is often appended to the entry interesting information about the condition, history, and, above all things, the present locale of the book. Such work as this requires labour, and skill, and knowledge of no ordinary kind. Now that Mr. Bradshaw is dead, there are few indeed who possess these qualities, and apparently only one who puts them at the service of his fellows. It has been often said of late that the bibliographer and indexer are more needed than the book-writer ; and if this is true, as we are inclined to think it, Mr. Hazlitt's work must, in relation to the age in which it is produced, be awarded a very high place. It enables us to ascertain what has been done in English literature, and therefore ought to enable us to do our work so much the better. Almost all departments of study are now occupied as much with a reconsideration of old facts as with the discovery of new, and for this purpose such books as Mr. Hazlitt's are indispensable. We are happy to say that a competent Cambridge student has undertaken to compile an index to the four volumes of bibliography issued by Mr. Hazlitt, and that this will be published by Mr. Quaritch as soon as it is ready."—*Antiquary,* April, 1887.

8. **Bibliographical Collections and Notes.** Supplements to the Third and Final Series. 2 vols. Medium 8vo. 1889–92.

9. **A General Index to Hazlitt's Bibliographical Works** (1867–89). By G. J. GRAY. Medium 8vo. [*In the Press.*]

This invaluable volume will assist the student and collector in using the several volumes of which the Series now consists, and will enable him to ascertain at a glance whether and where a book, tract, or broadside is to be found. It is a labour which Mr. Gray has undertaken *con amore,* and reflects the highest honour on his industry, discernment, and literary zeal.

** All these books are now on sale by MR. QUARITCH.

10. **Memoirs of William Hazlitt.** With Portions of his Correspondence. Portraits after miniatures by John Hazlitt. 2 vols. 8vo. 1867.

During the last twenty years the author has been indefatigable in collecting additional information for the *Life of Hazlitt,* 1867, in correcting errors, and in securing all the unpublished letters which have come into the market, some of great interest, with a view to a new and improved edition.

11. **Inedited Tracts.** Illustrating the Manners, Opinions, and Occupations of Englishmen during the 16th and 17th Centuries. 1586–1618. With an introduction and Notes. Facsimiles. 4to. 1868.

12. **The Works of Charles Lamb.** Now first collected, and entirely rearranged. With Notes. 4 vols. 8vo. *E. Moxon & Co.* 1868–69.

13. **Letters of Charles Lamb.** With some Account of the Writer, his Friends and Correspondents, and Explanatory Notes. By the late Sir THOMAS NOON TALFOURD, D.C.L., one of his Executors. An entirely new edition, carefully revised and greatly enlarged by W. CAREW HAZLITT. 2 vols. 1886. Post 8vo.

13A. **Mary and Charles Lamb.** New Facts and Inedited Remains. 8vo. Woodcuts and Facsimiles. 1874.
The groundwork of this volume was an Essay by the writer in *Macmillan's Magazine.*

14. **English Proverbs and Proverbial Phrases.** Arranged alphabetically and annotated. Medium 8vo. 1869. Second Edition, corrected and greatly enlarged, crown 8vo. 1882.

15. **Narrative of the Journey of an Irish Gentleman through England in** 1751. From a MS. With Notes. 8vo. 1869.

16. **The English Drama and Stage under the Tudor and Stuart Princes.** 1547–1664. With an Introduction and Notes. A series of Reprinted Documents and Treatises. 4to. 1869.

17. **Popular Antiquities of Great Britain.** I. The Calendar. II. Customs and Ceremonies. III. Superstitions. 3 vols. Medium 8vo. 1870.
Brand's *Popular Antiquities,* by Ellis, 1813, taken to pieces, recast, and enormously augmented.

18. **Inedited Poetical Miscellanies.** 1584–1700. Thick 8vo. With Notes and Facsimiles. 50 copies privately printed. 1870.

19. **Warton's History of English Poetry.** An entirely new edition, with Notes by Sir F. MADDEN, T. WRIGHT, F. J. FURNIVALL, R. MORRIS, and others, and by the Editor. 4 vols. Medium 8vo. 1871.

20. **The Feudal Period.** Illustrated by a Series of Tales (from Le Grand). 12mo. 1874.

21. **Prefaces, Dedications, and Epistles.** Prefixed to Early English Books. 1540–1701. 8vo. 1874. 50 copies privately printed.

22. **Blount's Jocular Tenures.** Tenures of Land and Customs of Manors. Originally published by THOMAS BLOUNT of the Inner Temple in 1679. An entirely new and greatly enlarged edition by W. CAREW HAZLITT, of that Ilk. Medium 8vo. 1874.

23. **Dodsley's Select Collection of Old Plays.** A new edition, greatly enlarged, corrected throughout, and entirely rearranged. With a Glossary by Dr. RICHARD MORRIS. 15 vols. 8vo. 1874–76.

24. **Fairy Tales, Legends, and Romances.** Illustrating Shakespear and other Early English Writers. 12mo. 1875.

25. **Shakespear's Library:** A Collection of the Novels, Plays, and other Material supposed to have been used by Shakespear. An entirely new edition. 6 vols. 12mo. 1875.

26. **Fugitive Tracts (written in verse) which illustrate the Condition of Religious and Political Feeling in England, and the State of Society there,** during Two Centuries. 1493–1700. 2 vols. 4to. 50 copies privately printed. 1875.

27. **Poetical Recreations.** By W. C. HAZLITT. 50 copies printed. 12mo. 1877. A new edition, revised and very greatly enlarged, is in preparation.

28. **The Baron's Daughter.** A Ballad. 75 copies printed. 4to. 1877.

29. **The Essays of Montaigne.** Translated by C. Cotton. An entirely new edition, collated with the best French text. With a memoir, and all the extant Letters, Portrait and Illustrations. 3 vols. 8vo. 1877. The only library edition.

30. **Catalogue of the Huth Library.** [English portion.] 5 vols. Large 8vo. 1880. 200 copies printed.

31. **Offspring of Thought in Solitude.** Modern Essays. 1884. 8vo, pp. 384.
Some of these Papers were originally contributed to *All the Year Round*, etc.

32. **Old Cookery Books and Ancient Cuisine.** 12mo. 1886.
" Full of curious information, this work can fairly claim to be a philosophical history of our national cookery."—*Morning Post.*

33. **An Address to the Electors of Mid-Surrey, among whom I live.** In Rejoinder to Mr. Gladstone's Manifesto. 1886. 8vo, pp. 32.
"Who would not grieve if such a man there be?
Who would not weep if Atticus were he?"—POPE.

34. **Gleanings in Old Garden Literature.** 12mo. 1887.

35. **Schools, Schoolbooks, and Schoolmasters.** A Contribution to the History of Educational Development. 12mo. *J. W. Jarvis & Son.* 1888. Pp. 300 + vi.
Survey of the old system of teaching—Dr. Busby—Early Dictionaries—Colloquies in the Tenth, Twelfth, and Thirteenth Centuries—Earliest printed works of instruction, Donatus and others—Stanbridge—Robert Whittington—Guarini of Verona—Vulgaria of Terence — School Classics — Erasmus and More — Dean Colet — Foundation of St. Paul's— Thomas Linacre— Wolsey's Edition of Lily's Grammar—Merchant Taylors' School—Old Mode of Advertising— Private Establishments—Museum Minervæ at Bethnal Green—Manchester Old School—Shakespear, Sir Hugh Evans, and Holofernes—Educational Condition of Scotland—Female Education—Shakespear's Daughters—Goldsmith—Ascham and Mulcaster—Ben Jonson and Shirley, writers of Grammars — Foreigners' English — Phonography — Bullokar — Charles Butler—Dr. Jones.

SELECTIONS FROM PRESS OPINIONS.

" A perusal of Mr. W. Carew Hazlitt's book is calculated to make both parents and boys thankful that they live in an age of comparative enlightenment. The work does not profess to be an exhaustive one, the object being ' to trace the sources and rise of our educational system, and to present a general view of the principles on which the groundwork of this system was laid.' In pursuing this plan, the writer has succeeded in producing a book which, though dealing with what some readers may consider rather a dry subject, is full of curious and interesting information, judiciously arranged and pleasantly conveyed."—*Morning Post.*

" This book contains a great deal of very curious information. After an introductory chapter on the system of teaching in the good old times when holidays were unknown and stick ointment laid the basis of all culture, an account is given of the various vocabularies, glossaries, and colloquies in use in mediæval times. Some interesting and amusing details are also given of sixteenth century school-books, and Mr. Hazlitt sketches the scholastic work done by Erasmus, Colet, Linacre, Lily, Ruddiman, and others, and gives us an insight into the methods followed in such schools as St. Paul's and the Merchant Taylors' Institution. . . . One of the most interesting chapters in the volume is that on female education."—*Glasgow Herald.*

" . . . Mr. Hazlitt knows his subject, and he also knows how to write. No small praise." —*St. Stephen's Review.*

" . . . Some of Mr. Hazlitt's pages are occupied with the humorous side of school life ; and as he tells a story well, these portions of the book come upon one with singular pleasure."— *Antiquary.*

" Mr. Hazlitt has evidently a favourite specialty in school-books. He has collected them, we should judge, with a good deal of zeal, and has acquired a really considerable amount of knowledge about them," etc.—*Spectator.*

36. **A Little Book for Men and Women about Life and Death.** 12mo. *Reeves & Turner.* 1891.
" Mr. Hazlitt believes that the only chance of shaking off the ignorance in which spiritual pastors help to keep the nation is to be found in the absolute secularization of education."—*Daily Telegraph.*

" This neat little volume discusses very ably and fairly several important questions."—*Newcastle Daily Chronicle.*

" This is a well-written attack on a few of the irrational doctrines, folly, and trumpery that go by the name of religion."—*Christian Life.*

" Mr. Hazlitt sees that to overthrow the superstition which selects and endows incompetence, there must be a general lift in the quality and efficiency of education all round ; and he sketches a plan or curriculum which does credit to his breadth of view."—*National Reformer.*

" Mr. Hazlitt is an original thinker. On the whole, he expresses himself moderately, temperately, and without needless offence. Those whose views Mr. Hazlitt voices are a growing number, and many will read his little book with sympathy."—*Birmingham Daily Post.*

37. **Tales and Legends of National Origin or Widely Current in England** from Early Times. With Critical Introductions. 8vo. 1891.

38. **A Survey of the Livery Companies of the City of London.** With a general Introduction and Preface, and numerous Illustrations.
[*For publication in December,* 1891.]

39. **A Manual for the Collector and Amateur of Old English Plays.** Sm. 4to. Only 250 copies printed.